Guide to California's Wine Country

By the Editors of Sunset Books and Sunset Magazine

Good wine *begins in a vineyard, ends in a glass.*

Lane Publishing Co.
Menlo Park, California

A constant challenge . . .

The rapid growth and change of California's wine industry is reflected in the history of frequent revisions of this book. Just to say that this is the third edition is not enough. The book was first printed in 1968, went through three revisions (1970, 1973, 1974), an expansion, and two updatings (1975, 1977) before the second edition appeared in 1979. And the wine industry marched on. So, often as we try, we cannot quite keep pace.

In recent years, Californians have developed the habit of launching wineries in leased space in existing wineries, and making several vintages of wine before building their own cellars. This, combined with such rapid construction techniques as tilt-up concrete, allows major new wineries to spring out of the landscape virtually overnight, and major new labels to burst upon the marketplace from no visible source.

This new edition anticipates a number of these newcomers, but undoubtedly misses several of them as well as any number of small, family wineries. We plan to keep after the situation.

Picker's job *is to be ready at the time when grapes are in perfect balance for wine.*

Research and Text: Bob Thompson

Supervising Editor: Barbara J. Braasch

Special Consultant: Margaret Smith, Sunset Magazine

Design: Cynthia Hanson, Lea Damiano Phelps

Illustrations: Rik Olson

Cover: Spring crop of mustard brightens vineyard at Rutherford in the Napa Valley. Photographed by Ed Cooper.

Editor, Sunset Books: David E. Clark

Third printing March 1985

 Library of Congress Catalog Card Number: 82-81743. ISBN 0-376-06945-7. Lithographed in the United States.

Hours, telephone numbers, and highway designations in this book are accurate as of the time this edition went to press.

Maps have been provided in each chapter for the special purpose of highlighting significant regions, winery locations, routes, and attractions in the area. Check automobile clubs, insurance agencies, and chambers of commerce or visitors bureaus in major cities for detailed highway maps.

Contents

"When one glass *of wine invites the second, the wine is good."—Samuele Sebastiani*

The Vintage Year

By dawn's early light, *harvest pickers in Napa Valley race to take advantage of cool morning air.*

It's growing time *for Almaden vineyard at Paicines. Vines soak up last warmth of spring evening.*

For most wine buffs, thoughts of the calendar revolve around the vintage. But the annual winegrowing cycle has crucial moments all through the year.

Spring. In an important sense, a vintage begins in March, when a pale fringe of new leaf begins to cover the bare bones of the winter vines. Wildflowers glow in the winter cover crops. After these are disked under at the end of the rains in April, luminous new grape leaves contrast with fresh-turned earth, the canes still short enough to make each row stand out separately.

Summer. Little happens in this season, but what does happen is important. The vines have made their growth, the cellars tend to be as idle as they get. By June, the fruit buds look very much like clusters of miniature grapes. In the middle third of the month, these buds unfold into one of the most insignificant floral displays in all of botany, but this flowering marks a critical stage. To set a full crop, vines must now have 10 to 14 days of dry, moderately warm weather. Rain is a disaster; extreme heat is not much better.

Autumn. The vintage moves to a peak as September moves to a close. A few grape varieties ripen early in the month and a few straggle into November and even December. But most California grapes ripen in the last three weeks of September and the first three of October. The business of crushing hundreds and thousands of tons of grapes is hectic and messy, but as soon as fermentations get going, matters begin not only to look better, but to smell just fine. A fermentation that smells sweet is sure to yield good wine for drinking regardless of how it looks at the time.

The harvest is enormously photogenic. Pickers, crushers, and presses are all in hurried motion from before sunup until well after nightfall. Demands upon winemakers at this time are incredible.

Winter. After Thanksgiving comes the quiet season. Pruners shear away last year's canes. New wines are racked clear; the fresh wines of the past harvest begin going to bottle for release in early spring. Crowds of summer and fall visitors dwindle, leaving winery hosts more time to answer questions. There is a price: December through February is the rainy season. However, with luck, visitors can catch the tail end of a storm and be treated to showy weather, with just enough warmth to promise spring.

Sheep mow *winter cover crop for independent vineyardist near Plymouth.*

Spring— a season for photographers

Diners *and sippers enjoy balmy weather on Domaine Chandon's terrace. With reservations, lunch or dinner can be combined with tour at Napa Valley showplace.*

Spring's soft light *adds glow to picturesque wineries in Sierra foothills. The barrel aging cellar (above) is at Monteviña. Tiny cellar (right) belongs to StoneRidge.*

Sparse spring rains *mean irrigation is a way of life in counties from Monterey south.*

Change of color *means harvest is about 45 days away.*

Summer— a time for getting ready

Getting ready, *cellarman at Barengo winery in Lodi washes down 30,000-gallon redwood tank.*

Workers at Paul Masson *vineyards near Soledad inspect wide-spaced rows of trellised vines.*

Autumn foliage *lends a fiery light to venerable vineyard in western Sonoma County.*

Autumn—the busy harvest season

Picker hoists *lug-sized container for trek to gondola. To beat the sun, harvesters get into vineyards about dawn, end days around 4 P.M.*

Hectic pace *of vintage can be seen, almost felt. At wineries, grapes go into crushers tons at a time.*

To beat midday heat, *mechanical harvesters pick throughout cool night hours.*

Winter—a period to pause

Toward end of winter, *pruners begin work in Lodi tokays as storm gives way to clearing skies.*

During winter tour *of HMR's ultramodern bottling line, visitors receive bonus view of rolling green hills outside picture window.*

After tumultuous arrival *of new-vintage wines, winemakers turn their attention to older vintages still in casks. Cellarmaster tastes each lot, decides to bottle now or wait longer. Scene is at J. Pedroncelli.*

Sampling the Wineries

Size *is a major factor in winery visitor policies. Tiny Hanzell (left) requires appointments; larger Novitiate (below) offers regularly scheduled tours through dim, cool cellars lined with ancient oak oval casks where wine sleeps.*

Twenty years of progress *have filled the Alexander Valley with more vines and more than twice as many wineries as in the 1960s.*

California's wine districts extend as far south as San Diego and as far north as Mendocino. Vines crown ridges looking out to the Pacific Ocean, carpet a score of coastal valleys, sprawl across the great Central Valley, and march up the slopes of the Sierra foothills.

California's first wineries, adjuncts to the Franciscan missions, were spaced a hard day's ride apart, from San Diego to Sonoma. Nearly all of their wine went to sacramental use, but some was also used to welcome neighbors, and some to settle the dusty thirst of summer travelers or drive the chill from winter visitors.

When the Franciscans abandoned their California winemaking in the 1830s, others were there to pick up the reins, not only in the original districts, but in areas farther north, and, above all, farther east in the Central Valley. In essence, winemaking in California had its present geographic shape by the late 1880s. Prohibition dimmed the outline from 1918 to 1934, but did not erase it.

From the viewpoint of visitors, however, there has been a tremendous revolution in the state's wineries since 1968, when the first edition of this book appeared. For example, the original edition described 18 wineries in the Napa Valley and the same number in Sonoma County. The current edition shows 107 for Napa and 90 for Sonoma. Even more striking: Monterey had but one winery in 1968, and Santa Barbara had none, while between the two of them, the total vineyard acreage ranged around 30. In this edition, Monterey shows 9 and Santa Barbara 13 wineries open to visitors, while Monterey's grape acreage reaches 34,000 acres and Santa Barbara's exceeds 9,800.

In the search for space, the Mother Lode area, Mendocino and Lake counties, and Temecula and Escondido areas add to the total winery count.

The new few pages hint at the rewarding diversity of the state's wineries, some large and many small. Napa and Sonoma have the greatest numbers of cellars of all sorts, but other districts challenge them in all respects save colorful history.

Wine *is made ofttimes in grand buildings such as The Christian Brothers Greystone Cellars.*

An architectural array

Flags fly *at Sonoma's Souverain Cellars. Building's size, spare lines, and twin towers built in style of old hop barns make it highly visible from freeway.*

Redwood siding *and shake roof of Lambert Bridge blend easily into oak-studded hill in background.*

Typical *of several area wineries, only part of Geyser Peak complex dates from 1880. Original building now contains wood-aging cellar.*

Some old favorites

Replica *of founder's Rhenish home, Beringer's tasting room was built in 1876. Winery tour also includes peek into century-old aging tunnels.*

A remnant *of the past, Inglenook's original cellar is particularly appealing in fall when draped by flaming ivy.*

Buena Vista's *historical plaque credits Agoston Haraszthy as being the father of California's modern wine history. Restored winery recaptures tranquility of another era.*

Classic *stone building at Charles Krug represents traditional old Napa winery estate.*

From vineyards below, *Sterling's hilltop architecture resembles rambling Grecian church. Tasting room offers incomparable valley views.*

. . . and some bold new statements

Towered and turreted *Chateau Chevalier is both old and new. Built in 1891, building underwent transformation, became winery again in 1973.*

Mock medieval tower, *old estate house, and romantic setting lend French touches to Chateau St. Jean.*

Robert Mondavi's *architecture may hark back to Franciscan mission days, but inside it's one of the more modernly equipped cellars in the state.*

Touring & Tasting

Currier & Ives *could not have printed a better Central Coast vineyard scene than one belonging to Almaden near Paicines. The company offers no tours at Paicines, but welcomes visitors at San Jose winery and in tasting room at Hollister.*

Most of state's *sizable cellars offer formal visitor facilities with scheduled tours and tasting rooms. Visits to smaller wineries are informal, may require appointments.*

Touring the wine country is not a new idea. Visitors have been crossing threshholds into California wine cellars for more than two centuries, 1969 having been the official bicentennial. But if the paths are well worn, they are more inviting than ever because of the presence of many new wineries, and more complicated because of the resulting diversity.

The old-line cellars, the ones that were around for the first edition of this book in 1968, were, in a great majority of cases, of a size to run formal visitor facilities, including tour guides and special tasting rooms. Some of the new names have followed their model, but a great many newcomers are too small to have either guides or tasting rooms, so they welcome visitors by appointment as personal guests, and offer tasting only when there is a bit of wine to spare.

One logical visitor approach to this situation is to use the cellars with developed tour programs as sources of primary information, saving the appointment-only places for a time when an hour's talk about the fine points of winemaking does not require a taste to be worthwhile. The other logical approach is to choose the sources of wines that are personal favorites, no matter what size or shape the cellar.

Whatever approach is taken to the state's wineries, they are rewarding for their diversity. Over the course of two centuries, California has acquired winemakers from every corner of the globe. They have contributed differing notions about how grapes should be grown, how wine should be made, how buildings should be designed, and even what kind of dog should stand sentry.

Someone bent on record-setting could visit as many as 20 cellars a day in some districts . . . but should not. Such a visitor would miss all the details, and details are what wine is all about. Experienced travelers in the vineyards limit themselves to three, or at most four, stops a day.

To many visitors, the words "touring and tasting" are synonymous. We offer some tips on tasting for serious bibbers in our special feature on page 129. Professional tasters judge wines by sight (wine's appearance), smell (aroma and bouquet), and taste. But in the end, judgment is a purely personal exercise.

Any visit to California's wine country can be rewarding. The seasons may govern timing of a trip: spring is the most picturesque, autumn the most dramatic. In winter, vintners may have more time to explain the winemaking process. Though summer can be hot in many wine districts, this is the season when some cellars offer accompanying entertainment (see page 87).

Bed and breakfast inns abound in the Napa and Sonoma valleys and in the Mother Lode regions. Hotels and motels throughout the state make it possible to extend wine forays.

Many veteran wine country visitors assemble picnic lunches using local cheese shops, delis, and bakeries. Many wineries offer picnic sites; a few have dining rooms.

Different lessons *come at different places. At Estrella River Winery, visitors are guided through big fermenting room full of stainless steel tanks.*

A peek behind the scenes

Tours *at Beaulieu Vineyards offer close look at its famed Cabernet Sauvignon and other reds.*

Guides at Beaulieu *need a sense of direction to keep up with expansions, but visitors get good look at winemaking from crushing station to bottling line.*

Automatic bottling lines *are endlessly fascinating. At blurring speed, they sanitize bottles, fill them with wine, cap or cork them, cover the neck with a capsule, and slap on labels fore and aft.*

Tall stacks *of barrels line walls at Stag's Leap. With appointment, winery owner explains how he makes wine; only tasting is by staff to check on aging process.*

Sipping and swirling —the final test

Tasters *take different poses at different places. At Mirassou, the job is done standing at a bar. In any case, the nose is a taster's most important asset.*

Tasting room *at Sterling is elegant, airy, and a pleasant end to self-guided tour.*

Informal atmosphere *reigns at Thomas Kruse and other small cellars around state where people just gather around an upturned barrel.*

From picnics to performances

Wineries *may offer more than a tour and a taste. Many cellars, such as Sonoma Vineyards (below), provide picnic tables; others present concerts. Paul Masson's old mountain winery (right) is setting for summer series.*

Tree-shaded picnic *between vines and winery is a relaxing interlude for Livermore visitors.*

Sterling's showmanship *starts at the parking lot. Visitors pay moderate fee to be whisked up to hilltop winery on aerial tramway.*

Fun among the vines

Festivals *crowd winery calendars. In May, Healdsburg's town plaza (left) draws tasters. At Soledad (below), footpower crushes a bit of ceremonial wine each October.*

A few wineries *maintain restaurants for luncheon or dinner; this one is at Souverain Cellars near Geyserville.*

For bird's-eye view *of Napa Valley vineyards, take a ride in a bright balloon.*

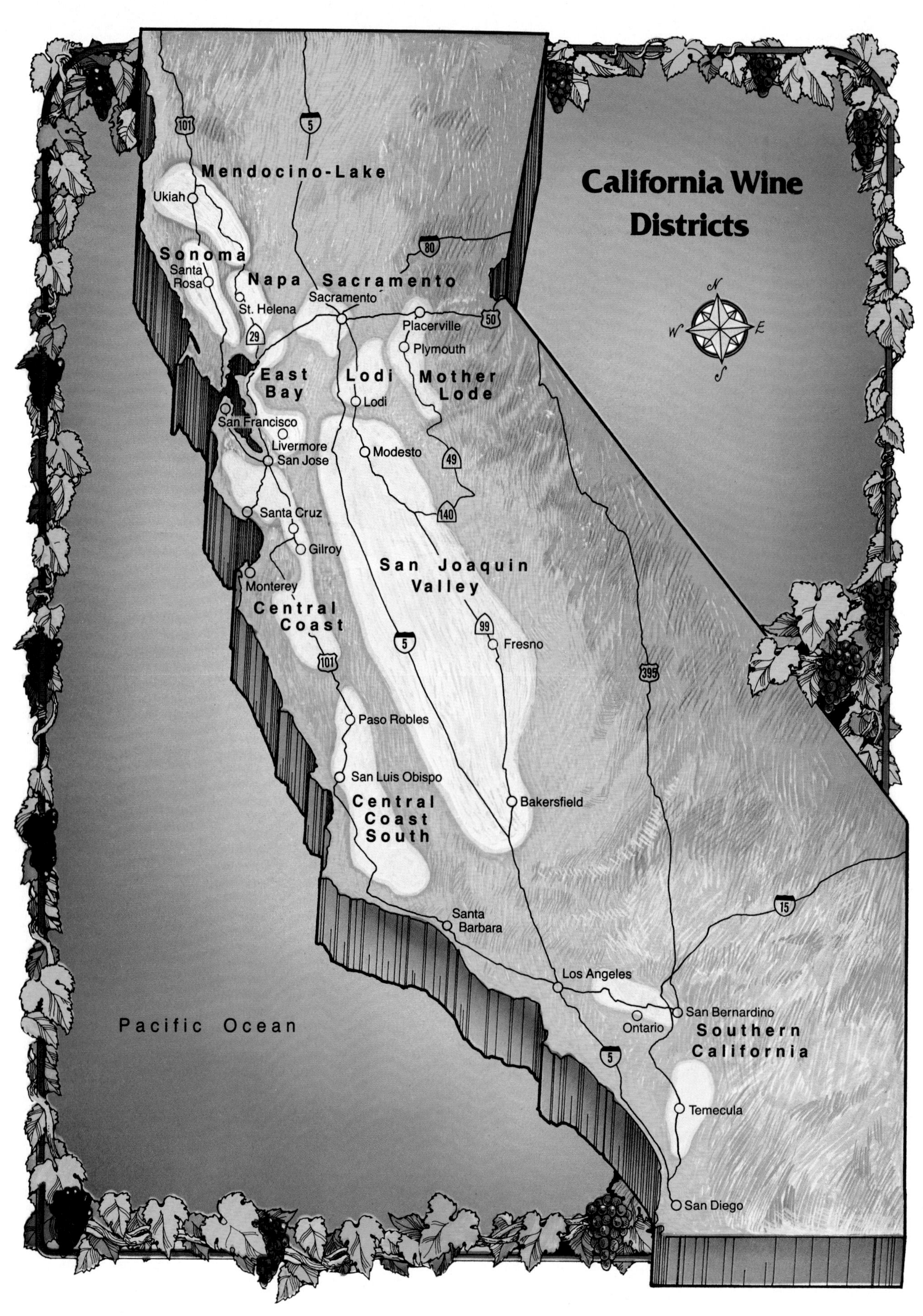
California Wine Districts
N
S
E
W
Mendocino-Lake
Ukiah
Sonoma
Santa Rosa
Napa
St. Helena
Sacramento
Sacramento
Placerville
Plymouth
East Bay
Lodi
Lodi
Mother Lode
San Francisco
Livermore
San Jose
Modesto
Santa Cruz
Gilroy
Monterey
Central Coast
San Joaquin Valley
Fresno
Paso Robles
San Luis Obispo
Central Coast South
Bakersfield
Santa Barbara
Los Angeles
San Bernardino
Ontario
Southern California
Temecula
San Diego
Pacific Ocean
101
5
80
29
50
49
140
99
395
15

About This Book

The following explanations will help make *California's Wine Country* a more useful and reliable guide.

The basic organization alphabetically lists wineries within a small region that can be covered easily by car on a day (or longer) of touring. Only the Napa Valley among the chapters takes all of its wineries in one chunk. Other, larger counties or districts have subdivisions focused, usually, on a single town. The purpose is to group all of the wineries within reach, allowing a potential tourist the fullest range of choice in planning a visit.

The system is best suited to newcomers to the pleasures of winery touring. Veteran hands often will wish to skip from district to district, singling out cellars of particular interest. Newcomers may wish to take similar tacks. There is a complete alphabetic listing of wineries in the index to assist in such planning.

Highway or Byway

Anyone slightly familiar with California geography knows that Napa, Sonoma, and Mendocino form a tight circle crowded with well more than half of the state's wineries. As the map on the facing page hints, it is possible to visit selected places in any two of the three counties in a single day's outing from San Francisco. But even well-informed Californians are less aware that San Luis Obispo and Santa Barbara counties now have enough cellars in a small radius to keep a studious visitor busy for almost a week, and are within weekend range of either Los Angeles or San Francisco.

Some districts lend themselves to byway visits. The Mother Lode, for example, is an easy detour between San Francisco and Lake Tahoe, or San Francisco and Yosemite National Park. In Southern California, Temecula is an equally easy detour for travelers between Los Angeles and San Diego.

Using the Maps

Within each chapter or subchapter is a useful locator map. Each map has accompanying tour information for wineries located within this area. While the maps are reasonably accurate and complete, their scale often makes winery locations a bit uncertain. Road directions in the accompanying winery listings supplement the maps. It is also wise to use detailed road maps, especially for such urban areas as the Santa Clara Valley in the Central Coast, and Cucamonga in Southern California, where maps in the book show only a few key roads.

In addition to road directions, the tour information lists the hours and days each winery is open to visitors. It must be recognized that these specifics may change without notice, even at large wineries. At small, family-owned cellars where the proprietor is also the winemaker and tour guide, hours may change from day to day because of business pressures.

Also in the tour information blocks are abbreviated notations on the winery's tour facilities. These should be translated as follows:

IT (informal tour) almost always means that visitors are free to poke about a small winery without a guide, usually with some advice from the host about any areas that might be off limits. This notation also is used in the cases of a few larger wineries which have developed sign-guided tours for visitors.

GT (guided tour), in the case of larger wineries, almost always means trained guides shepherd groups of visitors through a set route as often as enough people gather. These tours can be particularly useful for getting a handle on the basics of winemaking. Most of the time, such tours cover every aspect of wine production from the arrival of grapes for crushing through to the bottling line.

With the rapid increase in numbers of small wineries, many guided tours now are offered by the proprietor or winemaker. Such cellars offer tours only by appointment for the obvious reason: the winemaker has another, more timely job to do. These tours are of greatest value to connoisseurs and would-be connoisseurs trying to learn the fine points of production.

Ta (tasting) means the winery will provide samples of one or more of its wines at no charge. In the early days of this book, this was almost automatic; now, with the wineries often swamped with visitors and with many tiny cellars in operation, tasting is no sure bet. At many large wineries, visitors are offered only two or three set wines each day. At many small ones, they may be offered no tasting at all, either for lack of wine or because of governmental restrictions on a winery's use permit. The absence of a "Ta" notation does not mean there is no chance at all for tasting, but it does mean the proprietor has discretionary powers at the very least. If the notation is not there, it is wisest not to anticipate a sampling of the winery's wares.

At a minimum, wineries listed as welcoming visitors offer wines at retail. Usually, there is no minimum purchase; however in a few instances (usually because of use-permit restrictions), wineries sell in case-lot minimums. Most of these details are noted in the main description. Wineries which afford no chance to tour or buy wine at retail are not listed in the main section, but may be noted in sections headed "More wineries."

In & Around Sonoma

Rich in California history as well as vines

Few districts have more of the character of old California than Sonoma County. The town of Sonoma sprang up around the last of the Franciscan missions in the 1830s. Already the Russians had founded and abandoned their fur-trading outpost on the coast at Fort Ross. After Sonoma's mission days, the town served as headquarters for Mariano Vallejo during his term as governor of Mexico. The Bear Flag Revolt, a triggering incident in the union of California with the United States, unfolded on Vallejo's doorstep.

Later, horticulturist Luther Burbank did much of his work in and around Santa Rosa, proving incidentally that this region is a veritable garden spot. One of Burbank's friends, Jack London, labored at his home in the hills above Glen Ellen to prove that no place can be paradise.

Grapes and wine have been companions through all these historic episodes, a part of Sonoma from the beginning. The mission had vineyards in the 1830s. Vallejo took them over along with the rest of the property, and ran a lively competition with Agoston Haraszthy to see who was the better winemaker. In the judgement of history, Vallejo's fame is mostly political while Haraszthy is remembered for his long reign as the father of California winemaking.

Today the historical heart of Sonoma winemaking in the Sonoma Valley is but a small statistical part of the county's vineyards. By far the greatest acreage of vines and by far the greatest number of wineries are dotted along either side of U.S. Highway 101 from Santa Rosa north to the Sonoma-Mendocino county line near Cloverdale. Healdsburg is the hub of this larger district, nearly all of it within the watershed of the Russian River. All told, the county had a shade more than 25,000 acres of vines in 1982. Wineries numbered in the 90s.

Sonoma Valley

In a world often indifferent to yesterday, the town of Sonoma clings to much of its past. The town plaza was the heart of things after Fra Jose Altimira founded the mission in 1832. It remained the heart when the secular government of Mariano Vallejo supplanted the mission, and again when the Bear Flaggers did away with the Mexican regime. It remains the heart of town.

Time has changed the details of the plaza but not its essence. A good many of the adjacent buildings had weathered before California gained statehood in 1850. Most of the rest have had a chance to weather since. The square itself remained a patch of bare ground only until 1910 when the sizable city hall was built in its center using a buff-colored local sandstone. Sheltering trees have grown up since to shade the benches on which townsfolk and visitors take their ease in summer's heat.

West and north, a string of resort towns reaches back to the turn of the century, surviving in spite of losing their original purpose. The hot springs that made the district a favored spa for fog-chilled San Franciscans of the Gay Nineties cooled after the earthquake of 1906, never to heat up again.

Encircling the town of Sonoma and stretching away to the north beyond the resorts, vineyards and wineries were and are integral parts of the Sonoma Valley.

The Wineries

Winegrowing north of San Francisco had its beginnings at Sonoma. Today the wineries, like the rest of the valley, reflect old times and new in their architecture, sometimes even in their equipment.

In the spring of 1982, the valley has very nearly a score of cellars. One is among the oldest in the state. More than half of them date from this decade.

Adler Fels twice earns its name, which translates from German as Eagle Rock. Visitors drive up a steep hill to get to the winery gate, then up a steeper one to the aerie-high winery and its commanding views down the valley and up to landmark Eagle Rock.

Having given a German name to a California property, proprietors David Coleman, Ayn Ryan, and Lila Burford built a winery that mixes lines and materials from both places to appealing effect. The gambrel rooflines seem pure Californian. A tower nestled into an angle of the building has a Rhenish air. Redwood siding is local, but the patterns of its application borrow from Alpine half-timbering.

Within, the cellar is the typical California blend of new and old, from air-pressure press to European oak barrels. It was first used for the harvest of 1980. Older reds were made elsewhere. The list of wines produced in it includes Chardonnay, Gewürztraminer, Johannisberg Riesling, and Cabernet Sauvignon. There also is a tiny lot of sparkling wine sold only on the premises.

Buena Vista Winery has endured various fortunes since Agoston Haraszthy founded the firm in 1857.

Haraszthy, the now-a-colonel, now-a-count Hungarian who is widely credited as being the father of the modern California wine industry, set a tone. He brought the first really sizable importations of European grape varieties to northern California, but, because he had unacceptable political affiliations, he never received payment from the state for his effort in its behalf. The hapless Haraszthy disappeared in Nicaragua just a few years before phylloxera began to play havoc with his vines.

Haraszthy's sons, Attila and Arpad, and other partners carried on after his departure until the 1906 earthquake severely damaged the winery buildings. Finally, the sons went looking for greener fields and Buena Vista closed its doors. The old stone buildings were abandoned until 1943 when newspaperman Frank Bartholomew bought the property and started reconditioning the place.

The long of memory might have crossed their fingers when they saw the first new vines in very crooked rows. (They were planted by World War II submarine crews on rehabilitation leaves, presumably without their navigation officers.) It was not a bad omen however. Buena Vista has enjoyed prosperous good health since its reopening.

Bartholomew retained control until 1968, when he sold the winery to Young's Market Company of Los Angeles. Young's added a large new vineyard and a fermenting winery on a back road in the Carneros district before selling in turn to a German firm, A. Racke, in 1979. Throughout these changes, the old property has retained much of the appearance and all of the tranquility of 1860.

The larger, uphill building, built as the main cellar, now houses wines aging in a variety of cooperage. The stone barn and three tunnels carved into the hill behind it have a self-guiding tour with photographs and other memorabilia to illuminate past as well as present. Tasting takes place in the smaller, downhill building, originally the press house.

Outside are two picnic grounds, one directly in front of the main cellar, the other between it and the press house. In summer, this is the place to picnic on French bread from the bakery on the town plaza, fresh fruit from the market next door, cheeses from the factory diagonally across from them, and wine from the obvious source.

Buena Vista wines include Zinfandel, Pinot Noir, Cabernet Sauvignon, Chardonnay, Gewürztraminer, and Johannisberg Riesling.

Chateau St. Jean set out to look as romantically French as any property could given the fact that Sugarloaf Ridge, which looms up just behind the winery, is a quintessential California coastal hill.

A mock medieval tower is the architectural signature of the building. More than mere ornament, its secondary purpose is to provide a central vantage from which visitors on the self-guided tour can look down to see the entire winemaking process. At Chateau St. Jean this means state-of-the-art equipment designed to handle many small lots of wine. This winery has dedicated itself particularly to offering many wines of a single type, each from a specified vineyard, hence the great numbers of small fermentors rather than a fewer number of larger ones. The principal types are Chardonnay, Fumé Blanc, Gewürztraminer, and Johannisberg Riesling. The latter two vary not only by vineyard, but in degree of sweetness, late-harvest styles being another specialty (see the special feature, "Botrytis cinerea, the noble mold," on page 53).

(Continued on next page)

. . . Continued from page 35

Even before the new winery was built, the property had a romantic air about it. An old country estate house now used for the offices and tasting room dates back to the Roaring Twenties. From all accounts it helped the era earn its name.

Chateau St. Jean dates from 1974. Construction began then, and was completed in 1981. Not incidentally, the "Jean" is pronounced as in blue jeans rather than in the French fashion. The cellar is named in honor of the wife of one of the trio of owners.

H. Cotturi & Sons requires appointments of visitors because of its lack of size and staff, but the family proprietors of this small cellar hardly have to worry about floods of drop-in visitors. The property is miles off the beaten track in Sonoma Valley's west hills, and hidden at the end of a winding private drive to boot.

An aging cellar, well filled with a mixture of small fermentors and French and American oak barrels, is two small wood barns, or one barn with two roof peaks. Crushing takes place on a pad between the family house and the winery.

The wines from this small cellar make a surprisingly long roster. Included are Chardonnay, Gewürztraminer, Semillon, Cabernet Sauvignon, Pinot Noir, and Zinfandel.

Glen Ellen Winery restores to life one of the Sonoma Valley's historic wine estates, one less touched by time than almost any other.

A fine old house is at the shady center of a grove of trees growing in the midst of a rolling vineyard not far from Jack London's old ranch. Built by the pioneer Wegner family in the 1860s, it is being restored by the Bruno Benziger family, new owners in 1980. The Benzigers have kept grounds in which a horse and buggy would not look out of place, adding only a curiously appropriate flock of peacocks.

The white-painted winery is just behind the house and downhill from it. It is not the original, which was beyond redemption, but as near the spit and image of it as modern winemaking equipment would allow. In the form of a classic California barn, complete with twin cupolas, it hides stainless steel fermentors and other processing gear outside and inside its rear wall, leaving the front elevation peaceful and timeless. The Benzigers, father and sons, built it themselves, finishing just in time for the vintage of 1981.

Their roster of wines includes Chardonnay, Sauvignon Blanc, Cabernet Sauvignon, and a pair of proprietary generics.

Grand Cru Vineyards exemplifies several aspects of wine in contemporary California.

It is one of several wineries located in old cellars restored to use after decades of vacancy. It is one of several organizations in which scientists form the leadership, bringing with them extremely sophisticated notions about equipment and techniques. And it is a company that started almost as a weekend hobby, but quickly grew into a good-sized, full-time business.

Specifically, Grand Cru is located alongside and in the 1886 stone and concrete fermenting tanks of the Lemoine Winery. In 1970, the new proprietors erected a battery of stainless steel fermentors right next to the concrete originals, an instructive sight and, no doubt, a daily source of relief to the cellarmen who do not have to pitch pomace over the tops of the new models as their forebears did when concrete was all the style.

The old concrete tanks, with doors cut into them, have become surprisingly elegant vaults for the oak tanks and barrels in which Grand Cru wines age.

The mechanically minded will want to have a close look at Grand Cru. To give just one example, the crusher and Bucher tank press look conventional enough, but are powered by variable-speed hydraulic systems rather than standard direct-drive electric motors. Other touches visible on the self-guided tour are just as refined.

Grand Cru's tasting room is in an A-frame perched atop part of the old Lemoine fermentors. In time it is scheduled to move into a second building atop others of the old tanks, leaving the A-frame for offices. In addition to its tasting room, the winery has an oak-shaded picnic lawn with views of the fermenting area in one direction and of the vineyard in the opposite one.

Wines produced here include Chenin Blanc, Sauvignon Blanc, Gewürztraminer, Cabernet Sauvignon, and Zinfandel. A particular specialty is a sweet "Induced Botrytis" Gewürztraminer (see the special feature, "Botrytis cinerea, the noble mold," on page 53).

Gundlach-Bundschu was a famous winery name in Sonoma's early history. In 1976 its traditional label, still owned by the founding family, re-entered the ranks of the modern-day Sonoma wine community.

Jacob Gundlach and son-in-law Charles Bundschu had a world-wide market for their wines from the 1850s until the 1906 earthquake (and ensuing fire in their San Francisco warehouse), followed by Prohibition, caused them to close their doors. Though the Bundschus went out of the wine business, they retained ownership of their vineyards and orchards in Sonoma.

In 1970 the fifth generation in the form of Jim Bundschu began rebuilding on one of three original winery sites. In the summer of 1976 he formally re-opened the cellars to the public.

Behind an early-day quarried stone facade is a new building overflowing with both equipment and cooperage.

A tasting room just inside the front door is framed by tall stacks of European oak barrels. Behind the barrels come a bottling line, stainless steel fermentors, the press, a centrifuge, and other processing gear. Beyond these and the rear wall, a cluster of insulated stainless steel storage tanks nestles into an oak grove. (The odd shapes betray their origins as dairy tanks, much sought after by wineries for their superior quality, but too expensive to buy anywhere except from failing dairies.) The rest of the barrel collection is at another of the old family winery sites nearby.

Many of the grapes used for Gundlach-Bundschu wines come from the original vineyards, first planted in 1858. Wines from the old vineyard and two newer plots nearby include Sonoma Riesling, Gewürztraminer, and Chardonnay in whites. Cabernet Sauvignon, Merlot, and Zinfandel are primary reds. A particular specialty is a white called Kleinburger, from a little-known German grape variety.

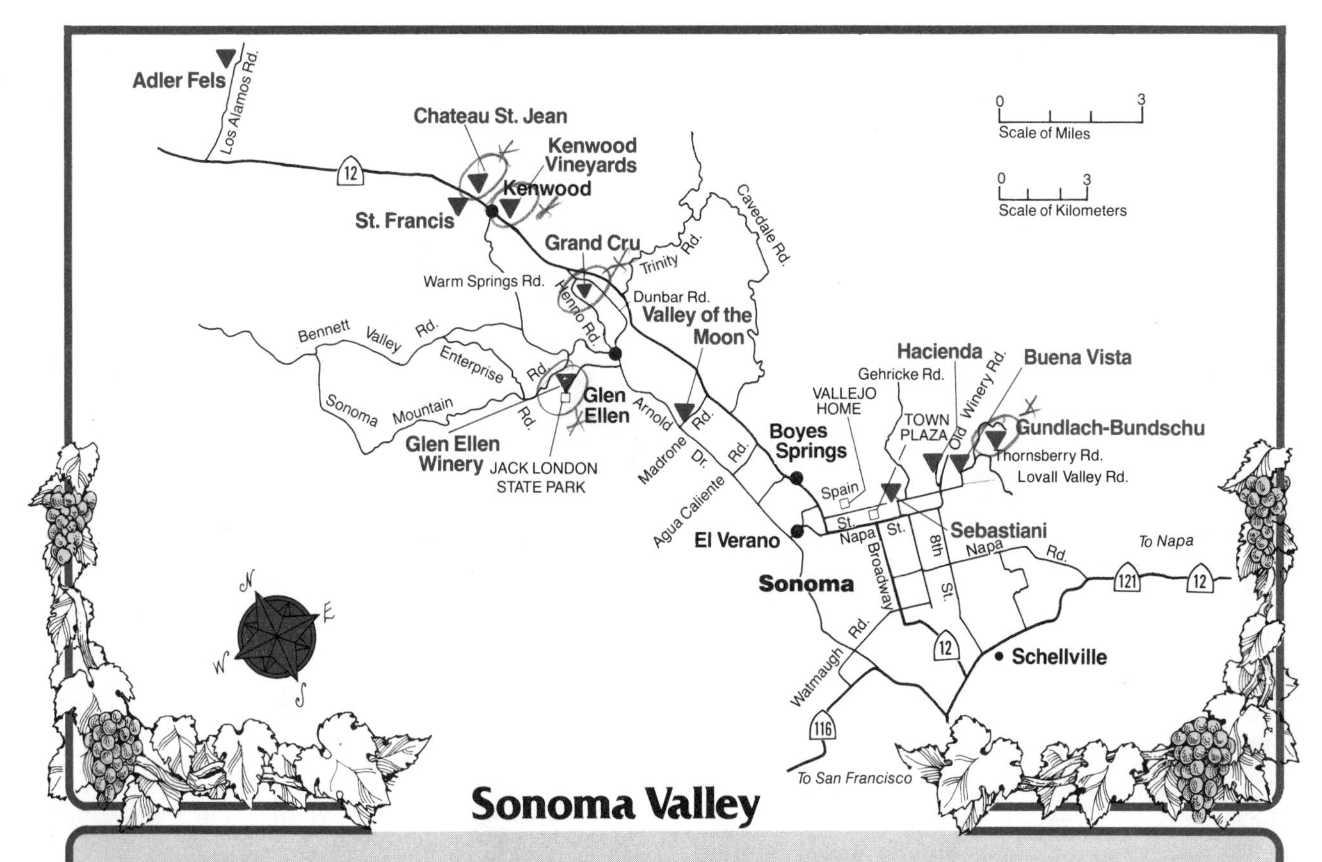

Sonoma Valley

Adler Fels. From Kenwood, N on State 12 to Los Alamos Rd., then E 2.2 mi. to winery drive, Corrick Ln. (5325 Corrick Ln., Santa Rosa, CA 95405) Tel (707) 539-3123. By appt. only.

Buena Vista Winery. From SE corner of Sonoma Plaza, E on E. Napa St. across RR tracks at 8th St. E. to Old Winery Rd., then NE to winery (P.O. Box 182, Sonoma, CA 95476) Tel (707) 938-1266. Picnic. Daily 10-5. IT/Ta.

Chateau St. Jean. From State 12 at N side of Kenwood, E on private winery drive, Goff Rd. (P.O. Box 293, Kenwood, CA 95452) Tel (707) 833-4134. Daily 10-4:30. IT (GT by appt. only)/Ta.

Glen Ellen Winery. From Glen Ellen, W .8 mi. on London Ranch Rd. to winery gate (1443 London Ranch Rd., Glen Ellen, CA 95442) Tel (707) 996-1066. By appt. only. GT.

Grand Cru Vineyards. From State 12 at Glen Ellen, W 100 ft. on Arnold Dr. to Dunbar Rd., N .3 to Henno Rd., then double back on private winery drive (No. 1 Vintage Ln., Glen Ellen, CA 95442) Tel (707) 996-8100. Picnic. Sa, Su, holidays 10-5. IT/Ta.

Gundlach-Bundschu. From SE corner of Sonoma Plaza, E on E. Napa St. to Old Winery Rd., N 4 blocks to Lovall Valley Rd., E 5 blocks to Thornsberry Rd., then continue E .8 mi. to winery (P.O. Box 1, Vineburg, CA 95487) Tel (707) 938-5277. Sa-Su 12-4:30 or by appt. IT/Ta.

Hacienda Wine Cellars. From SE corner of Sonoma Plaza, E on E. Napa St., N on 7th St. E./Castle Rd. to winery gate (P.O. Box 416, Sonoma, CA 95476) Tel (707) 938-3220. Picnic. Daily 9-5. GT by appt./Ta.

Kenwood Vineyards. On E side of State 12 opposite Warm Springs Rd. in Kenwood (P.O. Box 447, Kenwood, CA 95452) Tel (707) 833-5891. Picnic; groups must reserve. Daily 10-4:30. GT by appt./Ta.

St. Francis Vineyards and Winery. On W side of State 12 at N edge of Kenwood (8450 Sonoma Hwy., Kenwood, CA 95452) Tel (707) 833-4666. Daily 10-4:30. IT/Ta.

Sebastiani Vineyards. From NE corner of Sonoma Plaza, E 3 blocks on E. Spain St. to 4th St. E. (P.O. Box AA, Sonoma, CA 95476) Tel (707) 938-5532. Daily 10-5. GT/Ta.

Valley of the Moon Winery. From Sonoma, N 4 mi. on State 12 to Madrone Rd., W .75 mi. to winery (777 Madrone Rd., Glen Ellen, CA 95442) Tel (707) 996-6941. Daily except Th. 10-5. Ta.

Not on Map—Restricted or No Visitor Facilities

H. Cotturi & Sons. (6725 Enterprise Rd., Glen Ellen, CA 95442) Tel (707) 996-6247. By appt. only.

Hanzell Vineyards. (18596 Lomita Ave., Sonoma, CA 95476) Tel (707) 996-3860. By appt. only.

J.J. Haraszthy & Sons. (P.O. Box 375, Sonoma, CA 95476) Tel (707) 996-3040. By appt. only.

Haywood Winery. (18701 Gehricke Rd., Sonoma, CA 95476) Tel (707) 996-4298. By appt. only.

Kistler Vineyards. (2995 Nelligan Rd., Glen Ellen, CA 95442) Tel (707) 833-4662. By appt. only.

Laurel Glen Vineyard. (6611 Sonoma Mountain Rd., Santa Rosa, CA 95404) Tel (707) 546-2875. By appt. only.

Matanzas Creek. (6097 Bennett Valley Rd., Santa Rosa, CA 95404) Tel (707) 542-8242. By appt. only.

Ravenswood. (21415 Broadway, Sonoma, CA 95476) Tel (415) 474-2700. By appt. only.

Richardson Vineyards. (2711 Knob Hill Rd., Sonoma, CA 95476) Tel (707) 938-2610. By appt. only.

Sky Vineyards. (4352 Cavedale Rd., Glen Ellen, CA 95442)

Key: GT (guided tour); IT (informal tour); Ta (tasting).

Hacienda Wine Cellars looks more at home than any of its peers in Sonoma's old Spanish colonial setting because it is housed in a textbook example of Spanish colonial architecture.

The winery dates from 1973, when it was founded by the same Frank Bartholomew who restored Buena Vista to life in the 1940s. Though Bartholomew still has a hand in the winery, the principal owner now is veteran grape grower A. Crawford Cooley. The building goes back farther, to 1926, having formerly been the community hospital.

Tours of the well-appointed cellars are by appointment only, but the richly furnished tasting room is open daily. At one end of it, tasters can look through an iron grill to see the barrel aging cellar. The crusher, press, and fermentors are outdoors at the rear. Oak tanks and the bottling department are in an added wing next to the fermenting tanks.

Hacienda maintains a spacious picnic lawn next to the winery. Some of its tables are in plain sun, some nestle in the shade of oaks, but all look downslope to the town of Sonoma and the valley floor.

The winery produces Chardonnay, Gewürztraminer, Dry Chenin Blanc, Cabernet Sauvignon, Pinot Noir, and Zinfandel.

Hanzell Vineyards is the property of Barbara De Brye of London. With Bob Sessions as winemaker, Hanzell continues the revolution launched in the late 1950s by founder James D. Zellerbach.

The notion was and is that California can equal some of the great wines of Burgundy. The architectural statement of intent is a facade copied after that part of the Clos de Vougeot that comes into view at the end of the entrance tunnel. Inside the winery the effort becomes more concrete with a cellar full of barrels made from oak harvested in the forest of Limoges and coopered in Beaune.

But Hanzell is not mere copying. The production is so carefully planned that the crusher can handle exactly as many grapes per hour as required to fill one stainless steel fermentor with must, and so on, through the whole sequence of winemaking.

A visit is both instructive about thoughtful winery design and a sort of pilgrimage to a place where California wine found a new impetus toward a distinctive style. Hanzell is so small that appointments are required and tasting is not possible. Students of vinous California make the journey gladly to see the place and to buy Chardonnay or Pinot Noir when some of the small annual supply is available.

Haywood Winery occupies a bunkerish concrete cellar cut into a rocky hillside above Sonoma town.

On two levels, it has fermentors, press, and other working gear just inside the front door. A few steps up is a dim, cool parallel gallery given over to French oak barrels. The building had a short life as the winery of Views Land Company before it was purchased by Peter Haywood and rechristened with his family name.

Although a surprising amount of wine is made within a tight confines, the cellar is a one-man show, so visits must be by appointment only. All from Haywood's vineyards higher up the hill behind the winery, the wines are Chardonnay, Johannisberg Riesling, Cabernet Sauvignon, and Zinfandel. The first vintage was 1980.

Kenwood Vineyards, just off State Highway 12 on the south side of Kenwood, has grown from a typical country winery into a modern, sophisticated one without losing the earthy charms of old-fashioned wood barns that are its main cellars.

The place was built in 1906 by the Pagani Brothers, John and Julius, who were more than typically thoughtful. One example: the big crusher-stemmer rests in a notch cut into a bank between two roads. The proprietors can dump grapes into the crusher without lifting them very high, and let stems mound up below, out of the way of work. This is but one of several design factors the current owners have left intact for lack of any way to improve on them.

However, the Martin Lee family has changed the interiors of two old buildings into a thoroughly modern winery. At the upper level of the larger cellar are two long galleries of stainless steel fermenting tanks, Willmes presses, and self-emptying dejuicing tanks designed by the Lees. Below, next to the tasting room, and in a separate cellar building at one side are galleries of French and American oak barrels. (The barrels adjoining the tasting room replaced the last of the old Pagani redwood tanks in 1982.) Bottling and cased goods storage are in a new building designed and executed in 1982 to match the originals. Which building is which is instantly recognizable, but the unpainted board-and-batten exteriors form a pleasing whole.

In the tasting room, decorated with posters taken from Kenwood's artist series labels, Chardonnay, Chenin Blanc, Sauvignon Blanc, Cabernet Sauvignon, Pinot Noir, and Zinfandel are available.

Matanzas Creek occupies an interesting position in the current era of establishing legal boundaries for vineyard districts.

As a matter of hydrology, the winery and its surrounding vineyard are just barely in the Russian River watershed, a few score yards over the ridge that separates the Sonoma Creek drainage from that of the Russian River. However, the property is closer in space, climate, and soils to the Sonoma Valley than to any part of the larger Russian River area planted to vines, so, by government decision, the vines are part of the Sonoma Valley.

Whatever the fine points of geography, the cellar is built into and around a one-time small dairy. The old cold room now is stacked with rows of French oak barrels for the fermenting and aging of Chardonnay, and the aging of several other varietal wines. (This is one of a growing number of wineries both large and small that have taken to fermenting Chardonnay in barrels rather than stainless steel tanks.)

Outdoors are the temperature-controlled stainless steel fermentors, crusher, press, and other modern processing gear.

Proprietors Bill and Sandra MacIver cannot offer tours or tasting freely because of zoning restrictions, but do conduct scheduled open houses during the year for mailing list customers.

In addition to Chardonnay, wines produced at Matanzas Creek include Cabernet Sauvignon, Merlot, and Pinot Noir.

St. Francis Vineyards and Winery is the new kid among three cellars in the town of Kenwood.

Proprietor Joe Martin built his cellars in the classic form of a California barn in time for the vintage of 1979. Red-painted and neat as a pin, the winery has typical equipment: stainless steel fermentors, and an admixture of oak tanks and barrels. In a separate, matching building next to the cellars, the tasting and sales room offers the range of wines: Chardonnay, Gewürztraminer, Johannisberg Riesling, Merlot, and Pinot Noir, all from grapes grown in Martin's adjoining vineyard.

Sebastiani Vineyards anchors the northeast corner of settled Sonoma, starting at Fourth Street East and Spain Street and fanning out in several directions, but mostly northward toward sharply rising hills.

The main wood aging cellars, with the tasting room in one corner, are on the east side of Fourth Street next to a railroad track. In a corner opposite the tasting room, the Sebastiani family has gathered a small crusher, a basket press, and a single 500-gallon oak cask. With this equipment Samuele Sebastiani made his first wine, a Zinfandel, circa 1895. Here is the place to set a perspective for the astonishing changes that have come since then.

From this vantage, orderly rows of varnished, red-hooped redwood tanks extend not quite to infinity, but for a long way. Behind the main wood aging cellar is an ultramodern fermenting room filled with stainless steel tanks for the white wines. Behind this building, in an open space, are the crushers. Behind them, in a separate building, are red wine fermentors. Still farther along is a long, low building filled with oak barrels in which are stored the Sebastiani's most prized reds. Across the railroad track from all of this is the largest building of them all: the stainless steel storage cellar where wines that are ready await their turns for bottling.

Samuele no doubt bottled his early wines at any handy bench and table when he bottled any at all. Today, bottling and case storage require yet a fifth building, across Fourth Street from the others. In its current form it is far longer than the original.

In spite of the growth, the sizable collection of barrels stacked outside the main cellar is not there because the Sebastianis ran out of space within, but because they prefer to bake their sherry-types with the warmth of the sun.

The tour does not take in all of these points. It would tax a marathoner if it did. Rather, it focuses on some of the crucial elements. There is an elevated walkway around the outside of the white wine fermenting room that gives unobstructed views of the crushers and continuous presses as well as the fermentors. Visitors in harvest season may tarry as long as they wish to see how wine begins. Visitors also trek through the main aging cellar with its encyclopedic collection of cooperage. The fillip here is a collection of carved cask heads. Any number of wineries have the odd carved cask or

barrel. The Sebastianis have scores of them, nearly all the work of a local man, Earle Brown, who turned a retirement hobby into the task of Sisyphus.

Samuele Sebastiani died in 1946, leaving a prosperous but generally anonymous business to his son August. Most of the wines had gone into the world under other labels. In the mid-1950s August started abandoning bulk winemaking in favor of having the family name on the family product. He made enormous strides in that direction before his death in 1980. His widow, Sylvia, and son, Sam, continue the course he set.

A full range of table, appetizer, and dessert wines is on hand in a tasting room handsomely crafted from old wine tanks. The winery has three sets of labels: August Sebastiani wines are those in large containers; the regular Sebastiani label goes on regular lots; Sam Sebastiani signature wines are special reserve bottlings of varietal table wines. Under any of these labels, Barbera was and is a synonym for Sebastiani among reds. Green Hungarian is a specialty white; Gamay Beaujolais Nouveau is its red counterpart.

Valley of the Moon Winery, an agreeable collection of sturdy wood-frame buildings, perches on the banks of Sonoma Creek.

Enrico Parducci bought the old vineyard property in 1941, and eventually turned over the reins to his son, Harry, whose son in turn is coming up through the business. The vineyards go back to the 1850s, and were for a time owned by Senator George Hearst.

There is no tour of the new-in-1978 cellar filled with stainless steel fermentors, or of the wood aging cellar with its well-used assemblage of redwood uprights, oak ovals, and oak barrels. But there is tasting in a cool, dark room shaded by a huge California bay laurel that also serves as a sort of trademark for the Valley of the Moon label. This winery long has been a source of generic jug wines. It continues to be, but also has become a source of varietal table wines in fifths. Included in the roster: French Colombard, Semillon, Pinot Noir, and Zinfandel.

Plan a picnic

Sonoma County is a pleasing test of California's capacity for contrast. Its coast, however beautiful, leans toward cool and foggy summers rather than the warm, dry ones of its valleys.

At the expense of 2 or 3 hours' driving in pastoral countryside, a visitor can have a look at winemaking, cheesemaking, and oystering, crabbing, or clamming. At the expense of eight or ten dollars, he can assemble a picnic that combines all the joys of fermentation as company to a main course of seafood.

A well-warmed valley dweller can scoot west from U.S. Highway 101 at Santa Rosa on the Bodega Highway or take a slightly longer route from Sonoma west on State Highway 116 to Petaluma, then west on the Petaluma-Point Reyes Station Road ('D' Street). The latter route has few peers. It is its own pastoral symphony.

In the morning, with the dew still on the grapes, the valleys offer a kind of stillness. Just west of Sonoma, State 116 follows a curving course through dry, spaciously arranged hills, little populated and beginning to warm.

Once Petaluma is behind and the 'D' Street extension begins to be Point Reyes Station Road, the grass is greener and it begins to be dairy country. In the midst of these spacious rolling hills, the Marin French Cheese headquarters come into view. Here, especially with a bottle of wine and a loaf of bread aboard, is the place to lay in a stock of cheese and have a look at how it is made. From the cheese company, it is but a short jump after the retreating morning fog to Marshall and one of the Tomales Bay oyster markets.

What to take? Small individual cutting boards, steak knives (to double as personal cheese knives), wine glasses, and a corkscrew are the only utensils required for this picnic, though a large tray will come in handy.

More wineries. The Sonoma Valley has in addition to its regularly visitable wineries several more with extremely limited welcomes for the public, mainly owing to lack of size.

J.J. Haraszthy & Sons has an aging and bottling cellar in an old stone winery near the village of Glen Ellen. The firm offers a broad range of varietal table wines, but no visitor facilities.

Kistler Vineyards makes small lots of Chardonnay, Pinot Noir, and Cabernet Sauvignon in a cellar high in the hills east of Kenwood, almost on the Sonoma-Napa county line. The winery and a surrounding vineyard are owned by brothers Steven and John Kistler, who made their first wines in 1979.

Laurel Glen Vineyard, well up Sonoma Mountain, makes Cabernet Sauvignon as its primary wine, adding bits of Pinot Noir Blanc and Chardonnay. Proprietors Patrick and Faith Campbell have their winery at the end of a shared private road, so cannot offer tours or retail sales. The first crush was 1980.

Ravenswood is the small winery of Joel Peterson and partners. Located behind a woodworking shop south of Sonoma town, it specializes in Cabernet Sauvignon and Zinfandel. The winery began elsewhere in 1976.

Richardson Vineyards, on the flats south of Sonoma town, began in 1980. Dennis Richardson produces small lots of Cabernet Sauvignon, Gamay Nouveau, and Zinfandel among reds. Sauvignon Blanc is the white. Because winery and home are together, the proprietor offers no tasting or retail sales.

Sky Vineyards is a tiny vineyard and winery producing only Zinfandel. Owned by Lore and Aleta Olds, it is above Boyes Springs on a slope so remote that no electricity is available for the cellars. The proprietors made the first wine for their label in 1979.

Other Than Wineries

With all its history, the Sonoma Valley is a particularly easy place in which to find changes of pace from wine cellars. With all its people, it is not such an easy place in which to find uncrowded picnic parks.

On the old Sonoma Plaza and all around it, visitors cannot help but consort with the shades of history. Sonoma's mission, last in the Franciscan chain, stands on the northeast corner of the plaza, the most eye-arresting part of a complex State Historic Monument.

The chapel no longer serves a religious purpose but has been preserved in its original state, or nearly so. Other rooms in the lengthy adobe building house collections of mission appointments, pioneer memorabilia, civic documents, and Indian arrowheads and other tools of the times.

Across First Street East, the old Mexican army barracks have been restored to something like their original appearance. The most appealing section is a rear courtyard complete with roosting chickens and other homey touches, but reader boards inside provide clearer insights into the reason for the plaza's being.

Other buildings on the plaza date from mission or Mexican times, but are not open to tour as part of the state park. However the stately home of General Mariano Vallejo, last Mexican governor of California, is open as a major element of the park. Its long entry drive is three blocks west along Spain Street from the barracks. The house is a museum of family life at the top in the mid-nineteenth century. Its name, Lachryma Montis, after a spring on the property, also went on the label of Vallejo's wines.

Not far down Broadway from the plaza is privately owned Train Town, a narrow-gauge steam train that rambles around a meadow full of old-fashioned buildings rather larger than doll houses. It is the most exciting relief in the area for children who have walked through more wineries than they cared to visit.

Sonoma Plaza has become a major tourist stop in recent years. Whenever the weather is mild or better, the little park at its center bustles with picnickers, children playing on swings and other equipment, and park bench dozers. The ring of shops is just as crowded. But the average weekend horde pales in comparison to the throngs that show up for the oldest of the state's vintage festivals. It usually is scheduled for the last weekend in September.

The festival puts considerable emphasis on local history. Many Sonomans allow themselves to be conscripted for on-stage or back-stage service in a historical pageant or in one of the parades that celebrate the careers of the mission fathers, the Vallejo family, and the Haraszthys.

The wineries themselves play a quiet role. They elaborate on their daily welcome to visitors but do not invade the serenity of history. The effect is startlingly uncommercial.

A few miles north of Sonoma at Glen Ellen, Jack London State Park is another major visitor attraction in the Sonoma Valley. London finished his days on a ranch in the hills west of Glen Ellen, leaving some considerable marks on the property. His wife's staunch stone house is now a museum of family memorabilia. His own grandiose home, Wolf House, remains the burnt-out shell of stone walls it became on the eve he planned to occupy it. Higher up the hill is the old working ranch, which the author built around several big brick buildings that earlier had been the Kohler and Froehling Winery. The turnoff from State Highway 12 to the park is marked clearly.

Plotting a Route

The town of Sonoma lies 45 miles north of San Francisco. U.S. Highway 101 across the Golden Gate is the most direct northward artery from the city. It connects with State Highway 37 just north of Hamilton Air Force Base. That road runs east to an intersection with State Highway 121, which leads north toward the town of Sonoma. There is one more turn, clearly marked, onto State Highway 12, which runs right into the plaza as Broadway. All but the State 121 and State 12 legs are divided highway.

The main approach from the north is winding, scenic, two-lane State 12, which cuts inland from U.S. 101 at Santa Rosa.

Coming from the East Bay, the direct approach is Interstate Highway 80 to Vallejo, then west on State 37 to American Canyon, State 29 to Napa, and State 121 to the same intersection with State 12 that serves travelers on U.S. 101. For travelers coming from the Central Valley, substitute State 12 from Cordelia for the State 37 section of the route from the East Bay.

The Sonoma Valley is connected with other parts of the world by unhurried roads, too. These provide scenic if slightly slow access to the Pacific shore on one side and the Napa Valley on the other.

The dawdling route west toward the sea is State Highway 116 from Sonoma through Petaluma.

On any day of touring both Sonoma and Napa wineries, the back road from Sonoma through Vineburg to an intersection with State 121 trims a mile or two from the State 12/121 route. Another alternative is the Trinity/Oakville Grade road between State 12 near Glen Ellen and State 29 at Oakville on the Napa side. It crosses a steep-sided part of the Mayacamas Mountains. In either direction the climb is slow and grinding, the descent wearing on brakes. The rewards are superlative panoramas of both valleys and some pleasing smaller views in between. Yet another alternative is St. Helena Road/Petrified Forest Road, which connects with State 12 between Kenwood and Santa Rosa on the Sonoma side, and with State Highway 128 near Calistoga in the Napa Valley. This route is not quite as taxing as Trinity-Oakville, but doesn't fall far short of the mark. Part way along, Spring Mountain Road branches away to St. Helena. The latter is the steepest, curliest route of them all.

The Russian River Region

Between Geyserville and Forestville the Russian River suffers a period of extreme indecision before it turns west in a serious and successful bid to reach the Pacific Ocean.

Its meanderings create a whole maze of hillsides and benches favorable to the growing of fruit, especially apples and grapes. In a great crescent west and north of Santa Rosa, fruit growing remains the principal business of an agricultural district of diverse physical charms.

U.S. Highway 101 slices straight up the Russian River Valley, offering a surprisingly pleasant introduction to the region as it goes. But the truly joyous scenery is reserved for those who dawdle along the two-lane country roads flanking the freeway on either side. The differences of climate and soil reveal themselves at every turning. Redwood forests give way to grassy plains which give way in turn to oak-covered knolls. The oak knolls look up to bare, steep hillsides.

Through all of this change grapes stay in the landscape, not in the unbroken carpet that marks the Napa Valley, but in steady abundance. For students of the fine point of wine, Sonoma is yielding to a long list of more specific names almost before it is recognizable for itself. In the drainage of the Russian River alone, winemakers and bibbers alike speak of Alexander Valley, Dry Creek, the West Side, and Cloverdale with easy familiarity.

In the subtle geography of grapegrowing, the names have real meaning. Several are not far from winning federal government recognition as appellations of origin. (Sonoma Valley, the only major part of the county with a watershed draining into San Francisco Bay rather than the ocean, already has federal approval.) For purposes of touring, the lines are not of great importance. For all the important differences of climate and soil a fine network of roads unites the lot into one sprawling but easily usable district.

The Wineries

The Russian River watershed supports wineries every bit as diverse as its climate and soils might suggest, from gigantic Colony to tiny A. Rafanelli. The diversity is new.

From the end of Prohibition until the end of the 1960s this was mainly a region of middle-sized family wineries that sold most or all of their production to large firms with well-advertised labels. During the late 1960s there began a two-pronged shift. One prong was the development of several sizable firms owned by corporations and attuned to the production and marketing of vintage-dated varietal wines at comparatively modest prices. The other was a sharp increase of small, mostly privately owned cellars dedicated to small-lot winemaking, often of single-vineyard wines selling toward the top end of the price scale. Their arrival caused many of the old-line firms to turn to vintage-dated varietal wines for sale under their own labels.

With the advent of the 1960s newcomers, this became a rewarding region to visit. With the flood of new entries from the 1970s and early 1980s, it rivals Napa for numbers of opportunities, but does not have so many tourists crowded onto so few roads.

In the introduction to this section, one sentence suggests that the region does not need to be toured in subdistricts. True. But it can be. The wineries come in clusters closely paralleling the country's vineyard geography, with the added possibility of sticking close to U.S. 101 from end to end.

The regularly visitable highwayside cellars include, south to north, Landmark, Sonoma Vineyards, Sotoyome, Foppiano, Cambiaso, Simi, Souverain, Trentadue, Nervo, Geyser Peak, Pastori, Colony, Le Bay, and California Wine Co.

Around Forestville, in the area generally described as the West Side, are Davis Bynum, De Loach, Domaine Laurier, Hop Kiln, Iron Horse, Korbel, Mark West, Martini & Prati, and Topolos at Russian River.

Close to Healdsburg, west of U.S. 101 in or near Dry Creek Valley, are Dry Creek Vineyards, Fritz Cellars, Lambert Bridge, Mill Creek, Pedroncelli, Stemmler, and Rafanelli.

Still close to Healdsburg, but east of the freeway in Alexander Valley, are Alexander Valley, Field Stone, Johnson's of Alexander Valley, Sausal, and Soda Rock.

Cloverdale's wineries are close to the freeway, save for Cordtz Brothers and Pat Paulsen Vineyards.

This list of the more accessible cellars is expanded considerably by more private wineries. The following entries are alphabetic for a region a little more than 30 miles long and as much as 15 miles wide.

Alexander Valley Vineyards manages to bring several major historic themes in California winemaking together into one quietly attractive piece of architecture.

Set at the rear of its sizable block of home vineyard, the cellar building uses adobe block and weathered wood to evoke thoughts of colonial Spain, the Old West, and contemporary California. Built in 1975, it looks far more settled than its few years suggest.

As for the working winery, it offers to those who would take the appointment-only tour a mixture of typical and original ideas. The typical ideas are an outdoor pad with stemmer-crusher and Willmes basket press, and an indoor room full of temperature-controlled stainless steel fermentors. The original ideas are embodied in a lower cellar that is kept cooler and more moist than one on the upper level. The lower one is full of French oak for Burgundian varieties, especially Chardonnay, while the upper one is full of American oak for the aging of Cabernet Sauvignon. The notion, as old European hands will recognize, is to duplicate the environment of a *cave* in Beaune on the one hand and a *chai* in the Medoc on the other.

Tasting of Alexander Valley Vineyards' Chardonnay, Chenin Blanc, Gewürztraminer, Johannisberg Riesling, Cabernet Sauvignon, and Pinot Noir goes on indoors in a pleasant room, or, not infrequently, outdoors on a shaded porch overlooking the press and a block of vines. Picnickers may obtain permission to use the outdoor tables.

History buffs may wish to wander up a grassy knoll behind the winery to the gravesites of the Cyrus Alexander family, the pioneers after whom the valley is named, and whose sprawling ranch had its homestead on what is now the winery property of Harry Wetzel, Jr., and Harry Wetzel III.

Bellerose Vineyard is a try at bridging several gaps between California and France.

The property at the mouth of Dry Creek Valley is an old-time winemaking estate in California. As far back as the 1870s it was a stage stop, which explains some of the buildings. Not long after, circa 1887, it became the vineyard and winery of Capt. Everett A. Wise. Following Prohibition it came back as a typical Sonoma County mixed farm, growing grapes and prunes among other crops. In 1979 it was returned to winemaking.

Charles and Nancy Richard (pronounced Ri-shard in tribute to French ancestors in the family) have given the place a French name and set about making a red wine based in Cabernet Sauvignon but including all of the major grapes of Bordeaux (Cabernet Franc, Malbec, Merlot, and Petit Verdot), in tribute to the French ancestors of California Cabernets. The other wine on a short roster is a dry rosé called Rosé du Val.

Again after a French fashion, the winery comes in two separate buildings. Fermenting and bottling take place in a new wood-frame building that faces an imposingly large, solid nineteenth century barn, both set in a grove of trees part way up a long slope. Barrel aging goes on in the second cellar built up from surviving stone walls of the Wise winery.

Visitors, in addition to looking through the winery, will do well to stroll up to the top row of vines for a peaceful view across the Russian River Valley.

Davis Bynum Winery has evolved a good deal in getting to its present location on the site of a one-time hop barn above a sharp bend in the Russian River west of Healdsburg.

The property of a former San Francisco newspaperman after whom it is named, the firm started in 1965 in an ordinary store front on a busy commercial street in the East Bay town of Albany, feinted once in the direction of the Napa Valley, then moved to its current wooded, hilly location in time for the vintage of 1974.

The main working winery is in a big, unadorned masonry block building of two offset sections. The rearward one holds stainless steel fermentors and other large cooperage. The section nearer the entry drive has cased goods and a tasting area on its upper level and barrel aging cellars below grade. Crusher and press sit on a pad at one end. At the opposite side of the main building, an old barn left over from an earlier proprietorship contains the bottling line and empty bottles awaiting use. Both buildings are well back from West Side Road, behind a cluster of wood frame office buildings, equipment barns, and residences.

Visitors are mildly discouraged from taking tours because the buildings are crowded with working gear, but are warmly welcomed at the tasting bar, which sits as a sort of clearing amid stacks of cases.

Wines under the Bynum label come mainly from local grapes, but include some from as far away as San Luis Obispo County. The roster of varietals includes Chardonnay, Fumé Blanc, Cabernet Sauvignon, Merlot, Petite Sirah, and Zinfandel.

California Wine Company is a sheltering name for a quartet of labels, each representing a different grapegrowing region.

The roster includes Arroyo Sonoma for Sonoma Chardonnay, Cabernet Sauvignon, and Pinot Noir; Potter Valley for Mendocino Chardonnay, Johannisberg Riesling, and Sauvignon Blanc; Sage Creek for Napa Chardonnay, Sauvignon Blanc, Cabernet Sauvignon, and Zinfandel; and Bandiera for varietal and generic wines blended from one or more of the above districts. There are more details: selected lots of Arroyo Sonoma and Potter Valley bear individual vineyard designations.

Representative bottlings from all of these labels are available for tasting at a plain-on-the-outside, pleasant-from-the-inside highwayside building in Cloverdale.

The winemaking for all four labels goes on a few blocks away at the site of the old Bandiera winery, which is not the same thing as saying it goes on in the old Bandiera winery. There is a substantial, modern fermenting building upslope from the original winery, the latter completely revamped by new owners to make a storage cellar with one sizable gallery full of stainless steel, and larger one filled with French oak barrels.

Cambiaso Vineyards sits near the top of a round hill in the southeast quarter of Healdsburg, at the end of a narrow and twisting lane.

Visitors who remember the place from 1974 or earlier may recall a couple of weathered wood barns and a squat winery covered with corrugated sheet metal, a classic vision of the country jug cellar. It no longer is that.

Today, Cambiaso has a big, ultramodern cellar full of stainless steel fermentors and storage tanks, and an equally modern structure for its bottling line and cased goods warehouse. The old cellar now holds redwood tanks, a growing collection of oak tanks and barrels, and a retail sales desk.

The winery dates from 1934, when Giovanni and Maria Cambiaso started making wine in a wooden barn. The great expansion followed the sale of the property to Four Seas Investment Corporation by the second generation of Cambiasos.

Because neither the winding lane nor the sloping site permits many visitors at one time, Cambiaso offers neither tours nor tasting, but only sales.

The wine list still has jug generics, but emphasis is shifting toward varietals, notably including Chardonnay, Chenin Blanc, Sauvignon Blanc, Cabernet Sauvignon, Petite Sirah, and Zinfandel.

Colony is the new name for a winery that was known as Italian Swiss Colony for almost a century, or until marketing became a social force. Only the name has been changed. As when this was Italian Swiss, the wines offered under the label come from here, there, and elsewhere about the state, but the public face is at Asti near the town of Cloverdale.

Andrea Sbarbaro founded Asti in the early 1880s as a communal refuge for Italian Swiss who were out of work and out of money in San Francisco. The communal idea did not work out, but Sbarbaro reorganized the winery into a private company and persevered. After an enforced idle period during Prohibition, the winery and label were revived. Over the years since, the property has evolved through several forms and now is a subsidiary of the Heublein Corporation and a good deal shorter in the name.

It must have been hard to get visitors to Asti in Sbarbaro's time. An inveterate practical joker, he rigged the grounds of his mansion with all kinds of gadgets modeled after the ones at Hellbrunn Castle in Austria, which is to say most of them sprinkled or sprayed their victims with abundant water.

The mansion still is there but defused and, what is more, safely off the tour routes just in case some of the old booby traps escaped demolition. The winery, meanwhile, is one of the prime tourist attractions in all the California wine industry.

(Continued on next page)

. . . Continued from page 43

Colony sprawls parallel to U.S. 101 in a little valley between the roadway and the Russian River. It is an old winery, exhibiting many souvenirs of its past, but it also has much to show that is new. In sum, it is a good place to see how wine is made on a large scale.

Tours depart from a chalet-style reception building for close-up looks at a modern crushing station, an impressive array of big stainless steel fermentors, and an even more impressive collection of big redwood tanks. Included among the latter is the largest one known, an 80,000-gallon piece with enough room inside to sleep a platoon of infantry.

In the tasting room, hosts offer the wide range of wines labeled as Colony. The proprietors have explored the production of flavored wines more thoroughly than any other offering tasting. These include coffee-flavored, citrus-flavored, fruit-flavored, and lightly spiced wines. The roster also encompasses the full spectrum of varietal and generic table wines, appetizer, and dessert wines.

Cordtz Brothers Cellars occupies an old winery well known among winemakers but little known to the world at large.

A skillful winemaker named Hollis Black operated the cellars for years, selling almost everything he made to other wineries in bulk until late in his career, when he turned briefly to bottling wine under his own label. To a practiced eye, the place still gives evidence of its former role. One building is, in effect, two rows of concrete fermentors with a roof over them. The other is a well-made barn with still more concrete fermentors inside it.

Starting in time for the vintage of 1980, father and son, Dr. William and Dave, Cordtz built their new winery in and around the old concrete. They cut man-sized doors between the fermentors in one row, and turned them into a serial tasting room and barrel aging cellar. Still more French puncheons and barrels rest on top of the old concrete tanks. One wedge-shaped concrete fermentor in the barn has been made over to hold a library of Cordtz wines. The rest of the barn contains new stainless steel fermentors and other processing equipment.

From vineyards nearby along the Russian River southeast of Cloverdale come grapes for Chardonnay, Gewürztraminer, Sauvignon Blanc, Zinfandel, and Cabernet Sauvignon, plus a sweet Muscat Blanc sold only at the winery.

De Loach Vineyards belongs firmly in the new wave of small, family-owned and operated wineries in Sonoma County. Cecil De Loach is his own winemaker, son John manages the vineyards, and son Michael runs the sales side of the business.

Winery and vineyards are out at the west edge of the Santa Rosa plain, where the first low rolls lead to genuine hill country within a mile. At the middle of one block of family vines, the cellars are well-proportioned, sturdily made, impeccably maintained wood-frame buildings patterned on local barns. The original was built in time for the winery's first vintage in 1979. By 1982 it was so full of fermentors and French oak barrels that the proprietor had to go outdoors to get from one end of the place to the other, in his view reason enough to add a second structure so that barrels and fermentors could be separated and spaced out a bit.

The roster of wines, all from family vineyards, includes Chardonnay, Gewürztraminer, Fumé Blanc, Pinot Noir, Zinfandel, and a blanc de noir from zinfandel.

Domaine Laurier's vineyards stretch, long and narrow, between a quick creek and steep, wooded hills northwest of Forestville. They are the picture of idyllic charm in a region full of such beauty.

Proprietors Jacob and Barbara Shilo (pronounced shee-lo) have plans for an understated Tudor winery building worthy of the scene, but it was at least a year away in spring 1982. Meanwhile, the cellars are charmingly extemporaneous.

A solid, but hardly stylish, old red barn serves as the core. On two sides, wide overhanging roofs of plastic paneling shelter fermentors and other processing equipment. On the third side of the barn a pair of insulated freight containers expand Domaine Laurier's storage space. Against this backdrop of make-do architecture, the equipment is a thoughtful mixture of the best of modern and traditional. The mazelike old barn is full of French oak barrels. The fermentors for red wines are open-topped redwood, those for whites temperature-controlled stainless steel (or, in the case of part of the Chardonnay, barrels). Crusher-stemmer, press, and filter all are modern to the minute.

The winery dates from 1978. The roster of wines includes Chardonnay, Sauvignon Blanc, Pinot Noir, and Cabernet Sauvignon.

Donna Maria Vineyards ranks among the most beautifully set properties in a county full of them. On a long upslope separating Windsor from the upper end of the Alexander Valley, vines make a lush foreground to bare, grassy hills. This is a good place to talk about vineyard microclimates because it is steep enough that morning fogs stay on the lower slopes longer than the upper ones, hence separated plantings of varieties according to how much more or less sun each prefers.

The winery building—redwood board and batten on a steel frame—is well back from Chalk Hill Road, hidden in a little fold. Within is a typical modern California cellar: modern stemmer-crusher and press, stainless steel fermentors, French oak barrels.

Proprietor Fred Furth started the winery in 1980 amid vines planted several years earlier. The roster to date includes Chardonnay, Gewürztraminer, and Pinot Noir. Sauvignon Blanc and Cabernet Sauvignon are to join these.

Dry Creek Vineyard is located, appropriately enough, in Dry Creek Valley several miles west of Healdsburg.

The winery was founded in 1972. Proprietor David Stare completed the first stage of his handsome masonry block building in time for the harvest of 1973. In 1978 a new wing set perpendicular to the original one doubled the size of the cellars.

Though the comfortable tasting room is open daily, tours without appointment are chancy, depending on

How to read a California wine label

The first new rules since 1933 are scheduled to govern what California wine labels may or must say beginning in 1983. Most winemakers have been following these rules for some time.

Estate Bottled. Vines and winery must be within the geographic appellation shown, and the winery must control the grapegrowing.

1974. A vintage date can appear only if 95 percent or more of the grapes were harvested and crushed in the year stated. The margin simplifies topping up of wines aging in cask.

Napa Valley. Some statement of geographic origin is required. To be labeled "California," 100 percent of the grapes must be grown in the state. For "Napa County," at least 75 percent must be grown in the named county. As many as three counties may be used in a multicounty appellation if corresponding percentages are shown. For "Napa Valley" or other Official American Viticultural Area, 85 percent must be grown in the named area.

Cabernet Sauvignon. Varietal labeling requires that 75 percent of the wine be from the grape named. If used with an appellation, the minimum required percentage of the named grape must come from the appellation area. Generics (named for colors or after ancestral regions in Europe) have no requirements as to grape varieties used.

Produced and bottled by. At least 75 percent of the grapes were fermented by the bottling winery. **Made and bottled by** requires at least 10 percent of the grapes to be fermented by the bottling winery. **Cellared and bottled by, vinted and bottled by,** and other phrases do not require the bottler to have fermented any of the wine.

Alcohol 12½ percent by volume. The law allows a 1½ percent variation on either side of the stated amount. Some labels also give, voluntarily, residual sugar (unfermented grape sugar), total acid, and other specifics.

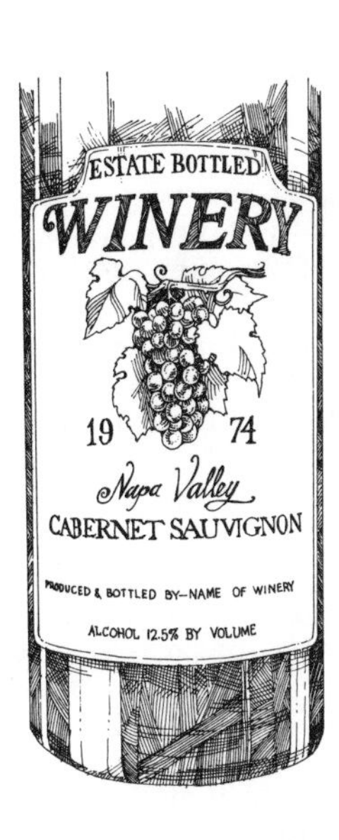

the availability of a small staff with more than enough work to do. Diligent scholars may wish to make arrangements for this is an instructive small winery.

Temperature-controlled stainless steel fermentors and other processing gear are along one outside wall of the original building. Inside that wall is the oak barrel aging cellar. The new wing holds stainless steel storage tanks, the bottling line, and stored cases awaiting sale to the retail market. It is possible to see all steps in wine production from a point where the two wings join, although the walls require a couple of steps one way or another to get the views clearly. Vineyards are but another few steps away. The tasting room is in the new wing. Dry Creek wines offered there include Chardonnay, Chenin Blanc, Fumé Blanc, Cabernet Sauvignon, and Zinfandel.

Visitors are welcome to picnic at tables set on a lawn in the angle formed by the two wings.

Field Stone Winery is dedicated to efficiency in several ways.

First, it was built underground to keep the cellars naturally stable in temperature. The building is not a cave. Rather, founder Wallace Johnson carved a trench into a soft knoll in the Alexander Valley, built the cellars in it, then covered the whole structure with earth from the excavation. The facade is field stone turned up during cultivation of the family vineyards, hence the name and the unobtrusive appearance of the winery in the landscape.

Second, the place is a veritable study in using every inch of space. For example, the stainless steel fermentors do not stand in rows, but are clustered so tightly together that a cat would have a hard time getting between them. However, gates and valves are turned in just such a way that a cellarman can reach five tanks without moving a step.

(Continued on next page)

. . . Continued from page 45

Finally, the working winery was designed to handle mechanically harvested, field-crushed must. Nothing is surprising about this, for the late Wallace Johnson was a pioneer developer of the mechanical harvester, and was experimenting with field crushers and field presses at Field Stone until his death in 1979. The winery continues in family hands, and the mechanical experiments continue, but such balky varieties as Gewürztraminer and Johannisberg Riesling are harvested by hand, and there is little or no field crushing pending more satisfactory designs of various pieces of equipment.

Amid all the steel and other modern gear, the tasting room is a comfortably old-fashioned, woody place. Wines available there include dry Chenin Blanc, Gewürztraminer, Johannisberg Riesling, a proprietary rosé called Spring-Cabernet, Cabernet Sauvignon, and Petite Sirah.

L. Foppiano Wine Company perches directly alongside Old Redwood Highway not far south of its exit from U.S. 101 at Healdsburg.

An aged, dark-painted main cellar building is due to acquire a new, less-plain face during the early 1980s. When it does, the modern touches inside will be less surprising. Not least among the visual shocks behind the original facade is a fermenting room full of stainless steel tanks which the family moved into place by the simple expedient of removing the roof and lowering them into position with cranes. Another new addition is a steadily growing collection of oak barrels. Among the traditional touches are some well-used redwood tanks, and a couple of long lines of unbreakable concrete aging tanks which also form exterior walls.(Since they cannot be destroyed, the Foppianos still use them as giant bottles, an easy trick after the invention of glasslike coatings.)

The Foppianos are a more durable presence in California winemaking than the brief existence of their label would suggest. The original Foppiano, John, bought the property in 1896. The first Louis Foppiano took over in 1910. His son, also Louis, re-established the business in 1934, and still directs it with help from his two sons, Louis and Rod.

They began bottling vintage-dated varietals in the late 1960s after a long career in the bulk and jug wine business. Production shifted sharply to varietal wines in the 1970s. The roster now includes Chardonnay, Chenin Blanc, Fumé Blanc, Cabernet Sauvignon, Petite Sirah, and Zinfandel.

With the coming of varietals the winery began to elaborate on its welcome to visitors. A new tasting room and picnic area opened in 1979. There are no regular guided tours, but visitors with an appointment may have a look around the sturdy old cellars.

Fritz Cellars stands out as individual in an era of distinctive winery architecture.

Buried in a steep hillside well above Dry Creek Valley, the winery is an extended round arch bent at the middle of its long axis at about the same angle as a boomerang. The main entrance announces the arch with tall, round-topped doors trimmed in the Art Deco style. The arch disappears for a moment in the tasting room, but reappears in a fermenting cellar painted pale blue for cheer and ribbed every few feet for support. Beneath rows of stainless steel fermentors—slanted at the top to fit the curving wall—is another cellar filled with upright oak tanks and fat, Burgundian barrels. This one is rectangular.

The roster of wines produced in this well-rounded environment includes Chardonnay, Sauvignon Blanc, a Rosé of Pinot Noir, Gamay Beaujolais, and Petite Sirah.

Tasters can stay inside, or, in fair weather, can examine the wines outdoors at umbrella-shaded tables in the entry court. Fritz also has tree-shaded picnic tables downhill from the winery along the bank of a sizable pond.

Geyser Peak Winery is one of several Sonoma County wineries that are both old and new.

As an old cellar it made both bulk wine and wine vinegar under the ownership of the family Bagnani. Long-time drivers of U.S. 101 through Geyserville still lament the disappearance of the old sign advising that no Geyser Peak wine was available for sale because the proprietors drank it all. However, it had to go. All of the Bagnanis in the world would have a hard time keeping up with current supplies. Even the new proprietors do not have enough bibbers to keep pace.

Under the ownership of the Jos. Schlitz Brewing Co., Geyser Peak is a great deal more than it used to be, and a little bit less. To get rid of the little bit less part, the firm no longer makes or sells vinegar. As for the great deal more: Two large concrete-walled buildings, flanking the stone-and-wood barn that was the original winery, were being joined in 1982 by a third, which will partially hide the old-timer from the freeway. The old cellar now holds bits of redwood and oak cooperage and a complex of packaging lines (the company uses not only bottles, but boxes and cans). Of the two flanking cellars, one contains the presses, stainless steel fermenting tanks, and other processing gear. The other is full of stainless steel storage tanks. The building under construction is to hold cased goods. Yet another building on the opposite side of U.S. 101 has much of the wood cooperage.

Tours of all this are limited to groups with appointments. However, all comers are welcome to taste Geyser Peak wines in a handsomely appointed room in the steel aging cellar next to the original building. Geyser Peak also offers picnic tables under shading trees on the opposite side of the original winery, and still more in a grove of trees east of the highway and next to a vineyard. A pair of hiking trails round out the public welcome. One runs along the river from the picnic ground there. The other courses through hills behind the winery.

The roster of Geyser Peak wines includes Chardonnay, Fumé Blanc, and Gewürztraminer in whites; and Cabernet Sauvignon, Pinot Noir, and Zinfandel in reds. A second label, Summit, goes on generic wines.

Hop Kiln Winery occupies the most outrageously dramatic building of any cellar in the whole of Sonoma County. As the name forthrightly states, it was a hop kiln, which is a guarantee of one tower, but not necessarily three. Neither is it a guarantee that all three will soar above the general roof line. However, at Hop Kiln, there are three, each soaring to the same point of improbability.

Hop Kiln belongs to Dr. Martin Griffin, hence the full name, Hop Kiln Winery at Griffin Vineyard. He uses the ground floor as his winery and a sort of mezzanine as the tasting room.

The view from the tasting room windows is of vineyards on a long bench above the Russian River southwest of Healdsburg. The interior view at tasting level is of antique woodworking—cabinets, bar, and more. The view below the rail is of working winery.

The winery itself is very small. A crusher and press are outside the back wall. Inside are a few small stainless steel tanks and several racks of oak barrels. To lean on the mezzanine railing is to see all, but the proprietors will take people downstairs so they can see the works up close, and also so they can have a look at the old hop-drying equipment.

The roster of varietal wines includes Chardonnay, Gewürztraminer, Petite Sirah, and Zinfandel. A proprietary white is called A Thousand Flowers. The counterpart red is known as Marty's Big Red.

Iron Horse Ranch & Vineyard is a new winery on a middle-aged vineyard planted on a pioneer property in sharply rolling hill country near Forestville.

In 1982, in fact, the winery was still expanding into a new, third building. The original, largest of the three, holds stainless steel fermentors and other processing equipment, plus some oak cooperage. The newest building, adjacent to the original, was to become the barrel aging cellar on completion. Both offer splendid views of the rolling vineyard and hills beyond it. The third building, downslope from the others, was on the way to becoming a separate cellar for sparkling wine after initial service as the main barrel aging cellar. All three are wood-frame structures with board-and-batten siding in the classic style of California barns.

Founded in 1978 by Audrey and Barry Sterling and Forrest Tancer, Iron Horse produces Chardonnay, Pinot Noir, Pinot Noir Blanc, and sparkling wines from previously planted vineyards at the winery; and Cabernet Sauvignon, Sauvignon Blanc, and Zinfandel from another vineyard in Alexander Valley.

The name, incidentally, comes from a former owner of the property who had a predilection for railroadiana and who had a zoo-sized rail line on the place.

Johnson's Alexander Valley Winery looks like a good many of the wooden barns that dot the countryside in northern Sonoma County. Vertical wooden siding and a sharply peaked metal roof mark the structure. However, this is another book not to be judged by its cover.

The winemaking equipment is modern from stemmer-crusher to temperature-controlled stainless steel fermentors, and the oak cooperage is of the same sorts to be found in wineries that just started operations this year.

More surprising, the building is also a sort of unofficial museum and repair shop for pipe organs, parts of which line the cellar walls.

Oak Casks

Once a month during the cool months, the cellar doubles as a concert hall for a guest organist. During the warm season, monthly concerts are held outdoors on a small stage next to a picnic lawn.

The tasting room is amidships, between the fermentors at one end and the wood aging cellar at the other. In it, visitors may sample Johnson varietal wines daily, the roster including Chenin Blanc, Johannisberg Riesling, Cabernet Sauvignon, Pinot Noir, Zinfandel, and a white wine from pinot noir grapes.

The winery and surrounding vineyards are owned by three brothers, Jay, Tom, and Will Johnson. Tom makes the wine. Jay is the business manager and organ buff.

F. Korbel and Bros. is a name most famous for sparkling wine. The winery was founded in 1882 by Francis, Joseph, and Anton Korbel, a trio of diligent brothers from Bohemia. The three settled first in San Francisco, then moved to the Russian River area to mount a large-scale redwood logging operation. When the trees were gone, they decided to plant grapes on newly bared hillsides above the Russian River.

A few of the stumps were too much for them, and remained implacable in the midst of vine rows for decades. Finally, time and larger machinery overcame them, but surviving trees ring Korbel vineyard blocks near Guerneville to give some hint of the labor required to clear these lands.

Since 1954 the winery has belonged to the Heck family. Alsatian by origin, the Hecks have mixed tradition and progress in the making of sparkling wine.

The process here is *methode champenoise*. Much of the basic method used at the winery is little changed from the earliest days of sparkling wine. What has changed has changed slightly and slowly. For example, sediment used to be moved down into the neck of each

(Continued on page 50)

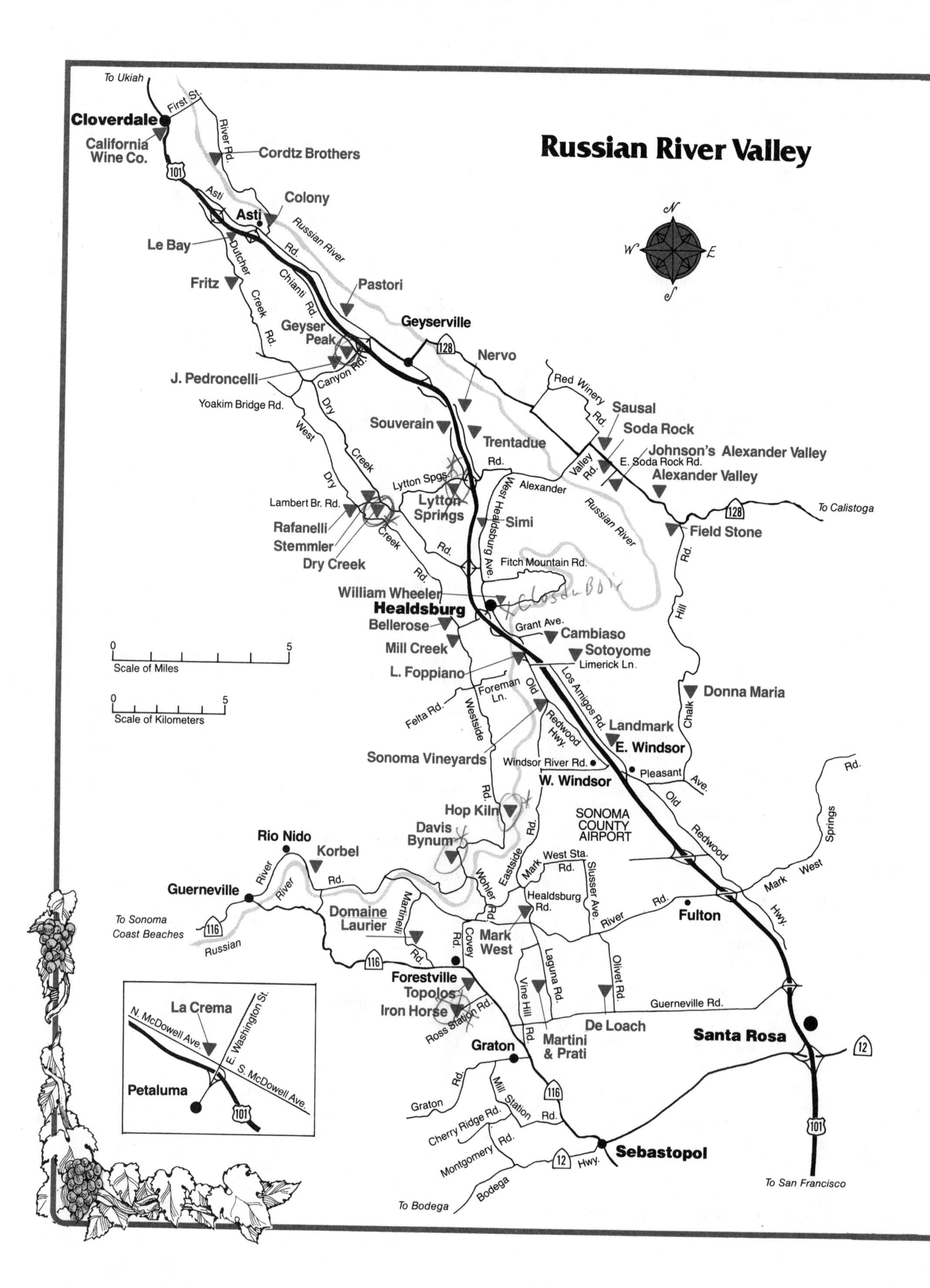

Russian River Valley
To Ukiah
First St.
Cloverdale
California Wine Co.
River Rd.
Cordtz Brothers
101
Asti
Colony
Russian River
Le Bay
Dutcher
Creek
Rd.
Rd.
Chianti
Rd.
Fritz
Pastori
Geyser Peak
Geyserville
128
Nervo
Canyon Rd.
J. Pedroncelli
Yoakim Bridge Rd.
Dry
West
Red Winery Rd.
Sausal
Soda Rock
Johnson's Alexander Valley
E. Soda Rock Rd.
Alexander Valley
Valley Rd.
Souverain
Trentadue
Rd.
Creek
Dry
Lytton Spgs.
Lytton Springs
West Healdsburg Ave.
Alexander
Lambert Br. Rd.
Rafanelli
Stemmler
Dry Creek
Creek
Rd.
Simi
Russian River
To Calistoga
128
Field Stone
Rd.
Fitch Mountain Rd.
William Wheeler
Healdsburg
Bellerose
Mill Creek
L. Foppiano
Grant Ave.
Cambiaso
Sotoyome
Limerick Ln.
Hill
0 5
Scale of Miles
0 5
Scale of Kilometers
Foreman Ln.
Felta Rd.
Westside
Old Redwood Hwy.
Los Amigos Rd.
Donna Maria
Chalk
Landmark
E. Windsor
Sonoma Vineyards
Windsor River Rd.
Pleasant
Ave.
W. Windsor
Rd.
Old
Redwood
Rd.
Springs
Hop Kiln
Davis Bynum
SONOMA COUNTY AIRPORT
Rio Nido
Korbel
River
River
Rd.
Eastside Rd.
Mark West Sta. Rd.
Slusser Ave.
Wohler Rd.
West
Mark
Hwy.
Guerneville
Domaine Laurier
Martinelli Rd.
Healdsburg Rd.
River
Rd.
Fulton
To Sonoma Coast Beaches
116
Russian
Covey Rd.
Mark West
116
Forestville
Topolos
Iron Horse
Ross Station Rd.
Vine Hill Rd.
Laguna Rd.
Olivet Rd.
Guerneville Rd.
De Loach
Martini & Prati
Santa Rosa
12
Graton
La Crema
N. McDowell Ave.
E. Washington St.
S. McDowell Ave.
Petaluma
101
Rd.
Graton
Mill Station Rd.
116
Cherry Ridge Rd.
Rd.
Montgomery
12
Hwy.
Sebastopol
101
To San Francisco
To Bodega
Bodega

Alexander Valley Vineyards. From intersection of Alexander Valley Rd. with State 128, E then S 2 mi. to winery drive at 8644, E to winery (P.O. Box 175, Healdsburg, CA 95448) Tel (707) 433-7209. Ltd. picnic. M-F 10-5, Sa-Su 12-5. GT by appt./Ta.

Bellerose Vineyard. From Healdsburg Ave., W on Mill St./Westside Rd., to intersection with W. Dry Creek Rd., then N .2 mi. to winery drive (435 W. Dry Creek Rd., Healdsburg, CA 95448) Tel (707) 433-1637. By appt. only.

Davis Bynum Winery. From junction of U.S. 101 and Westside Rd., SW 8 mi. to winery (8075 West Side Rd., Healdsburg, CA 95448) Tel (707) 433-5852. Daily 10-5 in summer, weekends 10-5 remainder of year. GT by appt./Ta.

California Wine Company (Arroyo Sonoma). Tasting room at S city limit of Cloverdale at 793 S. Cloverdale Blvd. (Mail: 155 Cherry Creek Rd., Cloverdale, CA 95425) Tel (707) 894-4295. Daily 10-4. Ta.

Cambiaso Vineyards. From U.S. 101, Healdsburg Ave./Old Redwood Hwy. exit, E .25 mi. to Grant Ave., then E to winery drive at end of Grant (1141 Grant Ave., Healdsburg, CA 95448) Tel (707) 433-5508. M-Sa 9-5.

Colony. From U.S. 101, Asti exit, E .25 mi. to winery (P.O. Box 1, Asti, CA 95413) Tel (707) 433-2333 or 894-2541. Picnic; groups by appt. Daily 9-5 summer, 10-5 remainder of year. GT/Ta.

Cordtz Brothers Cellars. From U.S. 101 in Cloverdale E on First St. .9 mi. to River Rd., S 2 mi. to winery (28237 River Rd., Cloverdale, CA 95425) Tel (707) 894-5245. W-Su 9-5. IT/Ta.

De Loach Vineyards. From U.S. 101, Steele Ln. exit, W 7.4 mi. to Olivet Rd., N .3 mi. to winery (1791 Olivet Rd., Santa Rosa, CA 95401) Tel (707) 526-9111. Daily 10-4:30. GT by appt. only.

Domaine Laurier. From Forestville, W on State 116 .8 mi. to Martinelli Rd., N 1 mi. to winery drive at 8075 (P.O. Box 836, Forestville, CA 95436) Tel (707) 887-2176. By appt. only.

Donna Maria Vineyards. From Old Redwood Hwy. in East Windsor, E .8 mi. on Pleasant Ave. to Chalk Hill Rd., NE 1.6 mi. to winery drive (10266 Chalk Hill Rd., Healdsburg, CA 95448) Tel (707) 838-2807. By appt. only.

Dry Creek Vineyard. From U.S. 101, Dry Creek Rd. exit, W 2.5 mi. to Lambert Bridge Rd., S .1 mi. to winery (P.O. Box T, Healdsburg, CA 95448) Tel (707) 433-1000. Picnic. Daily 10:30-4:30. IT (GT by appt.)/Ta.

Field Stone Winery. On W side of State 128 .2 mi. N of Chalk Hill Rd. (10075 Hwy. 128, Healdsburg, CA 95448) Tel (707) 433-7266. Picnic. Daily 10-4. GT by appt./Ta.

L. Foppiano Wine Company. From U.S. 101, Old Redwood Hwy. exit., SW .5 mi. to winery (12707 Old Redwood Hwy., Healdsburg, CA 95448) Tel (707) 433-7272. Picnic. Daily 10-4:30. GT by appt./Ta.

Fritz Cellars. From U.S. 101, Dutcher Creek Rd. exit, SW 3 mi. to winery drive on W side of rd. (24691 Dutcher Creek Rd., Cloverdale, CA 95425) Tel (707) 433-5177. Picnic. W-Su 12-5. GT by appt./Ta.

Geyser Peak Winery. From U.S. 101, Canyon Rd. exit, W .1 mi. to winery drive (Geyserville, CA 95441) Tel (707) 433-6585. Picnic. Daily 10-5. Ta.

Hop Kiln Winery. From junction of U.S. 101 and West Side Rd., SW 6 mi. to winery (6050 West Side Rd., Healdsburg, CA 95448) Tel (707) 433-6491. Picnic. Daily 10-5. IT/Ta.

Iron Horse Ranch & Vineyard. From Forestville, S 1.4 mi. on State 116 to Ross Station Rd., W to winery drive at end (9786 Ross Station Rd., Sebastopol, CA 95472) Tel (707) 887-1909. By appt. only.

Johnson's Alexander Valley Winery. From intersection of Alexander Valley Rd. with State 128, E then S 1.75 mi. to winery drive (8333 Hwy. 128, Healdsburg, CA 95448) Tel (707) 433-2319. Picnic.Daily 10-5. IT/Ta.

F. Korbel & Bros. From U.S. 101, River Rd. exit, W 14 mi. to winery (Guerneville, CA 95446) Tel (707) 887-2294. Daily 9-4:30. GT (9:45-3:45)/Ta.

Key: GT (guided tour); IT (informal tour); Ta (tasting).

La Crema Vinera. From U.S. 101, Washington St. exit, E .1 mi. to McDowell Ave., N .25 mi. to winery at 971 Transport Wy. (P.O. Box 976, Petaluma, CA 94952) Tel (707) 762-0393. By appt. only.

Landmark Vineyards. From U.S. 101, E. Windsor exit, N along Los Amigos (frontage road) .3 mi. to winery (9150 Los Amigos Rd., Windsor, CA 95492) Tel (707) 838-9466. Picnic. W & F 1-5, Sa-Su 10-5 or by appt. GT/Ta.

Le Bay Cellars. From U.S. 101, Dutcher Creek Rd. exit, S .2 mi. on Dutcher Creek Rd. to winery drive (26900 Dutcher Creek Rd., Cloverdale, CA 95425) Tel (707) 894-3191. W-Su 10-4. GT by appt./Ta.

Lytton Springs Winery. From U.S. 101, Lytton Springs Rd. exit, W .7 mi. to winery (650 Lytton Springs Rd., Healdsburg, CA 95448) Tel (707) 433-7721. M-F 8-5 by appt. only.

Mark West Vineyards. From U.S. 101, River Rd. exit, W 5.5 miles to Trenton-Healdsburg Rd., N .1 mi. to winery (7000 Trenton-Healdsburg Rd., Forestville, CA 95436) Tel (707) 544-4813. Picnic. Daily 9-5 . IT by appt.

Martini & Prati. From Santa Rosa, W on Guerneville Rd. 7 mi. to Laguna Rd., N 1.1 mi. to winery (2191 Laguna Rd., Santa Rosa, CA 95401) Tel (707) 823-2404. M-F 9-4. IT/Ta.

Mill Creek Vineyards. From U.S. 101, Healdsburg Ave. exit, W on Mill St./Westside Rd. to winery at 1401 (P.O. Box 758, Healdsburg, CA 95448) Tel (707) 433-5098. Picnic. Daily 10-4:30. GT by appt./Ta.

Nervo Winery. From U.S. 101, Independence Ln. exit, N .5 mi. to winery (19585 Old Redwood Hwy. S., Geyserville, CA 95441) Tel (707) 857-3417. Picnic. Daily 10-5. Ta.

Pastori Winery. From U.S. 101, Canyon Rd. exit, N 1.5 mi. on frontage rd. to winery (23189 Redwood Hwy., Cloverdale, CA 95425) Tel (707) 857-3418. Daily 9-4. Ta.

J. Pedroncelli Winery. From U.S. 101, Canyon Rd. exit, W 1 mi. to winery (1220 Canyon Rd., Geyserville, CA 95441) Tel (707) 857-3619. Daily 10-5. IT/Ta.

A. Rafanelli Winery. From U.S. 101, Dry Creek Rd. exit, W 3 mi. to Lambert Bridge Rd., S 1 mi. to West Dry Creek Rd. (4685 W. Dry Creek Rd., Healdsburg, CA 95448) Tel (707) 433-1385. Case sales by appt. only.

Sausal Winery. From intersection of Alexander Valley Rd. with State 128, E then S .7 mi. to winery drive (7470 Hwy. 128, Healdsburg, CA 95448) Tel (707) 433-2285. GT by appt. only.

Simi Winery. From U.S. 101, Dry Creek Rd. exit, E to Healdsburg Ave., N 1 mi. to winery (P.O. Box 698, Healdsburg, CA 95448) Tel (707) 433-6981. Picnic. Daily 10-5. GT/Ta.

Soda Rock Winery. From intersection of Alexander Valley Rd. with State 128, E then S .8 mi. to winery (8015 Hwy. 128, Healdsburg, CA 95448) Tel (707) 433-1830. Picnic. Daily 10-5. GT by appt./Ta.

Sonoma Vineyards. From U.S. 101, Windsor exit, W to Old Redwood Hwy., N 3 mi. to winery (P.O. Box 368, Windsor, CA 95492) Tel (707) 433-6511. Picnic. Daily 10-5. GT/Ta.

Sotoyome Winery. From U.S. 101, Old Redwood Hwy./Healdsburg Ave. exit, S .5 mi. on Old Redwood Hwy. to Limerick Ln., E .5 mi. to winery drive (641 Limerick Ln., Healdsburg, CA 95448) Tel (707) 433-2001. By appt. only.

Souverain Cellars. From U.S. 101, Independence Ln. exit, W .2 mi. on Independence Ln. (P.O. Box 528, Geyserville, CA 95441) Tel (707) 433-8281. Daily 10-4. GT/Ta.

Robert Stemmler Winery. From U.S. 101, Dry Creek Rd. exit, W 2.5 mi. to Lambert Bridge Rd., S on Lambert Bridge Rd. to winery (3805 Lambert Bridge Rd., Healdsburg, CA 95448) Tel (707) 433-6334. Case sales by appt. only.

(Winery listings continued on next page)

. . . Continued from page 49

Topolos at Russian River Vineyard. On State 116 at S limit of Forestville (5700 Gravenstein Hwy. N., Forestville, CA 95436) Tel (707) 526-0550. W-Su 11-5. GT by appt./Ta.

Trentadue Winery. From U.S. 101, Independence Ln. exit, N .5 mi. on frontage road to winery drive (19170 Redwood Hwy., Geyserville, CA 95441) Tel (707) 433-3104. Daily 10-5. Ta.

William Wheeler Vineyards. From Healdsburg Ave. at Healdsburg town square, E 1.2 blocks to winery (130 Plaza St., Healdsburg, CA 95448) Tel (707) 433-8786. M-F 9-5 or by appt. IT/Ta.

Wineries Not on Map— Restricted or No Visitor Facilities

Balverne Wine Cellars. (10810 Hillview Rd., Healdsburg, CA 95448) Tel (707) 433-6913.

Belvedere Wine Co. (4035 Westside Rd., Healdsburg, CA 95448) Tel (415) 435-2272. By appt. only.

C. Bilbro Winery. (P.O. Box 1260, Healdsburg, CA 95448) Tel (707) 433-2747.

Clos Du Bois. (Bus. Off.: 503 D St., San Rafael, CA 94901) Tel (415) 456-7310.

Dehlinger Vineyard. (6300 Guerneville Rd., Sebastopol, CA 95472) Tel (707) 823-2378. By appt. only.

Fenton Acres Winery. (6192 Westside Rd., Healdsburg, CA 95448) Tel (707) 433-2305.

Fisher Vineyards. (6200 St. Helena Rd., Santa Rosa, CA 95404) Tel (707) 539-7511. By appt. only.

Horizon Winery. (P.O. Box 191, Santa Rosa, CA 95401) Tel (707) 544-2961. By appt. only.

Hultgren & Samperton Winery. (2201 Westside Rd., Healdsburg, CA 95448) Tel (707) 433-5102. By appt. only.

Jade Mountain Winery. (1335 Hiatt Rd., Cloverdale, CA 95425) Tel (707) 894-5579.

Jordan Vineyard and Winery. (P.O. Box 878, Healdsburg, CA 95448) Tel (707) 433-6955.

Lambert Bridge. (4085 W. Dry Creek Rd., Healdsburg, CA 95448) Tel (707) 433-5855. By appt. only.

Pat Paulsen Vineyards. (25510 River Rd., Cloverdale, CA 95425) Tel (707) 894-3197.

Pommeraie Vineyards. (10541 Cherry Ridge Rd., Sebastopol, CA 95472) Tel (707) 823-9463. By appt. only.

Preston Vineyards. (9282 W. Dry Creek Rd., Healdsburg, CA 95448) Tel (707) 433-4748. By appt. only.

River Road Vineyards. (6109 Anderson Rd., Forestville, CA 95436) Tel (707) 887-1819.

Thomas Sellards Winery. (6400 Sequoia Cir., Sebastopol, CA 95472) Tel (707) 823-8273.

Sonoma-Cutrer Vineyards. (4401 Slusser Rd., Windsor, CA 95492) Tel (707) 528-1181.

Joseph Swan Vineyards. (2916 Laguna Rd., Forestville, CA 95436) Tel (707) 546-7711.

Viña Vista Vineyards. (P.O. Box 47, Geyserville, CA 95441) Tel (707) 857-3722.

Stephen Zellerbach Vineyard. (4611 Thomas Rd., Healdsburg, CA 95448) Tel (707) 433-9463.

. . . Continued from page 47

sparkling wine bottle by means of hand shaking, a process called riddling. Now a machine shakes whole batches of bottles at once, but the result is the same. This is but one of several ingenious devices developed at this winery to retain old methods in more efficient forms. The well-organized tour includes a collection of ancient machines to be compared to contemporary counterparts.

Tours start near the parking lot at a former Northwestern Pacific Railroad depot, acquired in 1935 for $5 in one of the best deals anyone ever made with a railroad. They end at Korbel's tasting and sales room in an elegantly refurbished one-time brandy barrel warehouse (the Hecks have re-introduced brandy to the Korbel roster, but make it elsewhere).

The list of regular sparkling wines includes—in ascending order of sweetness—Natural, Brut, and Extra Dry. Two special wines are Blanc de Blanc, from chardonnay, and Blanc de Noir, from pinot noir.

La Crema Vinera is one of many recent starts in California winemaking which has foregone fancy architecture in favor of getting started with good equipment.

The winery occupies half of a warehouse east of the freeway, U.S. 101, in Petaluma. Within the plain walls, the owning partners ferment Chardonnay in barrels, and Pinot Noir and Cabernet Sauvignon in custom-designed, open-topped stainless steel vessels resembling giant buckets. All three wines age in French barrels. There are several individual vineyard Chardonnays and Pinot Noirs each year.

The proprietors welcome visitors with appointments even when the small annual production has sold out.

Lambert Bridge is one of several new California wineries housed in a gracefully proportioned wooden building, but is surely the only one with a huge fireplace at one end of the main aging cellar.

Unstained redwood siding and a shake roof of the building cause it to blend easily into a site between vines in the foreground and an oak-studded hill in the background. The interior of the barrel cellar is finished in wood as well, except for the stone fireplace. Overhead illumination comes from chandeliers high in the rafters. These cause cellarmen working in soft shadows to curse now and again when they overfill one of the oak puncheons, but the effect for appointment-only visitors is one of fine romance.

Owner Gerard Lambert crushed his first vintage in 1975. The main cellar was completed in 1976. An expansion housing the stainless steel fermentors, press, and other working gear followed in 1979.

On the west side of Dry Creek Valley, the winery concentrates on producing Chardonnay and Cabernet Sauvignon from its own vineyards.

Landmark Vineyards draws its name from a long double row of old cypress trees lining the entry drive. The winery buildings draw their architectural style from the two-story Spanish colonial house at the head of that drive.

The owning William Mabry family launched the label from leased space in 1974, completed the first winery building at what is now the Home Ranch in Windsor in 1976, and made a substantial addition to it in 1979. The original wing holds stainless steel fermentors and part of the oak cooperage. The newer structure has the rest of the cooperage, a bottling room, and cased goods storage.

Tasting goes on in the old house, which has had its former living room turned into a retail sales area, and the erstwhile dining room into a gracious spot for tasting. Visitors also may picnic in the old gardens.

Landmark produces Chardonnay, Cabernet Sauvignon, and Zinfandel, primarily from family-owned grapes at the winery and in the Alexander and Sonoma valleys.

Le Bay Cellars may or may not be the name on the gatepost. It may be Diamond Oaks. Or it may be both of the above. In any case, the winery was Rege for years until two potential new owners began negotiations to buy it in 1982, and it almost surely will be open to the public for tasting and tours under whichever name.

The old cellar building perches on a knoll above the Dutcher Creek Road exit from U.S. 101 south of Cloverdale. The tasting room is in a small, separate, frame building across from the winery front door.

Lytton Springs Winery was founded in 1975 to focus on one wine, Zinfandel, from grapes grown in an old vineyard long known as Lytton Springs but now renamed Valley Vista. In recent years the proprietors have supplemented their own grapes with small lots from similar vineyards nearby as a matter of practical necessity, but the basic plan remains unchanged.

In classic coastal hills north and west of Healdsburg, the cellar is typical in equipment (stainless steel fermentors, oak barrels) and plain in architecture (prefabricated metal). For students of Zinfandel, the combination of old vineyard and new cellar make an altogether appropriate place to look at the techniques of making California's inimitable red. Because the cellar crew is one man, an appointment is required for any sort of visit. But there are tours, tasting, and sales in all seasons save for those times when the small annual supply of wine is sold out.

Mark West Vineyards perches on the crest of a round knoll just where the Santa Rosa plain gives way to the westernmost hills of the Coast Ranges. It has that happy facility, easily found in Sonoma County, of seeming remote from the rest of mankind without being very far off a major road.

The winery is an L-shaped building with re-sawn redwood siding and a shake roof, appropriate materials for the lightly wooded countryside all around. Vineyards form a skirt around the knoll.

Temperature-controlled stainless steel fermentors and processing gear occupy a pad at the rear side of the long leg of the L. Inside, a collection of French oak barrels fills most of that leg. A lab, bottling line, and retail sales room fill the short leg. A separate building houses case goods. Owners Bob and Joan Ellis have not finished building. The fermentors are yet to be enclosed, and a larger hospitality room is in the planning stages. Meanwhile, visitors may ask for informal tours of the cellars, and follow with a picnic at shady tables overlooking vineyards and the rest of a peaceful scenery.

Martini & Prati is a winery of few exterior charms. Wooden and concrete block buildings ramble in all directions across a small knoll planted to grapes. The major physical distinction is a high water tower.

Indoors, however, the firm has a vast array of aged redwood tanks, oak oval casks, and other sorts of cooperage. These cellars are pleasant to see.

The winery dates to the 1880s, including a previous proprietorship, and to 1902 under the Martini side of its present ownership. Its age explains both its external homeliness and its interior attractions.

In Sonoma County this winery was for years second in size only to Italian Swiss Colony (See: Colony, page 43), though a very distant second. Recently newcomers have dropped it several notches down the list even as it has continued to grow.

Most of the wine made here goes elsewhere in bulk, but wines sold in jug or bottle under the Martini & Prati label cover a range of types. The Zinfandel and Burgundy are much prized by the proprietors. The company also maintains the Fountain Grove label from a once-famous winery near Santa Rosa. It now is reserved for the most prestigious varietals made at Martini & Prati.

Only on weekdays does Martini & Prati offer tours and open its tasting room.

Mill Creek Vineyards, just west of Healdsburg, is the property of the Charles Kreck family.

Kreck and his two sons, Bill and Bob, planted their first vineyards in 1965, and began making wine in leased space in 1974. Their own winery saw its first crush in 1976.

The small cellars, hidden away well uphill from the tasting and sales room, are open to tour only by appointment because the family is virtually the entire work force. Those who persist in getting to the concrete block building will find a winery typical of California in all its equipment, but more crowded than most.

A new-in-1982 tasting room is, meanwhile, open to all daily. The two-story building looms out of vineyards just where they turn from flat to hilly. Patterned after a traditional mill house, it even has a sizable overshot waterwheel that works, although to no greater purpose than symbolizing the name of the winery. The Krecks cut their own timbers from family-owned property, and built their two-story visitor building themselves. An adjoining picnic area is available first-come, first-served.

Nervo Winery is a fine stone barn alongside a frontage road to U.S. 101 not far south of Geyserville. A landmark for years, it lasted two generations as a family enterprise. In 1974, manager Frank Nervo and his family sold the business to the Jos. Schlitz Brewing Co., which earlier had purchased the Geyser Peak Winery a short distance to the north. Since then, Nervo has been maintained as a separate label, and the winery has been kept as an aging cellar and tasting room.

Pastori Winery came into being in 1975 as a full-grown business, partly because wine is a tradition in the Pastori family and partly because the proprietor brought with him stocks he had made in earlier vintages as the winemaster of another cellar.

(Continued on next page)

. . . Continued from page 51

Frank Pastori's father, Constante, launched a winery near Geyserville in 1914. After Prohibition, Frank grew grapes on the family ranch but did not restart the winery. (He did, however, revive the old bond number, 2960, for his new start.) For some years before launching out on his own, he had served as winemaker at the nearby Nervo winery.

The old Nervo stocks were part of Pastori's initial inventory in his frame and concrete block cellar north of Geyserville.

With both old and new wines at Pastori, the emphasis is on varietal types. Reds, including Cabernet Sauvignon and Zinfandel, head the list. They are available for tasting in a no-frills tasting and sales room in a front corner of the cellar.

J. Pedroncelli Winery is a mile into the rolling hills west of Geyserville, on the ridge that separates the Russian River Valley from Dry Creek Valley.

The wood-frame main winery building, behind a finely crafted facade of redwood, dates from 1904, with additions in seven separate later years. It is flanked on one side by a masonry building, erected all of a piece, and on the other by a concrete block building that arose in three distinct phases.

Because the episodic additions have made the winery a bit difficult to walk through, the Pedroncellis do not mind when visitors forego a tour as a prelude to tasting. For those who insist, the whole picture is present. The old main winery has redwood tanks at the core, white wine fermentors in one extension, and red wine fermentors in the newest addition. The older concrete building contains stainless steel storage tanks. The newer, larger one across the drive holds oak barrels, the bottling room, cased goods, and, not least, the tasting room.

The tasting room is separated from stacked cases of aging wine by a sturdily wrought frame full of French oak barrels. These were brought from Europe in 1967 in time to hold a prized lot of Pinot Noir. Their arrival signaled the Pedroncellis' shift from bulk wine and generics to a focus on vintage-dated varietals.

The Pedroncelli family has owned the property since 1927. They sold grapes until 1934, made wine in that year, and have made it annually since. The founder was John Pedroncelli, Sr. The present proprietors are his sons, John, Jr., and Jim.

Grapes for Pedroncelli wines come primarily from hilly vineyards adjacent to the winery and a mile or so to the west, though the family had to give up one block of vines because they couldn't cultivate it after a particularly sure-footed horse died in 1965. The only livestock on the premises now are dogs that have been reduced to barking at tractors for a living.

The list of Pedroncelli varietals includes Chardonnay, French Colombard, and Gewürztraminer among whites, Cabernet Sauvignon and Zinfandel among reds, and a dry Zinfandel Rosé. The generics are cheerfully identified as Sonoma White, Rosé, and Red.

Pommeraie Vineyards hides its trim, barn-style winery building between a steep bank on one side and a row of thick, tall trees on the other.

The site west of Sebastopol was not chosen to be secretive, but it worked out that way to the satisfaction of two owning partners with full-time jobs elsewhere. They offer no retail sales, but gladly give weekend tours by appointment to anyone with an interest in their small lots of Cabernet Sauvignon and Chardonnay. Pilgrims are rewarded with looks at a conventional contemporary California winery: stainless steel fermentors under a roof overhang at one end of the building, and a mixture of American and French oak barrels in the main cellar.

Pommeraie was founded by the Ken Dalton and Robert Wiltermood families in 1979. The name comes from an archaic French word for apple orchard, fair tribute to the immediate neighborhood.

A. Rafanelli Winery comes as close as any spot is likely to get to a perfect vision of the family cellar. A gentle fold in a hillside above West Dry Creek Road cradles a trim red barn. A pasture full of sheep is visible on one side of the barn, a hillside covered in oaks is on the other, and a comfortable white frame house screens out the road on the remaining side. Inside the barn there is wood paneling in all three of its major rooms—one for fermenting, one for oak aging, and, above stairs, one for bottling and cased goods storage.

Americo Rafanelli built this quiet place for himself and his wife. He makes small lots of Gamay Beaujolais and Zinfandel more to please himself than to be in business, and for this reason sells only in case lots and only by appointment.

Sausal Winery started out purely in the bulk wine business, but, in 1978, began a slow turn toward offering its wines under its own label.

Set on a gentle slope in the Alexander Valley, the cellars are housed in an attractive wood-frame building with redwood siding. The main section is two long rows of good-sized stainless steel fermentors, similar rows of stainless steel storage tanks, and a comparative handful of oak tanks and barrels, all in neat order. The ratio of steel to wood is to tighten as planned shifts to bottled wines take place. The first Sausal wine released was a Zinfandel. A Chardonnay followed. The roster is to expand still more, primarily in reds. While the pace of change gathers speed, visits are by appointment only.

Though the winery dates only from 1973, the proprietors are long-time grape growers and winery proprietors in the Alexander Valley. Leo Demostene was a partner in the old Soda Rock Winery. His two sons and two daughters built Sausal as a tribute to him. They own and operate the winery and family vineyards today.

Simi Winery more than any other in Sonoma County reflects the ups and downs of wine in California. It has grown to its present size in an epic series of lurches.

The founders, Giuseppe and Pietro Simi, built the sturdy stone building that now houses wines aging in barrel in 1890, after a start in San Francisco and an interim stay in a since-disappeared cellar in downtown Healdsburg. The place prospered until both brothers died in 1904, and continued to prosper until Prohibition under the management of Giuseppe's daughter Isobel, even though she had to assume control as a teenager.

Botrytis cinerea, the noble mold

Since 1969, extra-sweet wines patterned after French Sauternes and German Beerenausleses and Trockenbeerenausles have become more and more a part of California winemaking. Most are simply called "late harvest;" a few have more fanciful names. A great majority come from White (or Johannisberg) Riesling grapes, as do their German counterparts. Some come from Sauvignon Blanc or Semillon (or a blend of the two), the two grape varieties used in making Sauternes. An occasional example is made from Chenin Blanc, the grape variety of another French sweet wine called Coteaux du Layon, or from Gewürztraminer.

Most of California's concentratedly sweet wines come from low-lying vineyards near rivers, where cool fogs can linger well into a morning. Particularly consistent areas include Sonoma's Russian River Valley, especially the section called Alexander Valley; the Napa Valley near Napa Creek between Rutherford and Yountville; and Monterey County along the Salinas River course from Greenfield northward. No district can deliver such wines every year.

The secret of making all of these wines lies with a mold called Botrytis cinerea, more commonly called The Noble Mold in the world of wine. And the secret of Botrytis lies with the weather.

It confers its curious benefits only when a cool, damp spell is followed by a warmer, drier one at about the time normal grapes might be harvested. Once it attacks ripe berries, it nibbles delicately at the skins until only a membrane is left. The job is so refined that water can evaporate, but larger molecules cannot. The result is unusual concentrations of sugar and flavor components in the grapes.

Where grapes for dry white table wines are harvested at about 21 to 23 degrees Brix (a winemaker's yardstick of measuring sugar content, and roughly equal to percentage of sugar), those thoroughly attacked by Botrytis weigh in at 28 to 30 degrees Brix, even, rarely, at 37°B.

When crushed, the grapes do not separate into free-running juice and solids, as is normally the case, but become a homely mush. (Typical fresh grapes yield about 140 to 160 gallons of wine per ton. Heavily Botrytised grapes may yield as little as 60 or 70 gallons.) This is clarified with great difficulty. (As one winemaker put it, filtering Botrytised must is a little bit like trying to pump corn syrup through a brick wall.) Then the juice is fermented, again with great difficulty. (Sugar inhibits the formation of alcohol above certain concentrations. Winemakers say a fermentation is complete when it uses up all of the fermentable sugars, or when it is deliberately stopped by chilling. Winemakers hardly ever say a late harvest fermentation is complete, only that it dwindles to no visible progress after a period of several weeks, or even months.)

To explain the wines in terms of technical balance: typical, slightly sweet table wines (Chenin Blancs, for example) have about 12 to 13 percent alcohol, and 1 to 2 percent of unfermented grape sugar (residual sugar, or RS in the trade). Partially Botrytised wines will have about 10 or 11 percent alcohol, and 4 to 8 percent RS. Thoroughly Botrytised wines will have 8 or 9 percent alcohol, and anywhere from 10 to 25 percent RS.

The numbers do away with sweet mystery and other poetic thoughts. Habitués ignore them and enjoy these rarities for what they are, nectar.

(The brothers had called their winery Montepulciano after their home village in Italy. Isobel renamed it after the family, though the Montepulciano name stayed in some evidence all the way into the 1960s.) The national dry spell just failed to bankrupt her and husband Fred Haigh. At repeal, Simi flowered again for a short time for the Haighs, then fell into a long, slow decline mirroring a general condition in the county's winemaking community.

At about the time the market for wine began awakening in the late 1960s, after 66 years in control, Isobel sold Simi to the Russell Green family. The Greens revitalized the place during a five-year proprietorship, then sold in 1974 to a British brewery firm, Scottish & Newcastle, which continued the refurbishing until it sold in turn to Schieffelin & Co. of New York in 1976. Schieffelin held the reins until 1980, when the French firm of Moët Hennessy acquired the property as a running mate to its Domaine Chandon sparkling wine cellars in the Napa Valley.

Between them, the latter two owners literally tore the lid off the old Simi from 1979 through 1981. First was added a state-of-the-art fermenting facility in a new building uphill from the stone original. Then the roof was removed from the old building, and a new aging cellar built inside the reinforced shell. Matching roofs tie the structures together aesthetically, but enough differences remain to symbolize two eras.

An informative tour takes in the whole winery and the complete process of winemaking, pausing long enough to explain the hows and whys of experimental lots of wine aging in barrels purchased from different coopers.

Since Simi has its tasting room in a separate building on the opposite side of a Southern Pacific rail line, it has the only tour that crosses a fully signaled, grade-level railroad crossing. Consequently it also has the only tours that wait for the afternoon freight to roll through.

The roster of vintage-dated varietal wines is dominated by Chardonnay, Chenin Blanc, Johannisberg Riesling, Cabernet Sauvignon, and Zinfandel.

Soda Rock Winery under the ownership of Charles Tomka, Jr., has, as one of its subsidiary goals, a desire to prove that good wine can be made using the museum pieces left as equipment by former owner Abele Ferrari.

Tomka bought the long-idle winery in 1979. Rather than throwing away decades' worth of equipment and material accumulated by a legendary pack rat, he sorted it all out, reconditioning the salvageable and putting the rest out of the way in case a new use develops. He has had to buy very little, for Ferrari designed and built things to last when he directed the long-time winery equipment supplier called Healdsburg Machine. Here, then, is where to see how winemakers lived in the years immediately after Prohibition.

The crusher sits in front of a handsome stone facade scavenged by Ferrari from a defunct schoolhouse. It looks like most. On the other side of the wall is a hydraulically operated basket press complete with tracks to roll the baskets to and fro. Some of the fermentors are open-topped redwood. Most of the tanks are redwood, too, with 3-inch staves milled from virgin heartwood. The biggest pump in the place is a masterwork of durability.

Amid all of this, in gleaming contrast, are a couple of stainless steel dairy tanks for fermenting youthful whites, and several rows of new French oak puncheons for fermenting and aging the Chardonnay.

In an appropriately dark, cool tasting room, the proprietors offer Chardonnay, Gewürztraminer, Cabernet Sauvignon, Zinfandel, and a pair of generics known as Charlie's Country White and Charlie's Country Red. These and the other Soda Rock wines (under a label that, in character, recycles the original design) are sold only here.

Out front, long-time landscape designer and gardener Charles Tomka, Sr., is developing a splendid country garden. Tree-shaded picnic tables provide close views of Tomka's handiwork and more distant views of grassy, oak-dotted slopes looming above the Alexander Valley.

Sonoma Vineyards is a sort of vinous Topsy, a winery that just "growed." Sizable though it is, it does not look nearly finished growing yet.

The company started as a small tasting room and mail-order business under the name of Tiburon Vintners. Headquarters was an old frame house in the Marin County town of Tiburon. A few successful years later, the company acquired an old winery in the Somona County town of Windsor, adding the Windsor Vineyards label to the earlier one. The business still was essentially mail order. Another few successful years later, in 1973, the corporation changed its name to Sonoma Vineyards and built a substantial winery a few miles north of the first Windsor premises.

The headquarters winery, set into one of the company's vineyards alongside Old Redwood Highway between Windsor and Healdsburg, is a striking combination of a cross and a pyramid.

Architect Craig Roland's notion was to establish separate work areas radiating from a central processing core. For a time things worked that way. Fermentors were in one wing of the cross, barrels in another, and so on. Several California wineries are descended from this prototype, but it grew out of its framework too far to keep the form. Consistent expansion has added a big battery of temperature-controlled stainless steel fermentors to the rear of the original building, and a huge aging cellar to one side.

In 1982, the huge aging cellar disappeared from ready view as the newest phase of activity began. The latest effort is a joint venture with the French Champagne producers, Piper-Heidseick. Piper-Sonoma, as the new sparkling wine facility is known, looks straight across a parking lot to the first building erected in what now looks like a whole community of wineries.

Visitors are welcome at both Sonoma Vineyards and Piper-Sonoma.

The Sonoma Vineyards half has a tasting room suspended high up among the roof beams. Visitors may taste at tables, then stroll out to a ring of balconies looking down into the working winery. The proprietors also offer a full tour of this building and the adjacent fermenting and aging areas.

The wines here cover most of the range of varietal and generic table wines. Some bottlings of Chardonnay, Johannisberg Riesling, Cabernet Sauvignon, and Pinot Noir carry the names of vineyards from which they came. In addition to Sonoma Vineyards labels, wines bottled as Windsor Vineyards, for mail-order sale, also are here.

Across the way, the striking Piper-Sonoma facility was scheduled for completion before the harvest of 1982. Vast expanses of glass and vertical concrete panels in stepped series give it an entirely different appearance from its older cousin. It will offer a complete tour of a modern, mechanically efficient *methode champenoise* champagne cellar from new cuvée through the processes called tirage, riddling, and disgorging (see page 83), and, finally, bottling.

Back at Sonoma Vineyards is a spacious lawn with picnic tables available on a first-come, first-served basis.

Sotoyome Winery, nestled among vines on a steep slope just south of Healdsburg, is one of a few California cellars that actively defy gravity.

In pre-electric days, most wineries were built so fresh fruit arrived at the high side of a building and bottled wine left by the low side, gravity having done most of the moving in between. The habit persists in most hillside cellars. But here the outdoor crushing and fermenting deck is downhill from the metal building that holds the miscellany of redwood tanks and oak barrels in which proprietor Bill Chaikin's estate-grown Cabernet Sauvignons, Petite Sirahs, and Zinfandels age.

People interested in small-scale winemaking will find much to engross them in this well-organized and impeccably kept cellar dating from 1974. Tours and tasting are by appointment only.

Historians have something to think about here as

well. The name, Sotoyome, comes from a huge Mexican land grant that one-time historian Chaikin is trying to establish as an appellation of origin. His label shows a map of the territory. The proprietor can point out his place in it.

Souverain Cellars is patterned on the old hop barns that still dot the Sonoma countryside. The stark profiles of its twin towers and its sheer size make the building highly visible from U.S. 101 even though it sits deep in a fold in the western hills between Healdsburg and Geyserville.

By design this winery lends itself to tours. Elevated walkways run throughout it, allowing clear views of every department from crushers to bottling lines. It is a very substantial winery to see. The stainless steel fermenting tanks outside at the rear of the building are both sizable and numerous. So are the stainless steel storage tanks inside. However, the most impressive perspectives are from walkways above long, unerringly straight rows of Slovenian oak tanks and both French and American oak barrels.

Tours end in a handsome tasting room on the upper level, with views out to rolling vineyard, or up through heavy beams of the east tower.

Souverain Cellars has packed a great deal of history into its brief existence, an exemplary demonstration of the speed with which life moves in these modern times. The winery was built in 1972 by Pillsbury Company as a younger sister to the original Souverain Cellars in the Napa Valley. It was first known as Ville Fontaine, while construction had not progressed enough to allow crushing on the current site. By 1973 the Sonoma cellar had progressed enough for wine to be made there. By this time the name had changed to Chateau Souverain. By the 1974 harvest the cellar was complete, but, shortly after the vintage, Pillsbury again changed the name, this time to Souverain of Alexander Valley. By 1976 the Pillsbury Company had sold both wineries. There is no Souverain at all in the Napa Valley now (its two homes there are now Burgess Cellars and Rutherford Hill Winery), and the Sonoma winery has taken the original name under its new owners, a limited partnership of growers banded together as North Coast Cellars.

Throughout all of the name changes, the focus at Souverain has remained on vintage-dated varietal wines, especially including Chardonnay, Colombard, Johannisberg Riesling, Cabernet Sauvignon, Pinot Noir, and Zinfandel. The company has released one port-type made from cabernet sauvignon.

This is another of the wineries that hosts art shows, musical and theatrical events, and even holiday fairs. For information, write the winery at the address on page 49.

Robert Stemmler Winery is the patiently achieved end product of a long winemaking career. The neat, sober, brown building next to the proprietor-winemaker's home in Dry Creek Valley is not large. Even so, it has been built and equipped in stages.

Stemmler, German-born and trained, made wine for several major firms in Napa and Sonoma counties from the 50s into the 70s before launching his own small cellar. Through the 70s he divided time between consulting work for others and his own growing business. Only in the 80s did he strike out entirely on his own.

The impeccably clean and orderly cellar is open to visit only by appointment, and sales are in minimum lots of a case. The list of wines includes Chardonnay, Fumé Blanc, and Cabernet Sauvignon.

Topolos at Russian River Vineyard is housed in a building just zany enough to look right in spite of its being on the southern outskirt of architecturally staid Forestville. Wooden towers in a Russian style soar above a concrete main cellar. Another tower alongside, equally Russian, has an office on the ground floor and a lab up under the eaves.

The structure preceded proprietor Mike Topolos, who has installed a conventional small winery in it. The tasting room is in a bottom corner of a separate, less-overstated building housing an affiliated indoor-outdoor restaurant. The list of Topolos wines includes Chardonnay, White Riesling, Cabernet Sauvignon, Petite Sirah, and Zinfandel.

Trentadue Winery nestles in the middle of its capacious vineyards at the end of a half-mile private lane leading east from the U.S. 101 frontage road between Healdsburg and Geyserville.

Owner Leo Trentadue crushed his first vintage in 1969 and has been expanding steadily since then. By 1972 he had gained enough size to build a substantial masonry block building as his main fermenting and aging cellar. He put a large tasting room on the second floor from which visitors can look down into the working parts of the cellar. The room also houses a miniature department store of wine-related merchandise.

Trentadue sells most of his wine on the spot. Principal on his list are Chardonnay, Chenin Blanc, Cabernet Sauvignon, Carignane, Petite Sirah, and Zinfandel, all made in a time-honored fashion that leans heavily on patience and hardly at all on fancy machinery or other sophistications of our technological age. There also is a specialty Aleatico.

William Wheeler Vineyards ferments its wines in an inaccessible part of Dry Creek Valley, but ages them in downtown Healdsburg.

Proprietor William Wheeler has a modern fermenting facility in a bare-bones building at his remote vineyard. Having decided it was easier to take the wines out than to bring supplies in, he acquired a one-time pool hall four doors off Healdsburg Plaza and transformed it into an elegant aging cellar and reception room for visitors.

On one side of a central wall, wines age in French oak barrels. On the other, the finely furnished reception area fronts a cellar full of stainless steel and upright oak tanks. Visitors wishing to have a look around can peer through curtained front windows or go in and climb a curving staircase to a mezzanine. The mezzanine extends as a little platform into the two cellars, so that a complete tour requires opening three doors and taking 10 steps.

The winery made its first wines in 1979. The roster includes Chardonnay, Sauvignon Blanc, and Cabernet Sauvignon. Zinfandel is a planned later addition.

More wineries. In addition to all those listed above, the Russian River watershed supports another score of cellars. A few are bulk producers without any reason to court visitors, but most sell bottled wine, or are about to begin doing so. They shrink from public attention in some cases because they are so new they have no wine ready to sell, in others because use-permit restrictions do not allow them to offer tasting or to sell at retail. In a few instances the privacy is simply a point of preference.

Balverne Wine Cellars is a dramatic estate in hills east of U.S. 101 between Windsor and Healdsburg. From its own rolling vineyards—each block with its own name—the winery produces, as its whites, Chardonnay, Sauvignon Blanc, Gewürztraminer, a rarity of German origin called Scheurebe, and a Riesling-based proprietary called Healdsburger after the home town. The reds are Cabernet Sauvignon and Zinfandel. Balverne offers neither tasting nor sales.

Belvedere Wine Company has a substantial cellar under construction on West Side Road in 1982. The plan is to produce wines from several individual vineyards, to be labeled with the vineyard name rather than the winery's. When the building is complete, it will be open to appointment-only visitors.

C. Bilbro Winery produces under its Marietta Cellars label only Cabernet Sauvignon and Zinfandel. The small winery is hidden away in steep hill country west of Healdsburg, and offers no tours, tasting, or sales.

Clos Du Bois, a well-established winery in the Dry Creek Valley/Alexander Valley district, was expanding its cellars in Healdsburg during 1982. The planned new construction, scheduled for completion in autumn, includes the first visitor facilities for the firm. Clos Du Bois makes Chardonnay, Gewürztraminer, Johannisberg Riesling, Pinot Noir, and Cabernet Sauvignon, sometimes under the names of vineyards from which the grapes come.

Dehlinger Vineyard, established in 1975 and located in its attractive permanent cellar since 1976, produces Chardonnay, Cabernet Sauvignon, and Zinfandel, primarily from its own rolling vineyards near Forestville. There are neither tastings nor retail sales, but winemaker Tom Dehlinger does give tours to friends of his wines by appointment.

Fenton Acres Winery, a near neighbor to Hop Kiln on West Side Road, produces Chardonnay as its primary wine. Processing goes on in leased space; aging is in a refitted barn on the property. Proprietor Joe Rochioli offers no tasting and no retail sales.

Fisher Vineyards, in the hills between Santa Rosa and St. Helena, produces only Chardonnay and Cabernet Sauvignon from winery-owned vineyards. Proprietor Fred Fisher sometimes extends invitations to visit his small, handsome redwood cellars.

Healdsburg Winegrowers may show up as a name in some lists of wineries. The label is Bacigalupi. Chardonnay and Pinot Noir are the only varieties. Owner Charles Bacigalupi offers no tours, tasting, or sales at the small aging cellar behind his home southwest of Healdsburg. For those who insist on getting close to the source, these wines are fermented at nearby Belvedere Wine Company and taken back there for bottling.

Horizon Winery specializes in Zinfandel. The cellar, near Martini & Prati, is part of owner Paul Gardner's residence. Gardner made his first vintage in 1977. Although production is too small to permit general tours and tasting, Gardner does sell wine by appointment.

Hultgren & Samperton Winery made its first wines at a hillside site southwest of Healdsburg in 1979. The list begins with Cabernet Sauvignon and ends with Chardonnay. The proprietors of the small cellar offer no tasting and no retail sales.

Jade Mountain Winery, near Cloverdale, is the tiny weekend winery of Dr. Douglass Cartwright, who makes small lots of wine from his own vineyard. There are no tours or tasting, and no wine for retail sale.

Jordan Vineyard and Winery produces Cabernet

Sauvignon and Chardonnay at a baronial building northeast of Healdsburg. It offers no tours, no tasting, and no retail sales.

Pat Paulsen Vineyards, tucked away at the end of a shared private lane southeast of Cloverdale, produces from its own vines Cabernet Sauvignon, Sauvignon Blanc, and a dry Muscat. Its location prohibits tours or retail sales. The first vintage was 1980.

Preston Vineyards is a family-owned and operated winery well up the Dry Creek Valley from Healdsburg. The principal wines are Sauvignon Blanc and Zinfandel. Begun in the late 70s, the winery was expanded in 1982, but remains small enough that the proprietors do not offer tasting or retail sales.

River Road Vineyards makes Chardonnay, Johannisberg Riesling, Sauvignon Blanc, and Zinfandel in leased space pending construction of a permanent cellar between Forestville and Guerneville. Proprietor Gary Mills plans to accommodate visitors.

Thomas Sellards Winery near Sebastopol was founded in 1980. The first small lots of Cabernet Sauvignon, Petite Sirah, and Zinfandel are not due to be bottled until 1983. The proprietor is accepting no visitors prior to that event.

Sonoma-Cutrer Vineyards is a dramatic new structure on the plain west of Windsor. Hidden away from traffic, the sizable cellar produced only Chardonnay from its first vintage, 1981. Future plans call for the addition of a sparkling wine from chardonnay grapes. No wine is to be available for sale before 1983; there will be no visitor facilities before then.

Joseph Swan Vineyards, near the intersection of Laguna Road with River Road, is the old-timer of this lot of wineries. Swan sells all of a very limited production of Chardonnay, Pinot Noir, and Zinfandel via a mailing list. Such has been the case since the cellar was founded in the late 1960s.

Viña Vista Vineyards has been growing at a steady but slow pace since the mid-1960s as a mail order winery. The cellars on a hill near Asti usually are not open to visit because the proprietor keeps an unpredictable schedule, but visits sometimes can be arranged by appointment. Production ranges across many of the familiar varietals.

Stephen Zellerbach Vineyard was under construction with plans for the cellars to be ready for the harvest of 1982 and for appointment-only visitors in 1983. The cellar is on Chalk Hill Road west of State 128 in the Alexander Valley. The firm has been making Cabernet Sauvignon in leased space since 1978.

In addition to these wineries Sonoma County still has several producers dealing only in bulk. Some are prominent enough in the landscape to attract attention. These include the Chris Fredson Winery, on Dry Creek Road west of Healdsburg; the Frei Brothers Winery (owned by E & J Gallo), a short distance farther west along the same road and somewhat secluded from view; Seghesio Winery, just west of the freeway, U.S. 101, and about a mile south of Asti; and the Sonoma Cooperative, in the village of Windsor. The old Sonoma County Cellars, a gloomily handsome brick building on Healdsburg Avenue not far from Dry Creek Road in Healdsburg, is used only for storage.

Other Than Wineries

The Russian River, in its endless tacking back and forth, is a diverse source of entertainment when wine has had its turn.

In winter the Russian River is a big, muddy, fast-flowing stream, its banks populated by steelhead fishermen. In dry summers it becomes a miles-long series of pools connected only by the merest of trickles. Between these extremes of its cycle, but especially in spring, the river is popular with canoeists and paddle boaters. For people who do not own boats, two rental firms have canoes at Healdsburg.

A county park at Healdsburg, Veterans Memorial, is near the bridge at the south edge of town. It has sandy bathing beaches and shady picnic sites.

The next-nearest parks are in Santa Rosa, none of them particularly handy for visitors trying to stay close to wineries in the Russian River watershed, though the fine Howarth Park is useful for anyone headed into or out of the Sonoma Valley.

The town of Healdsburg pays wine a direct tribute each year on a weekend in mid-May. At that time the town square comes alive with a friendly, increasingly crowded wine festival.

Santa Rosa is the commercial hub of the region, offering the widest range of hotels and restaurants, but both Healdsburg and Cloverdale have modest motels. They and Geyserville add restaurants to the list of possibilities. For lists, write: Cloverdale Chamber of Commerce, P.O. Box 476, Cloverdale, CA 95425; Healdsburg Chamber of Commerce, 217 Healdsburg Avenue, Healdsburg, CA 95448; or Santa Rosa Chamber of Commerce, 637-1st Street, Santa Rosa, CA 95404.

Plotting a Route

U.S. Highway 101 is the nearly inevitable means of heading into the Russian River area from either north or south, and it is an efficient route through the wine district. However, confirmed shunpikers can find local routes running alongside it on either side.

State Highway 128 is a particularly engaging road from end to end, one in persistent contact with wineries. It starts at a junction with State Highway 1 on the Pacific shore in Mendocino County, rambles through the Anderson Valley (see page 62), joins U.S. 101 from Cloverdale to Geyserville, then slides away into the Alexander Valley. South of there it slips through Knights Valley and over a shoulder of Mt. St. Helena on its way into the Napa Valley.

State Highway 12 is another road that passes through several wine districts. For immediate purposes, it connects the town of Sonoma, in the Sonoma Valley, with Santa Rosa, then continues through vineyards as far as Sebastopol, in what Sonomans call the West Side. There it connects with State Highway 116, which continues through Forestville and Guerneville.

Within the district a whole network of local roads ambles around the West Side. Some of the most useful and scenic of these are Dutcher Creek, Dry Creek, West Dry Creek, Westside, Eastside, and River roads.

Mendocino & Lake Counties

Quiet charm in the northernmost vineyards

Of all the effects of the boom in California wine, one of the most visible in literature on the subject is the fragmenting of the North Coast counties into smaller districts. Nowhere is the shift more visible than in neighboring Mendocino and Lake counties. Mendocino hardly had a name of its own not long ago. Now wine fanciers recognize Ukiah and Anderson valleys readily, and are beginning to know about McDowell, Potter, and Redwood valleys as well. Lake County was recognized only as a source of a few extra tons of red grapes for Mendocino, if it was recognized at all. Now it, too, has at least one named subdistrict, Guenoc, easing into the memories of wine bibbbers.

The reasons behind all of this awareness are new wineries scattered throughout these sprawling, colorful precincts. They have added hundreds of miles of new territory and at least two dozen new cellars.

Here more than in most California wine districts are grand diversions: the Mendocino coast is an anchor point on the west; Clear Lake is a warmer, easterly alternative.

Mendocino County

Northernmost of California's coastal winegrowing counties, Mendocino is the pick of the lot for winery visitors who want a little pioneering as part of the experience.

All along the north coast terrain alternates persistently between hill and valley, but, in Mendocino, steeper hills separate smaller valleys than in Napa and Sonoma counties. Settlements are fewer, the countryside between them wilder. Given these facts, local winemakers have scattered their small numbers across a remarkable amount of territory.

Like the rest of California, Mendocino has blossomed as a wine district since 1970, and especially since 1978. From the end of Prohibiton until the end of the 1960s, Parducci Wine Cellars at Ukiah carried the Mendocino flag almost unaided. All but a handful of the county's grapes flanked U.S. Highway 101 within a few miles. Now the county has a few more than a score of wineries and substantial vineyards in no fewer than five distinct valleys stretching well beyond U.S. 101 to both west and east.

The hub, and most logical headquarters for visitors bent on seeing most or all of Mendocino's wineries, is the agreeable town of Ukiah. Another approach, better suited to vacationers, is to stay at one of the scenic, old-timey coastal villages, visiting wineries near Philo as a day trip and those nearer Ukiah on the way to or fro.

Ukiah-Hopland Wineries

For crows, 17 of Mendocino's wineries are close to Ukiah or Hopland. Visitors with only casual interest do not have much more distance to cover than the crows. Several major wineries with well-developed visitor programs are within a few hundred yards of U.S. 101. However, for diligent seekers after particular cellars, the tumbled terrain here may add a good many miles to a day. To give the clearest example, Redwood and Potter valleys adjoin each other northeast of Ukiah, but are not connected by any road.

Braren Pauley Vineyards made its first wines in 1980 in an archetypal California barn refitted as a small winery inside, but untouched outside save for the little sign over the door that announces the firm as a member of the Wine Institute.

The site, next to young vineyards north and west of Potter Valley, puts the cellar farthest off the main routes in Mendocino County by some miles, but not in the least-settled neighborhood. Visits start two doors north at the residence of partner and winemaker William Pauley, then repair to the working cellar.

Standby wines are Chardonnay, Sauvignon Blanc, and Zinfandel.

Cresta Blanca Winery holds forth in two solid, square-cut buildings in the northeast quarter of Ukiah.

The one that has a barn roof goes back a ways, to the days when it was a fermenting winery for Guild Wineries and Distilleries and known as Mendocino Winery. The other, with exposed aggregate walls, was built after Guild turned the property into Cresta Blanca. In an eye-appealing switch, the older building is filled with stainless steel fermentors and other sleek new processing gear, while the new structure contains long rows of timeless oak casks and barrels along with the bottling line. A tour here is informative.

Both buildings sit behind a pleasingly cool, spacious tasting room and gift shop, an arbor-shaded picnic patio, and a green lawn with bordering gardens.

Chardonnay, Chenin Blanc, Gewürztraminer, Cabernet Sauvignon, and Zinfandel are offered in the tasting room. The firm also produces sparkling and dessert wines.

Readers of old books about wine may wonder how Cresta Blanca comes to be at the north edge of Ukiah. As a name, Cresta Blanca dates to 1882, when Charles Wetmore founded a winery and made famous wines in the Livermore Valley, east of San Francisco Bay. After Prohibition, his property was bought by Schenley Distillers, which later caused Cresta Blanca to move to several locations before finally settling into the old Roma Winery at Fresno. After Guild bought that facility, it re-established Cresta Blanca as an independent winery in its present home.

Dolan Vineyards is well hidden on a steep slope in Redwood Valley. The proprietors, Paul and Lynne Dolan, make only Chardonnay and Cabernet Sauvignon, and only in small lots.

The small, wood-sided cellar building, retrieved from an existing barn, is an impeccably orderly example of a one-man-sized winery. A pair of stainless steel fermentors, the crusher, and the press sit on a pad outside the front door. Inside, two rooms full of French oak barrels hold the aging wines. Appointment-only tours are informal. Tasting is subject to the Dolans having any wine on hand.

Fetzer Vineyards maintains its public face in what used to be Hopland High School on the west side of U.S. 101 in downtown Hopland.

One-time classrooms now serve as gift shops offering wine-related trinkets, picnic items, and several sorts of made-in-Mendocino crafts. However, wine tasting is the main event, and goes on in what must have been the assembly hall. The long list of Fetzer table wines includes Chardonnay, Sauvignon Blanc, Cabernet Sauvignon, Petite Sirah, Pinot Noir, and Zinfandel as well as Premium Red and Premium White.

The winery is some miles north of Ukiah in an attractive, hidden part of Redwood Valley west of U.S. 101. It is a remarkable story of growth. The company was founded by the late Bernard Fetzer in 1968. His background in forest products led to a small, handsome redwood winery building that since has been remodeled into offices. His business acumen led the family firm to far larger cellars, built on a flatter spot a hundred yards or so downhill from the hill-ringed original. Nine Fetzer children continue to manage the enterprise their father built.

Appointment-only visits reveal an attractive, well-organized winery that is now the largest in the county. Family-owned vineyards provide both fore and background scenery for the long, angular series of fermenting and aging cellars.

Frey Vineyards is an original. The winery building is both a classic expression of the wood butcher's art and a piece of history. Owned by a father and eight children, it was built in a Nordic style over a span of years, using timbers salvaged from the old Garrett winery at Ukiah. Well up in the Redwood Valley, it sits at the center of a sort of family compound containing a main residence in much the same style as the winery, other houses, a part of a school bus that might have appealed to Ken Kesey, and several piles of materials waiting for a use. A menagerie of amiable dogs and cats and more aloof chickens, ducks, and peacocks wander in and around certifiedly organic gardens and vineyard.

The small cellar is crowded with stainless steel dairy tanks converted to fermentors, barrels, and stacks of wines in cases. The Freys regularly make small lots of French Colombard, Gewürztraminer, Grey Riesling, and three different Cabernet Sauvignons. Fumé Blanc and Zinfandel joined the roster in 1981.

McDowell Valley Vineyards offers one of those staggered surprises of which California is almost routinely capable.

On winding, Model T-sized State Highway 175 east of Hopland, in a little valley all its own, is a sleek, low building instantly recognizable for a battery of solar panels integrated into the striking design of its front elevation. It looks lower than it is. In addition to being solar powered, it has 10 to 14-foot earthen berms to help conserve energy.

Inside, a good-sized winery is equipped to the minute, from Willmes membrane press to stainless steel fermentors to millipore filter and sterile bottling room. The old note is a huge gallery of European oak barrels. All of this—down to the computer program controlling the solar units—was designed by Richard Keehn, who, with wife Karen, owns both winery and vineyards.

In pleasing contrast to the straight-edged modernity, a huge tasting room at the upper level is all native oak and redwood worked into the sinuous forms of Art Deco. It is, if memory serves, the only tasting room in the state with its own baby grand piano and a big floor for dancing. (In a place designed for parties, there is a kitchen big enough for a cooking school directly behind the tasting bar.)

For those who would taste outdoors, a pair of wooden decks flanking the tasting room hold picnic tables, and offer fine panoramas of the vines or focused looks into the working winery.

The list of McDowell Valley Vineyards wines—all from the property—includes Chenin Blanc, Fumé Blanc, Chardonnay, Cabernet Sauvignon, Petite Sirah (in fact Syrah), and Zinfandel. Not incidentally, the Keehns have established McDowell Valley as an appellation.

Milano Winery occupies one of the most picturesque of several old kilns left from the days when the nearby village of Hopland was earning its name growing and curing hops.

Winemaker James Milone cofounded the winery in 1977 in a building his father and grandfather built. Father and son now are partners in the winery. The weathered wood structure has been refitted completely on one side of a central partition to make an all-purpose fermenting and aging cellar. The other side, beneath the kiln tower, is to be remodeled as the small winery grows to fit its large building.

Cased goods and a tasting room are at the upper level, over the cellar. In the tasting room, a quiet nook with natural redwood walls, one of the Milones pours wines from a short list that includes Chardonnay, Cabernet Sauvignon, and, most prominently, Zinfandel.

Mountain House Winery occupies a small, plain building behind a large house—sober as Victorians go, but hardly plain—on the site of a nineteenth-century stage stop near the southern boundary of the county.

The proprietors plan to enlarge the original winery with the addition of a second building during 1982. Also in the expansion plan is a tasting room. Meanwhile, visitors with appointments are welcome. The label covers Chardonnay, Cabernet Sauvignon, and a late harvest-style Zinfandel from Sonoma and Amador county grapes.

Parducci Wine Cellars, just on the north side of Ukiah, is the patriarch winery in Mendocino County. Founder Adolph Parducci came to Ukiah in 1931, having launched his first winery in Cloverdale, Sonoma County, in 1916.

Three generations of the Parducci family have had a hand in the steady evolution from country winery to the present one, which concerns itself mostly with varietal table wines.

The progress can be measured by the steady expansion of family vineyard holdings. In the early 1960s they owned about 100 acres; in the mid-1960s they doubled that figure. In 1972, they acquired another 100 acres, give or take a few. The newer plantings are principally of chardonnay, chenin blanc, white riesling, and pinot noir grapes. Their wines joined a roster dominated earlier by Cabernet Sauvignon, Petite Sirah, and Zinfandel.

A white masonry building of graceful proportions comes into view first for visitors to Parducci. Built in 1974, it is the bottling and cased-wine storage cellar. The older buildings of the producing winery nestle into a narrow draw a hundred yards or so west, on the first gentle slopes of a small hill. This is one of few small wineries in California that insists on aging wines in large redwood or oak tanks, completely excluding small cooperage. The fermentors in the spick-and-span cellar are all stainless steel.

The informative tour of all departments is not obligatory, but is a good introduction to winemaking for newcomers to the art. The Parduccis' large, comfortable tasting room, gift shop, and art gallery occupies a well-made Spanish-style building near one end of the big bottling cellar. Out back is an arbor-shaded, summer-only picnic area with several tables set on an adobe patio.

Parsons Creek Winery occupies three bays in a rent-a-warehouse complex toward the south limit of Ukiah. The only outward evidence of a winery is a rolling must tank (for field crushing) with the company name painted on the side. It sits in a little fenced yard at one end of a long, prefabricated metal building full of miscellaneous businesses.

Behind the anonymous facade is a well-designed and impeccably orderly winery. One bay holds two rows of stainless steel fermentors. The next one is filled with French-coopered American oak barrels. The last space has the bottling line and wine in cases.

Parsons Creek brings no whole grapes to the winery, but field-crushes instead, leaving stalks in the vineyard. The semiurban location imposes this bit of streamlining, which, in turn, thus far has limited the winery to white wines. Partner-winemaker Jesse Tidwell produces Chardonnay, Gewürztraminer, and Johannisberg Riesling.

Tijsseling Winery and **Tyland Vineyards** are not only near neighbors, but inextricably linked.

Tyland came first. Founded in 1977 by Dick and Judy Tijsseling, it is snugged away toward the head of a surprisingly long, narrow valley of vines running west from U.S. 101. A stemmer-crusher and press separate two tidy buildings of unpainted redwood, each with a

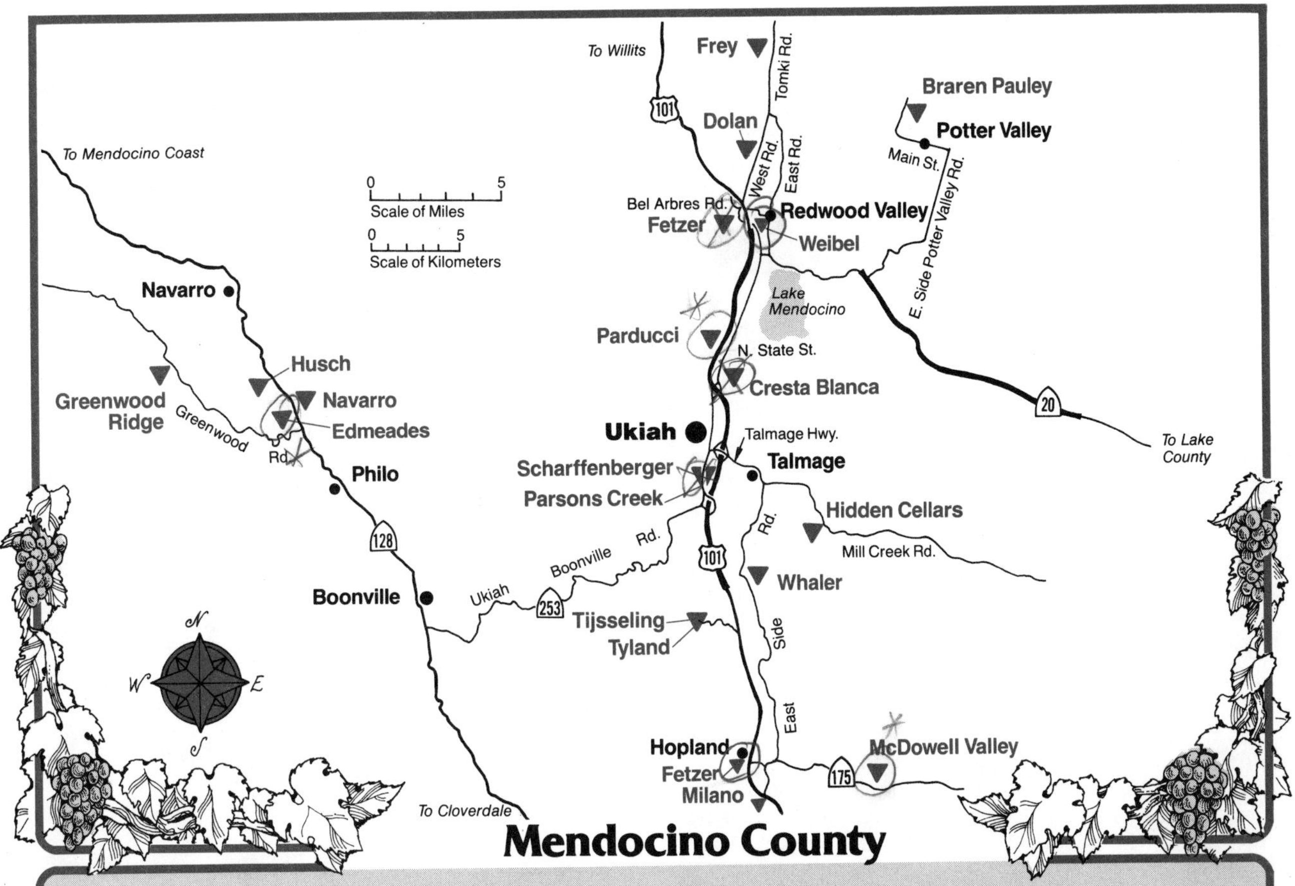

Mendocino County

Braren Pauley Vineyards. From Potter Valley, W on Main St. to end, then N .2 mi. to winery at 12507 Hawn Creek Rd. (Mail address: 1611 Spring Hill Rd., Petaluma, CA 94952) Tel (707) 526-6440. By appt. only.

Cresta Blanca Winery. From U.S. 101, Lake Mendocino Dr. exit, E to State St., then S 1 mi. to winery (2399 N. State St., Ukiah, CA 95482) Tel (707) 462-2987. Picnic. Daily 10-5. GT/Ta.

Dolan Vineyards. 1.6 mi. N of Redwood Valley via West Rd. to Inez Wy. (1482 Inez Wy., Redwood Valley, CA 95470) Tel (707) 485-7250. By appt. only.

Edmeades Vineyards. 3.5 mi. N of Philo on State 128 (5500 State 128, Philo, CA 95466) Tel (707) 895-3232. Daily 10-6 Jun-Sept, 11-5 Oct-May. GT by appt. only/Ta.

Fetzer Vineyards. Tasting room: on U.S. 101 at Hopland. Picnic. Daily 9-5. Winery: From U.S. 101, Uva Rd. exit, N 1 mi. on Uva to Bel Arbres Rd., then W .5 mi. to winery (1150 Bel Arbres Rd., Redwood Valley, CA 95470) Tel (707) 485-7634. By appt. only.

Frey Vineyards. From Redwood Valley, N 3.8 mi. on East Rd./Tomki Rd. (14000 Tomki Rd., Redwood Valley, CA 95470) Tel (707) 485-7525. By appt. only.

Greenwood Ridge Vineyards. From Philo, N on State 128 to Greenwood Ridge Rd. [county], then W 7.8 mi. to winery entrance (Box 1090 Star Rte., Philo, CA 95466) Tel (707) 877-3262. By appt. only.

Hidden Cellars. From Talmage, S .2 mi. on East Side Rd., to Mill Creek Rd., then E 1.1 mi. to winery (4901 Mill Creek Rd., Ukiah, CA 95482) Tel (707) 462-0301. By appt. only.

Husch Vineyards. 5 mi. N of Philo on State 128 (P.O. Box 144, Philo, CA 95466) Tel (707) 895-3216. Picnic. Daily 9-5.

Lazy Creek Vineyards. (4610 Hwy. 128, Philo, CA 95466) Tel (707) 895-3623. (Not on map)

McDowell Valley Vineyards. From U.S. 101 at Hopland, E 3.8 mi. on State 175 to winery (3811 Hwy. 175, Hopland, CA 95449) Tel (707) 744-1053. Picnic. T-Su 10-6 Jun 24-Oct 1. GT by appt./Ta.

Milano Winery. On U.S. 101 1 mi. S of Hopland (14594 S. Hwy. 101, Hopland, CA 95449) Tel (707) 744-1396. T-Su 10-5. GT by appt./Ta.

Mountain House Winery. On State 128 directly W of intersection with Mountain House Rd. (38999 Hwy. 128, Cloverdale, CA 95425) Tel (707) 894-3074. By appt. only. (Outside map area)

Navarro Vineyards. 3.5 mi. N of Philo on State 128 (5601 Hwy. 128, Philo, CA 95466) Tel (707) 895-3686. Picnic. Daily 10-5. GT by appt./Ta.

Parducci Wine Cellars. From U.S. 101, Lake Mendocino Dr. exit, E to N. State St., N .5 mi. to Parducci Rd., then W to winery (501 Parducci Rd., Ukiah, CA 95482) Tel (707) 462-3828. Picnic (summer only). Daily 9-6 summer, 9-5 remainder of year. GT/Ta.

Parsons Creek Winery. From U.S. 101, Talmage Rd. exit, W to S. State St., then .2 mi. S (3001 S. State St., Ukiah, CA 95482) Tel (707) 462-8900. By appt. only.

Scharffenberger Vineyards. From U.S. 101, Talmage Rd. exit, W .2 mi. to 303 (P.O. Box 537, Talmage, CA 95481) Tel (707) 462-8996. By appt. only.

Tijsseling Winery and **Tyland Vineyards.** From U.S. 101 6 mi. S of Ukiah, McNab Ranch Rd. W 2.5 mi. to wineries (2200 McNab Ranch Rd., Ukiah, CA 95482) Tel (707) 462-1810. Picnic. W-Su 10-5 or by appt. IT/Ta.

Villa Baccala. (185 E. Church St., Ukiah, CA 95482) Tel (707) 468-8936. (Not on map)

Weibel Champagne Vineyards. On U.S. 101 6 mi. N of Ukiah, and .1 mi. N of intersection with State 20. (7051 N. State St., Redwood Valley, CA 95470) Tel (707) 485-0321. Daily 9-6. Ta.

Whaler Vineyard. 5 mi. S of Talmage on East Side Rd. (6200 East Side Rd., Ukiah, CA 95482) Tel (707) 462-6355. By appt. only.

Key: GT (guided tour); IT (informal tour); Ta (tasting).

battery of stainless steel fermentors sheltered under the connecting roof. The remainder of the uphill building is given over to a bottling room and cased wine in storage. The downhill structure holds a mixed collection of American oak tanks and barrels and French oak barrels, used to age Cabernet Sauvignon, Gamay Beaujolais, Zinfandel, Chardonnay, and Chenin Blanc. (The Gewürztraminer spends little or no time in wood.)

The larger Tijsseling Winery is managed by Dick but owned by his father, Herman. A few hundred yards closer to the highway than Tyland, the sizable concrete building is divided into three parts: a cavernous room filled in part with stainless steel fermentors and in part with sparkling wine on tirage at one end, a bigger room sized to hold 5,000 French oak barrels at the center, and cased goods and bottling in the third section. This winery is designed to produce Cabernet Sauvignon, Chardonnay, and a pair of *methode champenoise* sparkling wines, all from surrounding family vineyard the two wineries share.

In spring, 1982, the tasting room was at Tyland, along with a tree-shaded patio and picnic area. Plans were afoot to build a tasting room where the entrance road branches away from U.S. 101, to save tasters a bumpy 2.5 mile drive alongside vineyards to the wineries. However, visitors will continue to be welcome in the cellars.

Weibel Champagne Vineyards, the long-time producer of sparkling and other wines at Mission San Jose in Alameda County (see page 125), established a producing winery and attractive tasting room north of Ukiah in 1973.

In time the Weibels plan to add aging cellars to their several banks of stainless steel fermentors. At that point, the Mendocino winery will make all Weibel table wines.

While sparkling wines will continue to be made at Mission San Jose, the Mendocino tasting room will be a reminder of them. It resembles an upside-down Champagne glass of the shallow style known as a coupe.

More wineries. New wineries have emerged rapidly in and around Ukiah since 1979. Several are at the brink of having wine to welcome visitors at deadline time for this book.

Hidden Cellars, which well and truly lives up to its name, began making wine on a small scale in 1981. Principal partner and winemaker Dennis Patton produced in that year Zinfandel, Gewürztraminer, Sauvignon Blanc, and late harvest Johannisberg Riesling. The first wines were to be released for sale during 1982. The winery buildings sit back from Mill Creek Road not far above a series of small reservoirs.

Scharffenberger Vineyards is running a neck and neck race with Tijsseling (see above) to become Mendocino County's first wholly local sparkling wine specialist. Operating in the same rent-a-space warehouse as Parsons Creek, it made its first cuvée in 1981, and got that debut lot on tirage in May, 1982, at least a few strides ahead of the rival. First release is not scheduled until 1984. The cellar also will produce Chardonnay and Pinot Noir Blanc table wines, the first due to appear in autumn, 1982.

During 1982, the firm, owned by local vineyardists George and John Scharffenberger, moved the major part of its winemaking operations to a more permanent home in a one-time pear packing shed on Talmage Road. Students of sparkling winemaking may make appointments to check on progress while the first cuvée ages.

Villa Baccala began construction of its permanent winery on a sloping site next to U.S. 101 north of Hopland in spring, 1982. Plans call for the sizable, early California-style building to be completed in summer, 1983, and for the vintage of 1983 to be the first crushed there. A tasting room and tours are to be part of the completed facility. Owner William Baccala plans to make Chardonnay, Chenin Blanc, Colombard, Cabernet Sauvignon, and Zinfandel as the major wines on his list. Meanwhile, the label is already on the market on wines made in leased space.

Whaler Vineyard belongs to the first Scandinavian sea captain to come into California winemaking since Gustave Niebaum launched Inglenook in the 1880s. Russ and Annie Nyborg made a small first lot of Zinfandel from their vineyard 5 miles south of Talmage in 1981. That wine is scheduled to appear in late 1982 or early 1983, at which time visitors will be welcome by appointment. The original winery was a spruce little barn painted a dusty blue, except for bright yellow doors. The family plan was to add a second, larger building in the same style directly behind it, probably for the harvest of 1982. With the expansion will come several styles of wine, but all Zinfandel and all from the property.

Anderson Valley Wineries

In this old-time apple-growing district near the Mendocino Coast, vines and wineries are beginning to be as important in the landscape as orchards. The first two wineries opened in 1971. Since then the number has grown to six, all small, all family-owned. Prospects are for still more of the same sort of friendly places. All but one of the currently existing cellars flank State Highway 128 near the wee village of Philo; the lone exception is well west on the road to Elk.

Edmeades Vineyards dates from 1971 as a winery, although its vines were among the first post-Prohibition ones planted in Anderson Valley, in 1963.

The property of Deron Edmeades, the winery proper is a tale of gentle growth. The original structure houses some of the aging cooperage. It perches on stilts on a steep bank just above the highway. A newer oak aging cellar is up on the crest of the same wooded hillock, overshadowed now by a more recent prefabricated metal building that houses the stainless steel fermentors and bottled wines. The tasting room is in none of these buildings. Rather it is in a comfortable room of rustic wood next to the proprietor's house. The entry is instantly recognizable by the basketball hoop over the doorway.

The roster of Edmeades whites includes Chardonnay, Gewürztraminer, a blend called Cabernet-Fumé, and a proprietary white called Rain Wine. The reds include Cabernet Sauvignon and several Zinfandels from ancient vineyards, usually identified on the labels.

Greenwood Ridge Vineyards is easily the most remote of western Mendocino's wineries and vineyards, and the most dramatically set in a neighborhood of handsome scenery.

The drive up Greenwood Ridge Road, marked as the turn to Elk where it leaves State 128, is one panorama after another of Anderson Valley. The drive from the county road into the winery does not offer any far views, but its curving path along the face of a steep hill does not lack for drama anyway. Once the drive is done, the scenery regains a spectacular scope. Proprietor Allan Green's vineyards run along the crest of the sharp ridge that gave them a name. Two connected, wood-sided winery buildings are cut into a slope just below the vines and just above a small pond, a quiet respite from the general grandeur of the place.

A tour of crusher, press, stainless steel fermentors, and oak barrels is quickly done. If any of a small annual production of White Riesling and Cabernet Sauvignon is on hand, the proprietor may offer a taste.

Husch Vineyards made the other early start in Anderson Valley when Tony and Gretchen Husch launched it in 1971. The property now belongs to a family of veteran Mendocino vineyardists named Oswald, who have a large vineyard near Ukiah as well as the trim winery and rolling vineyard begun by their predecessors in Anderson Valley.

There is no tour of the L-shaped, wood-frame winery building with its conventional array of stainless steel fermentors, oak upright tanks, and oak barrels. Neither is there tasting of a roster of wines that includes Chardonnay, Gewürztraminer, Johannisberg Riesling, Cabernet Sauvignon, and Pinot Noir. But the Oswalds offer all of their wines for sale from a refurbished onetime granary next to the winery, and provide several picnic tables shaded either by tall conifers or a robust grapevine trained onto an arbor.

Navarro Vineyards joined the roster of Anderson Valley wineries in 1975. Visitors are welcomed in an architecturally distinctive tasting room some hundreds of yards from the winery buildings, but right next to the highway.

The building, which somehow manages to be at once formal and countrified, has an indoor tasting and sales room and an outdoor picnic deck with umbrella-shaded tables. Glass doors allow tasters inside to contemplate the vineyards almost as clearly as picnickers can.

Looking around the weathered wood buildings of the winery requires an appointment. Proprietors Ted Bennett and Deborah Cahn built their small cellars to match an existing barn which they had earlier converted to a family residence. The winery also was built to spare some old oaks, which explains its irregular shape. The net effect is a visual pleasure, a cluster of tree-shaded, casual buildings on an impeccably orderly but not groomed knoll.

The sense of order extends into the winery; one cellar is devoted to reds (Pinot Noir and a bit of Cabernet Sauvignon), the other to whites (the specialty—Gewürztraminer, Chardonnay, and Johannisberg Riesling). The cooperage is European oak, divided about equally between puncheons and barrels. Stainless steel fermentors, a Howard basket press, and other modern processing equipment are on a deck at the rear.

More wineries. Anderson Valley has two other wineries. One, Lazy Creek, makes tiny lots of wine, to a total of about 500 cases. The property of Hans and Teresa Kobler hardly requires a tour, but the proprietors will sell wine to visitors who make appointments.

Other Than Wineries

Most of the diversions in Mendocino County, other than wineries, are outdoorsy and, above all, watery.

In the Ukiah region, manmade Lake Mendocino fills a sizable bowl in the hills northeast of town. The lake has three recreation areas, two accessible from State Highway 20, the road to Lake County, and the third by way of Lake Mendocino Drive from U.S. Highway 101. All routes are signed clearly. The shoreside parks have boat launches, swimming beaches, and picnic areas. The lake is stocked with fish. The Russian River above the lake also has trout.

In Ukiah a fine municipal park just west of the main business district amplifies the potential for picnics. Scott Street leads to it from the main business street.

For a list of accommodations and restaurants in the Ukiah area, write to the Chamber of Commerce, 495 E. Perkins Street, Ukiah, CA 95482.

In the Anderson Valley north of Philo, Hendy Woods State Park has picnic tables and campsites in the shade of redwoods. Entrance to the park is a mile west of State Highway 128 on the Greenwood Ridge Road to Elk. Indian Creek, a quieter, less known picnic park adjoins State 128 on the opposite side of Philo.

Plotting a Route

U.S. Highway 101 burrows straight and fast through the Ukiah Valley, the upstream end of the Russian

River watershed. The highway is part two-lane but primarily freeway. No other direct route leads into the region from either north or south.

State Highway 128 runs the length of the Anderson Valley. It connects with U.S. 101 at Cloverdale in northern Sonoma County, and with State Highway 1 on the coast near Albion.

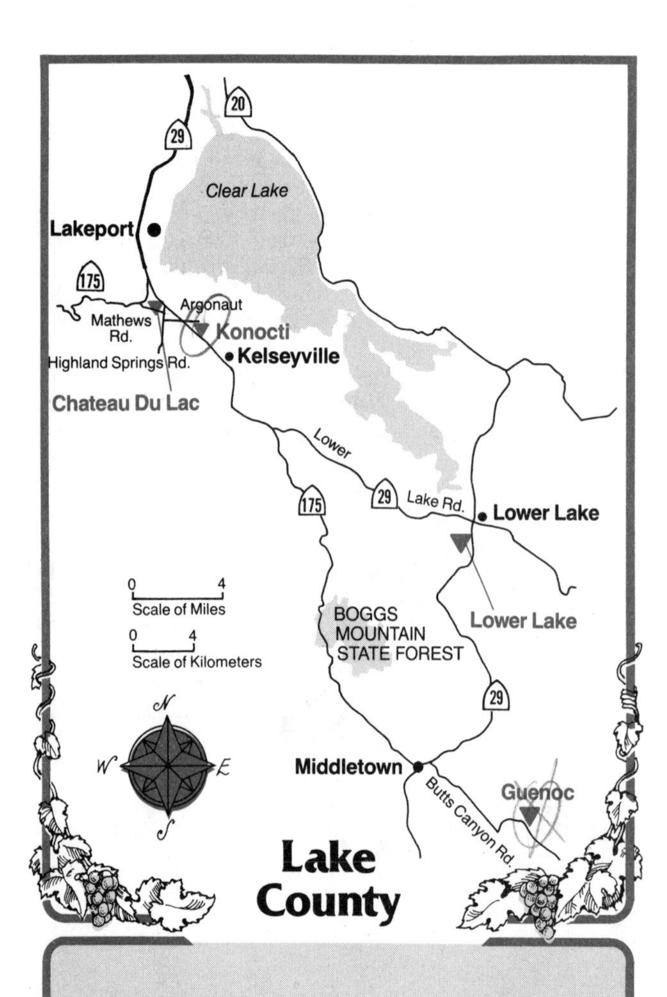

Chateau Du Lac. From State 29 3 miles S of Lakeport, W .1 mi. on Highland Springs Rd. to Mathews Rd., then N .1 mi. to winery drive (700 Mathews Rd., Lakeport, CA 95453) Tel (707) 263-9333. By appt. only.

Guenoc Winery. From State 29 at N side of Middletown, SE 5.5 miles on Butts Canyon Rd. to winery drive at 21000 (P.O. Box 1146, Middletown, CA 95461) Tel (707) 987-2359. By appt. only.

The Konocti Winery. From Kelseyville, N 1 mi. on State 29 to Thomas Dr. (P.O. Box 925, Kelseyville, CA 95451) Tel (707) 279-8861. Picnic. Daily 11-5. IT (GT by appt.)/Ta.

Lower Lake Winery. From Lower Lake, S 1 mi. on State 29 (P.O. Box 950, Lower Lake, CA 95457) Tel (707) 994-4069. Picnic. Sa-Su 10-5 or by appt. GT/Ta.

Key: GT (guided tour); IT (informal tour); Ta (tasting).

State Highway 20 is a winding way to get into the Ukiah Valley from the Sacramento Valley, and also connects Ukiah with the northern tip of Lake County's winegrowing area. In spring it has a glorious profusion of redbud as a scenic bonus. The other connector between Mendocino and Lake counties is State Highway 175 from Hopland to a point between Lakeport and Kelseyville. In a lot of spots it would keep a Model T well below peak speed.

One other connecting road to know about is State Highway 253, which runs a high, curving course across the Coast Ranges from Ukiah to Boonville, on State Highway 128. It is the shortest route between the Ukiah and Anderson Valleys, but its scenery discourages haste even more then its twisting, climbing turns.

Lake County

Of all the north coast counties of California, Lake is the most bucolic. It never has had a railroad. It has no city of size. Lakeport (population 3,688) is its county seat and largest town. The whole county has but 36,500 residents—and therein lies its charm.

Kelseyville, Middletown, and the other towns and villages of Lake County bring to mind scenes of Penrod and other Booth Tarkington characters of an era that pretty well has disappeared from more populous parts of the state. Businesses are small and local. There is a good deal of waving and talking among familiars along Main Street. A three-piece suit would be an oddity on almost anybody, even the banker. This is not to say Lake County is out of touch with the world. Its great geographic feature, Clear Lake, draws tourists by the hundreds on cool days and by the thousands on warm ones, and its resort owners and farmers know all the new tricks of their trades.

The county's recent spate of new vineyards and wineries fits into this picture well.

When California winemaking began to stagger back to life after Prohibition, it quickly became a truism that Sonoma fell into the shadow of Napa, that Mendocino struggled along behind Sonoma, and that Lake trailed in the wake of Mendocino. In a short time, Lake ran out of wineries altogether, and had only a scattered handful of surviving vineyards. Lake still is last in line in numbers of wineries and acres of vines among these four counties, but its reawakening is well advanced.

The wineries

In spring, 1982, Lake County had three wineries built and in full operation, a fourth beginning construction, and imminent prospects for two more. They are divided about half and half between the Lakeport-Kelseyville area alongside Clear Lake, and the Middletown district to the south of it.

Chateau Du Lac was beginning construction of its permanent main winery building in spring, 1982. The cellar was being cut into a round, oak-dotted knoll that rises out of its owners' vineyards next to State Highway 29 south of Lakeport. When it is complete, travelers on the highway will be able to see the crushing-pressing area at the rear, high side of the building. At the same time, the proprietors will bring their press, stainless steel fermentors, and Burgundian barrels from leased space as the first increment of equipment in the new cellar.

Chateau Du Lac's first vintage in 1981 yielded Chardonnay, Fumé Blanc, White Riesling, Cabernet Sauvignon, and Zinfandel.

Guenoc Winery revives winemaking in a storied place. The property once belonged to the British actress Lily Langtry, who imported a winemaker from Bordeaux and gave him instructions to do something a long cut above ordinary. Alas for history, her timing was off. Prohibition ended the attempt before it could make a fair start.

The current owners, a Hawaiian family named Magoon, have set about a plan that puts Lily's in the shade. Their winery, completed during the spring of 1982, perches atop a hill that was substantially reshaped for the purpose. It is a plain rectangle, if anything 180 by 300 feet and covered with clear, heart-grade redwood could be called plain. From one end, the view is across a small lake. From the other, the scene is mostly vines, although Lily's old house—now a family residence—can be seen in the middle distance.

The winery proper is impressive for its modern gear as well as for its size. The westerly end is a huge room containing a Willmes membrane press and a still-growing collection of stainless steel fermentors. A middle section of almost equal size houses a small number of upright oak tanks and what appears to be half an acre of French barrels. The easterly portion, the one facing Lily's house, is devoted to storing bottled wines, all made from grapes grown on the property.

The Guenoc label covers Chardonnay, Chenin Blanc, Cabernet Sauvignon, and Zinfandel. Sauvignon Blanc is to come.

The Konocti Winery hides among the last few trees of an old walnut orchard not far north of Kelseyville. The prefabricated metal building belongs to a cooperative of more than 20 growers with nearby vineyards ranging in size from 2.5 acres up to 40. They make visitors more than mildly welcome.

A tasting room and gift shop occupies most of a small frame building attached to the front of the winery. Outside, a number of picnic tables sit on a lawn well shaded by old walnut trees. On summer Sundays, the proprietors have local musicians on hand to complete Omar's famous triumvirate of treasures. On the second weekend in October, they stage a harvest festival with barbecue, art show, grape stomp, and, for those who would rather make distance than gallonage, a vineyard run.

Konocti will provide guided tours of its crowded cellars by appointment, but drop-in guests are allowed to stroll through on their own. The interior holds a diverse collection of stainless steel fermentors and storage tanks, redwood tanks, and American and French oak barrels. Out back, the roof extends to overhang more stainless steel fermentors.

The winery produces Fumé Blanc, late harvest Johannisberg Riesling, Cabernet Sauvignon, and Zinfandel in several styles ranging from fresh-fruity to a port-like specialty called Primitivo after the grape variety's suspected Italian ancestor.

Lower Lake Winery perches jauntily on the first rise of a small hill south of Lower Lake. Founded in 1977, it is the county's oldest winery in continuous production.

Two connected sections of a redwood-faced, steep-roofed building leave room for the owning Harold Stuermer family to enlarge their production a bit without new construction. Even when the buildings are filled with gear, this will be a small winery. In the rear, larger part of the structure, stainless steel fermentors fill only part of the area set aside for them. Adjacent neat stacks of French and American oak barrels also leave room for more to come. The front section is set aside for stored wines in bottle, the tasting room, and offices.

Winemaker Daniel Stuermer makes only Fumé Blanc and Cabernet Sauvignon. Most bottlings are from single vineyards identified on the labels. All are from Lake County grapes.

Other Than Wineries

The principal activity around Clear Lake is shoreside resorts. In fact the short roster of widely spread wineries makes them an adjunct to a lakeshore vacation.

For day-trippers or camping vacationers, sizable Clear Lake State Park is not far north of Kelseyville via Soda Bay Road. County-owned Buckingham Park is not far east of it via the same road. The state park ranges from 1400 feet elevation down to lake level, and has camping and picnicking sites, swimming beaches, and boat launches. Buckingham, on a peninsula sticking into the lake, has similar amenities. For lists of accommodations, write to the Lake County Chamber of Commerce, 875 Lakeport Boulevard, Lakeport, CA 95453.

Plotting a Route

Lake County does not have a U.S. Highway or Interstate Freeway in it, which is part of its charm. The main connecting road with other parts of the world is State Highway 20, which intersects with U.S. Highway 101 near Ukiah, and Interstate Highway 5 a little more than 50 miles north of Sacramento at Williams.

State Highway 175 runs, hilly and tightly winding, from U.S. 101 at Hopland to an intersection with State Highway 29 between Lakeport and Kelseyville.

The other ways to get into the county are through Napa County. Both are slow and mountainous routes in spots. State 29 continues from the Napa Valley northward. The alternative route is Deer Park-Howell Mountain Road from the Napa Valley east to Pope Valley, then north on Pope Valley Road-Butts Canyon Road into Middletown.

One other point of advice: State 175 between Clearlake Park and Middletown appears to be a short cut compared to State 29. It is not.

The Napa Valley

A small place synonymous with Wine Country

"Napa Valley" often is used interchangeably with "Wine Country," and not without reason. A few more than 100 wineries, most of them handsomely traditional but some handsomely contemporary, are spaced at close intervals all the way from the Carneros district near San Pablo Bay to the skirts of Mt. St. Helena, 25 miles northwest. Many of their names reach far back into the nineteenth century, and far back in the memories of knowledgeable wine hobbyists. Napa further earns the title of wine country because the cellars in this valley are surrounded by seas of vineyards, some 24,000 acres of them.

The vineyarded reaches of the Napa Valley may have an occasional peer for beauty in California, but they have no superior. Level and easy to negotiate as the floor of the valley is, it never becomes wide enough to lose the imminent sense of tall and consistently rugged hills on either side. Local roads burrow into the hearts of vineyarded land on flat and mountainside alike, offering visitors a whole gamut of views to admire.

The near end of the valley is just a little over an hour from San Francisco; the far end is not quite two hours away if one hurries, non-stop. However, it is of the essence *not* to hurry.

The Wineries

An old rule of thumb among veteran visitors to California wineries is this: three cellars a day, no more. If there is any district in the state that tempts people to stretch the rule, Napa is it, because distances between wineries are so short. In spite of the temptation, it is wise to resist, to keep details in perspective.

With the number of cellars having passed 100, it almost goes without saying that Napa has at least one of every sort of winery there is to see.

It is worth noting that most of the many new wineries in the valley are very small indeed, no few of them staffed by a single full-time man. Though the larger cellars are able to offer highly developed tour and tasting programs, the small cellars do not have enough hands to do that. More to the point, they cannot always give an appointment when someone calls for one, simply because the lone hand may have to spend the day delivering wine, or chasing after a replacement part for something that broke, or—the crux of it all—working on the winemaking itself. Serious bibbers almost always find that patience and persistence will pay in these cases.

There are no internal divisions in the alphabetical listing of Napa wineries because the cellars are so regularly spaced. However, they are so numerous that the map has been divided into two areas to fit them all in. Map entries are alphabetical within each area shown.

Alta Vineyard Cellar just downhill from Schramsberg (see page 84), revives a cellar immortalized by Robert Louis Stevenson in *Silverado Squatters,* the journal of his year in the valley.

Stevenson knew it as M'Eckron's. Vineyard and winery alike were brand new in 1880–81, but the writer thought his fellow Scot had an air of success. If he did, it was not a durable one. The cellars were idle for decades until Benjamin and Rose Falk restored them to their original use in 1979.

The small stone building remains as Stevenson saw it from the outside, but has been remade inside to produce only Chardonnay from nearby vines. The small cellar is almost full with fat French barrels used to age the wine.

Beaulieu Vineyard in Rutherford is one of the Napa Valley's more telling demonstrations of the state of international winemaking in modern times.

The crusher-stemmers are Garolla-types, made in Fresno after an Italian design. The presses are Willmes from Germany. The filters are both Italian and American. The cooperage includes American stainless steel for fermenting, and California redwood, Kentucky oak, and French oak for aging the wines. This equipment was gathered for years by the winemaker, Russian-born, French-trained Andre Tchelistcheff. His successors are American from start to finish, but no less globally oriented.

Touring Beaulieu (pronounced bowl-you, more or less) requires some sense of direction. The oldest part of the building dates (under another name) to 1885. Occasional expansion since then has not imposed any rigid order on the whereabouts of walls or working gear. Still, guides tack back and forth with expert ease and cover all departments from crushing station to bottling line.

Beaulieu was founded as a company in 1900 by a newly arrived Frenchman named Georges de Latour. The winery was continued first by his widow, then by his daughter, who married the eminently Gallic Marquis de Pins. The de Pins' daughter took a brief part in the management, but, in 1969, mother and daughter elected to sell the winery to the Heublein Corporation.

The buildings give some indication of their history. All of the parts painted a cream color date from the 1855 original or the de Pins' years. The parts left unpainted are additions since Heublein acquired the winery.

Though the physical plant is right in downtown Rutherford, Beaulieu spreads its vines over much of the valley.

The resulting wines include Chardonnay, Sauvignon Blanc, Cabernet Sauvignon in three separate styles, and Pinot Noir. They and their running mates are vintage-dated. Selected wines are available for tasting in a handsome building at one side of the winery. This building also is the beginning point for tours.

Beringer Vineyards dates from a modest migration of Germans into the Napa Valley in the mid-nineteenth century. Architecturally, it is German, but not modest.

The winery is fronted by Rhine House, built by Frederick Beringer as a replica of the Rhenish home he and brother Jacob left behind when they emigrated. Tours start at the front door and end in a tasting room handsomely turned out in period style.

Uphill from the stone and half-timbered house, about level with its steep slate roof, Beringer's original aging cellars include a thousand feet of tunnels. The founding brothers employed Chinese laborers to dig the tunnels, starting in 1876, the winery's inaugural year. In some sections pick marks still show plainly through a veil of dusty black lichen. After the caves developed a slight tendency to drop small chunks of rock on staff and visitors, the proprietors reinforced the weak spots and coated them with gray gunite, giving some sections a newer look.

These tunnels hold long lines of oak puncheons for fermenting and aging particular lots of Beringer Chardonnay, but are now only a small part of the story. Beringer has long since outgrown the tunnels and the finely crafted stone building that fronts them. The third generation of Beringers had expanded beyond the original capacity before they sold their cellars in 1969 to Nestlé, Inc. In 1975 the new owners built a more efficient if less picturesque cellar across the Avenue of the Elms to take care of a great majority of fermenting and aging.

Tasting at the Rhine House is of selected wines from a broad roster that includes Chardonnay, Fumé Blanc, Cabernet Sauvignon, Pinot Noir, and Zinfandel. Some bottlings are from identified single vineyards.

Burgess Cellars is well up in the hills east of the Napa Valley floor.

The main building is one of the few classic stone and wood-frame wineries still in operation in the county. When such cellars were built into hillsides in the 1880s, the upper wooden story held the fermentors and other processing gear while the cooler stone lower level held cooperage full of aging wines. Matters are still arranged somewhat along the original lines, although the premises now occupy three buildings rather than one.

The current name dates to 1972 when Tom and Linda Burgess bought the property. They offer barrel-fermented Chardonnay, Cabernet Sauvignon, and Zinfandel.

Cakebread Cellars occupies a distinctive wood-frame building. Part of its individual appearance comes from graceful proportion, part from impressive expanses of unornamented, unpainted redwood siding, but the unmistakable signature is a short, thick tower rising up at the intersection of its two crossing wings. Another sure sign of the place, in season, is a long bed of brilliant flowers alongside the entry.

This building, next to State Highway 29 north of Oakville, was completed in time for the vintage of 1981. The winery began in 1974 in a smaller wood-frame building some hundreds of yards farther back in the vineyard. The main building houses two rows of stainless steel fermentors, some imposing racks of

French oak barrels, and the bottling line. The original building now is used to make the barrel-fermented portion of the winery's Chardonnay.

The phased construction fairly typifies Napa's new wave of small, family-owned wineries. Owners Jack and Dolores Cakebread have complicated their own progress by sustaining other careers in professional photography and automotive mechanics, and simplified it by installing their son Bruce as winemaker after sending him through the enology course at the University of California at Davis.

Only four wines are made at Cakebread: Chardonnay, Sauvignon Blanc, Cabernet Sauvignon, and Zinfandel.

Carneros Creek Winery, founded in 1971, snugs into a hidden fold of the Carneros district south of Napa city, in a small, pleasantly understated structure built in two phases—one wing at a time.

In these conventionally equipped cellars, stainless steel fermentors occupy a roofed shed at the rear, while French oak barrels take up the majority of floor space inside the masonry block walls.

When work does not demand undivided attention, someone—possibly winemaker Francis Mahoney or one of the other owning partners—may stop to talk shop with casual visitors, but the staff is small enough that an appointment is a surer way to make a visit instructive at a winery where discussion can dwell on separate lots of wines from individually identified vineyards. There is some emphasis on Chardonnay and Pinot Noir. Sauvignon Blanc and Cabernet Sauvignon complete the list.

Cassayre-Forni Cellars provides a look at exactly the sort of small winery a winery systems engineer would design for himself given the chance, for that is exactly what it is.

The solid, square, masonry block building west of State 29 between Rutherford and Oakville was laid out by Paul Cassayre, a civil engineer who has done considerable winery work. The winemaking partner is Mike Forni.

Crusher and press sit on a concrete pad shaded by roof overhang at the rear. Inside are stainless steel fermentors, French and American oak barrels, and other gear familiar to any contemporary small cellar.

Cassayre-Forni dates from 1977. The roster of wines includes Chenin Blanc, Cabernet Sauvignon, and Zinfandel.

Caymus Vineyards straddles Conn Creek east of Rutherford, more or less at the heart of the huge nineteenth century Spanish land grant from which it draws its name.

Proprietor Charles Wagner is an old hand in the Napa Valley, the second generation of his family to grow grapes on the property. He is also not a man for frills. As a result of both facts, he and his son Chuck have assembled their winery in a trio of plain buildings and equipped it in part with gear that goes back almost as far as the family does. For example, the crusher-stemmer dates from 1909, which makes new parts hard to come by. Similarly, the presses are a pair of baskets with the same kind of hydraulic lifts used for automobile hoists, a device once common, but seldom seen in wineries these days.

This is not to say the Wagners turn a blind eye to the present. The four fermentors are made of jacketed and insulated stainless steel. Two of the buildings house thoughtful collections of European and American oak in the forms of barrels, oval casks, and upright tanks. The third structure houses a modern bottling line.

As a winery, Caymus dates from 1972. It was one of the earliest to produce an *Oeil de Perdrix* ("partridge eye" in French) from pinot noir. That wine continues as part of the list along with Chardonnay, Sauvignon Blanc, Cabernet Sauvignon, Pinot Noir, and Zinfandel. Caymus offers essentially the same list of wines under a second label, Liberty School.

Chateau Bouchaine will show visitors with long attention spans how it makes wine now, though none is scheduled for sale until early 1984.

On a rolling Carneros district hill overlooking San Pablo Bay, the winery building has been around for a good long time as a bulk cellar. Its current owners have transformed it from a weathered white barn into a striking redwood-sided building of impressive size. They also have made parts of it over from an obsolete winery into a modern cellar, but kept some old gear for the firm's second purpose, making and storing wine for others under contract.

For visitors, the net result of having a small, new winery inside a larger old one is a chance to look at working examples of present and past side by side. The stainless steel fermentors have open-topped concrete ones as neighbors, for example, and a long, low room full of French oak barrels adjoins a long, tall room full of well-seasoned redwood tanks.

The first substantial amounts of Chateau Bouchaine Chardonnay and Pinot Noir are to be made from the vintage of 1982.

Chateau Chevalier revives one of the Napa Valley's more flamboyant bits of nineteenth century architecture.

An aggressive businessman named F. Chevalier erected a towered and turreted stone building on a steep hillside in 1891. He called the place and its wines Chateau Chevalier.

After a long hiatus, the old building became a winery once again in 1973, although on a smaller scale than originally. The upper stories had been transformed into a residence during the property's non-vinous days and now are occupied by the family of owner Greg Bissonette. Only the lowest level of three is used for making and storing wine.

The vineyard land on the skirts of Spring Mountain above St. Helena was cleared in 1969 and replanted in 1970. The principal wines, some from the home vineyard, some from purchased grapes, are Chardonnay and Cabernet Sauvignon. Even with grapes from other vineyards, production is so small that tasting is at the proprietor's discretion.

Chateau Chevre got its name in whimsical tribute to a former use of the property. The translation from

French is Goat Castle. The building in question is a small, indestructible, oddly shaped, white-painted concrete structure that now is a compact cellar, but used to be an all-purpose barn. Milk goats grazed where owner Gerald Hazen's merlot vines now grow, not far south of Yountville.

Two-year-old wines in French barrels occupy one room. Year-old wines and the bottling line share the former milking room. Cased goods stack up in a narrow, tall wing that used to hold feed. A small crusher and press are outdoors on one side. Open-topped stainless steel tubs for fermenting sit outside the opposite wall. Hazen uses the tubs so he can stay with the old-fashioned technique of punching down red wine caps by hand.

The principal wine is Merlot. When a separate vineyard of Sauvignon Blanc matures, the proprietor plans to add a second building for it.

Chateau Montelena is both a new winery and an old one in the Napa Valley.

The finely crafted stone building dates back to the 1880s, when Alfred L. Tubbs had it built on its hilly site north of Calistoga, just where the road to Lake County starts over one shoulder of Mt. St. Helena.

In its present form, dating from 1968, the winery has revived the primary label name from the pre-Prohibition Tubbs days, but otherwise is a modern, efficient example of a small, estatelike property. Within the old stone walls, one half of the main cellar holds stainless steel fermentors; the other half is devoted to row upon row of oak barrels from a variety of sources. A flanking room contains the bottling line and bottled wines.

During the long interval between Tubbs's proprietorship and the current one, an owner named Yort Frank began to make the property into a showcase Chinese garden. Tea houses on two islands in a small lake still survive as picturesque souvenirs of that effort.

Chateau Montelena has but four wines on its list. Chardonnay and Johannisberg Riesling are the whites; Cabernet Sauvignon and Zinfandel the reds. One or another is selected for tasting each day.

The Christian Brothers began their California winemaking in Martinez shortly before the turn of the century. A bas-relief in the winery office at Mont LaSalle shows one of the brothers at Martinez crushing grapes in a horse trough with a wooden club.

By the time The Christian Brothers packed up to come to the Napa Valley in 1930, the equipment they barged across San Pablo Bay was much improved over the trough and club. Now their winery operations are the largest in Napa, far-flung, and a dazzling mixture of the traditional and the technically advanced.

Headquarters is at Mont LaSalle, west of Napa city and just below the Mayacamas Mountains' ridgetops. In the midst of 200 acres of rolling vineyard, a winery and a novitiate stand side by side against a backdrop of thickly wooded hills. The winery is the older building. A traditional stone barn, it was built in 1903 by Theodore Gier, whose pre-Prohibition Giersberger Rhine was a critical success in its time. The original home of the brothers in Napa, this winery now serves only as an aging and bottling cellar, its three stories filled with both old and new oak. The old uprights on the ground floor were Gier's fermenting tanks.

The other aging cellar in the valley is a good deal larger than the Gier place. It is the monumental Greystone Cellars at the northern edge of St. Helena. Greystone dates from 1888, when William Bowers Bourn used a small part of his great fortune to build the vast building as the largest stone cellar in the world. The Christian Brothers bought the property in 1950 when their stock of aging wines grew too great for Mont LaSalle to hold.

Crushing, fermenting, and sparkling winemaking all are done at the architecturally ordinary South St. Helena Winery, its big, ultramodern fermenting installation visible from State 29, but not open to visitors.

There are tours of both Greystone and Mont LaSalle and tasting at both cellars. Greystone has, as a bonus attraction, some of Brother Timothy's seemingly limitless corkscrew collection.

At the two tasting rooms, nearly all of The Christian Brothers' long list of wines is available for sampling. The roster includes several estate bottlings from selected vineyards. Of special pride are the Pineau de la Loire and Napa Fumé among whites, and the Pinot St. George among reds. A specialty is a light, sweet Muscat called Chateau LaSalle.

Clos du Val Wine Co., an altogether new winery at its founding in 1972, comes by its French name honestly, for both the principal owner and winemaker-manager Bernard Portet are French.

The winery building, elegantly proportioned and handsome in an understated, almost plain-faced way, occupies a square cut into one corner of the Chimney Rock Golf Course on the Silverado Trail north of Napa city.

Inside, it once offered a rather clear example of a typical Bordeaux chateau. Two rows of stainless steel fermentors and the press occupied one end. Echoing rows of oak upright tanks adjoined the fermentors for initial racking of new wines. Two-high stacks of French barrels next to the uprights carried the wine the rest of the way to bottling. The recent addition of wines other

(Continued on page 74)

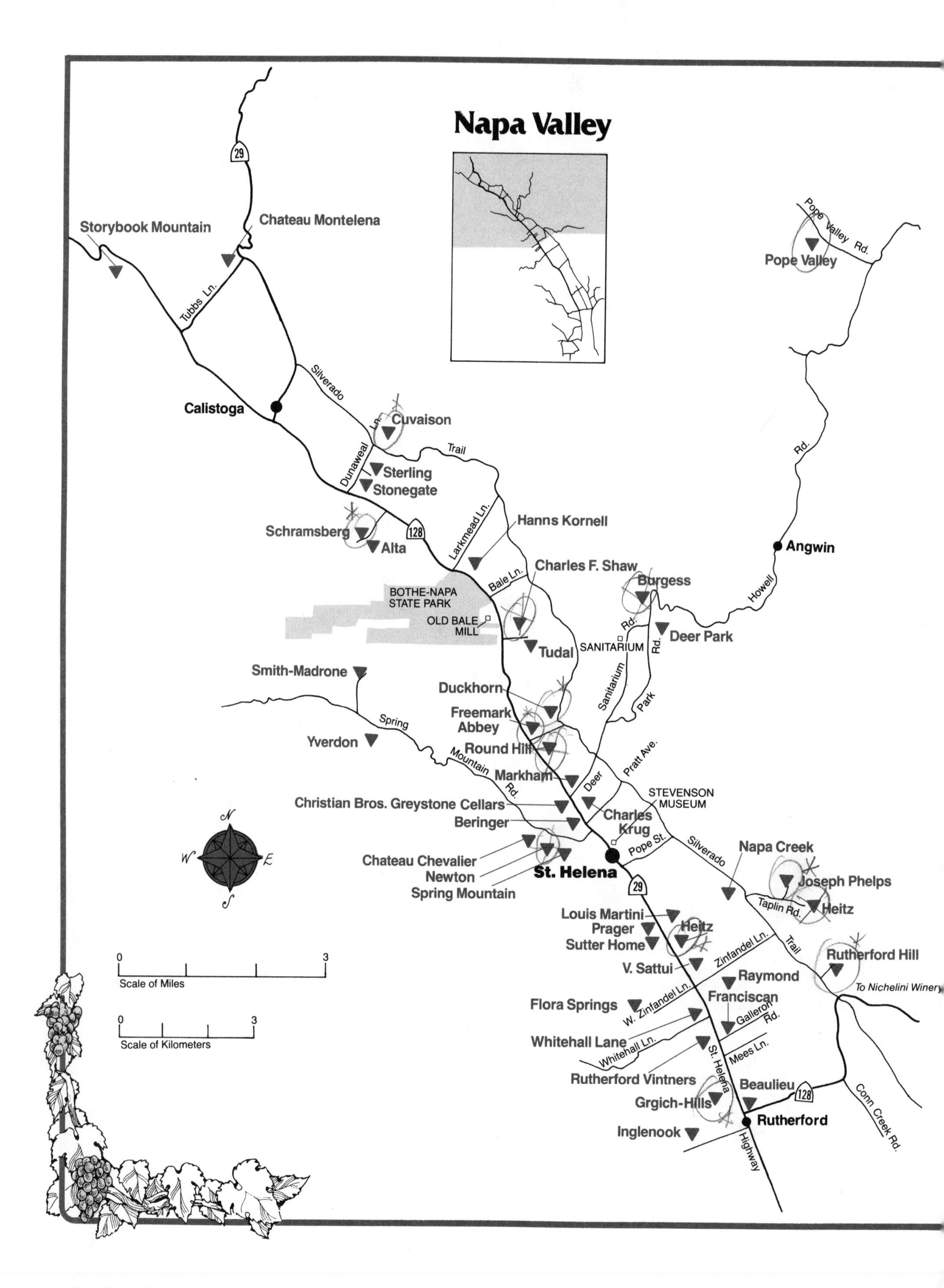

Napa Valley
Storybook Mountain
Chateau Montelena
Tubbs Ln.
Silverado
Calistoga
Cuvaison
Dunaweal Ln.
Trail
Sterling
Stonegate
Schramsberg
Alta
Larkmead Ln.
Hanns Kornell
Bale Ln.
Charles F. Shaw
BOTHE-NAPA STATE PARK
OLD BALE MILL
Tudal
SANITARIUM
Burgess
Rd.
Deer Park
Sanitarium
Park
Smith-Madrone
Duckhorn
Freemark Abbey
Spring
Yverdon
Round Hill
Mountain
Rd.
Markham
Deer
Pratt Ave.
Christian Bros. Greystone Cellars
Beringer
Charles Krug
STEVENSON MUSEUM
Pope St.
Silverado
Chateau Chevalier
Newton
Spring Mountain
St. Helena
29
Napa Creek
Joseph Phelps
Taplin Rd.
Heitz
Louis Martini
Prager
Heitz
Sutter Home
V. Sattui
Zinfandel Ln.
Trail
Rutherford Hill
To Nichelini Winery
Raymond
Franciscan
Flora Springs
W. Zinfandel Ln.
Galleron Rd.
Whitehall Lane
Whitehall Ln.
Mees Ln.
St. Helena
Rutherford Vintners
Beaulieu
128
Grgich-Hills
Rutherford
Inglenook
Highway
Conn Creek Rd.
Pope Valley Rd.
Pope Valley
Rd.
Angwin
Howell
N
W
E
S
0
3
Scale of Miles
0
3
Scale of Kilometers

Alta Vineyard Cellar. From State 29, .2 mi. N of Dunaweal Ln., W on pvt. rd. to winery (1311 Schramsberg Rd., Calistoga, CA 94515) Tel (707) 942-6708. IT/Ta by appt. only.

Beaulieu Vineyard. E side of State 29 at Rutherford (Rutherford, CA 94573) Tel (707) 963-2411. Daily 10-4 (last tour 3:15). GT/Ta.

Beringer Vineyards. W side State 29, N limit of St. Helena (2000 Main St., St. Helena, CA 94574) Tel (707) 963-7115. Daily 9-4:45 (last tour 3:45). GT/ Ta.

Burgess Cellars. From State 29, 1.5 mi. N of St. Helena, E on Deer Park Rd. 3 mi. to winery drive at 1108 (P.O. Box 282, St. Helena, CA 94574) Tel (707) 963-4766. Daily 10-4. GT by appt. Sa, Su, M 10:30 and 2:30.

Chateau Chevalier. From State 29 at St. Helena, W 3.3 mi. on Madrona Ave./Spring Mountain Rd. to winery drive (3101 Spring Mountain Rd., St. Helena, CA 94574) Tel (707) 963-2342. By appt. only.

Chateau Montelena. From State 29 N of Calistoga, W on Tubbs Ln. .2 mi. to winery dr. (1429 Tubbs Ln., Calistoga, CA 94515) Tel (707) 942-5105. Daily 10-12, 1-4. GT by appt.

The Christian Brothers/Greystone. W side of State 29 at N limit of St. Helena (707) 963-2719. (See also The Christian Brothers/Mont LaSalle, page 73.)

Cuvaison Vineyard. Just S of Dunaweal Ln., E side of Silverado Tr. (4550 Silverado Tr., Calistoga, CA 94515) Tel (707) 942-6266. Picnic. W-Su 10-4. Ta.

Deer Park Winery. From State 29 N of St. Helena, E 2.5 mi. on Deer Park Rd. (1000 Deer Park Rd., Deer Park, CA 94576) Tel (707) 963-5411. By appt. only.

Duckhorn Vineyards. On Silverado Tr. .2 mi. N of Lodi Ln. (3027 Silverado Tr., St. Helena, CA 94574) Tel (707) 963-7108. M-F 10-4. GT by appt. only.

Flora Springs Wine Company. From State 29 at Zinfandel Ln., W on W. Zinfandel Ln. to winery drive (1885 W. Zinfandel Ln., St. Helena, CA 94574) Tel (707) 963-5711. By appt. only.

Franciscan Vineyards. E side State 29 1.5 mi. S of St. Helena at Galleron Rd. (P.O. Box 407, Rutherford, CA 94573) Tel (707) 963-7111. Daily 10-5. IT/Ta.

Freemark Abbey. E side State 29 2 mi. N of St. Helena at Lodi Ln. (P.O. Box 410, St. Helena, CA 94574) Tel (707) 963-9694. Daily 10:30-4:45. GT daily 2.

Grgich-Hills Cellar. W side State 29 .5 mi. N of Rutherford (P.O. Box 450, Rutherford, CA 94573) Tel (707) 963-2784. Daily 10-4. IT.

Heitz Cellars. Tasting room: E side State 29 .5 mi. S of St. Helena at 439 St. Helena Hwy. S. Daily 11-4:30. Ta. Winery: 500 Taplin Rd., St. Helena, CA 94574. Tel (707) 963-3542. By appt. only.

Inglenook Vineyards. W from State 29 at Rutherford on pvt. ln. (Rutherford, CA 94573) Tel (707) 963-7184. Daily 10-5. GT/Ta.

Hanns Kornell Champagne Cellars. From State 29 5.9 mi. N of St. Helena, E .25 mi. on Larkmead Ln. (P.O. Box 249, St. Helena, CA 94574) Tel (707) 963-2334. Daily 10-4. GT/Ta.

Charles Krug Winery. E side State 29 at N limit of St. Helena (P.O. Box 191, St. Helena, CA 94574) Tel (707) 963-2761. Daily 10-4. GT/Ta.

Markham Winery. E side State 29 N of St. Helena at Deer Park Rd. (2812 St. Helena Hwy. N, St. Helena, CA 94574) Tel (707) 963-5292. Tu-Su 10-4. GT by appt./Ta.

Louis M. Martini. E side State 29, .5 mi. S of St. Helena (P.O. Box 112, St. Helena, CA 94574) Tel (707) 963-2736. Daily 10-4. GT/Ta.

Napa Creek Winery. E of St. Helena on Silverado Tr. .6 mi. S of Pope St. (1001 Silverado Tr., St. Helena, CA 94574) Tel (707) 963-9456. M-F 9-5, Sa-Su 11-5. GT/Ta by appt.

Newton Vineyard. From State 29 at St. Helena, W to winery dr. at end of Madrona Ave. (2555 Madrona Ave., St. Helena, CA 94574) Tel (707) 963-4613. M-F 9-5 by appt. only.

Nichelini Vineyard. From State 29 at Rutherford, E 11 mi. on State 129 (2349 Lower Chiles Rd., St. Helena, CA 94574) Tel (707) 963-3357. Picnic. Sa-Su, holidays 10-6. Ta. (Outside map area)

Joseph Phelps Vineyards. From Zinfandel Ln., N .5 mi. on Silverado Tr. to Taplin Rd., then E .2 mi. to winery dr. (200 Taplin Rd., St. Helena, CA 94574) Tel (707) 963-2745. M-Sa by appt. GT/Ta.

Pope Valley Winery. From State 29, E 11 mi. on Deer Park/Howell Mountain Rd. to Pope Valley, N 2 mi. on Pope Valley Rd. (6613 Pope Valley Rd., Pope Valley, CA 94567) Tel (707) 965-2192. Sa-Su 11-5, appt. preferred. IT/Ta.

Prager Winery and Port Works. From State 29 .1 mi. S of Sulphur Springs Ave., W on private lane to winery (1281 Lewelling Ln., St. Helena, CA 94574) Tel (707) 963-3720. Sa–Su by appt. only.

Raymond Vineyards and Cellar. From 29 1.5 mi. S of St. Helena, E on Zinfandel Ln. .5 mi. to Wheeler Ln./winery drive (849 Zinfandel Ln., St. Helena, CA 94574) Tel (707) 963-3141. By appt. only M-Sa.

Round Hill Cellars. From State 29 1 mi. N of St. Helena, E .3 mi. on Lodi Ln. (1097 Lodi Ln., St. Helena, CA 94574) Tel (707) 963-5251. M-F 8:30-5, Sa-Su 11:30-5. GT/Ta by appt.

Rutherford Hill Winery. From intersection with State 128, N on Silverado Tr. to Rutherford Hill Rd./winery drive (P.O. Box 410, St. Helena, CA 94574) Tel (707) 963-9694. Picnic. W-Su 11-4:30 Apr-Oct. GT 11 only/Ta.

Rutherford Vintners. W side State 29 1 mi. N of Rutherford (P.O. Box 238, Rutherford, CA 94573) Tel (707) 963-4117. Daily 10-4:30. GT by appt./Ta.

V. Sattui Winery. E side State 29 1.5 mi. S of St. Helena at White Ln. (111 White Ln., St. Helena, CA 94574) Tel (707) 963-7774. Picnic. Daily 9-6 Feb-Nov, 9-5 Dec-Jan. Ta.

Schramsberg Vineyards. From State 29 .2 mi. N of Larkmead Ln., W to winery at end of pvt. rd. (Calistoga, CA 94515) Tel (707) 942-4558. M-Sa by appt. GT.

Charles F. Shaw Vineyards & Winery. From State 29 3.5 mi. N of St. Helena, E on Big Tree Rd. .2 mi. to winery dr. (1010 Big Tree Rd., St. Helena, CA 94574) Tel (707) 963-5459. By appt. only.

Smith-Madrone Vineyards. From St. Helena, W via Spring Mountain Rd. to winery dr. at Sonoma County line, then N (4022 Spring Mountain Rd., St. Helena, CA 94574) Tel (707) 963-2283. By appt. only. GT.

Spring Mountain Vineyards. From State 29 at St. Helena, W 1.3 mi. on Madrona Ave./Spring Mountain Rd. to winery dr. (2805 Spring Mountain Rd., St. Helena, CA 94574) Tel (707) 963-5283. By appt. only. GT.

Sterling Vineyards. From State 29 7 mi. N of St. Helena, E .5 mi. on Dunaweal Ln. to winery drive (1111 Dunaweal Ln., Calistoga, CA 94515) Tel (707) 942-5151. Daily 10:30-4:30, except closed M-Tu Nov 1-Mar 31. IT/Ta.

Stonegate Winery. From State 29 7 mi. N of St. Helena, E .1 mi. on Dunaweal Ln. (1183 Dunaweal Ln., Calistoga, CA 94515) Tel (707) 942-6500. By appt. only.

Storybook Mountain Vineyards. From Calistoga, N 4 mi. on State 128 to winery dr. (3835 Hwy. 128, Calistoga, CA 94515) Tel (707) 942-5310. By appt. only, Sa preferred.

Sutter Home Winery. W side State 29 1.5 mi. S of St. Helena (P.O. Box 248, St. Helena, CA 94574) Tel (707) 963-3104. Daily 9:30-5. Ta.

Tudal Winery. From State 29 3.5 mi. N of St. Helena, E on Big Tree Rd. .2 mi. (1015 Big Tree Rd., St. Helena, CA 94574) Tel (707) 963-3847. By appt. only.

Whitehall Lane Winery. From Rutherford, N 1.1 mi. on State 29 to Whitehall Ln. (1563 St. Helena Hwy. S., St. Helena, CA 94574) Tel (707) 963-9454. Daily 12-6 Jun-Sept, F-Su 12-5 Oct-May. GT by appt.

Yverdon Vineyards. From St. Helena, W 4 mi. on Madrona Ave./Spring Mountain Rd. to winery dr. (3787 Spring Mountain Rd., St. Helena, CA 94574) Tel (707) 963-4270. M-F 8-3:30. GT by appt.

Key: GT (guided tour); IT (informal tour); Ta (tasting).

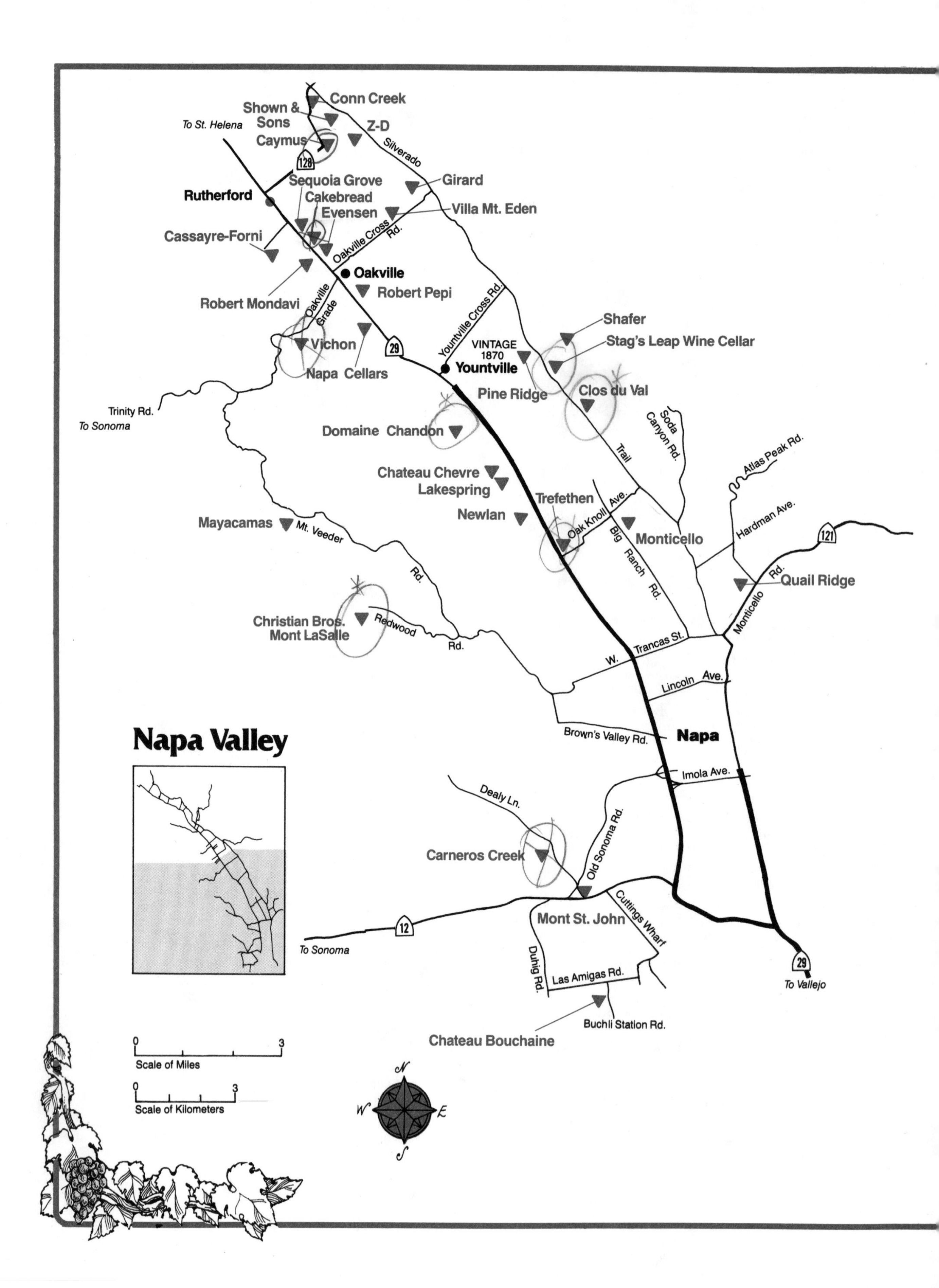
Napa Valley
Conn Creek
Shown & Sons
Z-D
Caymus
Silverado
To St. Helena
128
Sequoia Grove
Girard
Rutherford
Cakebread
Evensen
Villa Mt. Eden
Cassayre-Forni
Oakville Cross Rd.
Oakville
Robert Pepi
Robert Mondavi
Oakville Grade
Yountville Cross Rd.
Shafer
Stag's Leap Wine Cellar
VINTAGE 1870
Vichon
29
Yountville
Napa Cellars
Pine Ridge
Clos du Val
Trinity Rd.
To Sonoma
Soda Canyon Rd.
Domaine Chandon
Trail
Atlas Peak Rd.
Chateau Chevre
Lakespring
Trefethen
Newlan
Oak Knoll Ave.
Hardman Ave.
Mayacamas
Mt. Veeder
Big Ranch Rd.
Monticello
121
Rd.
Quail Ridge
Monticello Rd.
Christian Bros.
Mont LaSalle
Redwood Rd.
W. Trancas St.
Lincoln Ave.
Brown's Valley Rd.
Napa
Imola Ave.
Dealy Ln.
Old Sonoma Rd.
Carneros Creek
Cuttings Wharf
Mont St. John
12
To Sonoma
Duhig Rd.
Las Amigas Rd.
To Vallejo
Buchli Station Rd.
Chateau Bouchaine
Scale of Miles
Scale of Kilometers
N
W
E
S

Cakebread Cellars. On E side of State 29 midway between Oakville and Rutherford (P.O. Box 216, Rutherford, CA 94573) Tel (415) 832-8844. By appt. only.

Carneros Creek Winery. From intersection with State 121 5 mi. S of Napa, N on Old Sonoma Rd. .1 mi., then W on Dealy Ln. .4 mi. (1285 Dealy Ln., Napa, CA 94559) Tel (707) 253-9463. M-F 9-4:30. GT by appt.

Cassayre-Forni Cellars. From State 29 .5 mi. S of Rutherford, W .2 mi. on Manley Ln. (1271 Manley Ln., Rutherford, CA 94573) Tel (707) 944-2165 or 255-0909. M-F 9-5 by appt. only.

Caymus Vineyards. 1.5 mi. E of Rutherford at junction of State 128 and Conn Creek Rd. (P.O. Box 268, Rutherford, CA 94573) Tel (707) 963-4204. M-Sa by appt. only.

Chateau Bouchaine. From intersection with State 121 5 mi. S of Napa, S on Duhig Rd. 1 mi. to Las Amigas Rd., E .8 mi. to Buchli Station Rd., S to winery (1075 Buchli Station Rd., Napa, CA 94559) Tel (707) 252-9065. By appt. only.

Chateau Chevre. From State 29 .4 mi. S of Yountville, W .2 mi. on Hoffman Ln. (2040 Hoffman Ln., Yountville, CA 94599) Tel (707) 944-2184. By appt. only.

The Christian Brothers/Mont LaSalle. From State 29 at Napa, W 7 mi. on Redwood Rd. (P.O. Box 420, Napa, CA 94558) Tel (707) 226-5566. Daily 10:30-4. Ta.

Clos du Val Wine Co. On E side of Silverado Tr. 3 mi. S of Yountville Cross Rd. (5330 Silverado Tr., Napa, CA 94558) Tel (707) 252-6711. Picnic. M-Sa 9-4:30. GT by appt.

Conn Creek Vineyards. E of Rutherford at intersection of Silverado Tr., State 128 (P.O. Box 987, St. Helena, CA 94574) Tel (707) 963-9100. M-Sa by appt only. GT/Ta.

Domaine Chandon. From State 29 at Yountville, California Dr. exit W to winery dr. (P.O. Box 2470, Yountville, CA 94599) Tel (707) 944-2280. Daily 11-6 Jun-Sept, W-Su 11-6 Oct-May (last tour 5:30). GT/ Ta. fee

Evensen Winery and Vineyard. E side of State 29 midway between Oakville and Rutherford at 8254. (P.O. Box 127, Oakville, CA 94562) Tel (707) 944-2396. By appt. only, weekends preferred.

Girard Winery. On W side of Silverado Tr. .1 mi. N of Oakville Cross Rd. (7717 No. Silverado Tr., Oakville, CA 94562) Tel (707) 944-8577. M-F 1-4, Sa-Su 2-4. GT by appt.

Lakespring Winery. From State 29 .4 mi. S of Yountville, W .2 mi. on Hoffman Ln. (2055 Hoffman Ln., Napa, CA 94558) Tel (707) 944-2475. By appt. only. GT.

Mayacamas Vineyards. From State 29 at Napa, W and N on Redwood Rd./Mt. Veeder Rd. 8 mi. to Lokoya Rd., W .1 mi. to pvt. winery rd. (1155 Lokoya Rd., Napa, CA 94558) Tel (707) 224-4030. By appt. only.

Robert Mondavi Winery. W side of State 29 at N limit of Oakville (7801 St. Helena Hwy., Oakville, CA 94562) Tel (707) 963-9611. Daily 9-5 Apr-Sept, 10-4:30 Oct-Mar. GT/Ta.

Monticello Cellars. From State 29 at N limit of Napa, E on Oak Knoll Rd. to Big Ranch Rd., then S .1 mi. to winery dr. (P.O. Box 2500, Yountville, CA 94599) Tel (707) 944-8863. By appt. only.

Mont St. John Cellars. At intersection of State 121 and Old Sonoma Rd. 5 mi. S of Napa (5400 Old Sonoma Rd., Napa, CA 94558) Tel (707) 255-8864. Daily 9-4:30. Ta.

Napa Cellars. W side of State 29 2 mi. N of Yountville (7481 St. Helena Hwy., Oakville, CA 94562) Tel (707) 944-2565. Picnic. Daily 10:30-5:30. IT/Ta.

Newlan Vineyards & Winery. On State 29 frontage rd. at Darms Ln. 3.5 mi. N of Napa (5527 Hwy 29, Napa, CA 94558) Tel (707) 944-2914. IT/Ta by appt. only.

Niebaum-Coppola Estates. From State 29 at Rutherford W. 6 mi. to winery gates (1460 Niebaum Ln., Rutherford, CA 94573) Tel (707) 963-9435. By appt. only. (Not on map)

Robert Pepi Winery. E side of State 29 1 mi. S of Oakville Cross Rd. (7585 St. Helena Hwy., Oakville, CA 94562) Tel (707) 944-2807. M-F 9-5 by appt. only. GT.

Pine Ridge Winery. W side of Silverado Tr. 1.8 mi. S of Yountville Cross Rd. (5901 Silverado Tr., Napa, CA 94558) Tel (707) 253-7500. Picnic. W-Su 11-3:30 or by appt. IT/Ta.

Quail Ridge. On Atlas Peak Rd. .1 mi. N of State 121 (1055 Atlas Peak Rd., Napa, CA 94558) Tel (707) 226-2728 or 944-8128. By appt. only.

Sequoia Grove Vineyard and Winery. On E side of State 29 midway between Oakville and Rutherford (8338 St. Helena Hwy., Oakville 94562) Tel (707) 944-2945. F-Su 10-5. IT/Ta.

Shafer Vineyards. On E side of Silverado Tr. 1.2 mi. S of Yountville Cross Rd. (6154 Silverado Tr., Napa, CA 94558) Tel (707) 944-2877. By appt. only.

Shown & Sons Vineyards. From intersection with State 128, S .1 mi. on Silverado Tr. (8601 Silverado Tr., St. Helena, CA 94574) Tel (707) 962-7975. Picnic by appt. Daily 10-5. GT, appt. preferred.

Stag's Leap Wine Cellars. On E side of Silverado Tr. 2.2 mi. S of Yountville Cross Rd. (5766 Silverado Tr., Napa, CA 94558) Tel (707) 944-2020. By appt. only. GT.

Trefethen Vineyards. From State 29, E on Oak Knoll Ave. .4 mi. to winery dr. (1160 Oak Knoll Dr., Napa, CA 94558) Tel (707) 255-7700. By appt. only. GT.

Vichon Winery. From State 29 at Oakville, W 1 mi. on Oakville Grade Rd. to 1595 (P.O. Box 363, Oakville, CA 94562) Tel (707) 944-2811. By appt. only.

Villa Mt. Eden. N side Oakville Cross Rd. near Silverado Tr. (Mt. Eden Ranch, Oakville, CA 94562) Tel (707) 944-8431. M-F by appt. only.

Z-D Winery. From intersection with State 128, S on Silverado Tr. .7 mi. (8383 Silverado Tr., Rutherford, CA 94573) Tel (707) 963-5188. M-F 9-5. IT by appt.

Wineries Not on Napa Maps—Restricted or No Visitor Facilities

Acacia Winery. (2636 Las Amigas Rd., Napa, CA 94558) Tel (707) 224-8826.

Alatera Vineyards. (2170 Hoffman Ln., Napa, CA 94558) Tel (707) 944-2620.

S. Anderson Vineyard. (P.O. Box 3046, Yountville, CA 94599) Tel (707) 944-8642.

Buehler Vineyards. (820 Greenfield Rd., St. Helena, CA 94574) Tel (707) 963-2155.

Casa Nuestra. (3473 Silverado Tr. N, St. Helena, CA 94574) Tel (707) 963-4684.

(Winery listings continued on page 74)

Key: GT (guided tour); IT (informal tour); Ta (tasting).

. . . Continued from page 73

Chappellet Winery. (1581 Sage Canyon Rd., St. Helena, CA 94574) Tel (707) 963-7136.

Chateau Boswell. (3468 Silverado Tr. N., St. Helena, CA 94574) Tel (707) 963-5472.

Diamond Creek Vineyards. (1500 Diamond Mountain Rd., Calistoga, CA 94515) Tel (707) 942-6926.

Far Niente Winery. (P.O. Box 114, Oakville, CA 94562) Tel (707) 944-2861.

Frog's Leap Winery. (3358 St. Helena Hwy., St. Helena, CA 94574) Tel (707) 963-4704.

J. Heminway (Green & Red Vineyard). (3208 Chiles Valley-Pope Valley Rd., St. Helena, CA 94574) Tel (707) 965-2346.

William Hill Vineyards. (P.O. Box 3989, Napa, CA 94558) Tel (707) 226-8800.

Johnson-Turnbull Vineyards. (8210 St. Helena Hwy., Oakville, CA 94562) Tel (707) 963-5839.

Robert Keenan Winery. (3660 Spring Mountain Rd., St. Helena, CA 94574) Tel (707) 963-9177.

Long Vineyards. (P.O. Box 50, St. Helena, CA 94574) Tel (707) 963-2496.

Mt. Veeder Winery. (1999 Mt. Veeder Rd., Napa, CA 94558) Tel (707) 224-4039.

Napa Vintners. (P.O. Box 2502, Napa, CA 94558) Tel (707) 255-9463.

Pannonia Winery. (3105 Silverado Tr., Napa, CA 94558) Tel (707) 253-1821.

Robert Pecota Winery. (P.O. Box 571, Calistoga, CA 94515) Tel (707) 942-6625.

Ritchie Creek Vineyard. (4024 Spring Mountain Rd., St. Helena, CA 94574) Tel (707) 963-4661.

Roddis Cellars. (1510 Diamond Mountain Rd., Calistoga, CA 94515) Tel (707) 942-5868.

St. Andrews Winery. (2921 Silverado Tr., Napa, CA 94558) Tel (707) 252-6748.

St. Clement Vineyards. (P.O. Box 261, St. Helena, CA 94574) Tel (707) 963-7221.

Silverado Cellars. (6121 Silverado Tr., Napa, CA 94558) Tel (707) 257-1770.

Silver Oak Cellars. (P.O. Box 414, Oakville, CA 94562) Tel (707) 944-8866.

Stags' Leap Vintners. (6150 Silverado Tr., Napa, CA 94558) Tel (707) 253-1545.

Stony Hill Vineyard. (P.O. Box 308, St. Helena, CA 94574) Tel (707) 963-2636.

Sullivan Vineyards and Winery. (1090 Galleron Ln., St. Helena, CA 94574) Tel (707) 963-9644.

Traulsen Vineyards. (2250 Lake County Hwy., Calistoga, CA 94515) Tel (707) 942-0283.

Tulocay Winery. (1426 Coombsville Rd., Napa, CA 94558) Tel (707) 255-4699.

Vose Vineyards. (4035 Mt. Veeder Rd., Napa, CA 94558) Tel (707) 944-2254.

. . . Continued from page 69

than claret-style reds has complicated the picture somewhat, but this remains a good place to see how a Bordelais winemaker would arrange his working gear.

The roster of wines includes Cabernet Sauvignon, Merlot, Zinfandel, Pinot Noir, and Chardonnay. Several come in two differing styles. Wines under the main label often have a proportion of blended grapes for complexity. Those named Granval emphasize pure varietal character.

Conn Creek Vineyards plunges visitors into the core of things as soon as they step through glass doors at the front of a white stucco building that provides some refreshing turns on Mediterranean architectural themes other than Spanish mission.

A small entryway looks straight into a fermenting room with twin rows of stainless steel and a third row of oak upright tanks. The same entry looks obliquely into a gallerylike hall full of French oak barrels. Only the crusher and press (out back) and the bottling room of the working winery are not in instant view.

The reception area for visitors is at the top of a stairway immediately adjacent to the front doors. It consists of a round tasting table in a spacious room with views onto the fermentors or out to a small patio and, beyond it, the hills east of Rutherford. Proprietors William and Kathy Collins offer, under the Conn Creek label, Chardonnay, Cabernet Sauvignon, and Zinfandel, plus proprietary wines called Chateau Maja.

Cuvaison Vineyard houses itself in a deft architectural tribute to the Spanish colonial heritage of California wine, its white-walled, red tile-roofed cellars distinguished by a long row of graceful arches facing onto the Silverado Trail not far down the valley from Calistoga.

The winery has grown steadily since its founding in 1970, when a since-departed partnership opened it in a building that looked suspiciously like a depression-era hunting camp. Interim owners erected the main cellar and remodeled the original building into the present tasting room, matching the two structures with style and taste.

The current owner, a Swiss, offers no tours. (If there were tours, they would reveal the archetypal small Napa winery: modern crusher and press, stainless steel fermentors, and French oak barrels.) But the owner does offer for tasting all three of Cuvaison's wines: Chardonnay, Cabernet Sauvignon, and Zinfandel.

Deer Park Winery is one of several revivals of old Napa Valley properties that tucks a modern, efficient winery into a handsome old stone building. In this case, an energy-conscious proprietor is turning some inherited museum pieces to practical account.

The property first was the original Sutter Home location. After Prohibition, it was the John Ballentyne Winery until 1960. It became Deer Park when winemaker Dave Clark and partners bought it in 1979. For now, processing and aging both take place on the lower floor of a classic two-story, gravity-flow winery built into a hillside. In time the rehabilitated upper level will again hold the crusher, hydraulic press, and stainless steel fermenting tanks, leaving the lower story to hold ancient German oak casks, new French oak barrels and upright tanks, and the bottling line.

Sauvignon Blanc and Zinfandel are the mainstays, sometimes joined by Chardonnay and Petite Sirah.

Domaine Chandon, of all the new wineries in the Napa Valley, is the one that looks newest. It is the first (and so far only one) in the current era of heroic architecture to follow a purely modern style. Barrel vault roofs cover stone, concrete, and glass-walled buildings in a complex that flows across one slope of a gentle hill just west of Yountville.

Within the buildings the story is more complicated, for this winery was built to make sparkling wines only according to the ancient verities of the *methode champenoise*. There is no arguing the technical truths of this matter. Domaine Chandon is owned by Moët-Hennessy, the French proprietors of Moët et Chandon, and the winemaster in the Napa Valley is the same one as in Epernay. As a result, to see Domaine Chandon is to see sparkling wine made on a scale that the French tend to think of as right, using equipment and techniques favored there.

The main winemaking building has, on its curving upper story, twin rows of horizontal stainless steel fermentors, and on the underground lower story, row upon row of big, mechanized riddling racks. A glass-walled wing of this building holds the yeast culturing room and all of the bottling and disgorging equipment.

As a counterpoint to the working winery, the parent firm has loaned ancient equipment which is placed here and there about the premises, mainly in the separate building that houses the visitor center and an elegant French restaurant. The old gear includes pickers' baskets, vineyard cultivation tools, bottles, and more. The single most impressive piece is on the walk leading to the fermenting cellar. It is an ancient wooden press, a horizontal basket with remarkable similarities to such modern ones as Vaslins and Howards.

Well-conducted tours take in all of these details. There is a fee for tasting Chandon Napa Valley Brut or Blanc de Noirs.

The restaurant is popular enough that advance reservations are required for lunch or dinner.

Duckhorn Vineyards, on the Silverado Trail, has an air that would not be out of place in Bordeaux, appropriate enough since the winery makes only Cabernet Sauvignon and Merlot. Fermenting takes place in an open-walled building (*la cuverie,* if this were France); aging is next door in a cool, dim, quiet building *(le chai)*.

Limited in their ability to welcome visitors both by use-permit restrictions and the winery's small size, owners Margaret and Daniel Duckhorn nonetheless extend appointments to visitors who can take pleasure in discussing philosophical fine points of red wines modeled after traditional clarets.

The first wines released for sale were from the vintage of 1978.

Evensen Winery and Vineyard looks slightly Alsatian more by chance than design, but the image fits. In a small cellar beneath a half-timbered yellow house east of State 29 between Oakville and Rutherford, the owning Richard Evensen family makes only Gewürztraminer from its vineyards adjacent to the cellar.

Flora Springs Wine Company occupies a fine old stone building set at the back edge of a vineyard, tight against a wooded hillside west of St. Helena.

Originally built in the 1880s by a pair of Scots as the Rennie Brothers winery and later used for many years by Louis M. Martini, the building was to gain an addition to its upper story in 1982. The twin purpose was to keep the hill behind from pushing it another inch eastward, and to allow the owning Jerome Komes family to age its Cabernet Sauvignon up top and its white wines on the lower level. Until the addition is in place, Cabernet, Chardonnay, and Sauvignon Blanc will share the lower story.

However the aging wines are disposed, this is a flawless example of an ancient building turned into a modern cellar. The crusher, Willmes presses, and some stainless steel fermenting tanks stand on a pad at one end of the building. More stainless steel and several lofty racks of French oak barrels fill much of the interior. Not incidentally, it is a good place to talk about the effects of stainless steel versus barrel fermentation since the proprietors follow both practices.

Franciscan Vineyards is of a size that makes it highly informative to see. It is small enough that all of its departments fit together into a clear pattern, from freshly arrived grapes to finished wine. But it is big enough so that much of the equipment is kindred to gear at much larger wineries where patterns of production may not be so clear to see.

In addition, the tour is sign-guided, allowing visitors to pursue learning at their individual paces. Hosts in the spacious tasting hall will amplify on any subjects the signs do not explain to satisfaction.

Franciscan has grown steadily through several ownerships, but most spectacularly under the present proprietor, Peter Eckes Company. The original main cellar, built in 1973, was a plain box with concrete walls. A redwood-sided office and visitor area softened the front elevation. An addition in 1982 turned the redoubled cellars into an L, adding some niceties of design in the process. As originally, the stainless steel fermentors and other processing gear sit outside the north wall. Inside are stainless steel storage tanks and the bottling line. The new addition holds a much-enlarged collection of oak cooperage, most of it barrels from French and American coopers.

The tasting hall—too capacious to be called a room—offers the full range of Franciscan estate bottled wines, including Charbono and Merlot as well as Cabernet Sauvignon and Zinfandel in the reds. Principal whites are Chardonnay and Johannisberg Riesling.

Freemark Abbey revived an old label and older winery building at its founding in 1967.

The original label dated from 1939 and endured into the early 1960s. (There was no particular religious affiliation. The name derived from those of the original partners: Free from Charles Freeman, Mark from Mark

Foster, and Abbey from the nickname of Albert Ahern.) Seeing no way to improve on that ingenuity, the current partnership of seven owners applied it to a new generation of wines that includes Chardonnay, Johannisberg Riesling, Cabernet Sauvignon, Pinot Noir, and Petite Sirah. Some of the johannisberg riesling goes to make a late harvest Edelwein when conditions favor Botrytis *cinerea*.

The current owners have been required to improve upon their winery building, or at least to enlarge upon the fine old stone cellars built in the 1880s as Lombarda Winery. After the demise of the original Freemark Abbey, that building was turned into a complex of specialty shops and a restaurant. The new Freemark Abbey for a time crowded itself into the lower story, less than half the original space. In 1973, weary of making wine sideways, the partners built a new structure alongside the old one to house bottling and cased wine storage. In 1982, a third building was added to house red wines aging in French oak.

Tours begin in the middle building in a room furnished to break an antique collector's heart. They lead first into the original cellars, where stainless steel fermentors and oak barrels still are so closely packed that visitors must go single file, then through the newer buildings, both shaped after Spanish colonial models but finished with modern, dark materials that give them handsome individuality.

Girard Winery perches on a knoll alongside the Silverado Trail, its textured block walls half hidden in the dappled light of a small grove of oaks. Like most of the small wineries of recent vintage—its first crush was 1980—it is instructive to see from a single vantage.

The hopper and crusher are on a concrete pad just outside the entrance to a small sales area. Stainless steel fermentors and the press occupy a separate room at the north end of the building. Oak upright tanks and racks of French oak barrels greet the eye directly inside the entry. Bottled wines in cases are at the opposite end of the building from the fermentors.

Chardonnay, Chenin Blanc, and Cabernet Sauvignon labeled Girard come from an adjoining vineyard set into the angle formed by the Silverado Trail and Oakville Cross Road; those labeled Stephens come from purchased grapes.

Grgich-Hills Cellar, new in 1977, is yet another of the small California wineries that demonstrate the internationality of winemaking.

Its proprietors are Miljenko (Mike) Grgich and Austin Hills. Grgich studied formal enology at the University of Zagreb in Yugoslavia before emigrating to the United States to begin a long career in the Napa Valley. (He worked for several wineries before launching his own.) Partner Austin Hills is pure Yankee, a vineyard owner for some years before joining forces with Grgich.

The architecture of their trim building nods to the Spanish colonial heritage of California with white plaster walls, red tile roof, and arched entryways. The equipment includes, among other pieces, American stainless steel fermentors and French oak barrels.

Grgich-Hills offers no formal tours. A walk across the parking lot reveals the fermentors and other processing gear under an overhanging roof at the rear. A talk with the host at the sales room in one front corner of the aging cellar covers the fine points.

Production is dominated by Chardonnay and Fumé Blanc. Johannisberg Riesling and Zinfandel round out the roster.

Heitz Cellars comes in two parts. The original winery building now is the tasting room and a supplementary aging cellar. It is a small, redwood-faced structure on the St. Helena Highway just south of town. The present producing winery is tucked away east of St. Helena and the Silverado Trail in a small pocket called Spring Valley.

The Heitz family bought the Spring Valley property in 1964, having outgrown the original winery in 3 years. When the Heitzes acquired the second ranch it had not changed a great deal since 1898, when Anton Rossi completed a stone cellar as the capstone of his development of the property. Happily for the new owners, capable caretakers had occupied the buildings between 1914, when Rossi quit making wine, and the 1964 purchase.

Except for replanting abandoned vineyards and reequipping the cellar with stainless steel fermentors and a veritable library of oak casks and barrels, the new owners did not change the appearance of the place they bought until 1972, when progress dictated more space for the making and aging of wine.

There are several ways to go about expanding a winery. An old building can be enlarged or torn down for replacement or abandoned for a new site. The Heitzes elected to keep the fine old stone cellar intact and erect a whole new structure near it. The new building, an octagon of textured block, is the red wine cellar. The original holds the whites.

The replanted vineyard, stretching away south to the end of the little valley, is devoted almost entirely to Grignolino for red and rosé.

Other Heitz varietal table wines come from selected—sometimes identified—vineyards throughout the Napa Valley. The roster is dominated by several Cabernet Sauvignons and a Chardonnay, and includes Pinot Noir as well as the Grignolinos.

Regular tasting goes on only at the original winery

on St. Helena Highway South, where all of the wines also are available for retail sale. Because the Spring Valley winery buildings are behind the family home, visitors there must acquire an invitation beforehand.

Inglenook Vineyards is located in several buildings but for visitors all of the action is in the stately original cellar at Rutherford.

Built in the 1880s, the stone-walled building looks very much the way romantics think wineries should, though it was built by a Finnish sea captain and fur trader named Gustave Niebaum. The front wall has a long row of arched doors and another of arched windows. A cupola and several dormers serve as relief from the ordinariness of mere roof. Virginia creeper, which turns flame red in the fall, covers the exterior walls.

Inside, parallel tunnels contain row upon row of 1,000-gallon oak oval casks. Most of these casks came from the Spesart Mountains in Germany in the last decades of the nineteenth century and show very nearly flawless craftsmanship. Ordinary cask heads begin to buckle after a time; these still follow the curves formed by their German coopers. The wood has blackened with age but not bowed.

In its early days all of Inglenook was under the one roof. Now a new aging cellar big enough to house a dirigible faces the original cellar across a courtyard. It is filled with towering racks of oak barrels. Fermenting and some aging takes place in two other buildings at the intersection of State 29 and Oakville Crossroad. Affiliated wineries in other districts contribute still other wines to Inglenook.

The evolutions have come in stages. The founding family revived Inglenook after Prohibition under the proprietorship of the late John Daniel. Daniel ran Inglenook until he sold it in 1964 to a grower-owned marketing company called United Vintners. The latter expanded the business greatly before Heublein, Inc. acquired a controlling interest in UV in 1969. Heublein has made even more substantial additions to the business.

The tasting room, inside the original building, offers a broad sampling of selected wines each day. Tours start in the museum area at the entrance.

The Inglenook label covers three separate lines of wine. The Napa Valley varietals are presented under the premier label, and include Chardonnay, Johannisberg Riesling, Gewürztraminer, Cabernet Sauvignon, Pinot Noir and Zinfandel. A secondary line of North Coast varietal and generic wines appears under the Inglenook Vintage label. Inglenook Navalle wines come mainly from San Joaquin Valley sources belonging to its parent company.

Robert Keenan Winery is a spanking new cellar within a set of old stone walls. The walls were put there in 1904 according to a keystone over one arched doorway. According to the keystone over the other arch, their builder was Pietro Conradi.

Robert Keenan bought the long-idle property in 1974, and set about transforming it from a standard stone barn into an architecturally elegant modern winery. The revamped building has a centrally supported red tile roof and some redwood gables as its most visible new elements. Several compatible touches are to be seen within. The equipment is typical of contemporary small cellars in this part of the world: a Howard basket press, stainless steel fermentors, and, for aging the wines, French oak barrels. All of this tucks into a serene fold on one flank of Spring Mountain.

There are but two wines, Chardonnay and Cabernet Sauvignon. The winery offers no tasting. Minimum sales are in case lots.

Hanns Kornell Champagne Cellars is devoted entirely to the production of traditional, bottle-fermented sparkling wines.

On Larkmead Lane toward the north end of the valley, the old two-story, tree-shaded stone building started as Larkmead Winery early in Napa's vinous history. Other buildings have been added by interim owners and the current owner plans further remodeling. Hanns Kornell bought the property in 1958 after getting a head start during six years in a leased cellar in Sonoma. From a small beginning, Kornell has steadily built his inventory to its present level of 3 million bottles.

His is a remarkable one-man achievement. Kornell fled Germany in 1939 and followed a path set by earlier German liberals and political exiles (including winemaker Charles Krug several decades before). He landed in New York broke, worked his way west, in time got work as a maker of sparkling wine, and finally started producing his own Champagne in 1952.

The Larkmead property provides a textbook picture of traditional Champagne-making. A guide (sometimes the owner himself, sometimes daughter Paula or son Peter) conducts the tour to explain this quiet, slow process. The visitor can peer at yeast deposits in still fermenting bottles, observe wine as gravity brings it to perfect clarity in the riddling racks, watch the disgorgement and final corking, and, in general, stay within arm's length of the evolution of traditional, bottle-fermented sparkling wines.

There is a tasting room in the small frame office building to the rear of the winery. Visitors are always welcome to taste some of Kornell's authentic *methode champenoise* sparkling wines. The types include Sehr Trocken, Brut, Extra Dry, Demi-Sec, Rosé, Champagne Rouge, and sparkling Muscat Alexandria.

Charles Krug Winery, in a shady grove of tall oaks amid vineyards, presents a classic picture of an old Napa estate winery.

Charles Krug, the man, founded his winery in 1861. He built one massive stone building to keep his wines and another to keep his horses, both at 59°F/15°C.

Krug died in 1892, leaving two daughters to carry on. With help from a cousin they continued until Prohibition, when the winery closed. It remained in the hands of a caretaker-owner until Cesare Mondavi bought the property in 1943. Since his death in 1959, the winery has remained in his family's hands. His son, Peter, is now president.

Various aspects of the Krug ranch have changed over the years, but the two stone buildings remain and are the core of the present winery. The old main cellar continues in its original role. The one-time coach house now holds small cooperage for aging select wines. Over the years, the owners have erected three large buildings. The first holds the bottling operation, the second oak barrels. The newest, added in 1982, is a fermenting and processing area replacing an ancient collection of open-topped redwood tanks. Small frame buildings alongside the original cellar house the winemaker's lab, the offices, and, most important to visitors, the tasting room.

Tours of the sprawling premises are ably led and unusually complete. During harvest, the crushing and fermenting areas are out of bounds. Otherwise, visitors get to see every department. There are some fine, contrasting balances between old and new, between venerable redwood tanks or oak ovals on the one hand and glass-lined steel or stainless steel tanks on the other, between stone and insulated steel-frame cellars.

The tasting room offers a selection of three or four wines to those who complete the tour. They come from a complete range of varietal and generic table wines, including Chardonnay, Chenin Blanc, and Gewürztraminer, Cabernet Sauvignon, Pinot Noir, and Zinfandel. The winery keeps special selections of older reds at the tasting room for sale to visitors. At the other end of the price scale, the winery also has CK Mondavi generics in jugs.

Lakespring Winery, near Yountville, is a thoroughly Californian structure, and an imposing one in a quiet way. The red tile roof has cupolas vented to help cool the interior, a classic touch all up and down the rural coast counties. Windowless walls have enough spare ornamentation to suggest the considerable size of the building, and enough insulation to make easy work for the coolers.

Inside is a thoughtfully designed, neat-as-a-pin cellar with stainless steel fermentors and storage tanks at the middle, fat Burgundian barrels and puncheons at one end, and bottled wines in cases at the other. Owned by a San Francisco family named Battat, Lakespring's roster of wines includes Chardonnay, Chenin Blanc, and Sauvignon Blanc in whites; Cabernet Sauvignon and Merlot in reds.

Markham Winery is another of Napa's new starts in an old place. In this case the new start is by advertising executive Bruce Markham. He bought the first of his three vineyards in the valley in 1976. Then, in 1978, he bought a winery to have a home for his grapes.

The old place just north of St. Helena was founded in 1876 as the Laurent Winery, but for years had been known locally as The Little Co-op. Regular visitors to the valley may remember it as a plain building hidden by four steel tanks at State 29 and Deer Park Lane.

Markham's first moves included removal of those steel tanks to the rear of the cellars, which showed the stone-front building to be less plain than one might have thought. The subsequent addition of a tasting room enhanced an already appreciable front elevation.

The proprietor uses three of four long galleries in the main cellar for his own winemaking. The northernmost holds the stainless steel fermentors and other processing gear. The next two hold French oak barrels and other wood cooperage, plus an ultramodern bottling room. The south cellar is leased to other wineries in need of temporary storage.

Selected wines from the roster of estate bottlings are available for tasting in a large, comfortable room. The list includes Chardonnay, Johannisberg Riesling, and Muscat de Frontignan in whites; Cabernet Sauvignon and Merlot in reds. There also is a Gamay Blanc.

Louis M. Martini dates only from 1933 as a winery and yet is honored as one of the old-school labels in the Napa Valley. Family continuity is the key.

The founder, the late Louis M. Martini, began his career as a California winemaker in 1906 in Guasti and owned his first winery as early as 1922. Those facts, along with his immediate post-Prohibition start in the Napa Valley, earned him a secure reign as dean of California winemakers. His son and successor, Louis P., continues the family ownership in the traditional vein and in the original cellars, now with help from daughter Carolyn and son Michael.

Hosts at Martini do not insist on touring visitors through the buildings. They often skip that whole segment of the proceedings. Persuade them, if necessary, for the Martini cellars are instructive in several ways. The original Louis built his winery without costly adornments, but he built it to last, so it keeps some unusual old touches.

Most of the Martini fermentors, for example, now are the familiar stainless steel tanks. Yet, for a while at least, the original open concrete fermentors for reds will be around and in use. (The proprietor recalls how well they were constructed, and he shudders at the prospect of demolishing the things.) Then, too, the Martinis fermented white wines cold before refrigerated stainless steel tanks came into use; the huge, refrigerated room full of redwood tanks remains in the winery and in use because it does a couple of jobs very well.

The main aging cellar holds a diverse lot of redwood and oak cooperage as well as the bottling line. A short walk out back to the processing and fermenting area rounds out a complete look at all phases of winemaking. (The tour does not go to three flanking buildings that contain a majority of Martini's French and American oak barrels, nor does it go down into an underground cellar running most of the main building's length. In this latter room are ancient oak casks used to age particularly prized Special Selection wines purchased more readily at the winery than elsewhere.)

In the tasting room, in a building added to the main cellar in 1973, the complete roster of Martini wines is available for appraisal. It includes Chardonnay, Folle Blanche (made only at this winery as a varietal), Gewürztraminer, and Johannisberg Riesling among whites; Barbera, Cabernet Sauvignon, Merlot, and Pinot Noir among reds. The supporting cast includes generic table wines and Sherries.

Mayacamas Vineyards clings to the topmost ridges of the Mayacamas Mountains. Just getting to the winery taxes the suspension systems of most automobiles of ordinary manufacture. The road from the winery up to the highest vineyards is far more adventurous.

The owners are Bob and Nonie Travers, who acquired the site in 1968 from another family ownership.

The property centers upon an old stone winery erected by a man named J.H. Fisher in 1889, and operated as Mt. Veeder vineyards until 1910 or so. Restoration proceedings began in 1941 when a couple named Jack and Mary Taylor bought the property and renamed it Mayacamas. They got the cellars back in condition by 1947 and ran the estate until the Traverses bought it.

Mayacamas is cupped in the rocky rib of a long-extinct volcano, Mt. Veeder, and surrounded by several blocks of vineyard, mostly cabernet sauvignon. In a couple of places, sheer rock walls stick up out of the earth to set firm limits on vineyard size. Several hundred feet higher than the winery, ridge-top terraces with views clear back to San Francisco carry the chardonnay vines.

In addition to being a good example of traditional stonework, the original winery building provides a clear picture of how winemakers built on hillsides so gravity could move wine before electric pumps showed up. The crusher and press are on the uphill side of the main structure, level with the tops of the fermenting ranks. Below is a cellar full of a diverse mixture of cooperage ranging in capacity from 1,500 gallons down to 60. An adjacent building holds most of the French oak barrels.

The primary wines of Mayacamas, not opened for tasting for lack of volume, are Chardonnay and Cabernet Sauvignon, both vintage-dated.

Robert Mondavi Winery in Oakville crushed its first wine in 1966 while carpenters still were struggling to get the roof on the building, a first instance of what is now a tradition in California.

The winery does not look that new, mainly because founder Robert Mondavi commissioned designer Cliff May to pay strong architectural tribute to the role Franciscan missions had in developing California as a wine district. Appearance aside, most of the building is newer than 1966, steady growth having required Mondavi to expand thrice in one decade.

A faintly churchlike tower serves as the anchor point for two wings, one straight, one bent.

The south wing holds the tasting and sales rooms as well as other rooms designed for use in celebration of art, music, and dinners great and small. The sales room is furnished with early California pieces of interest. Also, one wall has an imposing demonstration for serious wine collectors. It is a stacked mass of agricultural tiles used as a wine rack. The tiles are light-proof, excellent insulators, and sized exactly to hold wine bottles.

To the north, the bent wing holds the offices and then a whole series of fermenting and aging cellars. Robert Mondavi, the man, is a ceaseless experimenter. As a result, his working winery is an ever-changing one, full of wizard equipment for visitors to gaze upon and learn from. Up in the roof rafters, for one example, are several horizontal tanks powered so they can rotate continuously. The original purpose was to keep red wines mixing throughout fermentation for maximum color extraction. At this task the tanks were failures, but the ingenious Mondavis experimented until they learned other, successful ways to use them. Guides have able explanations of these machines, as well as French continuous presses and German centrifuges.

A spacious open arch separates the two wings on the winery, framing a view across long rows of vines to the steep flanks of the Mayacamas Mountains beyond. A plush lawn behind the arch is the site of summer concerts, art shows, and frequent special tastings.

The wine list at Mondavi includes vintage-dated Chardonnay, Chenin Blanc, and Fumé Blanc in whites; a Gamay Rosé; and the reds, Cabernet Sauvignon and Pinot Noir. Selections from these and the rest of the roster are opened for tasting to those who take the tour.

Monticello Cellars is, in this international era of California winemaking, a straight throwback to American roots. Proprietor Jay Corley grew up in Virginia agriculture with a profound admiration for Thomas Jefferson. His winery is designed as a direct tribute to Jefferson as an architect and as a connoisseur of wine.

The cellars themselves are in a tall, spare box of a building still under construction in spring 1982. The offices and reception rooms, on which construction had not begun at the deadline for this book, are to be housed in a copy of Jefferson's masterpiece of design, the home he called Monticello.

Corley has made wines in leased space since 1980. All wines come from his vineyard surrounding the winery: Chardonnay, Gewürztraminer, and Sauvignon Blanc. There is to be no tasting.

Mont St. John Cellars offers no tours of its small, well equipped, conventional winery, but provides tasting of available wines in a Spanish colonial-style building at the front of the working winery in the Carneros district, at the southern tip of the Napa Valley.

The owners are a long-time Napa wine family. From the end of Prohibition until the mid-1970s, Louis Bartolucci owned the Oakville winery now used by Inglenook. He and his son, Andrea, dropped out of winemaking briefly, then dropped back in, in the current location.

The wines, all from their own nearby vineyard, include Chardonnay, Johannisberg Riesling, Moscato di Canelli, Cabernet Sauvignon, Pinot Noir, and Zinfandel.

Mt. Veeder Winery is one of the genuine mountainside wineries of Napa.

Housed in a trim wood-framed building well up the peak of which it is a namesake, Mt. Veeder can be visited only by appointment. For wine buffs, the major fascination is a vineyard growing all of the classic blending grapes used with cabernet sauvignon in Bordeaux, which is to say cabernet franc, malbec, merlot, and petit verdot. In addition, Mt. Veeder is of a scale to tempt newcomers with thoughts of joining the ranks of small, family-owned wineries.

Dating from 1973, the property of Michael and Arlene Bernstein specializes in Cabernet Sauvignon, and offers smaller lots of Zinfandel and Pinot Blanc.

Napa Cellars has a playful architectural appeal from the outside. The front section of the building bears some resemblance to an igloo. Directly behind it another section has walls that taper inward, while the rear and largest segment is conventionally rectangular in all planes.

Within, the playfulness gives way to a serene beauty. The igloo is in fact a slightly modified geodesic dome, much of it finished in stained wood. A skylight of stained glass casts a churchly kind of glow on upright oak tanks clustered under the peak, and on barrels lining the curved walls everywhere except for the short arc occupied by a tasting table.

The tapered center section allows for lofty stacks of European and American oak barrels in which age Chardonnay, Cabernet Sauvignon, and Zinfandel. The first two sections date to the winery's founding in 1975. The taller rear section was added in 1979 to hold stainless steel fermentors and still more barrels. Incidentally, the original name was Napa Wine Cellars, shortened in 1982 by a new owning partnership.

Napa Creek Winery ranks among the most ingenious examples of an obsolete building recycled from other use to a winery. Amid all the converted dairies, it is the only reworked meat packing plant.

Next to the Silverado Trail near St. Helena, the squat, solid old concrete and concrete block shell was made to stay cool and clean. Proprietor Jack Schulze put some of his fermentors outdoors at the rear, but the ones he wanted to keep particularly cool went into the old refrigerator room, to one side of a cellar full of French and American oak barrels. Behind these, in a little spot toward the rear, a short roster of wines is available for tasting. Whites dominate the list. Chardonnay, Chenin Blanc, Gewürztraminer, Johannisberg Riesling, and Sauvignon Blanc have only Cabernet Sauvignon to keep them company.

Newlan Vineyards & Winery occupies—at least for a time—a small modular metal building behind a white cottage at one side of a venerable vineyard near the city of Napa.

Within is a conventional small winery with stainless steel fermentors and oak barrels for aging.

The cellar started as Alatera (see page 89) in 1977, when Bruce Newlan was a partner in that firm. It became Newlan's exclusive property in 1982, but not his probable permanent site. He had tentative plans to build a newer, larger cellar on another of his vineyards nearby within two years of establishing his own label. Whether he moves north a half mile or stays put, the roster of wines is expected to remain the same: Chardonnay, Sauvignon Blanc, Cabernet Sauvignon, and Pinot Noir, plus an occasional late harvest Johannisberg Riesling.

Newton Vineyard does not have many peers for sheer drama. Its vines occupy steep, terraced slopes on the skirts of Spring Mountain near St. Helena. The cellars, having been dug into the earth to help keep them cool, compensate with a dramatic cap—an observation tower that helps to hide a ring of stainless steel fermentors which might otherwise bring to mind some such astronomical measuring device as Stonehenge. A formal garden with boxwood hedges covers the rest of the roof, giving good views of other landscaping as well as the valley below.

New wines descend by gravity from the fermentors to two galleries of French oak barrels in the main cellar. After bottling, they descend by truck in low gear to storage space in town. The list includes Sauvignon Blanc, Cabernet Sauvignon, and Merlot, plus one non-Bordelais varietal, Chardonnay.

Nichelini Vineyard is way up in the hills east of St. Helena. East of Conn Dam and the reservoir called Lake Hennessy, State Highway 128 curls along bare-shouldered hills forming one side of a steep canyon. Just at the head of the canyon the road slips into a grove of oaks. There, amid the trees and set into the downslope, is Nichelini.

Steps descend between an age-enfeebled barn and a solid frame house. The wine aspects of the place do not reveal themselves forcibly until the foot of the stairs, where it turns out that the rock foundations of the house shelter a substantial cellar full of redwood and oak cooperage.

Tasting goes on under clear skies (or cloudy ones) on a terrace just outside the cellar door and within the immense framework of one of the last Roman presses native to this hemisphere. It worked until the early 1950s, and still could be used, though proprietor Jim Nichelini much prefers to have it serve only ornamental purposes. There is scarcely a slower, more laborious way to press grapes.

The winery, founded in the late nineteenth century and now in the hands of the third generation, makes a number of varietal table wines. Sauvignon Vert is the specialty in whites. Cabernet Sauvignon, Zinfandel, and Gamay share honors among the reds.

There are no formal tours, but poking around is encouraged when the family-owned winery is open. Tree-shaded picnic tables have room for as many as 40 if everybody is convivial.

Niebaum-Coppola Estates must rank as the most patient new winery in the valley. Its first wine, from 1975, was scheduled to appear no earlier than 1983.

The name tells much of the history of the property. The vineyard is on part of what was Gustave Niebaum's land when he owned Inglenook. Motion picture-maker Francis Ford Coppola now owns a substantial porportion of the original property, and has his winery in the stately, cream-colored building Niebaum used as his stables.

The winery location is temporary. Plans are underway to build a more capacious cellar in a draw behind the current one. Meanwhile, visitors may make appointments to see where the first vintages of Niebaum-Coppola are undergoing their long upbringing.

Robert Pepi Winery crowns a steep knoll not far north of Oakville in fine style. One of several energy-conscious buildings added to the valley during the 1980s, it sacrifices no architectural drama to the point. Foam insulation hides as the sandwich layer between native stone outer walls and masonry block inner ones. These walls, and vents at the peak of a soaring slate roof, take care of most of the cooling needs.

The working winery is well laid out: a crusher stands outside the north wall. A Bücher tank press is just inside, directly beneath stainless steel settling tanks and alongside stainless fermentors. Medium-sized French oak tanks fill the middle space. French barrels are at the opposite end of a rectangular building from the fermentors. All of this is in easy view from glass-walled offices and labs at the upper level. From a dormer at one end, views across the valley are outstanding.

Sauvignon Blanc is the great specialty. Its running mates are Cabernet Sauvignon and Chardonnay. The first crush was 1981.

Joseph Phelps Vineyards winery building is set against a vine-covered slope in the first row of hills on the east side of the Napa Valley. It was built in 1974 by a proprietor who came to wine as a builder of other cellars and was so attracted that he changed sides of the fence.

The wood building is in effect two pavilions joined by a closed bridge that holds offices and labs. On the uphill side, a Brobdingnagian wisteria arbor is made of timbers salvaged from a one-time trestle bridge. (Much of the handsome entry gate was recycled similarly by the proprietor, Joseph Phelps.)

The northerly pavilion holds the fermentors—stainless steel ones in a mostly woody environment—along with a considerable number of oval oak casks from Germany and a smaller number of upright oak tanks. This pavilion also has the reception area, entered from the central court.

The other part of the building holds lofty racks full of oak barrels from French and American forests. A bottling room adjoins the barrel racks.

For the most part, the walls at Phelps are of large-dimensioned, rough-sawn redwood in keeping with the hay barn-inspired shape of the building. But as a pleasant study in contrasts, the reception room and offices have walls and ceilings with fine paneling and richly detailed decorative trims.

Tasting of selected wines follows appointment-only tours. The list includes Chardonnay, Fumé Blanc, Gewürztraminer, Cabernet Sauvignon, Pinot Noir, and Zinfandel. The specialties of the house are a true Syrah and Johannisberg Riesling made in a variety of styles from early harvest to late harvest. Some of the latter are comparable in sweetness to a German Trockenbeerenauslese.

Pine Ridge Winery is one of several pleasing blends of the new and the nostalgic in the Napa Valley. Most of the working winery is in a solid box of a building at the rear, but one of the aging cellars tucks under a frame building that used to be both the Luigi Domeniconi winery and residence.

The new part of the winery is typical of its era: stainless steel fermentors and storage tanks for the new wine, oak puncheons and barrels for the maturing stocks. Wilt Chamberlain would not have any trouble getting around in there, but only a handful of NBA guards could enjoy the old cellar with its rows of fat, Burgundian barrels. Pine Ridge produces Chardonnay, Chenin Blanc, Gewürztraminer, Cabernet Sauvignon, and Merlot. Not incidentally, this is a good place for serious students of wine to talk about the effects of wood on fermentation and aging. Proprietor-winemaker R. Gary Andrus has a ranging library of woods on hand to see which does what.

A more general attraction is a picnic ground in a shading grove of pines. Still another engaging prospect is a walking trail up onto the ridge that gives the winery its name.

Pope Valley Winery is located in the valley of the same name parallel to and well east of the Napa Valley.

The weathered, old-fashioned wooden barn exterior of the three-story winery fits comfortably into its hillside as it has since 1909. From then until 1959 it was operated as the Sam Haus Winery by Sam himself and his sister. In 1972 James and Arlene Devitt and their two sons bought the property and reequipped and restored the winery to modern standards.

Chardonnay, Chenin Blanc, Semillon, White Riesling, Cabernet Sauvignon, Gamay, and Zinfandel lead a long list of wines from Napa and Lake County grapes. Most are vintage-dated.

Pope Valley is a long drive over a winding, two-lane mountain road from the Napa Valley, so visitors are well advised to call ahead even during announced hours to make sure the gate is open.

Prager Winery and Port Works is a singular idea in the contemporary Napa Valley. While many wineries who have sold port-types were dropping the idea, Jim Prager was starting a winery substantially devoted to locally grown port-types. The small cellar has made half Port, half table wines since its founding in 1980.

Next to the proprietor's home south of St. Helena, the winery is one of few in the coast counties where visitors can talk about the details of dessert winemaking. As usual, all of the gear looks like gear in any other winery. The differences are in the winemaker's head, and, in this case, in the addition of brandy to still-fermenting young wines.

Quail Ridge belongs to a considerable school of new Napa wineries that have found homes in romantic buildings from the valley's era of growth in the 1880s.

The fine old stone building it occupies began in 1885 as Hedgeside Winery and Distillery, a firm owned by a California legislator named Morris M. Estee. In a mild irony, government shut it down during national Prohibition, and government reopened it to produce alcohol during World War II. No wine was fermented nor brandy distilled in the building from 1950 until recently. Quail Ridge succeeded a briefly present former proprietor in time for the harvest of 1981; the company was founded at another site in 1978.

Proprietor Elaine Wellesley uses the north end of the building and a hand-hewn 300-foot tunnel—sharper than a dogleg, but not quite a right angle—to barrel-ferment and age Chardonnay and French Colombard. Cabernet Sauvignon joined the white wines beginning with the vintage of 1980. It ferments in tanks at other premises, but comes to the picturesque caves for aging and bottling.

Visitors are invited to sit and talk around a table in the front part of the winery, in an atmosphere not unlike a French country inn save for the pleasing view of the cave stretching away in dim light, with the twin bottling tanks next to its mouth.

A real estate office and a plastics fabricator use the southern end of the building. Their signs shout louder than Quail Ridge's does, but the ivy-covered stone facade is hard to miss.

Raymond Vineyards and Cellar belongs to an old-line Napa Valley grapegrowing and winemaking family. Roy Raymond and sons Roy, Jr., and Walter established their own vineyard in 1971, and made their first wines from the harvest of 1974 after substantial careers with other firms.

The olive green-painted permanent winery building went up between 1979 and 1981 in the midst of the family's vines just south of St. Helena and just east of State 29. Stone lower walls and wood-sided upper walls echo traditional Napa winery architecture. The working gear—stainless steel fermentors, Willmes presses, and French and American oak barrels—typify the valley's modern era.

Full-fledged visitor facilities are in the future, but the Raymonds will conduct tours and sell wine by appointment. The list of wines from vines surrounding the winery includes Chardonnay, Chenin Blanc, Johannisberg Riesling (regular and late harvest), Cabernet Sauvignon, and Zinfandel.

Ritchie Creek Vineyard is the tiny winery of Richard Minor. Its only wines are Chardonnay and Cabernet Sauvignon from the steep vineyard near the Sonoma County line at the top of Spring Mountain.

The entry drive ends at the proprietor's house, at the top side of his forest-encircled vineyard. The winery tunnels into the slope just downhill from the bottom row of vines, the proprietor reasoning that it is easier to get boxes full of grapes downhill than it is to get them up.

Taking a look into the L-shaped tunnel with its double racks of French barrels requires an appointment. Tasting is at the discretion of the owner because production is so limited that a single bottle matters in the statistics.

Round Hill Cellars shares a sturdy building and a fine old garden with an antique shop. The whole place was a winery early in Napa's wine history; now the stone front part of the premises has the antiques, while the working winery tucks behind a stucco-walled structure shaded somewhere between rose and salmon pink to go with the flowers.

Proprietor Charles Abela used to build boats, and it shows in the cellars where each bit of equipment stows neatly in less space than usual. The gear itself is typical of time and place: crusher behind the building, stainless steel fermentors close inside the rear door, and French and American oak barrels up toward the high-ceilinged, white, airy sales and visitor room. The latter is entered from the west side of the building, via a path through the most aromatic parts of the garden.

The Round Hill label covers a wide spectrum of table wines, with more or less parallel rosters of all the familiar varietals from both Napa and Sonoma counties plus generics from a broader range of sources. An affiliated label, Rutherford Ranch, is used almost exclusively for Napa Valley varietal wines.

Rutherford Hill Winery is situated high on a steep slope east of Rutherford, overlooking an old olive grove, an elegant French restaurant, and a checkerboard of vineyards on the valley floor below.

The cellar is architecturally distinctive and efficient. The shake-roofed, wood-sided structure echoes old Napa hay barns in form, though its flying buttresses occurred to few or no farmers and it is a great deal bigger than any barn that might have inspired it.

A dramatic reception and tasting hall is just inside a pair of towering doors at the lower level. Beyond the tasting hall is a long, dim cellar filled with stainless steel and oak storage tanks. French oak barrels and the bottling line fill the upper floor. Willmes presses, stainless steel fermentors and other processing gear are on a deck at the rear.

The roster of available wines includes Chardonnay, Gewürztraminer, Sauvignon Blanc, Cabernet Sauvignon, Merlot, and Zinfandel.

There is reason other than wine for visiting Rutherford Hill. It is the California capital of *petanque,* the ancient Mediterranean game of bowls. All comers may play on the court, but betting against one of the cellar staff is a serious mistake.

Rutherford Vintners has a tasting and sales room open daily in a gray, wood-frame cottage next to State

Champagne: how the bubbles get there

Sparkling wine dates from the time of Dom Perignon, a Benedictine monk who made wine for l'Abbaye d'Hautvillers in the late 1600s. In a sense, effervescing wine had long since invented itself. Fermentation is the conversion of sugar by yeast into roughly equal parts of CO_2 and alcohol. Perignon only invented bottles and stoppers suitable for keeping the bubbles in.

His original method was chancy. It involved starting a secondary fermentation in the tightly corked bottle and hoping that the total accumulation of CO_2 would not explode the glass. Since Perignon and other early cellarkeepers took no notice of the interrelationship between sugar and eventual gas pressure, one scholar has it that the odds ran no better than 6 to 4 on any bottle in those pioneer years.

Now, with refined measurements, the same technique, called *la methode champenoise,* still is used. The Champagne master assembles a cuvée—a blend of still wines—to his taste, bottles it, and adds a mixture of sugar and yeast before capping each bottle. The wine is then stored "on tirage" while this mixture produces the bubbles during the secondary fermentation. After the yeast has finished its work it falls as sediment, and is allowed to remain in the bottle for at least a few months, sometimes for several years.

After this period, the sediment is worked into the neck of the bottle in a process called "riddling." Then the neck of the bottle is frozen in brine (or another solution) so that the sediment can pop out as a plug of ice (aided by an average gas pressure of 100 pounds per square inch) when the bottle is uncapped. After this process, called "disgorging," a syrup called "dosage" is added. It governs the sweetness of the finished wine. Then the cork is driven into the bottle and wired in place.

Latterly, science has added some variations. One is the German method called "Carstens transfer process." It starts out in the same way as the *methode champenoise.* But when the time comes to remove the sediment, the bottles are emptied under pressure into a holding tank, the wine is filtered, and then is returned to bottles with the desired dosage. Another method, French in origin, is called "Charmat" or "Bulk Process." In this case, the wine undergoes its secondary fermentation in a glass-lined tank, rather than in bottles. Then, as in the transfer process method, it is filtered on its way to the bottles.

A great many California wineries make sparkling wines; most have tours. Among the clearest demonstrations: Domaine Chandon, Hanns Kornell, Schramsberg, Korbel, and Mirassou for *methode champenoise;* Paul Masson for the transfer process; Weibel and Guild for Charmat.

29, a quarter-mile north of the Rutherford Cross Road.

To have a look at the workings of the trim winery in its grove of towering eucalyptus trees requires a group appointment since proprietor Bernard Skoda is the only tour guide as well as the winemaster.

Skoda has wedged a remarkable amount and variety of oak cooperage into his rectangular masonry block building. The back wall has German ovals for the Johannisberg Riesling. Both side walls have Slavonian oak ovals for mid-term aging of the reserve and regular Cabernet Sauvignons and Pinot Noirs. In the middle are a row of American oak upright tanks for initial aging, and separate racks of American and French oak barrels for final aging of the two reds. A separate rack of French oak barrels is for the Chardonnay. In one corner is a tall, refrigerated stainless steel tank for a specialty Muscat of Alexandria sold only at the winery.

The Willmes press and two rows of refrigerated stainless steel fermentors are under an overhanging red tile roof at the rear of the aging cellar.

St. Clement Vineyards occupies a fine old Victorian house near St. Helena. The winery is composed of a fermenting and processing area just behind the house, and a cellar full of fat Burgundian barrels under it. Because the building is the residence of proprietor Dr. William Casey, and because production is so limited, no visitors are allowed save those who make appointments to purchase St. Clement wines in case lots. The wines are Chardonnay, Sauvignon Blanc, and Cabernet Sauvignon.

V. Sattui Winery, just south of St. Helena, opened its tasting room in 1976 and was discovered quickly by wine country visitors looking for a place to picnic.

In addition to the winery and tasting room, the attractive building houses a gift, cheese, and deli shop. Flanking the white stucco, mission-style structure are many large, tree-shaded picnic tables.

The label dates not from 1976 but from 1885, when Vittorio Sattui established it for his own wines. It disappeared during Prohibition, but has been revived at the new site by Vittorio's great-grandson, Daryl, and several partners.

Sattui wines include Chardonnay, dry and late harvest-style Johannisberg Rieslings, Gamay Rosé, Cabernet Sauvignon, Zinfandel, and a Madeira blended from stocks going back 20 years.

Schramsberg Vineyards, having been founded by Jacob Schram in 1862, won quick immortality in the writings of Robert Louis Stevenson after the great British novelist visited the winery in 1880.

For a long time the immortality was more literary than practical. Stevenson's *Silverado Squatters* has gone on and on, but the winery began to fade as soon as Schram died. It closed altogether in 1921, experienced two ephemeral revivals in 1940 and 1951; then closed again.

The old property has lived up to Stevenson's hopes since 1965, when Jack and Jamie Davies launched Schramsberg anew, this time as a sparkling wine cellar. (Schram had made only still wines.)

It is a romantic place to visit for both its past and present. Stevenson's original description of the trail up from the main road remains fairly accurate, though the surface is a good deal better and the exact route has shifted somewhat. The original winery building still stands at the top of a large clearing next to the old Schram home. Two tunnels going back into the hill from the winery have been turned into modern fermenting rooms for production of the wines that become Champagne a few hundred yards away.

A short lane leads to the Champagne cellar itself, where a wood-faced building encloses a set of three more tunnels that hold the emergent Champagne in bottles, thousands of them piled row on row in the *methode champenoise* fashion. (New tunnels are under construction to add a bit of capacity.) Most of the techniques go back to early Champagne-making, but progress is being tested here. For one example, the old-fashioned riddling racks now have as company some experimental, octopodal contraptions that can simultaneously shake several hundred bottles and give them the required one-eighth turn per day.

Production is too limited to permit tasting of the five types of Schramsberg Champagnes. Four are finished in the dry style called Brut: Reserve, the premier bottling; Blanc de Blancs from white grapes; Blanc de Noirs from black grapes; and Cuvée de Gamay, a pale rosé. The fifth wine, Cremant, is finished demi-sec.

Sequoia Grove Vineyard and Winery is a rarity in the Napa Valley's current era of sleek, sizable new wineries. The winery is a well-weathered, sturdy, unpainted board-and-batten barn of a classic size and shape for this part of California. It hides modestly in the cluster of young redwoods from which proprietor James Allen drew the name.

An appropriately casual air clings to all of the property. For example, a crushing and fermenting area at the rear overlooks several elderly cars in varying stages of rebuilding. Against these easy-going touches, the equipment is more typical of modern Napa: a stainless steel horizontal basket press, stainless steel fermentors, and French barrels in a building that looks like a typical barn but is well-insulated and thoroughly air-conditioned.

There are but two wines, Cabernet Sauvignon and Chardonnay. The first vintage was 1979.

Shafer Vineyards occupies a striking corner of the district called Stag's Leap. Amid proprietor John Shafer's rolling vineyards is a modern, well-equipped, well-designed winery building that looks as if it has been around for years, but which was begun only in 1979, and completed a year later.

The architectural secret is a front elevation made part of stone wall, part of stained redwood siding, after a fashion once common in Napa. A signature stone next to the entry announces the founding date. The first Shafer wines came a year earlier, but were made in leased space nearby.

The working winery, along with conventional crusher, press, and fermentors, has an engaging library of wood cooperage ranging from stovepipe-thin American uprights to German oak ovals to fat, Burgundian barrels. The roster of wines produced here includes only Chardonnay, Cabernet Sauvignon, and Zinfandel from the property. Sales to appointment-only visitors are in case lots only.

Charles F. Shaw Vineyards & Winery, looks more than a little like a French farm building for a purpose. The owner, whose name the label bears, has set out to make a wine in the Beaujolais Villages style from his property on the valley floor between St. Helena and Calistoga. The architecture is part of the announcement.

The building is almost jaunty with its gray walls, red trim, and steep roof. A visit to learn what sorts of equipment are required to make a fresh, light-hearted red wine will show that much of winemaking is in the winemaker's mind. The crusher, Willmes press, and stainless steel fermentors at the rear look much like those at other cellars; so do the tidy ranks of French oak barrels inside. The story is in the fine points of how they and gamay grapes are used to make a Napa Valley counterpart to such as Morgon or Fleurie.

Shown & Sons Vineyards, east of Rutherford, is housed in a no-nonsense prefabricated metal building of a type designed to keep refrigerated goods both cool and moist, the notion being that wine will be hard put to evaporate in such surroundings. Aside from causing rusty tools, the building has worked entirely to the proprietor's satisfaction.

Romance is in the property, which bears the name of El Viñedo de los Aguacitas from Napa's Mexican days, and which, local legend insists, was a stopover point for the Bear Flag Party on the last leg of its march on Sonoma. A reservations-only picnic spot overlooks Napa Creek at a spot which could have suited the legend very well.

Proprietor Richard Shown makes Chenin Blanc, Johannisberg Riesling (in a late-harvest style when the weather cooperates), Cabernet Sauvignon, and Zinfandel, all from grapes grown on the property.

Smith-Madrone Vineyards belongs to brothers Charles and Stuart Smith and Stuart's wife Susan, the three having built what may be the ultimate image of a California cellar to house their wines.

The building is set on a shelf at the midpoint of a long, steeply sloping vineyard looking out across the valley from an upper slope of Spring Mountain. The lower half is masonry, the upper half wood-framed and wood-walled after a model common to the 1880s. But this building has some contemporary turns. The roof of the fermenting and main aging cellar is sod-covered for energy-efficient insulation. A separate section of overhead has been designed to accommodate a planned residence and offices, with steep roofs and offset walls that bring to mind contemporary seaside homes at such places as Sea Ranch.

As for the working winery, crusher and press rest on a pad outside. Inside, stainless steel fermentors occupy one end of the main level. French oak barrels occupy the other end and fill an underground cellar.

The Smiths make Chardonnay, Johannisberg Riesling, Cabernet Sauvignon, and Pinot Noir from vines they planted in 1972. Their first vintage was 1977.

Spring Mountain Vineyards evokes both of the great eras of building in the Napa Valley about as well as any single property can.

The first great era, the 1880s, gave rise to a splendid Victorian house, a less imposing but still fine barn, and a hand-hewn tunnel for storing wines in the cool earth. The original builder was Tiburcio Parrott, an enthusiastic participant in everything that made the late 19th century a golden age for most of man's tangible possessions.

In 1974, Michael Robbins bought the old property to house the winery he had founded in 1968 on another site. Parrott's legacy had fallen into considerable disrepair, so the new owner set about restoring it before adding to the current era of fine architecture in the Napa Valley.

By 1976, he had the old buildings tuned up, and was well advanced on the new construction. The new winery, built out from the face of the steep slope Parrott chose for his tunnel, reveals an eye every bit as romantic as Parrott's. To cite a single example, stained glass windows in the front wall cast soft light onto rows of French oak barrels, and are set so they can be seen sequentially as one walks toward the depths of the old tunnel. Cabernet Sauvignon ages in the new building. Chardonnay and Sauvignon Blanc age in the cooler tunnel. There is no tasting from a limited production. At times, all wines are sold out.

Stag's Leap Wine Cellars tucks neatly into its hillside amid a grove of oaks. The original 1972 building fit in so well that it was nearly invisible from the Silverado Trail no more than a hundred yards away. A second building added in 1976 sits out in fuller view. A third, dating from 1981, peeks out from behind the first two.

The original building holds the wood aging cellar—two rows of upright oak tanks, a row of fine old oak oval casks, and several tall stacks of barrels. Outside, on the uphill side, two rows of stainless steel fermentors run the length of the building.

The 1976 building houses stainless steel storage tanks, the bottling line, and newly bottled wines. The newest building, styled after a classic French country house, has the offices and more wine storage.

In all, Stag's Leap is so thoughtfully designed as to offer a virtual textbook example of how to put together a small, specialized winery. One example: both crusher and press straddle a single channel cut into the concrete work pad. Stems, pomace, and wash-water all course downhill, out of the way until the work is done and they can be disposed of at leisure.

Production at Stag's Leap is not great enough to permit tasting, but proprietor Warren Winiarski will arrange tours for all who call ahead, and explain how the winery works and how he makes his short list of wines: Chardonnay, White Riesling, Cabernet Sauvignon, Merlot, Petite Sirah, and Gamay Beaujolais.

Incidentally, there is another, unrelated winery called Stags' Leap Vintners (see the "More wineries" listing on page 90).

Sterling Vineyards looks from the outside like a fair approximation of the sort of church crusaders left on similarly craggy hilltops on Greek isles.

From the inside, it looks like the modern winery it is. The main cellar runs downhill from the first step in winemaking. Crusher, German presses, and jacketed stainless steel fermentors are at the top. A series of oak aging cellars descend from that level to the lowest point in the main building. A separate two-story cellar near the crest of the hill holds two years' worth of reserve wines aging in small oak. A separate bottling building hides behind the first two.

There is more than working winery to interest visitors here. An aerial tramway transports them from parking lot to winery and back for a $3.50 fee. The sign-guided tour is graphically and informationally excellent about grapes and wine, and also includes a room full of excellent antique furnishings and decorations. As an audible extra, the bells of St. Dunstans ring out the quarter hours.

In a separate building adjacent to the reserve cellar, the tasting room is an elegantly airy place, with awesome views down the valley plus tables and chairs for relaxed contemplation of the wines. In it the proprietors offer all of their short list: Chardonnay, Sauvignon Blanc, Cabernet Sauvignon, Merlot, and a Cabernet Sauvignon Blanc.

The present proprietors are The Coca Cola Co., which bought Sterling in 1977 from a trio of partners who had founded the winery in 1969.

Stonegate Winery, when it opened in 1973, was contained entirely within the small building at the rear of the present cluster of three. The original cellar now holds only white wines. Reds occupy the newer, larger structure directly alongside Dunaweal Lane not far down the valley from Calistoga.

Owned and operated by the James Spaulding family, Stonegate remains a small winery, but not such a crowded one as in the days when the whole enterprise squeezed itself into what had been a tractor shed.

Most small wineries are instructive for start-to-finish demonstrations of what goes into making wine. Because the red and white cellars are separate, this one is unusually so. The stainless steel fermentors common to both cellars sit outside along with other harvest-season processing gear, the anchor point for separate lessons to follow about the hows and whys and whens of oak aging.

With many other small Napa wineries, Stonegate does not have enough volume to offer tasting, but the wines are available for sale. The roster includes Chardonnay and Sauvignon Blanc in whites; Cabernet Sauvignon, Merlot, and Pinot Noir in reds. Some are special lots from identified vineyards.

Stony Hill Vineyard does not fit easily into a day of casual touring. An appointment is required to visit it, but that is only half the story. Stony Hill is at the top of a long, winding road, high in the westside hills. The drive up takes as long as a thorough look.

The cellar dates from 1951 when the late Fred McCrea and his wife Eleanor built it as a place to keep busy in retirement. The building, part stone, part plaster, nestles into a grove of trees at the foot of a sloping block of white riesling vines. A pair of handsome doors carved by the founder leads into a cellar containing European oak puncheons and barrels, and one of the last classic binning systems for bottled wines in California.

Stony Hill, under the direction of Eleanor McCrea and winemaker Mike Chelini, makes three vintage-dated wines, all white: Chardonnay, Gewürztraminer, and White Riesling. They ferment in the puncheons, the CO_2 dispelled through bubbler hoses with their noses stuck into water-filled wine bottles. Then the wines age in either the puncheons or barrels.

A visit is pretty much in the way of a pilgrimage. Once a year the winery dispatches a letter to its mailing list, and all the wine sells out within a few weeks. Thus, there are neither tastings nor sales, only an opportunity to see a cellar legendary to its followers.

Storybook Mountain Vineyards comes by its happy name and fabled label by a plausible set of literary word plays.

The winery was founded, and its three spacious tunnels dug, in the 1880s by a family named Grimm, which included a pair of brothers. With the brothers Grimm as a starting point, the name Storybook came easily. The label required a leap of imagination to get a picture of Aesop's fox and the grapes worked into the game, to compensate for the storytelling Grimms' failures to spin a tale on the subject.

Owner-winemaker Dr. J. Bernard Seps, a one-time professor, abandoned the study of history to make some. He is restoring the long-abandoned caves without harming their hand-hewn look, and has planted the steep amphitheater above them to zinfandel, the only wine he produces. The first vintage was 1980.

Visitors to Storybook Mountain will find a second winery parallel to the main one. Seps shares the underground cellars with Schug Cellars, a specialist in Pinot Noir. A carved head on a new German oak oval announces that presence, and also shows an old stone and concrete facade over the tunnels. That structure collapsed during the rainy winter of 1981–82, and is to be replaced by a complete building.

Sutter Home Winery, straight across State 29 from Louis M. Martini, offers various contrasts to its neighbor.

The winery is housed in a handsomely proportioned board-and-batten structure originally built to house the cellars of J. Thomann, one of the major forces in the early history of Napa wine. The 1880s building proves the durability of properly assembled, good wood, while pleasing the eye.

Sutter Home belongs, these days, to the Trinchero family. Theirs since 1946, it comes by its name honestly. John Sutter and son Albert built their first winery in the east hills of the valley in 1890. Sutter's son-in-law transferred the winery lock, stock, and barrels to its present site in 1906–1907, and operated it until 1930.

The Trincheros use their historic building with its historic name as a small and highly specialized cellar. Nearly all of the production is Zinfandel from Amador County grapes, most of it red, but a fair proportion White Zinfandel. The only other current wine in the roster is a small annual lot of Muscat Amabile. This specialization is relatively recent. Through the 1960s, the Trincheros offered a full range of wines.

There are no tours, but the three specialties (along with residual stocks from earlier times) are on hand to taste.

Trefethen Vineyards looks as if a good deal of history should surround it, and a good deal does. However, until the winery became Trefethen in 1968, that history was surprisingly quiet.

The vast, three-story, wooden building is the only survivor of its type in the valley. It is doubtful if it ever had a peer among wooden buildings in Napa. Its designer and builder was Captain Hamden McIntyre, who also designed Inglenook's original building and Greystone Cellars, now the property of The Christian Brothers. But while the other two cellars have had more or less famous labels attached to them down through the years, the Trefethen building was, until bought by the current owners, mainly a bulk winery, or leased as storage to a winery with its headquarters elsewhere. The Eugene Trefethen family has paid tribute to one of the winery's earlier careers with wines labeled Eshcol Red and Eshcol White, but rarely was there an Eshcol label when the winery went by that name.

Be all that as it may, the winery has a name now, and is a most agreeable and informative cellar to visit. The vineyards are harvested mechanically, so presses

Wine & the performing arts

Good music, art, and fine wine create festive occasions. Though spring and summer are many visitors' favorite seasons in the wine country, music and art accompany the clinking of glasses all year long at several wineries. Pick your afternoon or evening entertainment from the events listed below.

Call the individual wineries for more information on any of these activities. It's a good idea to plan well in advance for these popular attractions. Winery addresses can be found in the listings accompanying the maps in each chapter.

Barengo Vineyards hosts an annual art show the third weekend in May. Sponsored by the Lodi Art Club, this event attracts artists from across the nation. Paintings are hung throughout the winery, providing a perfect opportunity to stroll and sip complimentary wine. For more details, call (209) 369-2746.

Buena Vista Winery offers an annual Shakespeare in the Courtyard and Midsummer Mozart Concert series, in addition to art shows and other events. For information, call (707) 938-8504.

Concannon Vineyard and the Livermore Art Association cosponsor Art in the Vineyards every Memorial Day weekend. Member artists exhibit and sell their wares on the winery grounds. Wine is free, but you must buy the souvenir glass. For information on times, call (415) 447-3760.

Field Stone Winery features jazz, folk, and bluegrass at scheduled concerts throughout the summer. You'll need advance tickets for all but one free concert. For more details on tickets, dates, and times, call (707) 433-7266.

Guild Wineries offer the Winemasters Concert Series each summer at their Lodi facility. Past programs ranged from jazz to pops. Complimentary wines are served during intermission at the outdoor evening concerts, held on the lawn of the Winemasters' House. For information on programs and ticket prices, call (209) 368-5151.

HMR (Hoffman Mountain Ranch) presents their annual Mozart Spring Festival fund-raiser the first Sunday in May. Musicians play among booths of food, crafts, and spring wine releases. For information, call (805) 238-4945.

Johnson's Alexander Valley Winery has pipe organ concerts one weekend each month for wine-sippers. For performance details and times, call (707) 433-2319.

The Konocti Winery features musical talent every Sunday afternoon from the Memorial Day weekend through September. A variety of music is performed, primarily country or bluegrass with an occasional string quartet thrown in.

Local artists display their works at Konocti's annual Harvest Festival on the second weekend in October. The annual Vineyard Run, included in the festival, has attracted so much attention that the runners may have to wear numbers! For more details, call the winery at (707) 279-8861.

Charles Krug Winery hosts annual August Moon Concerts at their facility in St. Helena. Programs vary each year; for current information, call (707) 963-2761.

Paul Masson Vineyards originated the tradition of performances of classical music among the vines in 1957 with their "Music at the Vineyards" series. More recently they started a companion series of jazz and folk music concerts called "Vintage Sounds." For ticket and program information on both series, call (408) 257-4735.

Robert Mondavi Winery presents a Jazz Festival on the last Sunday in June and every Sunday in July at 7 P.M. You can picnic after 3:30 P.M.; wine and cheese tasting is offered during intermission. For additional information, call (707) 963-9611. For information on the Shakespeare Festival held at the winery in August, call the Napa Valley Association of the Performing Arts at (707) 944-2462.

Sonoma Vineyards offers a concert series as part of their summer Festival of the Performing Arts. Ballet, jazz, country, and symphonic performances take place in the vineyard's outdoor Greek Theater. For schedule information and tickets, call (707) 433-6511.

Souverain Cellars offers a variety of special events throughout the year. For information, call (707) 433-8281.

and other processing gear are set up to accommodate that fact. A new building to the rear of the original houses the stainless steel fermentors. The old cellar is filled with a mixture of American and French oak barrels used to age the Trefethen's estate-grown wines: Chardonnay, White Riesling, Cabernet Sauvignon, Pinot Noir, and the two Eshcols.

Tudal Winery makes a perfect example of the new wave of small, family-owned and operated cellars in the Napa Valley.

Two generations of the Arnold Tudal family tend the vineyard and make the wine from crush through bottling in a handsome barn next to a tennis court and an expert vegetable garden behind the family home. The cellar is so neatly organized that even casual visitors see at a glance how everything from French oak barrel to valve clamp is in use or precisely in its place.

Outside on a big L-shaped concrete pad are the temperature-controlled stainless steel tanks and other processing equipment.

There are only two wines, Cabernet Sauvignon from the property, and Chardonnay. The first vintage was 1979.

Vichon Winery perches on a dramatic slope right next to a swooping curve a few hundred feet up Oakville Grade from the valley floor.

Though the winery began only in 1980, this is its second home. The first one was in a small stone barn at the end of Ehlers Lane north of St. Helena, a building which has become a sort of nursery for new wineries. Vichon was the second born there, and has been followed by a third.

The current structure contrasts with the first one. Vichon's permanent home restates some old Spanish colonial ideas—covered walkways, balustraded balconies—in modern ways with modern materials well suited to contemporary winemaking equipment. The label, also modern, shows an abstracted outline of the Mayacamas Mountain ridges above the cellars. It covers Chardonnay, Chevrier Blanc (a proprietary blend of Semillon and Sauvignon Blanc), and Cabernet Sauvignon.

Villa Mt. Eden began as a vineyard in 1881 and has endured as both vineyard and winery property through numerous ownerships.

The best known of its earlier proprietors was Nick Fagiani, who used the place to make sherry-type wines just before Prohibition. The property now belongs to James and Anne McWilliams, who bought and named it in 1970 and installed sophisticated new equipment for a comeback as a table-wine cellar beginning in 1974.

Grapes for Villa Mt. Eden's estate-grown wines are field-crushed into rolling stainless steel tanks—a German system called the Mörtl—then fermented in stainless steel before aging in either American or French oak barrels.

The one-story, white stucco winery is one of several similar buildings grouped around an open courtyard in the classic fashion of a Mediterranean country villa. Vineyards surround the clustered buildings.

Current wine production is small, and plans are to keep it that way. All wines are varietals. The roster is Chardonnay, Chenin Blanc, Gewürztraminer, Cabernet Sauvignon, and Pinot Noir.

Winemaker-vineyard manager Nils Venge can accommodate visitors by appointment on weekdays only. He requests patience from phone callers; it is a long sprint from cellar to office telephone.

Whitehall Lane Winery advertises its location with its name. The jauntily designed building sits at the intersection of State 29 and Whitehall Lane, not far south of St. Helena.

The working winery is well designed and well equipped in the conventional way. Crusher, press, and stainless steel fermentors are in a semisheltered area at the rear. Barrels are in one section of the main cellar; more barrels and larger cooperage are in the other. What is startling about the place is its secondary role as a sort of art gallery, or modest museum. Prints, posters, and other pieces of art crop up here, there, and even way up the walls. It takes an appointment to get around to all the art, though casual visitors are welcomed in a tiny retail sales room at the front.

Proprietors Dr. Alan Steen and Art Finkelstein produce Chardonnay, Cabernet Sauvignon, and Blanc de Pinot Noir, some from designated vineyards. The winery also offers proprietary wines including a pinot noir known simply as Fleur d'Helene.

Yverdon Vineyards is a virtuoso one-man show of the building arts. Owner Fred Aves designed and built not only his two-story stone winery, but almost everything in it. He gathered and split local stone for the walls, designed and cast the flaring pillars that hold up the upper floor and gently sloping roof, designed and executed a series of quatre-foil stained glass windows, designed a Gaudi-esque metal spiral staircase with grape leaf motif, and even designed and cast concrete cradles for the oak casks he coopered himself.

About the only gear in the place which Aves did not build are the stainless steel fermentors, the Italian press, and some Swiss pumps and filters.

Tours are by appointment only. There is no tasting, but Yverdon Chenin Blanc, Johannisberg Riesling, Cabernet Sauvignon, and Napa Gamay are on sale weekdays. Finding the property is not easy; it is marked only by a plaque bearing the numbers 3787. The plaque is nailed to a tree next to a pipe and wire gate.

The name Yverdon is taken from the ancient Swiss town on Lake Neuchatel, ancestral home of the family Aves.

Z-D Winery is the first winery since Hanns Kornell to move from Sonoma to Napa. The purpose was to get into larger quarters than the original ones south of Sonoma town, selected when the enterprise was not much more than a hobby for partners Gino Zepponi and Norman De Leuze. Relief, as advertisements say, was only temporary. The business had become a full-time occupation by the time of the move in 1979, and has grown since. A good-sized prefabricated metal building on the Silverado Trail between Rutherford and Oakville is crowded not only from wall to wall, but in spots from floor to ceiling, with stacks of barrels and bottled wine in cases.

Z-D's production historically has focused on Chardonnay and Pinot Noir. The list also includes Cabernet Sauvignon, Merlot, and, on occasion, Johannisberg Riesling. Students of barrel-fermented white wines find some here done in American oak.

More wineries. The Napa Valley has a substantial number of wineries with extremely restricted ability to welcome visitors, or no ability at all. Their numbers are likely to grow because of recent ordinances prohibiting tasting and sales in several circumstances. These wineries are noted here to aid serious students of California wine who may have seen wines under their labels, and to explain their presence in the landscape.

Acacia Winery hides away on a back road in the Carneros district. The handsome cellars, newly built in 1982, are used to make only Chardonnay and Pinot Noir. Proprietor Mike Richmond offers no public tours, tasting, or retail sales.

Alatera Vineyards was in the process of moving a mile or so up the valley from its original home during the spring and summer of 1982. The new location is on Hoffman Lane south of Yountville. Alatera's proprietors planned to have their new building far along enough to handle the vintage of 1982, but completion of the structure and any visitor facilities were farther in the future. Alatera produces several varietal table wines plus a proprietary blanc de noir (from pinot noir) called Paradis.

S. Anderson Vineyard belongs to a southern California family which commutes weekends to its cellars near Yountville. The small winery produces Chardonnay from grapes grown on the property and a sparkling wine from pinot noir. Stanley and Carol Anderson are still planning their permanent winery building. Meanwhile, visitors are welcome to have a look around the temporary cellar, a prefabricated metal building set in their vineyard, on weekends only, and by appointment only.

Buehler Vineyards produces Sauvignon Blanc, Zinfandel, and other wines under the family label at an isolated location in Conn Valley. Proprietor John Buehler can offer neither tours nor sales. The private road leading to the winery and family home will not bear more traffic than residents already impose.

Casa Nuestra, a small, family-owned winery on the Silverado Trail north of St. Helena, was just getting into stride at publication time of this book. Owned by the Eugene Kirkham family, it was producing Chenin Blanc and Grey Riesling from its own vineyard. The proprietor accepted only written inquiries.

Chappellet Winery, east of Rutherford, is such an imposing hillside property that owner Donn Chappellet could afford to underplay the winery he had built in 1969. In the shape of a pyramid, it nestles into its slope at the bottom corner of a vineyard block. There are no visitor facilities here, and alas, for this is one of the most dramatic of California wine estates. Production focuses on Chardonnay and Cabernet Sauvignon.

Chateau Boswell is one of the more attention-getting wineries along the Silverado Trail north of St. Helena. The building with its short, round, cone-roofed tower and mansarded front elevation stands but a few yards off the road. The winery was under construction during the summer of 1982, but owner Dr. Richard Boswell had begun making Cabernet Sauvignon for his label in leased space in 1979. Chardonnay is to join the roster in the new cellar. The proprietors anticipate accepting visitors by appointment only.

Diamond Creek Vineyards does not offer conventional tours of its cellars on the slopes of Diamond Mountain. But proprietor Al Brounstein does welcome groups of wine buffs during selected weekends in June, July, and August, when he hosts picnics around a little lake at the high side of his vineyard. Groups can petition for reservations by writing to Diamond Creek at the address on page 74. The only wines are three separate bottlings of Cabernet Sauvignon from three different blocks of vineyard.

Far Niente Winery is a solid old stone barn with all sorts of cupolas and other frills on its roof. The building, set well back from State 29 near Oakville Grade Road, is also the residence of the proprietor, and not open for tours, tasting, or sales. The Far Niente label is used only for two wines, Cabernet Sauvignon and Chardonnay, both from vineyards surrounding the property.

Frog's Leap Winery earns its whimsical name. The cellar of Dr. Larry Turley flanks a creek north of St. Helena that is much favored by frogs. The winery's first crush was 1981. The roster of wines is Sauvignon Blanc and Cabernet Sauvignon. Visiting is by invitation.

The J. Heminway Winery, more formally known as Green & Red Vineyard, is located on the Chiles Valley-Pope Valley Road in Chiles Valley. Founded in 1977 to make Zinfandel and nothing more, it is so small as to have no capacity for visitors.

William Hill Vineyards is on the way to becoming a substantial winery with visitor facilities. Construction was to begin on permanent cellars in spring, 1982, at the end of Soda Canyon Road east of Yountville. Using leased space, the firm has been making Cabernet Sauvignon from its vineyards on Mt. Veeder since 1976.

Johnson-Turnbull Vineyards, near Oakville, produces only Cabernet Sauvignon from its own vineyard. The small winery, owned by a partnership of Reverdy

Johnson and William Turnbull, does not offer tours or retail sales.

Long Vineyards is another small family winery. Founded in 1978 it is the property of Bob and Zelma Long. The property, on a remote corner of Pritchard Hill east of Rutherford, is restricted from offering tasting or retail sales. Long Vineyards wines include Chardonnay, Johannisberg Riesling, and Cabernet Sauvignon.

Napa Vintners operates from yet another of the rent-a-bay warehouse buildings that have sprung up all over California to the benefit of small, growing winery companies. Proprietor Donald Ross first crushed in 1978. The principal wine is Sauvignon Blanc; others on the list are Cabernet Sauvignon and Zinfandel. Ross also produces wines for the Inverness label.

Pannonia Winery—the name comes from an ancient winegrowing province in Hungary—was being reorganized at publication time. Visitors were welcome to taste or buy (case minimums) on weekends only during spring, but the long-term visitor program was subject to immediate change. Pannonia was offering Chardonnay, Johannisberg Riesling, and Sauvignon Blanc. The prefabricated metal winery buildings are on the west side of the Silverado Trail not far north of Napa city, between Hardman Lane and Soda Canyon Road.

Robert Pecota Winery, north of Calistoga, crushed its first wines in 1978. The mainstays of the house are Sauvignon Blanc and Cabernet Sauvignon. An added specialty is Flora, made from a University of California-developed hybrid based in Gewürztraminer. Because the winery is very small and adjacent to the family home, it is not open to visitors.

Roddis Cellars, near Calistoga, makes only tiny lots of Cabernet Sauvignon from owner William Roddis's small vineyard. The first vintage, 1979, was scheduled to be released late in 1982. At present there are no visitor facilities.

St. Andrews Winery, housed in a prefabricated metal building on the Silverado Trail near the city of Napa, makes only Chardonnay, and can sell it only by appointment in minimum lots of a case. The small staff will make tour appointments for bibbers who wish to discuss the fine points of making Chardonnay.

Silverado Cellars, an impressive monument of stonework atop a steep knoll looming above the Silverado Trail, offers no tours, tastings, or retail sales. The winery makes Chardonnay, Sauvignon Blanc, and Cabernet Sauvignon.

Silver Oak Cellars, which makes only Cabernet Sauvignon, occupies a handsome, almost Gothic masonry building set 200 yards back from Oakville Crossroad. Patterned somewhat after Greystone Cellars architecturally, the building was erected in 1982 to supplement a small cellar dating back to 1973. Owned by Raymond Duncan and winemaker Justin Meyer, Silver Oak offers no tours, tastings, or retail sales.

Stags' Leap Vintners, owned by Carl Doumani and partners, dates from 1972. Its vineyards are at the old Stags Leap Manor property in the southeastern quarter of the Napa Valley, but the cellars planned for that site are not yet complete. While the winemaking goes on in leased space, there are no facilities to host visitors. (This is not Stag's Leap Wine Cellars, another company. For a description of that winery, see page 85.)

Sullivan Vineyards and Winery has begun to take shape on a site between Rutherford and St. Helena. Proprietor James O. Sullivan has planted most of his vineyards, and begun construction on a permanent winery building. The label is already established in the marketplace with 1981 wines made in leased space nearby. The roster includes Chenin Blanc, Chardonnay, and Cabernet Sauvignon. The Sullivans see visitors by appointment only at a site where residence and winery are side by side amid their vineyards.

Traulsen Vineyards is in an outbuilding styled after proprietor John Traulsen's handsome Mediterranean villa not far north of Calistoga on the highway to Lake County. The only wine at this tiny cellar is Zinfandel. The first vintage was 1980. There are no tours or tastings, but Traulsen does sell wine at retail by appointment.

Tulocay Winery is a tiny cellar adjacent to the home of its owners, William and Barbara Cadman, in the hills east of Napa city. The wines are Cabernet Sauvignon, Pinot Noir, and Zinfandel. There are no tours, tastings, or retail sales at the winery, which was founded in 1975.

Vose Vineyards, up in the dramatic folds of the Maycamas Mountains west of Oakville, sees visitors by appointment only, and limits retail sales to minimums of one case. Proprietor Hamilton Vose III makes Chardonnay, Cabernet Sauvignon, and Zinfandel from grapes at the property, and also produces Fumé Blanc and a proprietary white wine from zinfandel called Zinblanca.

In addition to these established firms, the Napa Valley has several others now operating in leased space, but with plans to establish their own wineries. Labels of such firms presently in the market include Calafia, Evilsizer, and Manzanita.

Finally, the Napa Valley has a scattered few bulk wineries. The Napa Valley Cooperative, on State 29 just south of St. Helena, sells all of its wine to E & J Gallo. Also on the south side of St. Helena, several blocks nearer the main business district, is the old Sunny St. Helena winery, now leased for storage by The Christian Brothers. At State 29 and Oakville Crossroad, two side-by-side buildings belong to United Vintners, which uses them for fermenting and aging Inglenook wines.

Other Than Wineries

The happy town of St. Helena is the hub of the Napa Valley, but attractions for visitors range from Yountville north beyond Calistoga.

A citizen's action committee called the Napa Valley Wine Library Association some years ago founded one of the valley's most enterprising allures for wine-oriented visitors. The association probably is best known for its summer weekend classes in wine appreciation, all taught by local winemakers and winery personnel, but it also earns its name with an excellent specialized library.

Wine courses begin in June and are scheduled intermittently through August. For information, write to Napa Valley Wine Appreciation Courses, P.O. Box 328, St. Helena, CA 94574.

The wine library, housed in St. Helena's public library two blocks east of Main Street via Adams Street, began largely with books from the shelves of then resident-writer M.F.K. Fisher and other local wine figures.

Another special possibility, located in a separate wing of the same building, is The Silverado Museum, a practical monument to the fine Scots writer Robert Louis Stevenson.

Stevenson followers have another, less formal opportunity at hand. The writer spent his honeymoon on the slopes of Mt. St. Helena, northeast of Calistoga. It was from a headquarters in an old miner's shack that he wrote *Silverado Squatters,* and also made the trips to Schramsberg chronicled in that cheerful little book. The cabin is long gone, burned in a forest fire, but the undeveloped Robert Louis Stevenson Park has a few markers commemorating the writer's presence. Reached by State Highway 29, connecting Calistoga and Middletown in Lake County, the park also offers scenic hiking trails.

Bothe-Napa State Park is the largest and most varied of several parks in the county. The gates are 5 miles north of St. Helena opposite the west end of Larkmead Lane.

An adjunct a few hundred yards to the south is the Old Bale Mill, a souvenir of the day when Napa County grew far more wheat than wine.

Three simple picnic parks are to be found in the valley. One is on Main Street toward the north end of downtown St. Helena. Lyman Park has a few picnic tables behind the lawn and old-fashioned bandstand facing St. Helena's Post Office. A larger park, Crane, sits behind St. Helena High School's campus on the south side of town. Finally, Yountville has several picnic tables in a small park flanking Washington Street at the north side of town.

Wine valleys seldom are paradises for children, and Napa is no exception, but it has a few enchantments for youngsters. Prime among them is the gliderport at the east end of Calistoga's main business street.

Last, but not least, the valley has a number of excellent restaurants and hostelries. These amenities are so heavily used that reservations are almost always necessary.

Plotting a Route

Napa County sandwiches neatly between U.S. Highway 101 to the west and Interstate Highway 80 to the east. State Highways 12, 29, 37, 121, and 128 connect the valley in various ways to the two great freeways.

Of all the possible combinations of access routes from San Francisco or Oakland, I-80, a short piece of State 37 north of Vallejo, then State 29 up the valley from Napa is the most direct, the flattest, and the least scenic. Driving at the speed limit, a typical lapsed time from the San Francisco-Oakland Bay Bridge toll plaza to St. Helena is about 1 hour 25 minutes. From Sacramento, the counterpart combination is I-80, State 12 from Cordelia, then State 29.

Another route from San Francisco that is slower (usually 1 hour 40 minutes), slightly hillier, and prettier goes across the Golden Gate and through Marin County on U.S. 101 to its intersection with State 37, then continues on the latter route, over State 121 through southern Sonoma County, and State 29 up the Napa Valley.

The slow, scenic way from Sacramento and points east is State 128 from Davis to Rutherford. This road follows Putah Creek for a time, then passes Monticello Dam and Lake Berryessa before climbing over the east hills and into the valley.

From the north, State 128 slips away from U.S. 101 at Geyserville, and runs through scenic vineyard country in Sonoma County before it crosses a shoulder of Mt. St. Helena into Calistoga.

As this latter route suggests, Sonoma and Napa combine well and easily. In addition to State 128 through Alexander and Knights valleys, other roads connect the two counties efficiently for wine tourists. From Santa Rosa, Petrified Forest Road crosses a scenic part of the Mayacamas Mountains on its way to Calistoga. Spring Mountain Road branches away from Pertified Forest Road on the Sonoma side of the mountains, ending in St. Helena. Trinity Road/Oakville Grade connects the Sonoma Valley with the Napa Valley from a point on State 12 near Glen Ellen. Of all the roads across the Mayacamas Mountains, this one is the most scenic, the steepest, and most winding.

Once in the Napa Valley, motorists have two main north-south roads paralleling each other along the valley floor. State 29, the westerly one, has a majority of the wineries and all of the towns on it. It cuts a wide swath a few hundred yards from the feet of the westerly hills. The eastern parallel is the Silverado Trail, which loops along a leisurely and almost purely noncommercial way on gentle slopes just a few feet above the valley floor. The slight elevation produces some striking vineyard panoramas. Once almost without wineries, it now has a considerable number on or near it.

Several crossroads tie the north-south routes together, making it easy for visitors to swap back and forth. The maps show the main ones. Several others may look promising on the spot, but, fair warning to the hurried, some east-west roads in the valley do not quite reach the other side.

The Central Coast

Santa Clara to Monterey – great vinous variety

The coastal counties south of San Francisco Bay are in a curiously unbalanced state at present. Though most of the vines grow in Monterey and San Benito counties, most of the visitable wineries are in Santa Clara and Santa Cruz counties.

The urban pressures that began to be inexorable on Santa Clara vineyards early in the 1950s will, no doubt, weigh ever more heavily on wineries through the 1980s. In the meantime, those who wish to see both vine and wine at the source have an enormous territory to consider when they go looking for the likes of Almaden, Paul Masson, Mirassou, and others in this divided region.

The north side of Santa Clara County around San Jose, where commercial winegrowing got its start south of San Francisco Bay, has been urbanized heavily since the late 1950s. Though vines almost have disappeared, this area remains a focal point for sizable wineries. West of the populous Santa Clara Valley, the Santa Cruz Mountains have fully a score of small to tiny cellars divided between Santa Clara and Santa Cruz counties.

The part suburban, part rural southern half of Santa Clara also has a considerable number of wineries. Some still have substantial vineyards around them, but housing tracts already have covered more acres than remain in vines around Gilroy.

Monterey County now supports a tremendous majority of the region's vineyards, but is only beginning to show wineries to go with its grapes. Neighboring San Benito County also has broad sweeps of the vine and a handful of wineries.

A serious student would need at least a week to cover all the ground between San Jose on the north and Greenfield on the south. More time would be better. Those with the advantage of living on the spot can carve the territory into several engaging two-day loops.

Santa Clara Valley

To remember the Santa Clara Valley as a beautiful bowl of cherries, plums, and grapes is almost impossible, even though it was dominated by orchards and vineyards well into the 1950s.

Now it is known as Silicon Valley after its prosperous electronics and space industries, and the roadsides are lined by manufacturing plants, car dealers, warehouses, and just plain houses.

Driving through the region to see its wineries is hardly a pastoral experience. Still, for all the gritty aspects of getting around, there are some pleasing moments to savor and some agreeable lessons to learn. Most surprising, the number of wineries is increasing.

The Wineries

The long-established firms are easy to visit. Several small-to-tiny newcomers require appointments, which often are restricted to one or two days a week.

Almaden Vineyards dates back to 1852, counting all the ancestors, and since has spread out mightily without ever losing its original home.

The founders were two frenchmen named Etienne Thée and Charles Lefranc, who planted vines on the site of the present Almaden home winery in San Jose. (Lefranc, having married a Thée daughter, watched history recycle a few years later when his own daughter married his junior partner, Paul Masson.) The property eventually passed out of Lefranc's hands, fell idle during Prohibition, then was restored by Louis Benoist. In 1967 Benoist sold to the present owners, National Distillers.

While all of this was going on, San Jose grew to surround the original property. And, while the suburbs were surrounding the home place, Almaden was growing in several new directions. The original property is now a sparkling wine cellar and bottling arena. Almaden has two producing wineries near Hollister in San Benito County, another near Bakersfield, a big aging cellar at Kingsburg, and, finally, a warehouse for bottled wines on the southern fringes of San Jose.

Almaden welcomes visitors only at the old home place among these facilities, but also maintains a tasting room at Hollister (see page 111).

The home property on Blossom Hill Road holds one of the largest and fastest bottling operations in the California wine industry. It is open to view. In the same building a historical museum records the company's growth from early times onward. The company has kept enough vines on the site for the setting to be handsome.

Vintage-dated varietals head the list of table wines under both the Almaden label and the more expensive (and much more limited) Charles Lefranc label. The Almaden label also covers ranges of sparkling and dessert wines.

Kathryn Kennedy Winery, a tiny cellar on a residential road not far from downtown Saratoga, is the Santa Clara Valley's ultimate specialist.

The principal wine is Cabernet Sauvignon made entirely from a small block of vines surrounding the winery and reaching up a gentle slope to the owner's house. A *vin gris* from purchased pinot noir rounds out the list.

Visitors will find a little more to see than first glance reveals. The small, gray-painted building with its adjacent concrete pad for crushing and pressing is only the top half of the winery. A below-ground cellar full of French oak barrels is the hidden part.

Paul Masson Vineyards spreads across much of the state, as do many of California's sizable wineries. For visitors, though, things are centralized at a complex of buildings on the valley floor just east of Saratoga's business district.

There the Paul Masson Champagne and Wine Cellars depart completely from traditional winery architecture. Out front, a free-form metal sculpture sets the tone. The cellars themselves show a glass front wall and a wavy, modern roofline, not quite so sharply arched as barrel vaults, but close.

However the outside may strike the eye, the inside is an efficient aging cellar and has much to recommend it to visitors. A raised walkway permits bird's-eye views of an expanse of handsome cooperage (glass-lined steel, oak ovals, and redwood uprights all nestled together in harmony), five model bottling lines, and all the steps in making sparkling wines.

Masson, in fact, offers one of the few chances to study what is called the "transfer process" of making sparkling wine. The lesson is presented clearly at listening station 8 on Masson's electronically guided tour. On the tour, each visitor is given a one-station radio receiver of the sort familiar to museum-goers, allowing each to set a personal pace in listening to taped presentations at a series of stations. Hosts are posted along the way to answer any questions the tapes do not.

The Champagne and Wine Cellars were opened in 1959, then expanded in 1967 and again in 1971, long after the owning Joseph Seagram Co. had decided to move the main body of Masson's vineyards south into Monterey County. No crushing or fermenting goes on at this older site. That part of the work takes place at the Pinnacles vineyard near Soledad where a big producing winery was completed only a few days before the harvest of 1966 began, and at the Paul Masson Sherry Cellars in Madera, built in 1974. But Saratoga is where all Masson wine comes for final aging, bottling, and packaging, and this is where it is at hand for sampling in a spacious and comfortably appointed tasting hall. Masson makes a broad range of wines. The flagships are vintage-dated varietals from Monterey. Also available are nearly all of the familiar varietal and generic table types, some proprietary table wines such as Emerald Dry, and sparkling and dessert wines.

Paul Masson Vineyards goes back to the turn of the century, when the flesh-and-blood Paul Masson ended his partnership with Charles Lefranc and built a handsome cellar of his own in the hills west of Saratoga. The original cellar was carved into a hillside in 1900, rebuilt after the earthquake in 1906, and rebuilt again after a gutting fire in 1941. (The old man did not have to deal with the fire. He had died a year earlier after 58 years of winemaking in California and 4 years of retirement.)

The old cellar still holds small lots of dessert wines, but its interest for visitors is on a stage out front. Paul Masson Vineyards presents several music and drama series in an amphitheater facing a Romanesque church wall that serves as the building's facade (see page 87).

Mirassou Vineyards, now in the hands of its owning family's fifth generation, is one of the oldest wine companies in Santa Clara, but the family began marketing wines under its own label only in the mid-1960s.

A French vineyardist, Pierre Pellier, established the dynasty in 1854 in what is now downtown San Jose. (Following an exploratory visit in 1848, he returned to France to gather a wife and thousands of vine cuttings.) Subsequently another Frenchman, Pierre Mirassou, met and married a Pellier daughter. That was in 1881. The Mirassou family has figured in every California vintage since.

An old photo on the tasting room wall shows wooden tank trucks loading Mirassou bulk wines into railroad cars for the long voyage east in the era before World War I. After the enforced respite of Prohibition, the third and fourth generations resumed commercial winemaking, again anonymously. Only the diligent knew to go to the winery, which bottled tiny lots for sale to familiars. Now, with the fifth generation firmly embarked on the path of family identity with family vintages, Mirassou wines may be found all across the country.

The main winery building, with a richly appointed tasting room in one front corner, is a squarely built, solid masonry structure nestled into the beginnings of a steep slope southeast of San Jose. Once, not so many years ago, it was the whole winery. Now it holds only a small proportion of the aging cooperage and a bottling line.

A second building just uphill holds the sparkling wine cellar and bottled wines. A third building at the rear stores only bottled wines. (A fourth building a couple of miles away holds much of the wooden cooperage including all of the barrels.)

Outdoors, at the rear of the original cellar, is a complex assemblage of processing equipment. The usual stainless steel fermentors, a crusher, and two big Willmes-type presses are there. So are some specialized hoppers and dejuicers for handling the must of field-crushed grapes. Most Mirassou grapevines are in the Salinas Valley of Monterey County, which led the family to pioneer in mechanical harvesting and field-crushing of quality grapes for varietal wines.

As a result, this is one of Santa Clara's most instructive wineries to visit during the October-November harvest season for both traditional and innovative approaches to winemaking. The main works are far enough out in the open to permit sidewalk superintending. The sparkling wine cellar also is instructive for looking at traditional *methode champenoise* techniques.

Only still wines may be tasted. The roster includes Chardonnay, Gewürztraminer, and a specialty called Fleuri Blanc among whites, and Cabernet Sauvignon, Pinot Noir, and Zinfandel among reds.

Novitiate Wines has few peers for handsome setting. The winery building cuts into a narrow shelf halfway up a hill of some size. Drivers approaching Los Gatos, westbound on State Highway 17 or southbound on Monte Sereno Road, can see the white winery building and, on the crest above it, some old vineyards are visible.

Within the winery building, amid observable outlines of still older buildings, dim tunnels lead off in several directions. There is no telling which are the oldest of the oak casks lining the tunnels. The Novitiate has been making sacramental wines since 1888 and has acquired cooperage whenever possible. Some casks came to the hillside winery without pedigree papers at the end of Prohibition.

But not all is cobwebby romance. The Jesuit fathers and brothers who run the winery are an experimental lot. A since-reassigned winemaker-priest designed and installed a battery of highly efficient stainless steel fermenting tanks after having studied the subject at the University of California at Davis. Down in one of the deeper regions stands a stainless steel tank shaped somewhat after the fashion of a Mercury space capsule and equipped with a porthole. On view inside is the yeast culture used in the Novitiate Flor Sherry. (Other flor cultures crop up throughout the winery in a wild variety of bottles, flagons, and demijohns. The winemaker waits patiently to see if variant strains of yeast might develop.)

Getting around to see all of this involves a considerable amount of climbing spidery iron stairways, since the office building is at the lowest level and the start of the tour is at the highest, and there is no alternate route. The tour ends in the cellar-level tasting room, where the good owners offer table, appetizer, and dessert wines for leisurely tasting and consideration of their merits.

Pendleton Winery is quartered in a space-for-rent warehouse on an industrial street in San Jose. If the surroundings are not altogether romantic, the notion is eminently practical for small winery owners who own no grapes, but buy from districts at every point of the compass in search of exactly what they want.

Owner R. Brian Pendleton has been one of this increasingly numerous breed only since 1979, but has had a winery since 1975. The business began as Arroyo Winery, acquiring its present name in time to use it on wines from the vintage of 1977.

The specialty is Chardonnay. It is supplemented by Cabernet Sauvignon and Pinot Noir.

Sommelier Winery occupies one bay in one of those space-for-rent warehouses that have sprung up by the dozens in recent years. This one is just off Old Middlefield Road not far from San Antonio Road in deepest Mountain View. Behind one part of its concrete block front is a full-fledged producing winery, with everything from crusher to bottling line.

Founded in 1976 and owned by Robert and Laverne Burnham, Sommelier makes small lots of a short list of varietal wines using grapes from as far north as Sonoma, as far south as San Luis Obispo. They are available for tasting at specified times when stocks are not sold out.

Turgeon & Lohr, like several others in the district, has its winery in San Jose and its vineyards in the Salinas Valley of Monterey County.

Owned by Bernard Turgeon, Jerry Lohr, and winemaker Barry Gnekow, the cellar opened to the public in 1975 when its first wines were ready for release.

(Continued on page 96)

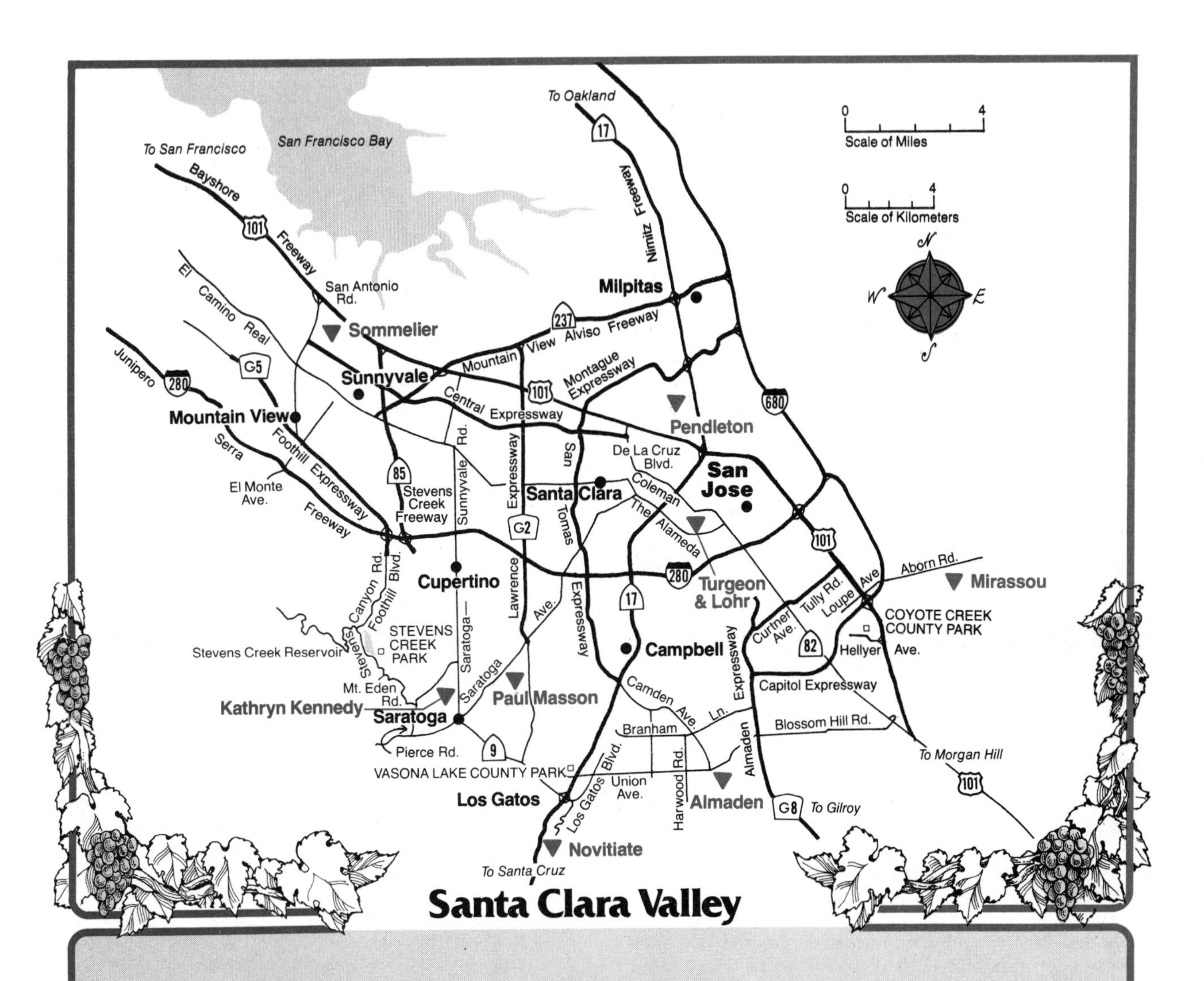

Santa Clara Valley

Almaden Vineyards. On Blossom HillRd. at intersection with Camden Ave. (1530 Blossom Hill Rd., San Jose, CA 95118) Tel (408) 269-1312. M-F 10, 11, 2. GT.

Kathryn Kennedy Winery. On Pierce Rd. .5 mi. N of State 85/Saratoga-Sunnyvale Rd. (13180 Pierce Rd., Saratoga, CA 95070) Tel (408) 867-4170. Su 12-4 or by appt. IT/Ta.

Paul Masson Vineyards (Champagne and Wine Cellars). From Saratoga, NE 3.25 mi. to 13150 Saratoga Ave. (P.O. Box 97, Saratoga, CA 95070) Tel (408) 257-7800. Daily 10-4. GT/Ta.

Mirassou Vineyards. From U.S. 101, Capitol Expwy. exit, E to Aborn Rd., then E on Aborn 2 mi. to winery (3000 Aborn Rd., San Jose, CA 95135) Tel (408) 274-4000. M-Sa 10-5, Su 12-4. GT/Ta.

Novitiate Wines. From Main St. in Los Gatos, S on College Ave. to Prospect, W (up hill) on Prospect to winery drive (P.O. Box 128, Los Gatos, CA 95030) Tel (408) 354-6471. Daily 10-5. GT (M-F 1:30 & 2:30, Sa 11 & 1)/Ta.

Pendleton Winery. From State 17, Montague Expwy. exit, W to O'Toole Ave., then S to winery (2156G O'Toole Ave., San Jose, CA 95131) Tel (408) 946-1303. By appt. only M-F 9-5. IT/Ta.

Sommelier Winery. From U.S. 101, San Antonio exit, W to Middlefield Rd., S on Old Middlefield Rd. 2 blocks to Independence Ave., E 1 block to Wyandotte Ave., N 1 block to winery (2560 Wyandotte Ave., Sec. C, Mountain View, CA 94043) Tel (415) 969-2442. By appt. only Sa-Su. IT/Ta.

Turgeon & Lohr. From State 17, SE on The Alameda to Lenzen Ave., N 1 block (1000 Lenzen Ave., San Jose, CA 95125) Tel (408) 288-5057. Daily 10-5. GT/Ta.

Not on Map—Restricted Visitor Facilities

Gemello Winery. (2003 El Camino Real, Mountain View, CA 94040) Tel (415) 948-7723.

Llords & Elwood Winery. (Bus. off.: 315 S. Beverly Dr., Beverly Hills, CA 90212) Tel (213) 553-2368.

Key: GT (guided tour); IT (informal tour); Ta (tasting).

. . . *Continued from page 94*

The brick-front winery just off The Alameda occupies what once was the shop building of a brewery. Tours keep going in and out of little buildings inside a big one. Just inside the front door is a cool, spacious, redwood-paneled tasting room. The working cellar begins on the other side of an interior door, where temperature-controlled stainless steel tanks and other modern processing equipment are sheltered by a tall, airy, steel-framed building. To one side, an insulated substructure holds almost 2,000 barrels of aging wine.

From there it is back to the tasting room. The roster of wines includes Chardonnay, Chenin Blanc, and a proprietary called Jade among whites, and Cabernet Sauvignon, Monterey Gamay, and Zinfandel among reds. Also, there is a Gamay Rosé. In all cases the label is J. Lohr.

More wineries. Two old-timers with limited visitor facilities are to be found in the valley.

Gemello Winery, the old-timer, dates from 1934, always with a member of the founding Gemello family active in it. Located behind a bowling alley off El Camino Real in Mountain View, the red-wine specialist (Cabernet Sauvignon, Zinfandel, Barbera and others) offers neither tours nor tasting, but does have a retail room in front of the architecturally modest cellar building.

Llords & Elwood Winery crushes and ferments most of its wine in leased space, ages and bottles it in a downtown San Jose location, and sells it from a business office in Los Angeles. On occasion the San Jose aging cellar is opened to visitors. The long list encompasses varietal table wines and several dessert types.

Other Than Wineries

Urban distractions abound in the neighborhood. These notes cover only two with historic ties to wine, some potential picnic sites, and a few attractions around San Jose, the area's largest city.

Leland Stanford in his day ranked as one of the state's most enthusiastic winegrowers, though histories suggest his skills did not come anywhere near matching his hopes. Skilled or not, he established three major wineries, one of them on the north side of the present Stanford University campus. The handsome brick building, on Quarry Road between the Stanford Shopping Center and the university's hospital, still stands. Today, it is filled with shops and restaurants.

Farther south, the Mission Santa Clara has similarly dim ties to the vine. Santa Clara is something of a curiosity piece because vines did not prosper there during the mission era. The failure mystified the mission fathers but has been cleared up since. Santa Clara is too cool for the mission variety of grape to ripen properly. This was one of the earliest, if unheeded, hints at the complexity of microclimate zones in the coastal counties. The mission adjoins the campus of Santa Clara University on The Alameda a few blocks north of State Highway 17.

For picnickers on the west side of the valley, Vasona Lake County Park straddles a creek and reservoir directly alongside State 17 at Los Gatos. It has abundant picnic and recreation facilities on well-kept lawns.

A more remote possibility is Stevens Creek Park, a long strip along a narrow and shaded creek, that offers picnic sites aplenty in March or April. But as spring wears into summer, the park begins to be crowded. The shallow creek is a fine playground for children, which accounts for a good part of the traffic. The sheltered and wooded nature of the place contributes the rest of the allure.

The park is west of Cupertino on the same road that leads to Ridge Vineyards (see page 100).

Just west of Los Gatos, where the Coast Ranges begin to climb, Lexington Reservoir's shoreline is a developed picnic and water sports park—but a less manicured one than Vasona.

Picnickers who prefer to be on the east side of the valley will find a county park alongside U.S. Highway 101, not far south of Mirassou. Long, narrow Coyote County Park has a small lake as well as several tree-shaded picnic sites.

A potpourri of attractions in the greater San Jose area may appeal to families with children: Winchester Mystery House, Rosicrucian Egyptian Museum (with mummies), Kelley Park's petting zoo, and Marriott's Great America. For information, write to the San Jose Chamber of Commerce (see address below).

Fuller descriptions of the Santa Clara Valley region may be found in the *Sunset Travel Guide to Northern California*.

Plotting a Route

Getting around the Santa Clara Valley in the modern era is mainly a matter of picking the most efficient sequence of freeways and expressways.

U.S. Highway 101 (the Bayshore Freeway) steams straight and fast through an industrial corridor from San Francisco into San Jose. Interstate Highway 280 connects the same two cities almost as quickly, and has the advantage of coursing through scenic coastal hill country.

On the industrialized east shore of the bay, State Highway 17 (the Nimitz Freeway) connects Oakland and San Jose, then continues westward to Santa Cruz. It intersects with both U.S. 101 and I-280.

Finally, Interstate Highway 680, the easterly equivalent to I-280, connects with U.S. 101 and I-280 at San Jose, providing an alternative to State 17 for anyone coming from Alameda County east of Oakland. For anyone coming from the south, U.S. 101 is the only quick approach.

The choice of expressways and major arterials within the region is almost limitless. The map on page 95 shows the most efficient ones for getting to wineries.

Accommodations and restaurants are as plentiful as the large population would indicate. The quietest location is Los Gatos. For lists of visitor facilities, write to the San Jose Chamber of Commerce, 1 Paseo de San Antonio, San Jose, CA 95113; the Saratoga Chamber of Commerce, P.O. Box 161, Saratoga, CA 95070; or the Los Gatos Chamber of Commerce, P.O. Box 1820, Los Gatos, CA 95930.

California Wine Chart

Table wines

Varietals

Named for the grapes from which they are made.

White wines

Light, freshly fruity flavors. Most bottlings slightly sweet. Meant for early drinking.

Chenin Blanc
Emerald Riesling
French Colombard
Gewürztraminer
Green Hungarian
Grey Riesling
Sylvaner
White Riesling (Johannisberg Riesling)

Full-bodied, flavorful enough to withstand aging in oak. Dry. Many made to age well in bottle.

Chardonnay (Pinot Chardonnay)
Dry Chenin Blanc
Pinot Blanc
Dry Semillon
Sauvignon Blanc (Fumé Blanc)

Richly fruity. Sweet enough to serve with dessert rather than dinner.

Malvasia Bianca
Muscat of Alexandria
Moscato Canelli
Sweet Semillon
Late Harvest White Riesling

White wines from black grapes. Sometimes dry. Should be white to salmon color but usually pink, slightly sweet, more akin to rosé than to white.

Pinot Noir Blanc
Zinfandel Blanc
Cabernet Sauvignon Blanc
White Barbera

Rosé wines

Light, freshly fruity. Sometimes dry, more often slightly sweet. Meant for early drinking.

Rosé of Cabernet Sauvignon
Gamay Rosé
Grenache Rosé
Grignolino Rosé
Rosé of Pinot Noir
Zinfandel Rosé

Red wines

Fresh, fruity. Dry or just off-dry. Light-bodied, meant for early drinking.

Carnelian
Gamay
Gamay Beaujolais
Grignolino
Pinot St. George
Ruby Cabernet

Full-bodied, with distinctive flavors. Sturdy enough to require oak aging. Aging in bottle improves them.

Barbera
Cabernet Sauvignon
Charbono
Merlot
Petite Sirah
Pinot Noir
Zinfandel

Generics

Named—usually after European wine districts—to hint at style.

White wines

Light, relatively dry. Meant for early drinking.

Chablis
Dry Sauterne
Mountain White

Light, noticeably sweet, but suitable with meals.

Rhine

Medium-sweet to very sweet, meant for dessert rather than dinner.

Haut Sauterne
Light Muscat
Sweet Sauterne
Chateau ____ (winery name)

Rosé wines

Fruity, slightly sweet to sweet.

Vin Rosé
Rosé

Red wines

Dry or just off-dry. Versatile with meals. Meant for early drinking.

Burgundy
Chianti
Claret
Mountain Red

Full-bodied, noticeably sweet, but suitable with meals.

Barberone
Vino Rosso

Appetizer wines

Made with higher alcohol content than table wines (17 to 20 percent compared to 12 to 13 percent), usually with deliberate oxidized flavors or with added herbal flavors.

Sherry (Cocktail, Dry, Medium-dry)
Vermouth (Dry, Sweet)

Special natural wines: These are appetizer wines flavored with fruit juices or natural essences. Citrus is especially popular as a flavoring. Also used: mint, coffee, chocolate, several herbs. Most carry proprietary names.

Dessert wines

Made with higher alcohol content than table wines, as in the case of appetizer wines, but markedly sweeter.

Angelica
Cream Sherry
Madeira
Marsala
Muscatel
Port (Ruby, Tawny, White)
Tokay

Sparkling wines

Made in a variety of styles, with a range of colors. Meant as versatile accompaniments to appetizers, entrées, desserts.

Champagne (white sparkling wine; subtitled by degree of sweetness)
- *Natural*—very dry
- *Brut*—dry
- *Extra Dry*—hint of sweetness
- *Sec*—noticeably sweet
- *Demi-Sec*—very sweet

Blanc de Noir (White champagne from black grapes, usually styled as Brut)

Cremant (Fewer bubbles than regular Champagne, usually sweet)

Sparkling Muscat, Sparkling Malvasia (From muscat grapes, usually sweet)

Pink Champagne (usually sweet)

Sparkling Burgundy, Champagne Rouge (Red sparkling wine, usually off-dry)

PROPRIETARIES: Some wines of each major type are labeled with special names coined by the proprietors of wineries. These proprietary names frequently echo generic place names; the wines parallel generics in range and use.

The Santa Cruz Mountains

The Santa Cruz Mountains offer almost the perfect fantasy of specialized, hand-crafted winemaking.

Tumultuous slopes make every vineyard a scenic wonder, and keep every vineyard small. Only here and there is the soil deep enough and the sun reliable enough for grapes to mature. So specialist winemakers fit themselves—one here, one there—into forests or onto mountaintops, or both at once.

This makes touring a demanding business. The distances are considerable on winding, narrow roads. With a few exceptions, the wineries are too small to have daily tastings and tours. Many are part-time enterprises of people with other jobs. But the rewards are singular for wine buffs who wish wine to be an enchanted product from enchanted places.

Even without wine these mountains are enchanted. Thick forests give way without warning to grassy meadows, which in turn give way to forests again. The enchantment is not undiscovered. The whole region is a vacationland for people who think rustic is better.

The Wineries

A few more than a score of wineries are in operation in the Santa Cruz Mountains or near them, from Half Moon Bay down to Soquel. An exact census is always hard to get in this region because the part-time cellars tend to start with little fanfare. Now and again one ends its career more quietly still.

Bargetto Winery, in the town of Soquel, is the largest and oldest winery in the area, and still is small by general standards. It is housed in a trimly painted red barn that looks just as solid as it is.

The second generation of Bargettos owns it now. John Bargetto and a brother founded it in 1933, and John had a firm hand in the business until his death in 1964. His son Lawrence continues the operation.

Tours of a typical small cellar start at the crusher out front and end in an agreeable tasting room and gift shop at the west end of the building. In the tasting room, Bargetto offers a substantial range of varietal wines, including Cabernet Sauvignon, Merlot, Chardonnay, Johannisberg Riesling, and Gewürztraminer. The winery also specializes in fruit wines.

David Bruce Winery is up in the hills southwest of Los Gatos on Bear Creek Road. The building is plain, but some distinctive touches in the equipment make this an unusual winery to visit.

Outside are a French Demoisy crusher and a German Bucher membrane press. Both could be explained, but are more believable if seen. Inside, the original number of oak barrels hang from the walls on cantilevered racks designed by the proprietor and still unique almost 20 years later. The first lot of barrels has been augmented by many more, stacked conventionally on the floor, and by a modern stainless steel fermenting room.

The other singular touch at David Bruce is a series of solar collectors on the roof of the fermenting room. They supply hot water to the winery.

Dr. David Bruce launched his winery in 1964, completed the sizable concrete block aging cellar in 1968, and added the steel fermenting building in 1975.

A physician by profession and a winegrower by avocation, Bruce makes principally Chardonnay, White Riesling, Cabernet Sauvignon, Petite Sirah, and Zinfandel.

Congress Springs Vineyards, new in 1971, is, in spite of the present winery's youth, an old property and one dedicated to preserving old vineyards and an old cellar.

Now the property of the Dan Gehrs and Vic Erickson families, Congress Springs was a winery as early as 1910 under the ownership of a Frenchman named Pierre Pourroy. Now, as then, the working winery is housed on the lower level of a sturdy concrete building while the upper level is home to the winemaker. And, as in the past, the principal vineyard sweeps east from the winery down a rolling slope. The view across Saratoga is worth the trip by itself.

The current proprietors also lease other old mountain vineyards in the region, and buy small lots of grapes from local growers. The roster of Congress Springs wines includes Pinot Blanc, Semillon, Sauvignon Blanc, Cabernet Sauvignon, Pinot Noir, and Zinfandel.

Although the wines are opened for tasting only semiannually, visitors are welcome every Saturday.

Felton-Empire Vineyards somehow gives an impression of being away from it all, even though the winery and vineyard tuck in behind a row of houses just above the main business street in Felton.

This is a winery property with some history. It was the famous Hallcrest Winery of San Francisco lawyer Chaffee Hall until his death in the 1960s. In Hall's day the winemaking was organic, even primitive in some respects. It is no such thing now.

Owners John Pollard and James Beauregard brought in a microbiologist, Leo McCloskey, as their winemaker and partner. He has transformed the cellars into as technically impeccable a place as imagination can conjure.

On the upper level, along with a roomful of stainless steel fermentors and the tasting room, is a laboratory equipped to measure things and creatures only dimly known outside academic halls. On the lower level of a building cut into a hillside are some oak barrels and a tiny but scientifically sterile bottling room. (Medical people will recognize the air filter from hospital and laboratory applications.) The crusher and press are state-of-the-art types in keeping with the rest of the enterprise.

The production of this winery focuses on sweet white wines, especially White Riesling. It includes dry Riesling and Gewürztraminer, and tiny lots of Cabernet Sauvignon and Pinot Noir. One other product of the house is an unfermented varietal grape juice.

Frick Winery, one of the new breed of downtown wineries that have sprung up in California since the 1970s, is in a one-time sash mill in Santa Cruz.

(Continued on page 100)

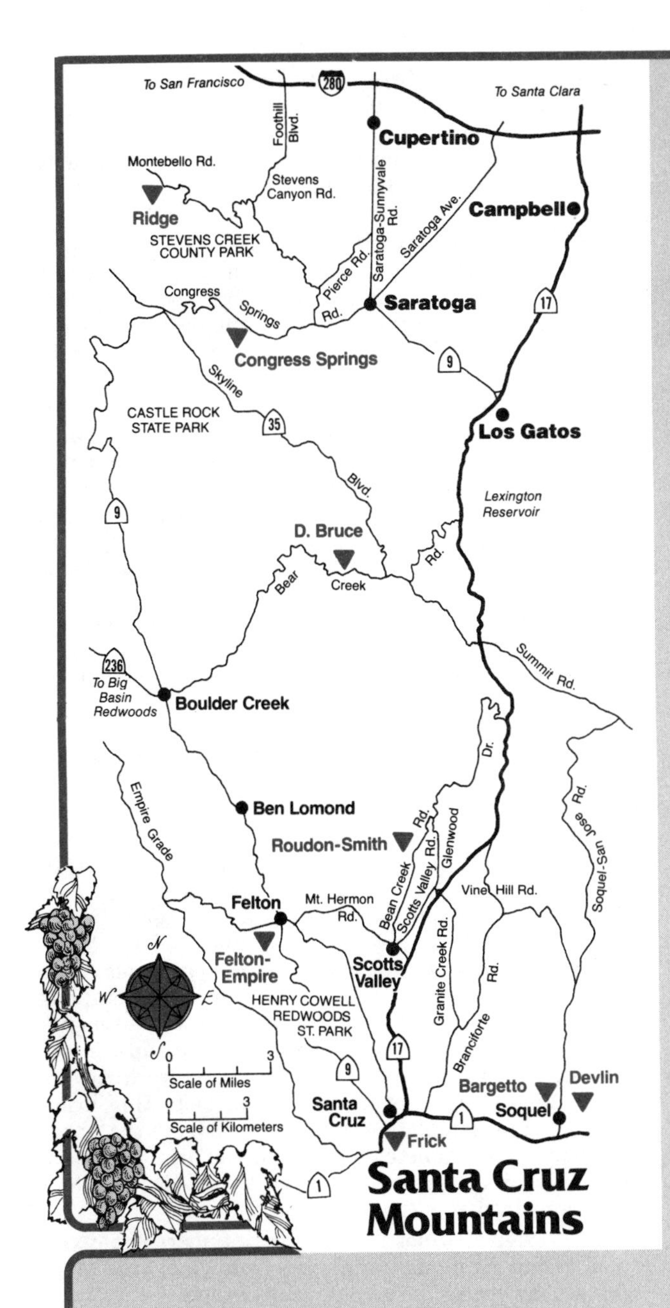

Bargetto Winery. From State 1, Soquel exit, E on S. Main St. to Soquel Dr., then .25 mi. N on N. Main St. (3535-A N. Main St., Soquel, CA 95037) Tel (408) 475-2258. Daily 10–5:30. IT/Ta.

David Bruce Winery. From State 17, Bear Creek Rd. exit, 2 mi. W (21439 Bear Creek Rd., Los Gatos, CA 95030) Tel (408) 354-4214. Sa 12–2 by appt. GT/Ta.

Congress Springs Vineyards. From Saratoga, 3.5 mi. W on State 9.to private drive at 4.09 mi. marker (23600 Congress Springs Rd., Saratoga, CA 95070) Tel (408) 867-1409. Sa–Su by appt. GT.

Devlin Wine Cellars. From State 1, Park Ave. exit, E to end of Park Ave. extension (P.O. Box 723, Soquel, CA 95073) Tel (408) 476-7288. By appt. only.

Felton-Empire Vineyards. From downtown Felton, .25 mi. W on Felton-Empire Rd. (379 Felton-Empire Rd., Felton, CA 95018) Tel (408) 335-3939. Sa–Su 11–3. GT/Ta.

Frick Winery. From State 1, S 3 blocks on River St., W on Potrero to winery (303 Potrero St. #39, Santa Cruz, CA 95060) Tel (408) 426-8623. F-Sa 12-6 June 15-Sept. 15 or by appt. IT.

Obester Winery. At 12341 San Mateo Rd. (State 92) 2 mi. E of State 1 or 6 mi. W of I-280 (Rt. 1, Box 2Q, Half Moon Bay, CA 94019) Tel (415) 726-9463. GT by appt. only Ta Sa–Su 10–5. (Outside map area)

Ridge Vineyards. From jct. of I-280 & Foothill Expwy., 3.1 mi. S on Foothill Blvd./Stevens Canyon Rd., 4.4 mi W to 17100 Montebello Rd. (P.O. Box AI, Cupertino, CA 95015) Tel (408) 867-3233. Sa 11–3. Ta.

Roudon-Smith Vineyards. From State 17, Scotts Valley exit, N .5 mi. on Mt. Herman Rd. to Scotts Valley Rd., 1 block to Bean Creek Rd., 2 mi. NE on Bean Creek (2365 Bean Creek Rd., Santa Cruz, CA 95066) Tel (408) 438-1244.

Sherrill Cellars. From jct. of State 84 and State 35 W of Woodside, 2.2 mi. S on State 35/Skyline Blvd. to 1185 (P.O. Box 4155, Woodside, CA 94062) Tel (415) 851-1932. Sa by appt. (Outside map area)

Not on Map—Restricted Visitor Facilities

Ahlgren Vineyard. (P.O. Box 931, Boulder Creek, CA 95006) Tel (408) 338-6071.

Crescini Wines. (P.O. Box 216, Soquel, CA 95073) Tel (408) 462-1466.

Cronin Vineyards. (11 Old La Honda Rd., Woodside, CA 94062) Tel (415) 851-1452.

Grover Gulch Winery. (7880 Glen Haven Rd., Soquel, CA 95073) Tel (408) 475-0568.

Mount Eden Vineyards. (22020 Mt. Eden Rd., Saratoga, CA 95070) Tel (408) 867-5783.

Page Mill Winery. (13686 Page Mill Rd., Los Altos Hills, CA 94022) Tel (415) 948-0958.

Martin Ray Vineyards. (22000 Mt. Eden Rd., Saratoga, CA 95070) Tel (415) 321-6489.

Santa Cruz Mountain Vineyard. (2300 Jarvis Rd., Santa Cruz, CA 95065) Tel (408) 426-6209.

Silver Mountain Vineyard. (P.O. Box 1695, Los Gatos, CA 95030) Tel (408) 353-2278.

P and M Staiger. (1300 Hopkins Gulch Rd., Boulder Creek, CA 95006) Tel (408) 338-4346.

Sunrise Winery. (16001 Empire Grade Rd., Santa Cruz, CA 95060) Tel (408) 423-8226 or 286-1418.

Walker Wines. 25935 Estacada Dr., Los Altos Hills, CA 94022) Tel (415) 948-6368.

Woodside Vineyards. (340) Kings Mountain Rd., Woodside, CA 94062) Tel (415) 851-7475.

Key: GT (guided tour); IT (independent tour); Ta (tasting).

(Continued from page 98)

Proprietor William Frick started his winery in the more rural precincts of Bonny Doon in 1977, but moved soon after to his more spacious present quarters. Two wooden buildings face each other across a courtyard; the open space is used for crushing. The buildings house fermentors, French oak barrels, and other gear.

Pinot Noir is the specialty of the winery. Also on the roster are Chardonnay, Petite Sirah, and Zinfandel.

Obester Winery was founded by Paul and Sandy Obester in 1977 in the unlikely environs of Half Moon Bay.

It has some instant history. Sandy Obester is the granddaughter of John Gemello, founder of the Gemello Winery in Mountain View (see page 96). John was not only the inspiration, but, at 95, the overseer of the construction and equipping of a winery that was, thus, three generations old at its birth.

The winery proper is located in an old pole barn with corrugated sheet-metal roof and siding. Set in a narrow draw in hills behind town, the one-time small box factory now houses a conventionally up-to-date small cellar with stainless steel fermentors, oak barrels, and the other familiar pieces of winemaking equipment. The tasting room is in a separate building with a picture window looking across a particularly fine coastal meadowland. The wood covering the walls once was meant to be fashioned into boxes by the former user.

The emphasis is on Johannisberg Riesling from Monterey grapes and Sauvignon Blanc from Mendocino. Obester also has limited lots of Cabernet Sauvignon.

Ridge Vineyards started in 1959 as a weekend winery. It has long since grown past that stage, and become one of the largest of the Santa Cruz Mountain wineries. At this point there is enough Ridge to fill the original cellar and a much larger second building. Or, as its proprietors put it, Ridge is about the size of a large chateau in Bordeaux.

Ridge's two locations, almost a mile apart, are both spectacular. The name comes from the fact that the winery does indeed sit on a ridge due west of Cupertino. The topmost vineyard yields views out to the Pacific Ocean and down into a vast portion of San Francisco Bay. The rest of the premises is also scenic.

Visitors are welcomed Saturdays at the rustic original winery, now a bottling and case storage building. It is hidden in a little fold 100 yards or so off Montebello Ridge Road. Drivers need to watch mailbox numbers carefully for the cue to angle left into a drive that, from the road, appears to go nowhere.

When the weather is reasonably good, tasting and talking go on outdoors, at one edge of a small patch of vines, but there is indoor space for gloomy days.

From time to time the hosts are moved to cart visitors up to the producing winery, a handsome old frame building that covers a sizable cellar dug into the stone hillside. The equipment there is modern, but the building goes back to before the turn of the century, when it housed the Montebello Winery.

The labels on Ridge Wines are among the most explicit of any in California. The dominant wines are Cabernet Sauvignon and Zinfandel, supplemented on occasion by Petite Sirah.

Roudon-Smith Vineyards moved into its current home in the Scotts Valley district of Santa Cruz county in 1978 after being launched in 1972 on a nearby property. Like several other wineries of its era, it began as a cross between a hobby and a business, and quickly grew into a full-sized business.

The wood-sided structure of owners Robert Roudon and James Smith is best described as prim. Indeed, it would look at home somewhere in New England. But it is cut into a side slope above a fine meadow, and is hedged all about by conifer forests that leave no doubt about its California location.

The well-equipped and tidily kept winery has stainless steel fermentors and other processing gear outside, barrels for fermenting and aging on the lower level, and an upper story for storage of cased goods and relaxed Saturday tastings. The roster of wines is led by Chardonnay and Zinfandel. Also on the list are Gewürztraminer, Cabernet Sauvignon, and Petite Sirah.

Since Bean Creek Road was underdesigned even for the Model T, the atmosphere is almost certain to be tranquil for those who make appointments to visit.

Sherrill Cellars, one of many husband-wife partnerships in this part of the wine country, moved into its current quarters in 1979 after several years of operating under the post office at Woodside.

The roof peak of the new building peeks out of trees from the downhill side of Skyline Drive some miles to the south of the original location. The two-story, wood-frame, redwood-sided winery came into being in the old-fashioned American way. Nathaniel and Jan Sherrill threw a fine winery-raising party patterned after a midwestern barn raising as far as the work went, but with a distinctly different flavor to the refreshments served the friends and neighbors who raised up the roof beams. The sturdy result of their handiwork awaits such finishing touches as an upper-story tasting room, scheduled for completion in spring, 1983, but the working winery is completely equipped, and an airy deck is a comfortable, appropriate place to welcome visitors with appointments in good weather.

The roster of wines is mostly red: Cabernet Sauvignon, Petite Sirah, and Zinfandel from vineyards ranging southward as far as San Luis Obispo.

More wineries. Connoisseurs of California wine will recognize some prestigious names on this long list, and see some new ones. They are grouped here for a variety of reasons that make each almost as hard to get into as Harvard. In most cases, the main reason is lack of size. For those willing to work patiently for an invitation, the addresses are noted with the regional map.

A man named Martin Ray managed, from 1943 onward, to create vast interest in a tiny winery high in the hills west of Saratoga. Ray died in 1975 shortly after his property had been divided into two parts.

The new owner, son Peter Martin Ray, now operates the property, which is still called Martin Ray Winery. A second winery, Mount Eden, is operated by a consortium of vineyard owners who used to sell their grapes to Ray.

The property never was large enough to allow casual

visits. Now neither of the two wineries is large enough to accept visitors other than established friends, even though both buy grapes to supplement their own small vineyards.

In addition to continuing on their own, their successes have helped inspire a whole school of similar enterprises, most of them operated as second careers on evenings and weekends as changes of pace from regular jobs.

Ahlgren Vineyard is a tiny, family-owned winery located under the home of the Dexter Ahlgren family. The aim is to learn which grape varieties fare best in the complex microclimates around Boulder Creek.

Crescini Wines in Soquel was a new start in 1980. A husband and wife partnership makes Chenin Blanc, Cabernet Sauvignon, and Petite Sirah from Napa and Monterey grapes. This is one of the few wineries in the district which offers no tours, tastings, or sales at the door.

Cronin Vineyards, in Woodside, uses some local grapes as well as imports from Napa, Sonoma, and Monterey. Owner Duane Cronin's list of wines includes Chardonnay, Cabernet Sauvignon, Pinot Noir, and Zinfandel.

Devlin Wine Cellars, the Santa Cruz winery of Chuck Devlin, has made small lots of Cabernet, Chardonnay, and Zinfandel from a broad range of coast counties' vineyards since 1978.

Grover Gulch Winery of Soquel, a partnership of Dennis Bassano and Reinhold Banek, makes Zinfandel and other reds from old vineyards near Gilroy and Paso Robles.

Page Mill Winery, in Los Altos Hills beneath the home of the owning Richard Stark family, makes small lots of Napa Chardonnay and Cabernet plus a local Chenin Blanc.

Santa Cruz Mountain Vineyard, in the hills above Santa Cruz, was founded by Ken Burnap primarily to explore the possibilities of Pinot Noir.

Silver Mountain Vineyard, west of Los Gatos, is owned by Jerry O'Brien, who makes only Chardonnay and Zinfandel.

P. & M. Staiger, another family winery housed under its owners' residence, is tiny and inaccessible on its mountaintop above Boulder Creek. Its vineyard is planted to Cabernet Sauvignon and Chardonnay.

Sunrise Winery, on a high peak west of Felton formerly occupied by the old Locatelli Winery, makes a range of varietals from a broad spectrum of coastal vineyards under the direction of partner-winemaker Keith Hohlfeldt.

Walker Wines, in Los Altos Hills, is the property of the Russell Walker family. The label covers tiny lots of Chardonnay, Petite Sirah, and other varietals, mostly from San Luis Obispo grapes.

Finally, in this alphabetic listing, comes Woodside Vineyards, property of Bob and Polly Mullen, who use their small winery to make—among other wines—a Cabernet Sauvignon from the last few vines of the legendary LaQuesta estate of Dr. E.H. Rixford. LaQuesta Cabernet Sauvignons were much treasured in pre-Prohibition California.

Other Than Wineries

Entirely in keeping with the wooded nature of this part of the world are two fine redwood parks with both picnic and camping facilities.

Big Basin Redwoods State Park is the larger of the two. On a loop road off State Highway 9, it is slightly more distant from the wineries than its running mate, but not far enough to disqualify it as a respite, or refuge.

The other is Henry Cowell Redwoods State Park, which straddles State 9 on the south side of Felton. It has several fine picnic grounds accessible from the highway. Its campground is reached via Graham Hill Road from Felton.

In addition to the parks, one other important diversion is the Roaring Camp & Big Trees Steam Railroad, a narrow-gauge line that was built for loggers but now amuses small fry and impresses their elders with some superior forest scenery.

From Boulder Creek down to Felton, State 9 is fairly regularly lined with visitor accommodations ranging from rustic cabins to fancy motels.

Santa Cruz Convention and Visitors Bureau, P.O. Box 921, Santa Cruz, CA 95061, will provide lists of accommodations in the county. See the Santa Clara Valley section for addresses of chambers at Los Gatos and Saratoga.

Wineries away from this core area can suggest parks and accommodations near them.

Plotting a Route

State Highway 9 forms a properly pastoral loop into the heart of the Santa Cruz Mountains from State Highway 17, the freeway connecting San Jose and Santa

Cruz. One end of the loop is at Los Gatos, the other at Santa Cruz. From it, local roads need give only modest help to get visitors to wineries from Scotts Valley north to Saratoga.

Interstate Highway 280, a freeway, and State Highway 35, a curving, hilly two-laner, are the main north-south routes to most of the cellars from Saratoga north. State Highway 1 is the route for cellars from Santa Cruz south through Soquel.

For anyone driving from San Francisco, I-280 is the fast way while State 1, more affectionately called Coast One, is a low-key route between the city and Santa Cruz. Another possibility is State 1 to Half Moon Bay, State Highway 89 east to State 35, then the latter road south to the neighborhood of Saratoga, where it intersects with State 9.

South Santa Clara

Time was when South Santa Clara was all of a piece, vinously speaking. Its wineries offered good, sound jug wines from local vines, and almost nothing else. That day is gone.

Increasing urbanization, a wine boom that placed strong emphasis on varietal wines, vintage dates, bottles with corks, and new blood in the region's community of winemakers all combined to broaden the spectrum of wines from Gilroy and Morgan Hill until it included high-priced varietals along with solid values in jugs.

If some new styles have joined the old ones, the countryside remains quietly appealing for winery visitors to seek out. U.S. Highway 101 cuts a straight swath through it, giving a hint of the character, but the nature of the region reveals itself more truly from byways close to the hills.

West of U.S. 101, beyond the tract homes, the district called Hecker Pass is made of vine-filled bottomlands, grassy hills, oak knolls, cactus farms, wandering creeks and reservoirs, the beginnings of conifer forests just below the namesake pass, and a nest of small, distinctly casual wineries.

Rapidly growing Gilroy is the focal point for touring. It has revitalized its downtown since being bypassed by the freeway. What used to be a tedious stretch of stop-lighted highway now has become a stylish shopping street. But, still, in season, a heavy, sweet aroma of drying fruit hangs in the quiet air, even in the middle of town, for this is prune and apricot as much as grape country, and the dehydrators perfume the district for week after warm summer week. Gilroy's other aroma comes later when the town is beyond any shadow of a doubt the Garlic Capital of the World.

The Wineries

Most of the south county's wineries are several miles west of U.S. 101, especially in the Hecker Pass district. However, Morgan Hill has a fair share of the roster close to the freeway on either side.

Fortino Winery is one of several cases in the region in which a new proprietor shifted the production of a one-time jug winery over to vintage-dated varietals.

Ernest Fortino bought the old Cassa Brothers winery in 1970, and has been upgrading the property ever since, although without modernizing it very much. A Willmes press bought for the harvest of 1978 is one concession to contemporary winemaking. An automatic bottling line is another. Otherwise, Fortino is the sort of man who believes that the old ways are best.

His fermentors, in a building to the rear of the stucco-covered main cellar, are open-topped redwood. In the main cellar he ages his wines—nearly all of them reds—in redwood and good-sized oak tanks. Time is his favorite filter.

Fortino's list of wines includes Carignan (spelled here without the final "e"), Charbono, Cabernet Sauvignon, Petit Syrah, and Zinfandel, plus rosés and a Sylvaner. All are on hand in a spacious tasting room and gift shop at the front end of the winery. So are occasional limited bottlings of white wines from black grapes.

Emilio Guglielmo Winery, a mile east of U.S. 101 at Morgan Hill, recommends itself to visitors for several reasons.

Most directly to the point, the owning family has taken pains to make its tasting room and picnic area inviting. Inside, the tasting room is quiet and cool. The focal point is a serving bar fashioned entirely from tank staves, but there is ample space to step back between tastes. Outside, vines trellised along one side of the building allow the picnic area to be as sunny and warm as a winter day can get, or as cool as a summer day can be. Umbrellas over four tables add shade in summer.

An appointment to tour the winery can be worth the effort because of its unusual aspects. Foremost of these is a double file of stainless steel fermentors patterned after a type developed in Australia. The tank floors, instead of sloping in one direction, are conical so that grape solids empty automatically through doors at the very bottom of the cone. At the other end of tradition, the Guglielmos keep a sizable collection of oak oval casks that predate Prohibition. Some are in a cellar beneath the residence—the original winery. The rest of the casks are in the main aging cellars along with steel and redwood tanks and a growing collection of oak barrels.

The Emilio Guglielmo label was new in the 1970s, though the winery dates back to 1933. It reflects a shift from jug generics to vintage-dated varietals. (The jugs are still available under the original Emile's label.) The list includes Semillon, Sylvaner, and Johannisberg Riesling in whites, a Grignolino Rosé; and Barbera, Cabernet Sauvignon, Ruby Cabernet, and Zinfandel among reds.

One final reason to visit is the availability of small lots of selected older wines only at the winery.

Hecker Pass Winery belongs to Mario and Frances Fortino, who launched their small cellar in 1972, but did not open it for tours until their first wines were ready for tasting in 1974.

Mario Fortino came to the United States from Italy in 1959 and worked for other cellars in the Santa Clara region—full-time until he founded his own winery, part-time until the business was well established. Some outgrowths of his earlier employment show up in the working winery. The basket presses and redwood fermenting tanks at the rear of the small stucco building are typical of old-line Gilroy, but inside it the proprietor has a temperature-controlled stainless steel fermenting tank for his whites, sophisticated pumps, and other equipment to suggest he learned a great deal while he was getting ready to launch his own venture. The aging cellar has redwood tanks and oak barrels.

The table wines, most of them vintage-dated and labeled as "Estate Bottled" include Chablis, Carignane, Petite Sirah, and Zinfandel. There also are dessert wines on the list.

Kirigin Cellars occupies one of the oldest properties in the Hecker Pass district but is one of its newer wineries.

Nikola Kirigin Chargin bought the one-time Bonesio vineyards and winery in 1976, and forthwith gutted the time-weary main cellar. The building now houses three rows of temperature-controlled stainless steel fermentors and racks of oak barrels in place of the old redwood tanks that once filled it. The cellar also holds modern filters and bottling equipment, all visible on the leisurely tour.

Even the exterior of the cellar got a face-lift, with buff stucco walls replacing the old, barn-red, board-and-batten ones.

The proprietor, fifth generation of a Croatian wine-making family, had university training in his homeland and experience in other California wineries to lead him toward modern equipment and techniques.

The results are on hand for tasting in a pleasant building next to the cellar, and at another tasting room on Business U.S. Highway 101 in Morgan Hill. The roster includes Chardonnay, Malvasia, Opol Rosé, Cabernet Sauvignon, Pinot Noir, and a dessert specialty called Vino de Mocca.

In front of Kirigin Chargin's residence—originally the home of a local cattle baron named Henry Miller—a pine-shaded picnic ground can accommodate as many as 30 people.

Thomas Kruse Winery, across the Hecker Pass Highway (State Highway 152) from the end of County Road G8, more or less started the revolution that is changing this region from a country jug producer to a source of vintage-dated varietals.

A Chicagoan until wine caught his interest, Kruse acquired the property in 1971 and forthwith set about doing things differently from his neighbors of that time. He has not changed since. He ferments all his wines in oak barrels or small plastic tubs, sticks to varietals, and insists on bone-dry wine as his style.

The list is uncommon, too. It includes a white sparkling wine from Zinfandel, a Carignane, a dry rosé from Cabernet Sauvignon, Pinot Noir, Grignolino, and, now and again, a bottling of Thompson Seedless.

The winery is a classic wooden barn, or rather two of them about a hundred yards apart. Kruse spent several years rehabilitating a weather-weakened main building, but never violated its appearance inside or out. The tasting room, in a back corner, is all old wood, a serene nook in keeping with the rest of an unfailingly cheerful and informal atmosphere.

Live Oaks Winery advertises itself best of the several cellars along State 152. A platoon of signs on the north side of the road invites visitors to turn and drive along beside an eclectic lot of frame buildings until the drive dips downhill and ends alongside a yellow-painted, board-and-batten winery.

In all its casual and good-humored aspects, this winery typifies what the Hecker Pass used to be in its entirety: a source of modestly priced, unpretentious, everyday wine made in and offered from an appropriate kind of cellar.

Live Oaks' tasting room has a paneled wall on one side, stainless steel bottling tanks on the other, stuffed birds and animal heads wherever space permits, and case goods stacked as owner Peter Scagliotti's need requires. The tasting room is at the lower level, at the rear of the building. Tours of the upper-level fermenting area go on only during the vintage season.

The Live Oaks label, which has been around since 1912, appears on red, white and rosé—two wines of each type, one in inexpensive bottles, the other in even less expensive jugs.

Pedrizzetti Winery is most accessible at its roadside tasting room and gift shop on Business U.S. 101 at the north side of Morgan Hill. However, visitors who make appointments can tour the producing winery and taste its wines there.

The building's history goes back to 1946 with the Pedrizzetti family, having begun in 1923 when Camillo Colombano first made wine on the property. Inside the rectangular cellar, two rooms full of well-seasoned redwood tanks are much as they have been from the beginning. However, the rest of the property has gone modern. Outside, two rows of stainless steel fermentors flank a processing deck with a new continuous press. Another row of stainless steel tanks snugs against an outside wall, and still more stainless tanks fill the white wine aging cellar inside.

The office and tasting room are in a small building at the rear of a courtyard on the opposite side of the

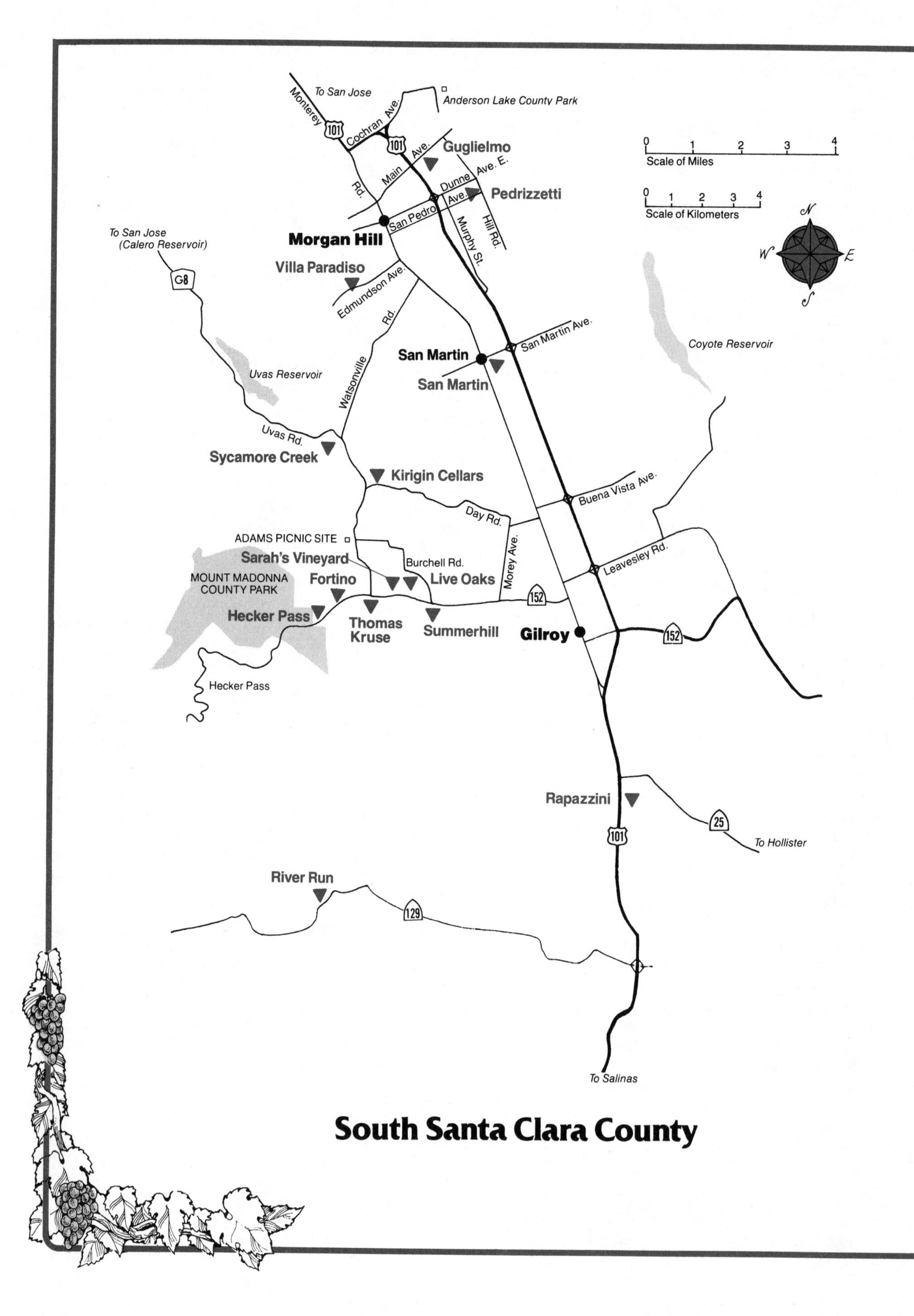
To San Jose
Anderson Lake County Park
Monterey
101
Cochran Ave.
Main Ave.
Rd.
Guglielmo
Dunne Ave. E.
Ave.
Pedrizzetti
San Pedro
Murphy St.
Hill Rd.
Scale of Miles
0 1 2 3 4
Scale of Kilometers
0 1 2 3 4
N
W
E
S
To San Jose
(Calero Reservoir)
G8
Morgan Hill
Villa Paradiso
Edmundson Ave.
Rd.
Watsonville
San Martin Ave.
San Martin
San Martin
Coyote Reservoir
Uvas Reservoir
Uvas Rd.
Sycamore Creek
Kirigin Cellars
Buena Vista Ave.
Day Rd.
ADAMS PICNIC SITE
Sarah's Vineyard
Burchell Rd.
Morey Ave.
Leavesley Rd.
MOUNT MADONNA
COUNTY PARK
Fortino
Live Oaks
152
Hecker Pass
Thomas
Kruse
Summerhill
Gilroy
152
Hecker Pass
Rapazzini
25
101
To Hollister
River Run
129
To Salinas

South Santa Clara County

Fortino Winery. N side of State 152 5.2 mi. W of Bus. U.S. 101 (4525 Hecker Pass Hwy., Gilroy, CA 95020) Tel (408) 842-3305. Daily 9-6. GT/Ta.

Emilio Guglielmo Winery. From Bus. U.S. 101 in Morgan Hill, E on Main Ave. 1.5 mi. (1480 E. Main Ave., Morgan Hill, CA 95037) Tel (408) 779-2145. Picnic. Daily 9-5. GT by appt./Ta.

Hecker Pass Winery. N side of State 152 5.4 mi. W of Bus. U.S. 101 (4605 Hecker Pass Hwy., Gilroy, CA 95020) Tel (408) 842-8755. Picnic. Daily 9-6. IT/Ta.

Kirigin Cellars. From State 152, N on County G8 2.5 mi. (11550 Watsonville Rd., Gilroy, CA 95020) Tel (408) 847-8827. Picnic (groups must reserve). Daily 10-6. GT/Ta.

Thomas Kruse Winery. S side of State 152 5 mi. W of Bus. U.S. 101 (4390 Hecker Pass Hwy., Gilroy, CA 95020) Tel (408) 842-7016. Picnic. Sa-Su 12-5 or by appt. IT/Ta.

Live Oaks Winery. N side of State 152 4 mi. W of Bus. U.S. 101 (3875 Hecker Pass Hwy., Gilroy, CA 95020) Tel (408) 842-2401. Daily 8-5. Ta.

Pedrizzetti Winery. From U.S. 101, Dunne Ave. exit, E to Murphy St., S to San Pedro Ave., then E .8 mi to winery (1645 San Pedro Ave., Morgan Hill, CA 95037) Tel (408) 779-7774. By appt. only. GT/Ta.

Rapazzini Winery. E side of U.S. 101 3 mi. S of Gilroy (P.O. Box 247, Gilroy, CA 95020) Tel (408) 842-5649. Daily 9-7 Jun-Sep, 9-6 Oct-May. Ta.

River Run Vintners. From U.S. 101, NW 5.5 mi. on State 129, then SW .2 mi. toward Aromas on Rogge Ln./Carpenteria Rd. (65 Rogge Ln., Watsonville, CA 95076) Tel (408) 722-7520. By appt. only. IT/Ta.

San Martin Winery. E side Bus. U.S. 101 .1 mi. S of San Martin Ave. (P.O. Box 53, San Martin, CA 95046) Tel (408) 683-4000. Daily 9:30-5:30. GT (only groups by appt.)/Ta.

Sarah's Vineyard. N side of State 152 4.1 mi. W of Bus. U.S. 101 (4005 Hecker Pass Hwy., Gilroy, CA 95020) Tel (408) 842-4278. Sa-Su 12-4 or by appt. GT/Ta.

Summerhill Vineyards. S side of State 152 4.1 mi. W of Bus. U.S. 101 (3920 Hecker Pass Hwy., Gilroy, CA 95020) Tel (408) 842-3032. Daily 12-dusk. GT (Jun-Sept by appt.)/Ta.

Sycamore Creek Vineyards. From State 152, N 3.3 mi. to Uvas Rd., then W .1 mi. (12775 Uvas Rd., Morgan Hill, CA 95037) Tel (408) 779-4738. Sa-Su 12-5 or by appt. GT/Ta.

Villa Paradiso Vineyards. From Bus. U.S. Hwy. 101 in Morgan Hill, SW 2 mi. on Edmundson Ave. (1830 Edmundson Ave., Morgan Hill, CA 95037) Tel (408) 778-1555. Picnic. Sa-Su 11-5. GT/Ta.

Not on Map—Restricted Visitor Facilities

Conrotto Winery. (1705 Hecker Pass Hwy., Gilroy, CA 95020.) Tel (408) 842-3053.

Peter & Harry Giretti Winery. (Bus. off.: 791-5th St., Gilroy, CA 95020.) Tel (408) 842-3857.

Ronald Lamb Winery. (17785 Casa Ln., Morgan Hill, CA 95037.) Tel (408) 779-4268.

Key: GT (guided tour); IT (informal tour); Ta (tasting).

winery from the fermenting area. The roster of wines is mostly varietal and vintage-dated. Included are Chardonnay, Chenin Blanc, and Petite Sirah. Also on the list are both reds and whites from Zinfandel and Barbera.

Rapazzini Winery is new in 1982 as a building, but goes back to 1962 as a business.

Jon and Sandra Rapazzini had to rebuild after fire destroyed their original premises in 1980. The new winery, on exactly the same highway-side spot as the old one, is a sizable prefabricated metal building; the new tasting room is a stone building attached to the front of the working cellar. Both parts of the replacement are more handsome than the 75-year-old, stucco-covered structure they replace.

There are no tours. A window at one end of the tasting bar gives a clear view of the entire working winery. The Rapazzinis open for tasting all of a wide range of wines from vintage varietals to fruit and specialty wines. The owners operate a second tasting room on the plaza at San Juan Bautista.

River Run Vintners is not, technically speaking, part of South Santa Clara. The winery of Will and Terra Hangen is near Aromas in that skinny, scenic tail of Santa Cruz County that separates Santa Clara and Monterey counties. Technicality aside, the wineries around Gilroy are River Run's nearest neighbors.

The place is simplicity itself. In a barn set back from Rogge Lane in the owners' apple orchard, the cellar is equipped with a basket press, a trio of open-topped redwood fermentors, and a double row of neatly stacked American oak barrels. Tasting goes on across a card table next to the aging wines.

The River Run roster is dominated by Zinfandel, made in two or more styles each vintage. Cabernet Sauvignon and Pinot Noir round out the winery's regular list.

San Martin Winery makes life easy for people who would like to taste its wines near the source, but asks potential cellar visitors to work a bit harder.

The company maintains three sizable tasting rooms within a close radius of its producing winery in Morgan Hill. The main one is on Business U.S. 101 near San Martin Avenue, and just across the railroad tracks from the cellars. Another is on the east frontage to freeway U.S. 101 near the Dunne Avenue exit at Morgan Hill. The third is a shade more than 3 miles south of Gilroy.

At all three, wines are offered in sequences governed by the traditional rules of professional tasters. A host comments on each wine as it is poured. These exercises—frequent, brief, and never formidable—show wine in its wide diversity of flavors.

The roster of San Martin wines is dominated by vintage-dated varietals. It includes Fumé Blanc, Johannisberg Riesling, and Chardonnay among whites. Cabernet Sauvignon and Zinfandel are the principal reds. A specialty of the house is a separate line of wines labeled "Soft" because they have a lower than normal alcohol content. In this group are Chenin Blanc, Johannisberg Riesling, and Gamay Beaujolais.

(Continued on next page)

. . . Continued from page 105

San Martin is open to group tours only, and only by appointment. After an end-to-end rehabilitation of some once-archaic cellars by the owning Somerset Wine Company, this largest of the district's wineries is also its most modern. Temperature-controlled stainless steel fermentors are outdoors next to stainless steel dejuicing screens and continuous presses. White wine storage is in stainless steel in a huge, refrigerated cellar. Reds and selected whites age in oak barrels in a separate building.

Tours conclude with private tastings in a romantic room in the oldest and finest building on the property, a brick structure once full of redwood tanks, but now primarily used for bottling.

Sarah's Vineyard is one of the new-era Hecker Pass wineries concentrating on varietals aged in French oak rather than jug generics aged in venerable redwood tanks.

The tiny, well equipped, neat-as-a-pin winery is around on the back side of a steep knoll from the entry and parking area. To get from the car to the natural wood cellar, one strolls around the knoll between blocks of vines and with an escort of geese. In the words of winemaker and co-owner Marilyn Otteman, the purpose is to "get the city off your back" before settling down to talk wine. The rest of a visit is similarly designed to lower blood pressure rather than raise it. The price of a bottle of wine may include a rose, a bit of fresh fruit from the family orchard, or even a goose egg or two.

Principal wines on the list are Cabernet Sauvignon and Zinfandel. There is a bit of late harvest-style White Riesling. Chardonnay will follow as the home vineyard matures.

Summerhill Vineyards is a new start in one of the old-timer wineries in the Hecker Pass district.

Hilton (Red) Johnson, Debra Dodd, and partners have begun the long task of modernizing the old Bertero Winery, which opened in 1917 and had not seen much change during its long career. Soon after their 1980 purchase of the property, the new owners fitted stainless steel fermentors, a small collection of American oak barrels, and a new bottling line in among the ancient redwood tanks and oak casks. Visitors may check the progress before or after tasting in a handsome pavilion set among vines about halfway between the highway and the several winery buildings.

The list of wines is a long one, encompassing Cabernet Sauvignon, Zinfandel, and other varietals in bottles, generics in jugs, and a number of fruit wines.

Sycamore Creek Vineyards joined the roster of South Santa Clara wineries in 1976. Its proprietors, Terry and Mary Kaye Parks, had acquired the old Marchetti winery and vineyards earlier, and could think of no better use of the old property than to resume making wine.

The producing winery is a classic wooden barn cut into a gentle slope and neatly refitted to modern standards. Crushing and pressing take place on a concrete pad on the uphill side of the steep-roofed white building. Just inside, on a sort of mezzanine, is the bottling department. Below it, at the downhill grade level, is a fermenting and aging cellar full of neatly stacked barrels and a trio of small oak tanks.

Tasting takes place on the upper level of a second barn just far enough from the first to give even better views across rolling vineyards. The roster of wines is anchored by estate-bottled Chardonnay, Cabernet Sauvignon, and Pinot Noir from new vines, and Carignane and Zinfandel from old ones.

Villa Paradiso Vineyards houses itself in an impressive hulk of a building, one with concrete walls imposing enough to summon up thoughts of a fortress.

However, there is nothing formidable about the welcome. All comers on weekends get a leisurely look through cellars just beginning to be filled with wines. Proprietors Hank and Judy Bogardus made Zinfandel and Petite Syrah from their debut vintage in 1981. Those wines will follow a lot of Zinfandel from an earlier vintage. The proprietors offer easygoing tasting, and visitors are invited to spread a blanket under a shade tree and picnic if they wish.

Visitors in earlier times will recognize the property as having been the Richert and Sons Winery before the Bogarduses took over and named it half for the accompanying Italianate villa and half for its location in what is locally known as Paradise Valley.

More wineries. Several more cellars are located in the district, but are too limited in visitor facilities to be readily tourable.

Conrotto Winery, an old-timer dedicated to making house wines for the restaurant trade, offers neither tours nor tasting, but does sell its red and white wines at the cellar door in Gilroy. The Peter & Harry Giretti Winery is another local fixture, selling jug wines to a long-established clientele from an old cellar in Gilroy. Ronald Lamb Winery at Morgan Hill makes tiny lots of several varietals including Chardonnay, Cabernet Sauvignon, and Zinfandel. Lack of size prohibits public visits. De Santis, a new winery in Gilroy, is not yet ready for visitors.

Other Than Wineries

Several pleasing and temptingly diverse parks line the hills on either side of southern Santa Clara County.

Dry and parched as the east hills appear from U.S. 101, they hide a string of reservoirs, each developed for recreation.

The most highly developed of the lot, Anderson Lake County Park, is in the first range of hills east of Morgan Hill. Cochran Road goes directly to the main area. Though primarily designed for boaters, the park has a large picnic area. At the southern tip of the same lake is a second, smaller picnic area, this one reached via East Dunne Avenue.

Henry W. Coe State Park lies directly east of Anderson Lake on an extension of East Dunne Avenue. The distance from downtown Morgan Hill is 14 miles. A one-time working ranch, the park has its headquarters in old ranch buildings at an elevation of 2,600 feet. These buildings attract almost as many watercolorists as the park's rolling, grassy hills, except in late April and early May when the wildflowers capture every eye. There is a small day-use fee for picnic sites. The park also has a few campsites.

Farther south, Coyote Lake County Park offers picnickers another choice. Again, a cooling reservoir is the prime attraction. Access is from Gilroy via Leavesley Road.

Over in the west hills, Mt. Madonna County Park has its main entrance at the summit of Hecker Pass. Like Henry W. Coe State Park, this park has been built out of a one-time working ranch. Cattleman Henry Miller owned it, and left some formal gardens for posterity. Also, the park has a herd of albino deer as a special attraction. Roads meander through oak forests at the higher elevations. At the foot of the hills, next to a creek and pond, picnic sites nestle in the shade of oaks and other trees. The entrance to this area is from State 152 just before it starts climbing. There is a day-use fee.

Finally, a small county park called Adams Picnic Site sits next to County Road G8 opposite the end of Burchell Road.

Plotting a Route

U.S. Highway 101 brings traffic into southern Santa Clara County from both north and south. State Highway 152, called the Hecker Pass Highway west of U.S. 101 and the Pacheco Pass Highway east of it, handles the cross traffic.

U.S. 101 is scheduled to be a divided highway in Santa Clara County before the end of 1982. The last stretch of stop-lighted business road between southern San Jose and Morgan Hill has been a vantage throughout 1981 for watching construction of the last link of freeway. The freeway is flat and straight, but close enough to hills to be pleasant driving.

The Pacheco Pass Highway, winding and scenic, carries a great amount of truck traffic in and out of the San Joaquin Valley, and also serves as a link in a much-used route to Yosemite National Park. It is hardly ever lonely. The Hecker Pass Highway to Watsonville does not climb so high or serve so many purposes, but does offer some fine panoramas of coast hills.

Not many local roads supplement the major highways. County Road G8 pokes and dawdles through fine hill country betwen Gilroy and San Jose. Where G8 starts into the hills north of Gilroy, Watsonville Road eases northeast toward Morgan Hill through a pretty countryside.

Monterey County

In the mid-1970s Monterey County exploded into prominence as a vineyard district. Between 1963 and 1973, vineyard acreage shot from a few hundred to more than 30,000. Today, there are 33,773 acres planted to grapes.

Much of the early acreage is concentrated in the Salinas Valley between the towns of Gonzales and King City. Most of the more recent plantings stretch south

from King City almost to the San Luis Obispo County line. One tiny patch is across the west hills in Carmel Valley.

Except for a couple of spots, vines do not come close to U.S. Highway 101 between Gonzales and King City. The rich, thick soils at the bottom of the valley still hold the more traditional crops of this part of the world: strawberries, peppers, and all sorts of leafy vegetables (above all, lettuce). The vines are up on steeply photogenic alluvial fans at each side of this long, broad furrow in the Coast Ranges, more easily seen from local roads than the highway.

In spite of all its vineyards, Monterey remains relatively modest as a district for vinous touring. Only a handful of wineries have formal visitor policies, and they are widely scattered in a valley that is as much as 10 miles wide, and well more than 100 miles long. This curious state of affairs owes itself to the fact that vineyards in Monterey County originally were a response to urban pressure farther north in Santa Clara and Alameda counties, so great volumes of Monterey grapes belong to or are bought by Almaden, Paul Masson, Mirassou, Wente Bros., and other firms with long histories and most of their winemaking capacities in the more northerly counties.

The Wineries

The Monterey Vineyard and its colossal sibling, Taylor California Cellars, loom up right next to the freeway and to each other. Except for them, a trip to Monterey County wineries requires taking local roads for anything from a quick detour to a genuine pilgrimage.

Chalone Vineyard occupies a special niche in Monterey in every sense of the term. It is in an aerie of its own, and both vineyard and winery are the oldest in the county.

(Continued on next page)

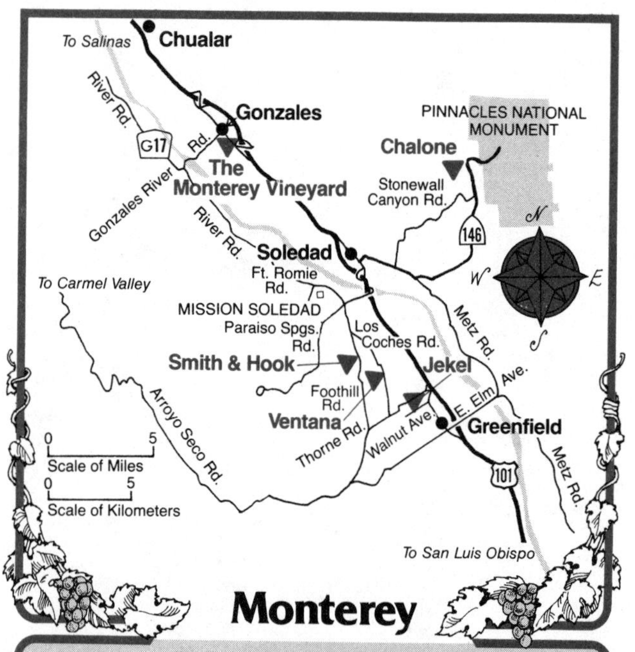

Chalone Vineyard. From Soledad, State 146 10 mi. E to Stonewall Canyon Rd., NW .3 mi. to winery road (PO Box 855, Soledad, CA 93960). M-F (except Sept-Oct) by appt. only. GT/Ta.

Durney Vineyard. Directions to winery with appt. (P.O. Box 222016, Carmel, CA 93922) Tel (408) 625-5433. By appt. only (Outside map area)

Jekel Vineyard. From U.S. 101, Walnut Ave. exit, W 1 mi. (40155 Walnut Ave., Greenfield, CA 93927) Tel (408) 674-5524. Th-M 10-5. GT/Ta.

Monterey Peninsula Winery. Jct. of State 68 and Canyon Del Rey (2999 Monterey-Salinas Hwy., Monterey, CA 93940) Tel (408) 372-4949. Daily 10-dusk. Ta. (Outside map area)

The Monterey Vineyard. From U.S. 101, Alta St. exit, N .5 mi. to winery (800 S. Alta St., Gonzales, CA 93926) Tel (408) 675-2481. Daily 10-5. GT/Ta.

Smith & Hook Winery. From U.S. 101, Arroyo Seco Rd. exit, W on Arroyo Seco Rd./Paraiso Springs Rd. to Foothill Rd., then N 1.8 mi. to winery at No. 37700 (P.O. Box 1010, Gonzales, CA 93926) Tel (408) 678-2132. By appt. only.

Ventana Vineyards. From U.S. 101, Arroyo Seco Rd. exit, W then S on Arroyo Seco Rd. to Las Coches Rd., then SE on Las Coches 3 mi. to winery (P.O. Box G, Soledad, CA 93950) Tel (408) 678-2306. By appt. only.

KEY: GT (guided tour); IT (informal tour); Ta (tasting).

. . . *Continued from page 107*

The vineyards roll across limestone slopes high above the east side of the Salinas Valley floor. The topmost rows almost reach the foot of a striking geologic curiosity, the Pinnacles. (An abstraction of the near-vertical basalt outcrop decorates Chalone's labels. Another representation of it is set in tile in the bottling room walls.) The next nearest vineyards are miles west and hundreds of feet lower.

The oldest Chalone vines go back to 1919, planted then by a man named Bill Silvear, who put his grapes on the site of a still-older vineyard. After Silvear died in 1957, the vines endured ups and downs until 1965, when more than 100 wine buffs formed Gavilan Vineyards, Inc., and bought the property.

First, the proprietors put the old vines right. Then, beginning in 1972, they began to expand their plantings. The original plot approached 30 acres. Current acreage is a bit more than 100.

Interim owners between Silvear and Gavilan Vineyards had built a tiny winery. The white-walled, oak-shaded original served through 1974. Now dwarfed by a new cellar upslope, it holds bottled wines.

Scaled to hold the expanded vineyard's full production, the handsome newer building cuts into its hillside so that crusher, press, and red wine fermenting tanks adjoin the high side. The upper floor holds cased goods, lab, and bottling room. Underneath are three cavelike galleries filled with fat, French barrels from Burgundy, used to ferment the whites and age all of the wines.

Getting up to see the place requires an appointment and considerable effort, especially when rains soften unpaved roads between Stonewall Canyon Road and the winery, but diligent admirers of California wine make the trip gladly.

The shy-yielding vineyards produce a predominantly Burgundian list of wines: Pinot Noir, Pinot Blanc, and Chardonnay, plus Chenin Blanc.

Durney Vineyard stands in the same sort of lonely splendor as Chalone, but on the other side of the county, on the seaward side of the Santa Lucia Mountains.

William and Dorothy Durney's vineyards and winery occupy one of a mere handful of reasonable slopes in some seriously steep hill country a few miles east of Carmel Valley Village.

For dedicated students of California wine, a visit well repays the effort of assembling the required group, arranging an appointment, and making the trek up Cachagua Road to a genuine estate winery. Founded in 1977, the cellar occupies a handsomely renovated hay barn and a newer second building. Crusher and press are just outside the rear wall of the original, and stainless steel fermentors fill most of the interior. The newer building is the oak aging cellar.

Vineyards run across a series of gentle hills and dips on the downhill, north side of the winery. The roster of wines made from their grapes includes Chenin Blanc, Johannisberg Riesling, Cabernet Sauvignon, and Gamay Beaujolais. Chardonnay is in the near future.

Jekel Vineyard lies just northwest of the main business district of Greenfield.

The winery is housed in a classically red, barn-shaped building, but this is mostly illusion. A steel building with eight inches of insulation sandwiched between its inner and outer skins, the Jekel winery is modern to the minute. A fermenting room full of stainless steel tanks is directly behind the front wall. Just outside stand a big crusher rigged to handle machine-harvested grapes and a horizontal basket press. Alongside the fermenting room is a cellarful of oak barrels. Adjacent to it is a sterile bottling room, and so it goes.

A comfortable tasting room is but a few paces from any of these elements in the compact winery, so tours are effortless. Because mechanical pickers work in Jekel-owned vineyards right around the winery, it is a particularly good place to see them in action during harvest.

Wines from those vines include Chardonnay, Pinot Blanc, Johannisberg Riesling, Pinot Noir, and Cabernet Sauvignon.

The owning Jekel brothers, William and August, planted the vineyards in 1972 and built the winery in 1978.

Monterey Peninsula Winery nestles into various corners of the mazelike bottom story of a fine stone building alongside State Highway 68 near the east end of Monterey airport's main runway.

A tasting room is at the front door, wherein a knowledgeable staff helps sort out the differences between wines from a wide range of districts. The grottolike room makes as romantic an impression as one might wish. Dim light and stone walls are supplemented by barrels that cannot so easily be fitted anywhere else in the winery's crowded space.

Because the cellars are so crowded and built on such uneven floors, the tasting room is as far as visitors may go, except on one day of each year, when long-standing customers of the winery are invited to an old-fashioned, barefoot grape stomp staged to help local charities.

Deryck Nuckton and Roy Thomas launched the winery in 1974 after some years as hobby winemakers. The focus is on reds, especially Cabernet Sauvignon and Zinfandel; however, the list ranges wider to include Chardonnay and other varietals.

The Monterey Vineyard winery building looms up alongside U.S. 101 on the south side of Gonzales. In a region with very few large buildings, it would be huge except for the dwarfing colossus of its running mate, Taylor California Cellars, located next door.

The architectural style at TMV is a remarkable mixture of early and late California. Arches, towers, and red tile roofs are the main distinguishing marks of the early corner containing the tasting room. Diagonal steel end walls and buttressed concrete side walls provide the modern counterpoint.

Visitors work their way through the whole building on a carefully engineered route that takes them past crushers and presses, into a large fermenting hall, through aging cellars full of large and small oak cooperage, and, finally, the tasting room.

Close attention to the gear will show any number of unusual details, most of which were designed by winemaker-president Dr. Richard Peterson. One example is a system of closed conveyors for moving pomace and lees (solid residues) out of the fermentors and into presses or filters. Another is a metal pallet for barrels in the small wood aging cellar. Most of these details bask in warm light from rows of towering stained-glass windows in the two side walls.

In the second-story tasting room are available vintage-dated Chardonnay, Chenin Blanc, Fumé Blanc, Gewürztraminer, Pinot Noir, and Zinfandel, plus generics. When nature agrees, there is a Botrytis Sauvignon Blanc.

The original scheme for The Monterey Vineyard, under another ownership, was a grand one. After the company was purchased by The Coca Cola Co., that notion was abandoned in favor of keeping The Monterey Vineyard a small, prestigious part of a winery complex dominated in size by Taylor California Cellars. Its huge facility, adjacent to the north, is not yet scheduled to open for touring.

Smith & Hook Winery, one of the newest wineries, looks to be one of the oldest. It gets its name and its fine old buildings from horse ranchers who were the previous occupants of a dramatic hillside site west of Soledad.

The winery occupies the old stable, a long, low, board-and-batten building painted pale blue and refitted to its new purpose in time for the vintage of 1979. Old tack hangers still line one wall of the laboratory, but all traces of horse have been cleared out of the stalls, now two barrel aging cellars at opposite ends of the building. Open-topped redwood fermentors out back look across vineyards divided by original corral fences judged too handsome to be removed when the property was planted to vines.

Smith & Hook makes only one wine, Cabernet Sauvignon, from grapes grown on the more tractable parts of a steep property cut in places by apprentice canyons.

McFarland Land Co. manages the property for a partnership of which the McFarland family is a part.

Ventana Vineyards opened its winery doors in 1978, using grapes from a substantial vineyard planted some years earlier by owners J. Douglas and Shirley Meador.

The winery building is a well weathered, gap-sided, leaky-roofed barn which stands as a considerable testimonial to a local climate so temperate it can be allowed to pass through unchanged. In striking contrast, the stainless steel fermentors, French oak barrels, and other equipment are modern to the minute. (The bottling line and bottled wines are pampered in a well insulated prefabricated metal building next to the old barn.)

The roster of wines is headed by Chardonnay, and includes White Riesling, Chenin Blanc, Pinot Noir, and Petite Sirah. When harvest-season weather encourages it, there also is a Botrytised Sauvignon Blanc. If the name, Ventana Vineyards, seems familiar from other labels, it is because the Meadors sell grapes to a number of wineries, some of which identify the source on their label.

More wineries. As Monterey gathers speed as a wine district, it has begun to acquire its share of tiny cellars. Carmel Bay Wine Co. is perhaps the tiniest. Owned by stockbroker Fred Crummey, it is located in a one-time airplane hangar at the Monterey Peninsula airport. Zampatti's Champagne Cellar, another very small firm, sells to a local trade from its location in Carmel Valley Village.

Other Than Wineries

In addition to its vineyards and wineries, the Salinas Valley has an engaging mixture of the works of God and of the works of man on behalf of God.

The pure article is Pinnacles National Monument, an imposing array of columnar basalt and caves left over from one of the more explosively formative moments of the local landscape. The monument is high in the

Gavilan Mountains, which form the east side of the valley.

Much the greater development—including the visitor center and campgrounds—is on the east side of the monument, accessible via State Highway 25 from Hollister or King City. But a fair sampler of the lunar landscape may be had by driving to the end of State Highway 146 from Soledad.

Incidentally, the fogs and breezes that cool the valley floor do not penetrate to the Pinnacles in summer, when it becomes downright hot.

Two of California's 21 Franciscan missions are in the vineyarded reaches of the Salinas Valley. They are at Soledad and west of King City.

Soledad Mission—Mission Nuestra Señora de la Soledad, to give it its full name—has one mostly melted adobe wall surviving from the original complex. (A chapel of newer style flanks it.) In its forlorn way the old wall tells the history of the region. Soledad was essentially a desolate, lonely failure. Very little, including grapes, would grow for the missionaries in this place of scarce rainfall. And the padres had no idea that the Salinas River was full of water because none showed on top.

West of U.S. 101, the mission is reached via Paraiso Springs and Fort Romie roads.

A far truer look at how life went in the mission days can be had at Mission San Antonio de Padua, located in a high valley west of the main Salinas River Valley, approximately at the latitude of King City. Jolon Road leads to it from U.S. 101 at King City or near San Miguel.

Within, the nearly complete building has restorations or replicas of a great deal of working mission gear. Included is the old wine cellar, a structure guaranteed to gladden the hearts of all who drink wine from newer, more manageable fermentors and aging cellars.

Picnickers in search of a table in the Salinas Valley have only one choice in the neighborhood of the wineries. A few tables flank the chapel grounds at Mission Soledad. A municipal park at King City is the next nearest opportunity.

Plotting a Route

Monterey County is long on its north-south axis and slender on its east-west one. More important, two lofty ranges of coast hills—the Gavilans on the east and the Santa Lucias on the west—trend northwest to southeast.

The coast side of the county has two-lane State Highway 1, and the Salinas River valley has freeway U.S. Highway 101 to transport people along the long axis. The trouble for wine fanciers is that the wineries string themselves out east and west at about midcounty. Local roads tying them together get into and over the hills as best they can, but expressways they are not.

State Highway 68 from Salinas to Monterey links coast and valley, and passes near two wineries in the process. It is a fairly level two-laner for most of the distance.

Arroyo Seco-Carmel Valley Road is the other, more southerly cross route. It is sometimes two lanes, sometimes a lane and a half, high, winding, and mostly glorious for scenery.

State Highway 46 (Stonewall Canyon Road) echoes on the east what Carmel Valley Road does on the west.

River Road, Foothill Boulevard, and Fort Romie Road are the most useful local roads for getting to several of the wineries. River Road also is an alternative to U.S. 101 for those who would rather look at the flowers.

San Benito County

San Benito County is a considerable curiosity within the larger curiosity of a region with its wineries in one place and its vineyards in another. Almaden Vineyards owns or operates nearly all of the county's 4,500 acres of grapes, has two large wineries there, but welcomes visitors only at a tasting room well north of the vineyards. Meanwhile, three small-to-tiny wineries with no more than 200 acres among them do accept visitors, though their size and remoteness limits the welcomes a great deal.

Except for Hollister and San Juan Bautista on its northern boundary, this is a sparsely settled county.

The Wineries

All of the visitable wineries in the county are in the Cienega district, along the west side of the San Benito

River valley, in the shadow of the Gavilan Mountains. Almaden's tasting room is near Hollister.

Almaden Vineyards welcomes visitors to taste and talk about its wide range of wines at a tasting room on Pacheco Pass Road. Though its wineries are not open for tours, a drive past one or both is worth the effort, for it will give some impression of the scope of the winery's vast acreage. The cellar on Cienega Road devotes itself primarily to reds; the one off State Highway 25 at Paicines produces both reds and whites.

Calera Wine Company is a dramatic place built on the still-born frame of a huge limekiln in the Gavilan Mountains. Its name (Spanish for limekiln) was chosen when the winery began operations in 1975.

In March, 1982, the seven levels of the working winery were completed on a steep site above Cienega Road. From every level the view is spectacular: down an oak-clad slope to a small pond, then out across a low range of hills, a higher one, and, finally, on clear days, to the distance-hazed Diablo Range.

There was a functional reason for choosing the property. Proprietor Josh Jensen's winery is arranged so that gravity will do much of the work once grapes arrive on the premises. They come in at the top, level with the crusher. Stainless steel fermentors are one step down, the press another. Then come holding tanks, barrel cellars, and, at the bottom, the bottling and case storage.

The wines are Pinot Noir from winery-owned grapes and from a vineyard in Santa Barbara, and Zinfandel from several sources.

Cygnet Cellars occupy a modest prefabricated metal building on an oak-studded, grassy site just off Cienega Road. Within, the small cellar is conservatively equipped with basket press, small crusher, and American oak barrels. An unusual note is 500-gallon fermentors made of fiberglass.

Cygnet is directed by two partners, James Johnson and C. Robert Lane. Their principal wine is a late-harvest Zinfandel. They also produce small lots of Cabernet Sauvignon.

Enz Vineyards is tucked away toward the top of Limekiln Canyon in a spot so peaceful and agreeable that it looks like the setting for a Disney movie, or maybe an episode from the nostalgic days of *The Waltons*.

This is almost an anachronism: a small winery run along the lines of a family farm. In the midst of the vineyards—the oldest blocks date back to 1895—are the family home, a white barn converted to an aging cellar, fermentors and crusher set on an open pad, and, well upslope, a metal building which serves as both barrel and bottle aging cellar.

All hands in the family turn to. Bob is the winemaker, Susan the business manager. The children work without titles.

The roster of wines is relatively short, focused on Pinot St. George and Zinfandel, and on a proprietary aperitif called Limekiln in tribute to a former use of the property.

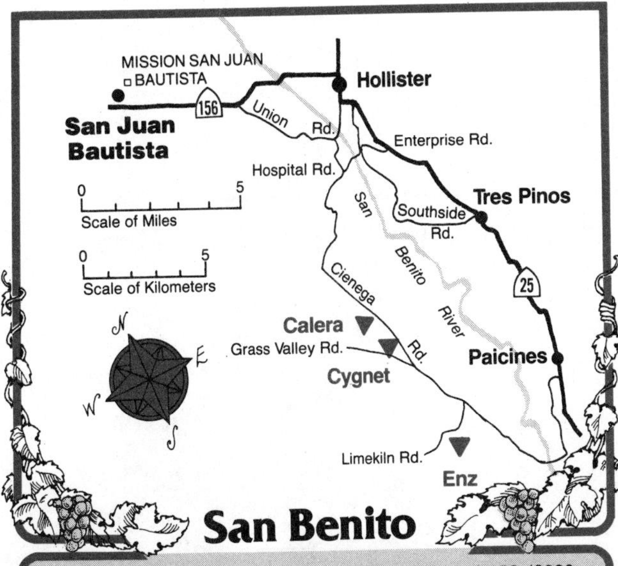

Almaden Vineyards. At junction of State 152 and 156 (8090 Pacheco Pass Rd., Hollister, CA 95023). Daily 10-6 April-October, 10-5 November-March. Ta. (Outside map area)

Calera Wine Company. From Hollister, State 25 (San Benito St./Nash Rd.) to Cienega Rd., S on Cienega 11 mi. to private lane (11300 Cienega Rd., Hollister, CA 95023) Tel (408) 637-9170. Sa 11 a.m. by appt. only. GT.

Cygnet Cellars. From Hollister, State 25 (San Benito St./Nash Rd.) to Cienega Rd., S on Cienega 11.2 mi. to winery drive (11736 Cienega Rd., Hollister, CA 95023) Tel (408) 733-4276. By appt. only.

Enz Vineyards. From Hollister, State 25 (San Benito St./Nash Rd.) to Cienega Rd., S on Cienega 16 mi. to Limekiln Rd., then W on Limekiln to winery (1781 Limekiln Rd., Hollister, CA 95023) Tel (408) 637-3956. Weekdays by appt. only.

KEY: GT (guided tour); IT (informal tour); Ta (tasting).

Other Than Wineries

The agreeable old mission village and stagecoach stop of San Juan Bautista is a gateway to the winery district, and the most notable change of pace from touring cellars. In addition to Mission San Juan Bautista and San Juan Bautista State Historic Park on the original plaza, the nearby main street is lined by an inviting miscellany of shops and restaurants.

Plotting a Route

Since all three of San Benito's visitable wineries flank Cienega Road, the only question is where to pick up that road.

From downtown Hollister, San Benito Street runs west to its end. A left turn onto Nash Road leads in two blocks to the head end of Cienega Road.

Those coming from the west via State Highway 156 can turn south short of Hollister at Union Road (marked by a round-backed hill planted to grape vines), which joins Cienega Road a shade less than 5 miles later.

Central Coast South

Handsome new territories for the vine

Mission Santa Barbara

Even by California's swift standards, the coastal valleys of San Luis Obispo and Santa Barbara counties have emerged as vineyard districts with unusual speed.

When wine began to boom in the early 1970s, San Luis Obispo was puttering along with a handful of wineries making small lots of rustic red from a few patches of zinfandel. Santa Barbara, virtually without grapes, had one local winery. In spring, 1982, San Luis Obispo County has 18 cellars and 4,150 acres in vineyard. In Santa Barbara County the counts were 14 cellars and 5,270 acres of vines. More wineries and more vineyards were in the works in both counties.

Though district boundaries still are blurred in many spots, the region has at least three distinct, tourable areas within it, and early promise of a fourth. One is the old wine area of San Luis Obispo County near Paso Robles, now much enlarged. The second, lying south of San Luis Obispo city, is called Edna Valley. Santa Barbara County has a fully tourable district centered on Solvang and called the Santa Ynez Valley. Adjacent on the north is the Santa Maria district, which has substantial vineyards but is just beginning to have wineries.

Before the vines came, these districts had much to appeal to visitors. San Luis Obispo is an agreeable university and mission town close to Hearst Castle and ocean beaches at Pismo and Avila. Solvang is a well-developed gateway to beautiful ranching country in the Santa Ynez Valley and the site of another of the old Franciscan missions.

Paso Robles

The northern part of San Luis Obispo County has a bit of vinous history in the forms of three old wineries near Templeton, and a great deal of new development both east and west of Paso Robles.

In addition to being a useful road, U.S. Highway 101 marks the dividing line between two very different terrains. To the west is steep, thickly wooded hill country. To the east, only a few oaks poke up out of gentle, grassy hills. Most of the vines are out with the grasses. Most of the cellars are up in the woodsy hills.

This is a bigger territory than it appears at first glance. A good many miles separate the wineries east of U.S. 101 from each other. On the west side, distances are less, but no road goes in a straight line for more than a few hundred feet at a time, and some are spurs.

The Wineries

As the combination of old and new promises, there is variety to be found among the several cellars in this sprawling district.

Caparone Vineyard is owned by two sorts of a specialist. Owner-winemaker M. David Caparone makes only Cabernet Sauvignon and Merlot and only from Central Coast grapes. But he also is an experimental grower of Nebbiolo and Brunello. As his young vineyard matures, varietal wines from these two Italian grapes will join the roster, though in very small lots.

Caparone's winery is a no-nonsense, chocolate brown, prefabricated metal building kept in impeccable order. Stainless steel fermentors fill one end. Racks of American oak barrels take up most of the rest of the space, save for an aisle given over to bottled wines, and a small lab. In harvest season the proprietor rolls a small crusher and horizontal basket press onto a concrete pad outside the main cellar door to get new wines started.

Caparone is not only the owner-winemaker, he is the whole staff, and a jazz trombonist on the side. Wine buffs can acquire the necessary appointment to visit whenever he does not have an out of town gig.

Estrella River Winery became a landmark on the road between Paso Robles and Shandon as soon as the building went up in 1977.

It could not be otherwise, given the size of the stucco-walled main cellar, its lofty observation tower, and its location at the high point of some 700 acres of rolling vineyard, the whole owned by a private corporation.

The observation tower looks north to the Gavilan Mountains and west to the Santa Lucia Mountains. Both views are striking. The foreground scene of rolling vineyards falls easily on the eye, too.

Below the open-air tower, a closed-in gallery gives close views of the crusher-stemmer and adjoining continuous press.

Inside the main walls an open platform looks first across a spacious fermenting room full of stainless steel tanks, then into an aging cellar full of oak upright tanks and barrels, the latter piled high on metal pallets. At the foot of stairs leading down from the platform, a large window looks into a modern, sterile bottling room.

There is a particular effort here to court visitors, beginning with the observation tower, continuing with a well-mapped tour route, and ending with a good-sized tasting room and gift shop.

Estrella River offers only varietal table wines from selected lots of its own grapes. The roster includes Chardonnay, Fumé Blanc, and Muscat Canelli among whites; Cabernet Sauvignon and a rarely bottled French Syrah among reds.

HMR (Hoffman Vineyards) wines can be tasted with little trouble. Having a look around the winery requires a fair journey into dramatic hill country west of Paso Robles.

The firm maintains its most accessible face one long block west of the State Highway 46-East exit from U.S. 101 at Paso Robles. Tasting and sales are housed there in a red building that looks as if it were designed by a man who wanted to invent the caboose, but was too late.

The winery itself is several winding miles west along an extension of the same road. For the serious student of wine, getting an appointment and trekking up Adelaida Road repays the effort. Hoffman Mountain Ranch (hence the HMR label) lives up to every part of its name. It is the property of Dr. Stanley Hoffman and his sons, winemaker Michael and vineyardist David. Its vineyards range in elevation from 1,100 up to 1,800 feet, sometimes on breathtaking slopes. Finally, the property yields other crops, and looks entirely the part of a traditional ranch, white rail fences and all.

The winery building fits its steep site. A broad roof has its off-center peak above the open-walled fermenting room and a see-through bottling room with a fine view of grassy hills. Parallel and downhill, the aging cellars hold upright oak tanks on the ridgepole side, and barrels on the downhill side, where the roof sweeps low toward the ground. The whole building is built of unpainted wood. It was completed in 1975.

The HMR label is used only for varietal table wines, including Chardonnay and Riesling among whites; Cabernet Sauvignon, Pinot Noir and Zinfandel among reds.

Las Tablas Winery is a recent start in the oldest active winery property in the Templeton district.

Late in 1976, John and Della Mertens bought the property, which had been the Rotta Winery since 1907, and before that the Adolph Siot Winery going all the way back to 1856.

The Mertens continue the patient process of upgrading outworn cooperage and equipment. While they renovate the winery proper, they are making essentially the same list of wines as their predecessor: dry, off-dry, and sweet Zinfandel, and a Muscat. The lone addition is a white table wine.

The tasting room is housed in a reshaped old redwood tank attached to the front of the white-faced main aging cellar. There is no tour of that cellar or a processing cellar located upslope in an ingeniously elevated and insulated Quonset-type building.

Martin Brothers Winery perches amid its own young vines near the top of an eye-pleasing slope west of Paso Robles.

The owners have wrought a remarkable rejuvenation of a faded one-time dairy ranch. Their main cellar occupies the old barn, a jaunty board-and-batten structure painted pale gray. Its natural wood-finished interior is trim enough to satisfy a sea captain. Three stainless steel fermentors march in a row beneath the roof peak. Racks of French oak barrels fill the two wings so tightly that the proprietors do not offer tours for lack of room.

The Martin family does, however, welcome visitors with appointments in an equally shipshape concrete

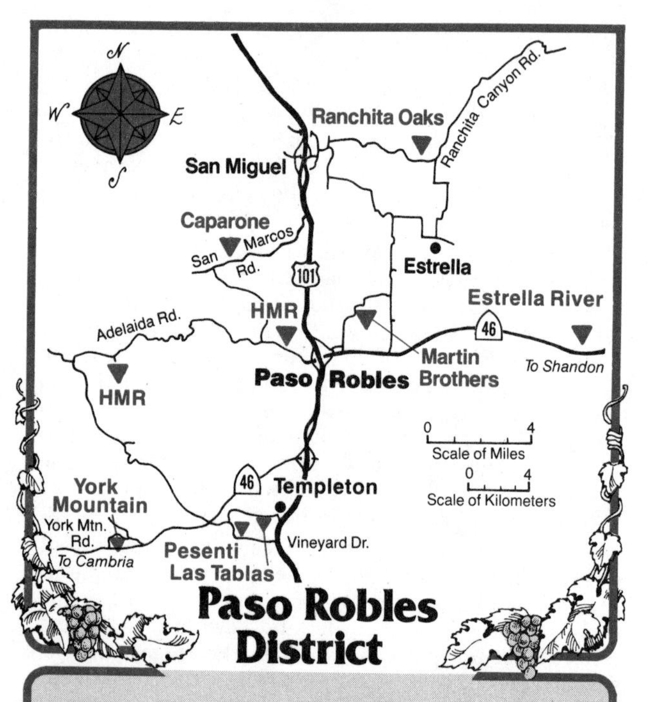

Caparone Vineyard. From U.S. 101, San Marcos Rd. exit, 3 mi. W (Rt. 1, Box 176-G, Paso Robles, CA 93446) Tel (805) 467-3827. By appt. only.

Estrella River Winery. From U.S. 101 at Paso Robles, 6.5 mi. E on State 46 (Shandon Star Rt., Paso Robles, CA 93446) Tel (805) 238-6300. Picnic. Daily 9–5. GT/Ta.

HMR (Hoffman Vineyards). Tasting room in Paso Robles 1 block W of State 46-East exit from U.S. 101; directions to winery available there (Adelaida Rd., Star Rt., Paso Robles, CA 93446) Tel (805) 238-4945. Tasting room daily 11–5. Winery tours by appt. only.

Las Tablas Winery. From U.S. 101, Las Tablas Rd. exit, 3 mi. W to winery drive (P.O. Box 697, Templeton, CA 93465) Tel (805) 434-1389. Daily 9–6. Ta.

Martin Brothers Winery. From U.S. 101, State 46-East exit, 1 mi. E to Buena Vista Rd., 1.1 mi. N (Rt. 2, Box 622, Paso Robles, CA 93446) Tel (805) 238-2520. By appt. only.

Pesenti Winery. From U.S. 101, Vineyard Dr. exit, W 2.5 mi. (Rt. 1, Box 169, Templeton, CA 93465) Tel (805) 434-1030. M–Sa 8–6, Su 10–6. Ta.

Ranchita Oaks Winery. From San Miguel, 7 mi. E on Cross Canyon Rd. to intersection with Ranchita Canyon Rd. (Estrella Rt., San Miguel, CA 93451) Tel (805) 467-3422. Sa–Su by appt. only IT/Ta.

York Mountain Winery. From U.S. 101, State 46-West exit, 9 mi. W, then N .4 mi. on York Mountain Rd. (Rt. 1, Box 191, Templeton, CA 93465) Tel (805) 238-3925. Daily 10–5. Ta.

Not on Map—Restricted Visitor Facilities

Mastantuono Winery. 101 3/4 Willow Creek Rd., Paso Robles, CA 93446. Tel (805) 238-1078.

Watson Vineyards. Adelaida Rd., Star Route, Paso Robles, CA 93446. Tel (805) 238-6091.

Key: GT (guided tour); IT (informal tour); Ta (tasting).

and concrete-block building once the milking barn, now an office and storage for bottled wines.

The Martins make small lots of four wines: Sauvignon Blanc, Chenin Blanc, Chardonnay, and Zinfandel. The winery crushed its first grapes in 1981, and planted its first vines the same year.

Pesenti Winery finally has escaped the title of the youngest winery in Templeton. Founder Frank Pesenti opened the doors in 1934 as a home for grapes from vineyards he had planted earlier, and his cellar stayed the youngest kid on the block until Mastantuono (see next page) came along in 1978.

The winery reached its present size in 1947, and continues almost unchanged in the second and third generation hands of its founding family. Tours are by appointment only because the white-walled cellars and their rows of venerable redwood and oak tanks do not lend themselves to casual wandering. However, the spacious tasting room is open to all comers.

The Pesenti label ranges from varietal table wines through several dessert types.

Ranchita Oaks Winery and vineyards occupy part of a long sideslope directly above a remote stretch of Ranchita Canyon Road, well east of the old mission village of San Miguel.

The first vintage for Ranchita Oaks was 1979. Owner Ron Bergstrom makes only Cabernet Sauvignon, Petite Sirah (the particular specialty), and Zinfandel from his vines, which surround a winery housed in a neatly maintained prefabricated metal building. Like most other cellars of its small size, this one provides a coherent picture of winemaking from start to finish.

Not incidentally, the steep dirt road leading up to the cellars becomes impassable after heavy rains in the winter.

York Mountain Winery is the westernmost cellar around Templeton, and several scores of feet higher in the hills than its neighbors.

Andrew York established the winery in 1882 to use surplus grapes from his own vineyard. The property went two more generations in York family hands, until 1970, when a veteran winemaker named Max Goldman bought it.

Goldman's original intention was to turn the onetime Zinfandel winery into a *methode champenoise* sparkling wine house. The first cuvées went down from the vintage of 1981, a tribute to patient endurance. Meanwhile, Zinfandel and other table wines have been, and continue to be, the staples. The founder and his family have replanted the first 10 acres of York's old vineyard, and are making small lots of Chardonnay, Pinot Noir, and Cabernet Sauvignon from them. The Goldmans also buy grapes in the district to round out the line.

The winery, wearing a properly aged air, is not big enough to require a tour. Its racks of old redwood tanks and oak barrels can be seen from the entry door. The brick-walled tasting room makes a comfortable stop in any season with its big fireplace and miscellaneous memorabilia of earlier days (the most surprising of which is an ancient motorcycle).

More wineries. Several more wineries are just getting into stride in the district.

Eberle Winery began construction on its permanent cellars on Union Road east of Paso Robles during 1982. W. Gary Eberle, one of the founders of Estrella River, is the winemaker and proprietor. Eberle has been making wine for his label in leased space since 1979.

Farview Farms is also an established label belonging to the proprietors of a vineyard of the same name. Construction of a winery on the property at the intersection of State 46-West and Bubble Road is pending. Meanwhile, the wine is being made in leased space.

Watson Vineyards, on Adelaida Road west of Paso Robles, produced a tiny first vintage of Johannisberg Riesling in 1981. Chardonnay and Pinot Noir are to join the roster in 1982. The winery is not open for tours, tasting, or sales at this time.

A small, rustic cellar specializing in Zinfandel is Mastantuono, owned by Pat Mastan, who made his first wine in 1978. In hilly country west of Templeton, the property may be visited only by appointment. Three other tiny, rustic wineries also have begun operations. El Paso de Robles Winery and Old Casteel Vineyards are near neighbors of Mastantuono, west of Templeton. Tobias Winery is southwest of Paso Robles.

Other Than Wineries

This is not an easy part of the world for picnickers, or for families needing to offer small children a respite from tasting rooms and winery tours.

A county picnic park is on the east side of U.S. 101 at Templeton. The big recreational park in the region is Nacimiento Reservoir, several miles into the hills west of Paso Robles.

Accommodations and restaurants are plentiful at Paso Robles. A listing may be obtained from the Paso Robles Chamber of Commerce, P.O. Box 457, Paso Robles, CA 93446.

Plotting a Route

Major routes in the region are simplicity itself; U.S. Highway 101 traverses it north and south. State Highway 46 crosses the territory east to west, with a slight jog. However, the roads to many of the wineries are narrow, ill-marked, and winding. Several do not connect to other roads, requiring at least some back-tracking. The map on page 114 shows all of the useful ones.

Edna Valley

As wine districts go, Edna Valley blossomed overnight. It remains small in vineyard acreage, but has three wineries nestled into superbly scenic coastal hill country a few miles south of the city of San Luis Obispo.

Chamisal Vineyard, the smallest winery of the three, occupies a tall stucco box of a building at one end of a long, rolling vineyard. The property of the Norman Goss family, Chamisal made its first wines in 1981, though the vines go back several years more than that.

As in the case of many small wineries, the lack of size makes a visit instructive. The crusher and an old-fashioned basket press sit on a small pad between the winery and a mobile home. Inside, stainless steel fermentors and French oak barrels share a single room, so the whole process can be seen step by step.

These are specialists. The vineyards are planted entirely to Chardonnay and Cabernet Sauvignon. Selected lots of grapes from the family vineyards make the only two wines regularly on the list. From time to time the owners buy grapes and make a bit of Sauvignon Blanc.

Edna Valley Vineyard is an unusual joint venture by the owners of the local Paragon Vineyards on one hand and the Monterey County winery called Chalone Vineyards on the other.

The Chalone influence is easily visible to anyone who has visited there. The stucco-covered cellars at Edna Valley are architectural and technical copies of those at Chalone. The state-of-the-art upper level has inside it a laboratory, modern bottling line, and space to store bottled wines. Outside at the rear are the crusher, press, and red wine fermentors. In the ultra-traditional underground cellars are three purposefully damp galleries filled with French oak barrels. Here the white wines ferment and both white and reds age in conditions imitating those in the great underground cellars at Beaune, in France's Burgundy.

As the Burgundian connection promises, the wines are Chardonnay and Pinot Noir, the latter made both as a red and a *vin gris* (a pale wine somewhere between blanc de noir and rosé for color, and made dry). An appointment to visit will reward the studious with both tastes of the wines and explanations of the techniques behind them.

Lawrence Winery is by far the biggest and showiest of the three pioneers located in Edna Valley. A substantial, Spanish colonial-style main building holds the offices, a big tasting room, a small collection of barrels, and the fermenting and bottling departments. Prefabricated metal buildings to the rear hold the aging wines in bulk and bottle.

There is no tour here because none is needed. The tasting room has a window wall looking into the main cellar. Visitors can see the gear used in winemaking without taking more than a few steps. Hosts gladly explain what is in view.

The long roster of Lawrence wines includes a Gewürztraminer Rosé and Chardonnay Nouveau along with more usual varietal types.

Other Than Wineries

Edna Valley proper is mostly ranches. It has no parks or other diversions aside from its wineries. However, it is at the center of an attractive vacation area. The San Luis Obispo mission is only a few miles north. Also within easy distance are Hearst Castle at San Simeon, and ocean parks at Avila and Pismo beaches.

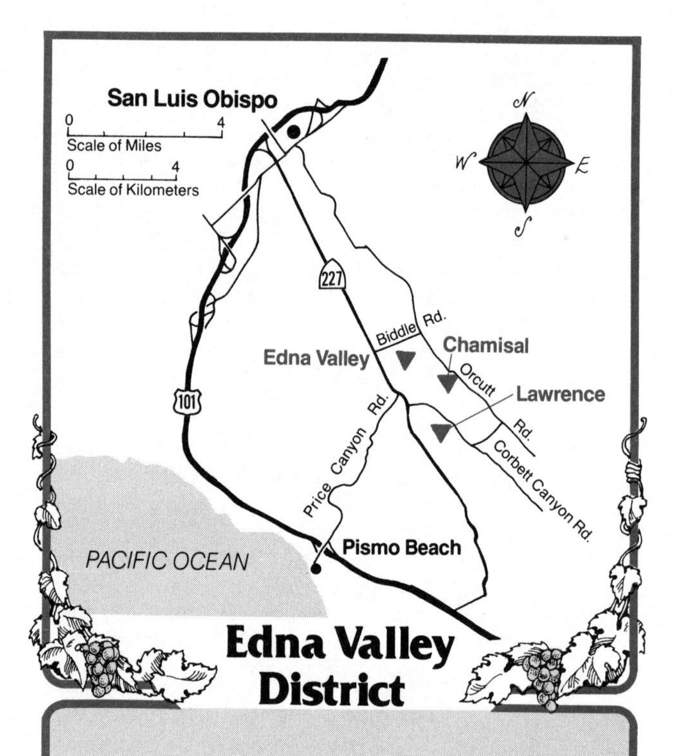

Chamisal Vineyard. From State 227, E on Biddle Rd. to Orcutt Rd., then 2 mi. SE (Rt. 3, Box 264-M, San Luis Obispo, Ca 93406) Tel (805) 544-3576. M–F by appt. only.

Edna Valley Vineyard. From State 227, .3 mi. E on Biddle Rd. (Rt. 3, Box 255, San Luis Obispo, CA 93406) Tel (805) 544-9594. By appt. only. GT/Ta.

Lawrence Winery. On Corbett Canyon Rd. 1.3 mi. S of its intersection with State 227 (P.O. Box 1151, San Luis Obispo, CA 93406) Tel (805) 544-5800. M–Sa 10–4, Su 12–4. Ta.

Key: GT (guided tour); IT (informal tour); Ta (tasting).

Plotting a Route

State Highway 227 runs east of U.S. Highway 101, from San Luis Obispo on the north to Arroyo Grande on the south. (At the San Luis Obispo end, it crosses Higuera, the main street, under the name of Broad Street.)

The wineries are on a neat rectangle east of State 227. From the north, it is best to follow State 227 about two miles south of the San Luis Obispo Airport to Biddle Ranch Road. From there, the sequence of Biddle Ranch Road, Orcutt Road, Tiffany Ranch Road, and Corbett Canyon Road passes each of the wineries, ending up on State 227 again. This avoids making an uphill left turn from State 227 into Corbett Canyon Road in the middle of a blind curve. Drivers coming from the south can take the loop in either direction with equal safety.

Santa Barbara County

Having started well behind San Luis Obispo in numbers of wineries and acres of vines, Santa Barbara shot to the forefront on both counts during the decade from 1972 to 1982.

The focal point, well-known to vacationers in this part of the world, is the polyglot town of Solvang, where a thick layer of Danish all but hides old traces of Franciscan missionary times and a more recent era of cowboys.

Vineyards and wineries alike hide in beautiful, rolling hill country on either side of U.S. Highway 101 from Buellton north to Santa Maria, but are not so far off the freeway as to make visiting difficult. Quite the opposite, a well-articulated web of secondary roads allows easy access to the wineries at a very small price in extra miles.

In time, this sprawling area is likely to become two distinct wine districts called Santa Ynez Valley and Santa Maria Valley. For now, the two blend rather easily into one district for touring.

The Wineries

All but one of the county's cellars have been founded since 1970, most since 1978. If history lacks, variety does not, and more is in the planning stage.

Ballard Canyon Winery sits in the shade of a fine old oak tree part way up a long, gentle, vine-clad slope.

A small winery, it has stainless steel fermentors, office, and lab in a prefabricated metal building, and French oak barrels in a wood-frame lean-to attached to the rear. Tours are informal, and can be quick. Tasting, on the other hand, tends to be leisurely. In fair weather, the proprietors prefer to present their wines on a deck beneath the same oak that shades the winery buildings.

The owning Gene Hallock family made the first Ballard Canyon wines in 1978. The roster includes regular and Botrytised Johannisberg Riesling, Chardonnay, and partridge eye and red Cabernet Sauvignons.

Brander Winery is the ultimate specialist in the region. It offers only estate wines from grapes native to the Bordeaux region of France. Sauvignon Blanc dominates a small production. There are tiny lots of Cabernet Sauvignon, Cabernet Franc, and Merlot.

Owner-winemaker C. Frederic Brander has been making wine in the area since 1976. His own cellar dates from 1981.

The brown-painted winery, visible from State Highway 154 but approachable only via Refugio Road, is an ingenious adaptation of a pole barn. Tall, steep-roofed, it has a small open-walled crushing and fermenting area at one end. The aging cellar full of French oak barrels and bottled wines uses a far larger proportion of the space, in part because Brander is a proponent of starting fermentations in tanks, then moving quickly to barrels for the major part of that process. His reasons for doing so take up a fair part of the tour.

J. Carey Cellars looks like one of the oldest wineries in the region because it is housed in a 50-year-old barn painted exactly the correct shade of red. In fact, the first winemaking was in 1978.

The much-refurbished original barn holds stainless steel fermentors and oak upright tanks. An expansion at the rear holds French oak barrels for final aging of the wines. Tasting goes on in an informal corner of the fermentation cellar directly inside the door. Picnic tables are around at the other end of the building, next to the crushing area.

The winery and adjoining vineyard are owned by a trio of Dr. J.s, all physicians, not NBA forwards. Dr. James Carey, Sr., and his sons, Dr. James, Jr. and Dr. Joseph, make Gewürztraminer, Chardonnay, and Cabernet Sauvignon (partridge eye and red) from their own vineyard, and buy grapes for their Sauvignon Blanc.

Firestone Vineyard's winery building soars dramatically above the southernmost ridgeline of the mesa called Zaca. Rooflines set at varying angles to each other give the place a bold, sculptured quality. Beneath those roofs the architectural drama continues. The highest peak gives the fermenting room an almost cathedral atmosphere, while the lowest eave swoops so close to earth that barrels can be stacked only two high along the downhill wall, and then only because the floor drops a level to make a separate gallery.

Well-trained tour guides explain winemaking from beginning to end, starting with vineyards that surround the cellars, and ending with tastes in a wood-walled room in which an upper set of windows looks out to nearby hills while a lower set gives views into the cool darkness of a wood-aging cellar.

Founded in 1974, Firestone is the largest winery in the Santa Ynez Valley and likely to remain so for some time to come. A partnership of the Leonard Firestone family and Suntory, the Japanese distillers and winemakers, the firm offers estate-grown varietal wines, including Chardonnay, Gewürztraminer, Sauvignon Blanc, Cabernet Sauvignon, and Merlot.

Los Viñeros, new in 1981, occupies a large box of a building in an industrial area on the western edge of Santa Maria. The vineyardists who own the winery took the sensible, Swiss approach of putting their building where nothing would grow.

Because the staff is small, visitors are not discouraged from starting and ending in the tasting room, in an adobe addition at the front of the main cellar building. The persistent can earn a look at a well-organized winery. The crusher and press sit beneath an overhanging roof at the rear. Stainless steel fermenting and storage tanks and French oak barrels share the main cellar with a bottling line and wines aging in bottle.

The Los Viñeros roster includes Chenin Blanc, Chardonnay, Sauvignon Blanc, and whites from pinot noir and cabernet sauvignon grapes. Reds are to join the list in 1983.

Rancho Sisquoc hides away about as well as a winery can. It is deep in the Sisquoc River canyon, two miles beyond public roads, and about halfway between the town of Los Olivos and the village of Sisquoc.

Most California vineyard properties are known as ranches. This one puts the rest in the shade, not because of its 200 acres of vines, but because of the other 38,000 acres, most of it grazing land for cattle.

The winery building is quietly unobtrusive, hidden among older work buildings and dwellings at ranch headquarters, as the vines are hidden in rangeland. Still, even as a miniature cog in a giant wheel, the cellars are pleasing to visit.

The first crusher is nailed to one wall of the cozy tasting room. It is a baseball bat, too short and light to do the work now, but not by much.

Behind the tasting room, with its front wall of local river rock, lies the small barrel-aging cellar. Fermentors, presses, and other working gear are in the other wing of an L-shaped, board-and-batten building.

Behind the winery is a pleasant picnic lawn. All around it, the ranchhouse grounds come close to being an unofficial arboretum, with oaks, peppers, palms, peaches, avocados, pecans, and pines growing in harmonious confusion.

Although the ranch goes back beyond the turn of the century, the first major block of vines dates only from 1970. Owner James Flood of San Francisco bonded the winery just in time for the harvest of 1977.

The list of wines includes Franken Riesling, Johannisberg Riesling, and Cabernet Sauvignon.

Ross Keller, like several other relatively new wineries, occupies three bays in one of those rent-to-fit warehouses that have sprung up throughout the state during the past decade. Howard and Jacqueline Tanner have equipped their Buellton winery with stainless steel fermentors and a mixture of French and American oak barrels to make a surprisingly long list of generic and varietal table wines including White Riesling, Chardonnay, a rose of Cabernet Sauvignon, and a Pinot Noir Blanc.

Once out of the tasting room and into the cellar, the tour can be taken at a standstill.

Not incidentally, the name translates from German as Horse Cellar, and is a nod to the proprietors' principal occupation, racing harness horses.

Santa Barbara Winery occupies a one-time warehouse near the waterfront of the city for which it is named.

It is the old-timer in the county. Proprietor Pierre LaFond in 1962 bonded his first cellar. The business grew enough to require a move to the present premises in 1965. Continued growth has required several expansions since then.

Though the cellars are well apart from the others in the county, the vineyards are not. LaFond grows grapes for his varietal table wines along the lower reaches of the Santa Ynez River west of Buellton. The varieties include Chardonnay and Chenin Blanc among whites, Cabernet Sauvignon and Zinfandel among reds. The whole list of varietals plus some jug generics may be tasted at the winery.

Santa Ynez Valley Winery is one of a considerable number of new California cellars housed in old dairy

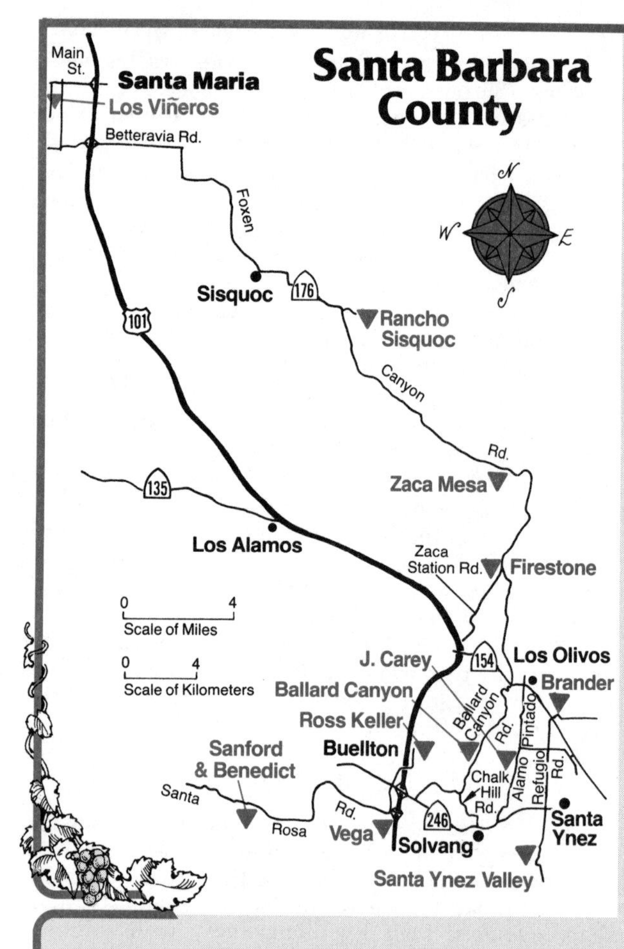

J. Carey Cellars. From Solvang, 1 mi. E on State 246 to Alamo Pintado Rd., N 3 mi. (1711 Alamo Pintado Rd., Solvang, CA 93463) Tel (805) 688-8554. Picnic. Tu-Su 10-4. IT/Ta.

Firestone Vineyard. From U.S. 101 N of Buellton, 2 mi. E on Zaca Station Rd. (P.O. Box 244, Los Olivos, CA 93441) Tel (805) 688-3940. M-Sa 10-4. GT/Ta.

Los Viñeros. From U.S. 101, Main St. exit, 2 mi. W to Hansen Way, S 1 block to 618 (P.O. Box 334, Santa Maria, CA 93454) Tel (805) 928-5917. M-F 12-5 or by appt. IT/Ta.

Rancho Sisquoc. From U.S. 101 N of Buellton, 2 mi. E on Zaca Station Rd. to Foxen Canyon Rd., N 18 mi. to winery drive, then E 2 mi. (Rt. 1, Box 147, Santa Maria, CA 93454) Tel (805) 937-3616. M-Sa 10-4. GT/Ta by appt.

Ross Keller. At Buellton, on E frontage road to U.S. 101 (900 McMurray Rd., Buellton, CA 93427) Tel (805) 733-4324. Daily 11-4. GT/Ta.

Sanford & Benedict. 9 mi. W of Buellton on Santa Rosa Rd. (Santa Rosa Rd., Lompoc, CA 93463) Tel (805) 688-8314. Sa 10-4 by appt. only. GT/Ta.

Santa Ynez Valley Winery. From Solvang, E 2 mi. on State 246 to Refugio Rd., S 1 mi. to winery drive (365 Refugio Rd., Santa Ynez, CA 93460) Tel (805) 688-8381. Sa-Su 10-4 or by appt. GT/Ta.

Vega Vineyards. From downtown Buellton, .7 mi. S on Santa Rosa Rd. (9496 Santa Rosa Rd., Buellton, CA 93427) Tel (805) 688-2415. Fri-Su 11-4 or by appt. GT/Ta.

Zaca Mesa Winery. From U.S. 101 N of Buellton, E 9 mi. on Zaca Station/Foxen Canyon rds. (P.O. Box 224, Los Olivos, CA 93441) Tel (805) 688-3310. Picnic. Daily 10-4. GT/Ta.

Ballard Canyon Winery. From downtown Solvang, 2.8 mi. N on Atterdag Rd./Chalk Hill Rd./Ballard Canyon Rd. (1825 Ballard Canyon Rd., Solvang, CA 93463) Tel (805) 688-7585. By appt. only. GT/Ta.

Brander Winery. From U.S. 101 N of Buellton, 3 mi. E on State 154 to Roblar Ave./Refugio Rd. intersection, NW .3 mi. on Refugio Rd. (P.O. Box 92, Los Olivos, CA 93441) Tel (805) 688-2455. By appt. only. IT/Ta.

Outside Map Area

Santa Barbara Winery. From U.S. 101, 1 block W on Anacapa St. (202 Anacapa St., Santa Barbara, CA 93101) Tel (805) 962-3812. Daily 10-5. Ta.

Key: GT (guided tour); IT (informal tour); Ta (tasting).

buildings. This bespeaks a trend toward more small wineries and fewer small dairies, and saves the pouring of a great many new concrete floors. In this case it also causes a good deal of extra walking for winemakers and visitors.

Inside the plain walls at Santa Ynez, bottled wines are stored at one level in two separate rooms; wines aging in oak barrels and stainless steel tanks are at three other levels in two rooms; and the stainless steel fermentors are outdoors on still another level. If the floor plan is a bit unorthodox, the equipment is not, and tours are as instructive here as in other small wineries where the parts come in logical sequence.

Santa Ynez Valley Winery was founded in 1976 by a trio of partners, all residents of the region. Their vineyards—most of them at the winery, some a few miles away at Los Olivos—supply the grapes for a list including Chardonnay, White Riesling, Sauvignon Blanc, and Merlot. These wines and the rest of the list may be sampled in a spacious tasting room in a front corner of the building, dead-level with the bottled wines.

The property, not incidentally, once held the forerunner of St. Mary's College, hence the signpost reading "Old College Ranch" at the head of the entry drive.

Vega Vineyards has its cellars in a classic red barn so close to U.S. 101 south of Buellton that drivers on the freeway sometimes can catch a fleeting whiff of newly fermenting wine during the harvest season.

The old barn and an 1853 adobe house next to it gives the property an enduring air, but the winery is a recent development. Owners Bill and Jeri Mosby made their first wines on these premises in 1979, having started the business a year earlier in leased space.

Visitors can have an informal look around a thoughtfully designed cellar as a prelude to tasting. The Mosbys used a little slope at the rear of the building to great mechanical advantage. Their bin dump sits directly above the grape hopper, which in turn looks down to the crusher. Similarly, the press sits over a conveyor that hauls pomace to a still lower spot. Inside, the winery is mostly stainless steel tanks because the primary production is Gewürztraminer and White Riesling. A small collection of oak between fermentors and cased goods is for Pinot Noir. All three wines are from winery-owned vineyards nearby.

Zaca Mesa Winery offers a complete look at a well-designed, flawlessly equipped cellar of the sort that draws bits and pieces from everywhere and still manages to look as native as the oak trees growing on grassy hills all around it.

Wine follows a wayward, international course through a prim, cedar-sided refinement of a classic California barn. It begins at the rear in a new, French-designed crusher that looks like cockle shells whirling around inside a metal sleeve, advances to an equally modern German press, or to American stainless steel fermentors located where the building's waist pinches in. It ages in French oak barrels or American oak tanks toward the front of the building before heading to the rear again for bottling on a German-made line, sometimes in Canadian glass. Visitors follow the same route, though more quickly.

The propriety of Marshall Ream, a retired oil executive, Zaca Mesa nestles into a small hollow along the Foxen Canyon Road side of the mesa from which it takes its Spanish name.

Weathered wood on some inside walls reveals a 1981 expansion of the original cellar of 1978. One of the added parts is a spacious, high-ceilinged tasting hall in the rear wing. Available in it are Chardonnay, Johannisberg Riesling, Cabernet Sauvignon, Pinot Noir, and other varietals from winery-affiliated vineyards up on top of the mesa.

Tree-shaded picnic tables are just outside the tasting room and up on a gentle slope behind the winery.

More wineries. Santa Barbara County, like neighboring San Luis Obispo, is developing rapidly. Some of its existing wineries are changing course. New ones continue to appear.

Sanford & Benedict made its first wines in 1976. Now under the direction of Michael Benedict, the winery located on Santa Rosa Road between Buellton and Lompoc continues with its original specialties, Chardonnay and Pinot Noir, plus Johannisberg Riesling and Cabernet Sauvignon, all from the vineyards surrounding it. Because of a small staff and the remote location, visitors must have appointments. The winery asks, to use its words, "serious inquiries only."

Sanford Winery made its first wines in leased space in 1981, and planned to begin construction of its own cellars in the Santa Ynez Valley early in 1982. Owner Richard Sanford intends to limit his list of wines to Chardonnay, Sauvignon Blanc, and Pinot Noir.

La Zaca appears as a Santa Barbara County label. It is a vineyard whose proprietor has his wines made in leased space, then returned to their home ranch for bottle aging and sale. There are no visitor facilities.

The California Central Coast Wine Growers Association maintains an up-to-date list of visitable wineries in Santa Barbara and San Luis Obispo counties. Copies may be ordered from the association, 1000 E. Betteravia Road, Santa Maria, CA 93456. There is a modest charge.

Other Than Wineries

This region, though new as a wine district, has been a major destination for tourists for years. Solvang alone draws as many as 5 million visitors annually with its Danish flavors. Pea Soup Andersen's at Buellton seems to get almost as many.

The *Sunset Travel Guide to Southern California* provides detailed information on this town, the missions of Santa Ynez and La Purisima, and ocean shore parks and resorts at Santa Barbara and Gaviota.

For picnickers, the closest parks to wineries are Santa Rosa County Park, on Santa Rosa Road west of Buellton, and Los Alamos County Park, on the west outskirts of Los Alamos town. The biggest, most versatile park in the region is some miles east of Santa Ynez via State Highway 154. It is Lake Cachuma County Park, which has swimming and boating as well as picnic grounds.

Accommodations and restaurants are abundant in and around Solvang, Buellton, and Santa Maria. For lists, write to the Solvang Chamber of Commerce, P.O. Box 465, Solvang, CA 93463, or the Santa Maria Chamber of Commerce, P.O. Box 277, Santa Maria, CA 93456.

Plotting a Route

U.S. Highway 101 neatly divides the vineyarded reaches of northern Santa Barbara County into western and eastern sectors. It is a freeway for the whole of its run through the winemaking district, though rolling hill country keeps it from being monotonously straight and out of touch with the countryside.

When speed is required, the freeway can be used in getting from one winery to another. However, local roads east of the freeway are bucolic, but straight and uncrowded enough to add very little time and very few miles to a tour, while improving the scenery and the feeling of being in the country.

As the map on page 118 shows, most of the county's wineries can be reached on a single loop with its ends at Buellton and Santa Maria.

From Santa Ynez, Refugio Road connects with State Highway 154 at Los Olivos; from Los Olivos, Foxen Canyon Road rambles north to a junction with State Highway 176. The latter rejoins U.S. 101 at Santa Maria. Getting to all of the wineries on or east of U.S. 101 involves a minimum of backtracking. Only two cellars are any distance west of the freeway.

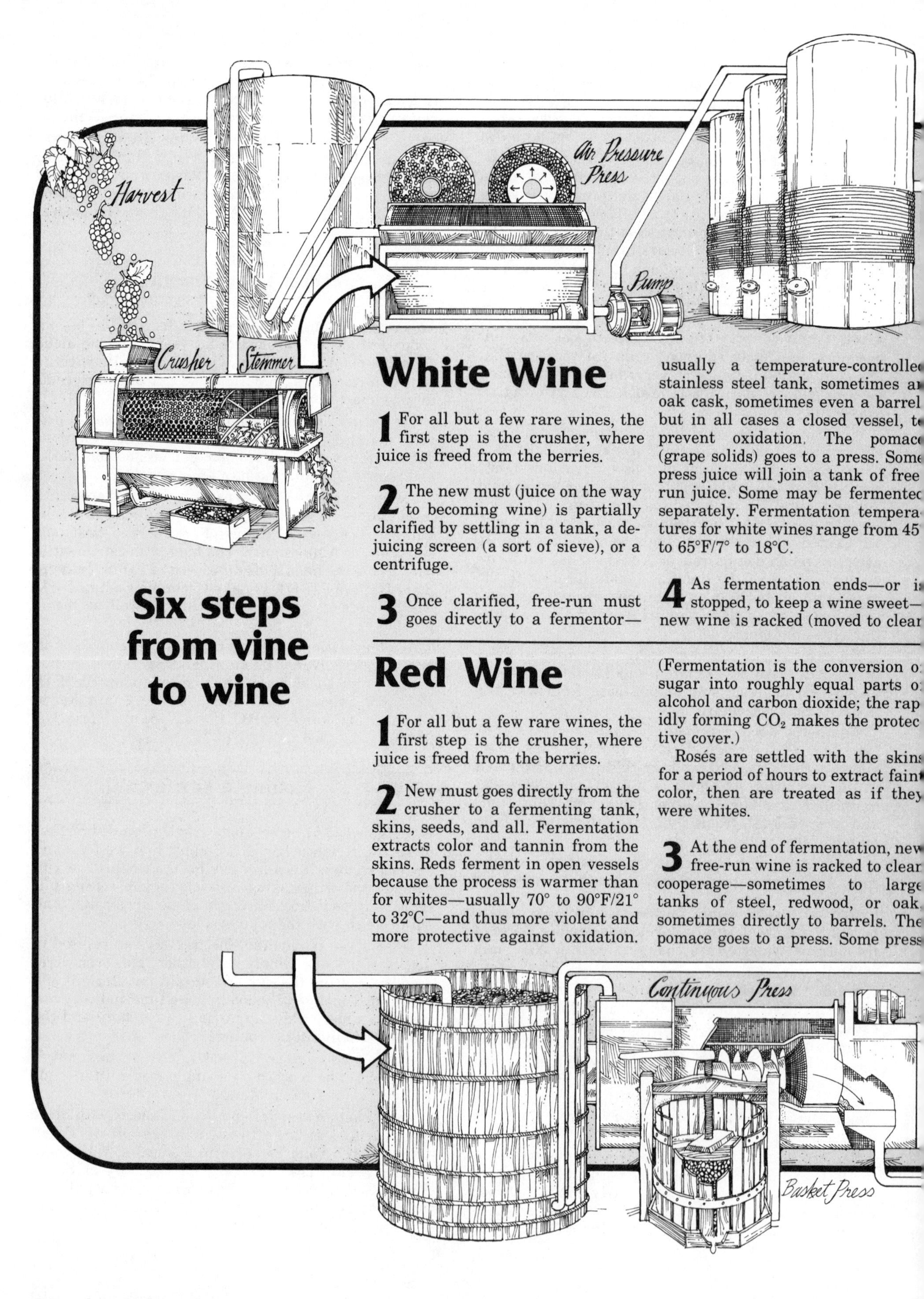

Six steps from vine to wine

White Wine

1 For all but a few rare wines, the first step is the crusher, where juice is freed from the berries.

2 The new must (juice on the way to becoming wine) is partially clarified by settling in a tank, a dejuicing screen (a sort of sieve), or a centrifuge.

3 Once clarified, free-run must goes directly to a fermentor—usually a temperature-controlle stainless steel tank, sometimes a oak cask, sometimes even a barrel but in all cases a closed vessel, t prevent oxidation. The pomac (grape solids) goes to a press. Som press juice will join a tank of free run juice. Some may be fermente separately. Fermentation tempera tures for white wines range from 45 to 65°F/7° to 18°C.

4 As fermentation ends—or i stopped, to keep a wine sweet— new wine is racked (moved to clea

Red Wine

1 For all but a few rare wines, the first step is the crusher, where juice is freed from the berries.

2 New must goes directly from the crusher to a fermenting tank, skins, seeds, and all. Fermentation extracts color and tannin from the skins. Reds ferment in open vessels because the process is warmer than for whites—usually 70° to 90°F/21° to 32°C—and thus more violent and more protective against oxidation. (Fermentation is the conversion o sugar into roughly equal parts o alcohol and carbon dioxide; the rap idly forming CO_2 makes the protec tive cover.)

Rosés are settled with the skin for a period of hours to extract fain color, then are treated as if the were whites.

3 At the end of fermentation, ne free-run wine is racked to clea cooperage—sometimes to larg tanks of steel, redwood, or oak sometimes directly to barrels. Th pomace goes to a press. Some pres

ɔoperage) to separate it from the
es (spent yeasts and grape solids).
ne wine may or may not be filtered
centrifuged during racking.

5 As wine ages and clarifies, it may be racked again. Clarify-
g is done by time and gravity, or
a fining agent such as a fine clay
lled "bentonite." Fresh white
ines—those meant to be drunk in
eir youth—may age entirely in
ainless steel or other neutral coop-
age. Wine meant for keeping in
ottle often ages in small oak.

Champagnes and other sparkling wines require an extra process (see page 83). Sherries also demand an extra process (see page 139).

6 When any wine is judged ready, it is bottled, often with a light, or polish, filtration just as it goes to the bottling line. Sweet whites may be given a sterile filtration in a millipore filter, so yeasts cannot start a refermentation in the bottle.

---

ine may be added to free-run wine
om the same fermentation. Some
ill be kept for blending with other
ften weaker) wines. Some wines
re filtered at this point.

4 Most red wines are racked twice or more to help clarify them.
hey also may be fined with benton-
e or albumen (egg white) to speed
arification.

5 Some wineries rack their wine more than once in order to fla-
or it with more than one kind of
ood—or to limit its exposure to

wood. Woods, like grapes, have regional and varietal characteristics. These are pronounced in new cooperage, then fade with succeeding uses.

6 When any wine is judged ready, it is bottled, often with a light, or polish filtration just as it goes to the bottling line.

The East Bay

Mostly urban, but famous for white wines

Although Alameda and Contra Costa counties have long traditions as sources of wine, both had long sinking spells lasting into the early 1970s. The Livermore Valley was the last remaining district with not only a reputation, but a sizable acreage in vines. Mission San Jose and other early districts had long since replaced vines with houses and factories.

With the wine boom has come a considerable new technology for handling grapes, and a curious resurgence of winemaking on the east side of San Francisco Bay. There are not many new vineyards growing in this populous part of the world, but numerous new wineries have sprung up to use grapes grown elsewhere around the state.

The Livermore Valley, with its open spaces, continues to look the part of a wine district, as it has since the 1880s. However, the greater number of East Bay wineries are located on the populous bay shore from Fremont north to Berkeley.

To the north, Contra Costa County and neighboring Solano County make a tidy loop drive that touches pretty vineyard country as well as wineries.

The Livermore Valley

Say "Livermore" to a student of California wine, and he will make the automatic associations of "white wine" and "gravelly soil."

Pioneer vineyardists Charles Wetmore and Louis Mel brought cuttings of vines from Chateau d'Yquem very early in Livermore's wine history and made Sauterneslike wines from the resulting grapes. The original Carl H. Wente and the original James Concannon concentrated on white wines, too. Winemakers have branched out from white wines, but never left them.

The whole county of Alameda produces much less than 1 percent of the state's wine each year. However, the families making wine in Livermore still include families that made wine there in the beginning—in the 1880s.

The Wineries

The pioneer names of Concannon and Wente reach back to Livermore's earliest days of winegrowing, the last two names from that era. In recent years several other, smaller wineries have joined them, some in old buildings, some in new.

Concannon Vineyard for almost a hundred years has proved conclusively that Irishmen can make wine if given a reasonable climate to do it in.

As with any Irish enterprise, there is a fine story about how it got started. In the 1880s the then Archbishop of San Francisco, Joseph S. Alemany, was a bit short of sacramental wine. His solution was to suggest to James Concannon, printer and stamp maker, that he should buy a vineyard and make wines. Concannon had a flexible enough mind to make the professional jump.

While the printing talent has lapsed in all subsequent Concannons, the winemaker has stayed in them. Although the winery has been sold to Agustin Huneeus, a veteran of winemaking in California and in his native Chile, Concannons still are active in management of the cellars in which four generations of them have grown up.

For the most part, the cellars appear unhurried and informal. The oldest part of the building dates from the early years of the winery. Subsequent additions have been made out of need for space rather than any desire to add frills. Some sections of wall are brick; others are clapboard. A fair proportion is made of corrugated iron to match the roof. Inside, old oak upright tanks and oval casks from the founder's day run in orderly but crowded rows.

An instantly visible reflection of modern thought is the collection of stainless steel fermentors along the winery's west wall. A less dramatic but equally effective announcement of contemporary thinking is an ever-growing collection of French oak barrels.

Appearances aside, the winery always has had an eye to the future. It is not only abreast of research at the University of California at Davis and other centers; it actively participates in the research itself. For example, Concannon has contributed a few acres from its small vineyards to serve as test plots for grape varieties not commonly grown in Livermore, and for experimental combinations of rootstocks with fruiting varieties. (Vines, like humans, marry for better and for worse. California needs rootstocks resistant to both phylloxera and nematodes to carry its classic grape varieties. Some combinations work. Some do not. Some work in certain conditions but not others. Researchers are very busy at the mating game.)

White wines under the Concannon label include Chenin Blanc, Sauvignon Blanc, and Livermore Riesling. Among the reds are Cabernet Sauvignon, Petite Sirah (which the winery was the first to offer as a California varietal), and Zinfandel. From time to time the owners offer Sauvignon Blanc, Cabernet Sauvignon, and Petite Sirah in limited bottlings.

The Concannon tasting room is as easy-going as the rest of the property. A large room lined with rough-sawn redwood, it has a small tasting bar at one side, and some picnic foods and gifts along the other two walls. The bottling room is where the fourth wall might be. On special occasions the regular bar is supplemented with extra tables. Across a small parking lot from the tasting room door, picnic tables under shading trees look out across winery-owned vineyards.

Livermore Valley Cellars is by miles the smallest established winery in the district.

The propriety of Chris Lagiss, it occupies a small prefabricated metal building at the rear of the family home. Both buildings are surrounded by the winery's 34-acre vineyard.

Tours do not take much time here. Stainless steel fermentors run along one wall of the winery, barrels along the other, and cased goods or new bottles pretty much fill the middle. The press is out back.

Tasting, on the other hand, may last for a while. The tasting counter is set up next to a three-car parking area and beneath an overhanging roof outside the small building in which Lagiss stores wines available for sale. Trees cast more shade and flowers grow around the edges. Hand-lettered signs carry quotes from Maynard Amerine, advice from the proprietor, and current prices of a roster of white wines grown on the property. Pinot Blanc, Grey Riesling, and French Colombard are the mainstays.

Stony Ridge Winery dates only from 1975, but houses itself in a cellar that goes back to 1887.

The current partnership is refurbishing and updating a building that went a long while without much change. A man named John Crellin founded the winery, then named Ruby Hill, and it remained in his family until 1921, when Ernest Ferrario bought it. Ferrario kept the property through a little bit of thick and a lot of thin until, in 1973, he sold it to Southern Pacific Land Company without having done much modernization during his long tenure.

Interim proprietors started rehabilitating the place late in the 1970s. Although some museum qualities remain—gravel floor in one section, ancient redwood fermentors in another—the functional winery is now up to date. A battery of stainless steel fermentors is outdoors at the rear, and much of the cooperage is now French oak barrels.

Crellin's eye for architecture gave the new proprietors something to work with. He set his 60 by 185-foot brick and stone building into a gentle hillside, and capped it with some graceful cupolas. Photogenic old vineyards slope away from its skirts.

The current proprietors still make Sauvignon Blanc and Semillon from the old vineyards, along with Chardonnay, Cabernet Sauvignon, and other varietals from Livermore and Monterey vineyards.

Villa Armando Winery in Pleasanton is less well known among Californians than among Atlantic Seaboarders, because most of the wine made at this middle-aged cellar historically has gone east for sale.

Anthony D. Scotto acquired the winery from the founding Garatti family in 1962, coining the current name then. In 1971, Scotto opened a tasting room designed in a Spanish style. It was only then that the wines became available to the home audience. Though recently the wines have become broadly available, the tasting room is still a prime local source. Wines are also available in a restaurant the Scottos operate next door.

(Continued on next page)

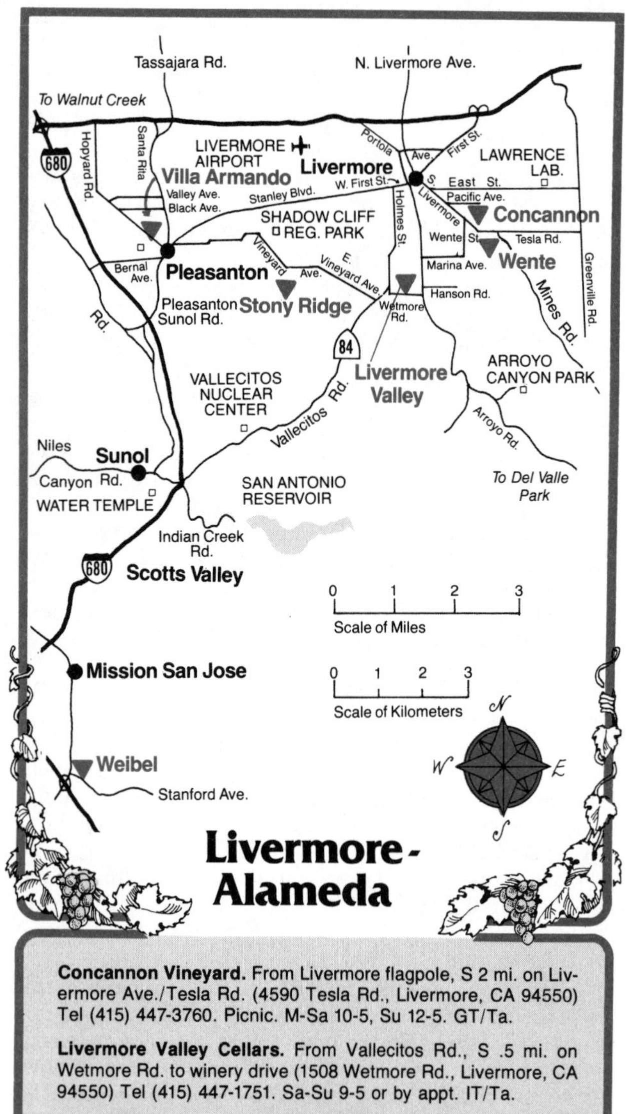

Concannon Vineyard. From Livermore flagpole, S 2 mi. on Livermore Ave./Tesla Rd. (4590 Tesla Rd., Livermore, CA 94550) Tel (415) 447-3760. Picnic. M-Sa 10-5, Su 12-5. GT/Ta.

Livermore Valley Cellars. From Vallecitos Rd., S .5 mi. on Wetmore Rd. to winery drive (1508 Wetmore Rd., Livermore, CA 94550) Tel (415) 447-1751. Sa-Su 9-5 or by appt. IT/Ta.

Stony Ridge Winery. From Main St. in Pleasanton, E on Ray St./Vineyard Ave. 3.5 mi. to winery drive (1188 Vineyard Ave., Pleasanton, CA 94566) Tel (415) 846-2133. Picnic. Daily 12-5. Ta.

Villa Armando Winery. From Main St., N 1/2 block on St. John St. (553 St. John St., Pleasanton, CA 94566) Tel (415) 846-1451. Ta daily 12-5.

Weibel Champagne Vineyards. From Mission San Jose, S 1 mi. on State 238, E on Stanford Ave. .5 mi. to winery (1250 Stanford Ave., Mission San Jose, CA 94539) Tel (415) 656-2340. Picnic. GT M-F 10-3/Ta daily 10-5.

Wente Bros. From Livermore flagpole, S 2.5 mi. on Livermore Ave./Tesla Rd. (5565 Tesla Rd., Livermore, CA 94550) Tel (415) 447-3603. GT M-F 9-5/Ta M-Sa 9-5, Su 1-5.

Key: GT (guided tour); IT (informal tour); Ta (tasting).

. . . Continued from page 123

There are no tours of the old, workaday winery building directly behind the Pleasanton Hotel. Most of the gear is conventional, but students of winemaking techniques would find some unusual fermentors to think about. The Scottos extract color from red wine grapes before—rather than during—fermentation, the latter being the conventional way. (Frank Garatti, who founded the winery in 1902, doubtless would be amazed.)

The winery built its original reputation with proprietary types (Vino Rustico, Rubinello, Orobianco). These now accompany a long list of familiar varietals, many grown in Scotto's nearby vineyard.

Wente Bros. is the oldest wine business and the newest working winery in the Livermore Valley, in one of those odd turnabouts that is not at all uncommon in vinous California.

The first Wente in Livermore was Carl H. Wente, who arrived in 1883, a year or so ahead of James Concannon. The two men were close in age. Subsequent generations of the two families have grown up within a stone's throw of each other. But there is no stone-throwing; they get along so well that it is traditional for the oldest child to take charge of both broods when the parents go somewhere together.

The Wentes, on the opposite side of Tesla Road from Concannon and a few hundred yards east, retained their original cellar until 1966. By then the old frame building had become a small part of the winery and had to yield to a more efficient structure. With the original building's dismantling, all of Wente took on a modern appearance. There have been subsequent additions to the concrete cellars, the age of the ivy on various walls helping to peg the different construction dates.

Few wineries offer visitors a clearer picture of how wine is made from start to finish than Wente. Behind the main aging cellars, four horizontal basket presses adjoin several rows of temperature-controlled stainless steel fermenting tanks. Next to the presses are some specialized devices used to handle field-crushed grapes hauled up from the family's distant vineyards in Monterey County. The whole works is out-of-doors and accessible for close inspection (except during harvest time). Guides on weekday-only tours explain the fine points.

The aging cellars, for their part, contain a remarkable diversity of cooperages: stainless steel, glass-lined steel, redwood uprights, oak ovals, and oak barrels. Again, the purpose of each type is well-explained.

Finally, the visitor can get within arm's reach of an automatic bottling line. Automatic bottling lines have a hypnotic effect on mechanically minded people. They have dozens of moving parts, all going at a synchronized rate. Bottles get washed, filled, corked or capped, topped with a capsule, and labeled fore and aft, all with little or no human assistance.

In front of the winery, the tasting room is an adobe building designed expressly for the comfort of guests. The basic notion is an Arthurian round table at which all comers are welcome to taste the full range of Wente wines, now being made by the young fourth generation. The Sauvignon Blanc, Semillon, and Grey Riesling are traditional in Livermore, going back to the earliest days. More recent additions include Chardonnay and Pinot Blanc. The most recent members of the roster come from the family's vineyards in Monterey County's Salinas Valley, notably including Gewürztraminer and Johannisberg Riesling.

Other Than Wineries

Reliably warm and sunny, the Livermore Valley has spawned several picnic parks.

The handiest of the lot is Shadow Cliffs Regional Park, nestled into the old arroyo bed alongside Stanley Drive between Livermore and Pleasanton. It has tree-shaded picnic sites, some playground gear, and a bit of water to splash in. Stanley Drive, not incidentally, has a bike path connecting the two towns.

Del Valle Regional Park, another part of the fine East Bay Regional Parks system, hides away in beautiful rolling hills southeast of Concannon and Wente. The park encompasses much of a reservoir lake's shoreline. It has abundant picnic sites in the shade of oaks, as well as swimming beaches and a boat launch. The park entrance is a bit more than 7 miles south of Tesla Road by way of Mines and Del Valle roads. The junction with Tesla Road is midway between the Wente and Concannon wineries, and is well marked with signs.

A lower-key park is Arroyo Canyon, on the road that passes the old Cresta Blanca winery and the veterans' hospital.

At Sunol, the San Francisco Water District maintains picnic tables and other comforts around its water temple. The entrance to the grounds is at the intersection of State Highway 21 with State Highway 84, just at the head of Niles Canyon.

Pleasanton's main street has an early American flavor about it still, in spite of the town's being ringed with contemporary housing tracts. The focal point is just west of St. John Street, where the landmark Pleasanton Hotel and the Pleasanton Cheese Factory face one another across the roadway. The cheese factory is a useful source of picnic fare to go with whichever of the local wines one might choose.

The Alameda County Fair, July 1–15 at Pleasanton, demonstrates that a good many cows remain in the area—and encompasses much more, including local winemaking.

For information on restaurants and overnight accommodations, write to the Livermore Chamber of Commerce, P.O. Box 671, Livermore, CA 94550.

Plotting a Route

The Livermore Valley is crisscrossed by a pair of freeways. Interstate Highway 580 goes east-west; Interstate Highway 680 runs north-south. One or the other will get a visitor into the region from almost anywhere.

I-580 turns toward Livermore from the San Francisco Bay basin at Hayward and connects with Interstate Highway 5 in the San Joaquin Valley. Heading east, the first real vista is the Livermore Valley, which springs into full view at the crest of a long upgrade. A second and much larger panorama is the San Joaquin Valley from the top of Altamont Pass on the east side of Livermore.

I-680 courses for most of its length in the shelter of the East Bay hills. The route begins at its junction with Interstate Highway 80 and ends at its intersection with U.S. Highway 101 at San Jose, so it is useful to visitors from the Sacramento Valley or the South Bay.

For the traveler heading up to Livermore from the south end of San Francisco Bay, State Highway 84, through Niles Canyon, offers a low-speed alternative to the freeway.

South Alameda

Alameda County's southwest corner was a flourishing vineyard district before Prohibition and remained a fairly sizable one through the years before World War II. But by 1965, the roster of surviving wineries and vineyards had dwindled to one, and there it remains.

The last survivor fits tidily into a day of touring the Livermore district, which is fewer than 20 miles distant via State Highways 238 and 84.

Weibel Champagne Vineyards leans east into a steep and photogenic line of hills and looks west out over baylands at Warm Springs. Look from Weibel toward the hills and time has changed nothing: except for vine rows, the hand of man shows but little. Look the other way and the story is different: westward, beyond a tract of houses, lies an automobile assembly plant which advertised itself as the world's largest building under one roof. It is the south end of an industrial-residential chain that runs unbroken to Oakland and beyond.

Being caught on the boundary between the worlds causes certain difficulties for the Weibels, but they go on in good humor at a winery that once belonged to Governor Leland Stanford.

Some of the buildings still would be recognizable to Stanford if he could stop by today, but the originals of 1869 have been supplemented since the Swiss family Weibel acquired the site in 1940. The winery is several hundred yards off State Highway 238. The access road, bordered on one side by eucalyptus trees and on the other by olive trees, runs alongside the vineyard until it comes to the small adobe-style building which houses Weibel's tasting room. Just north of it, a long, low, red brick building houses all of the Champagne-making and most of the stored still wines aging in bottle. Uphill from these are two rows of stainless steel aging tanks, the outdoor Sherry soleras, and the original winery building. A good deal of the redwood and oak cooperage in it holds Weibel table wines, most of them made at a new-in-1972 Weibel winery near Ukiah, in Mendocino County (see page 62), and transported to Mission San Jose for aging and bottling. Some wine is still made at Mission San Jose, the crusher being at the topmost level of the winery complex.

The brick Champagne building gives a clear view of the equipment for making both bottle-fermented and Charmat sparkling wines; this is one of the few cellars in which visitors can make a direct comparison between the two methods of winemaking and then go taste the results. The tasting room host pours sparkling wines of several sorts ranging from a Champagne Brut to a Charmat Sparkling Burgundy. The range of table wines encompasses nearly all of the generic and varietal types, and finally, there are several appetizer and dessert wines. Weibel, unlike other wineries, chooses to make its Green Hungarian a fairly sweet table wine. Among its dessert types is a relatively unusual Black Muscat. A house specialty liqueur is called Tangor.

The Weibels have several arbor-shaded picnic tables alongside the tasting room.

North Alameda

There is no growing of grapes in Berkeley or Emeryville, but the industrialized east shore of San Francisco Bay is right in the center of other places where grapes grow abundantly and well: Napa and Sonoma are not far north; Livermore is across the hills to the east; Santa Clara, Monterey, and San Luis Obispo stretch away to the south. Once freeways, field crushers, and other technical solutions had come into being, no great difficulties stood in the way of making wine downtown. And, lo, an urban wine country grew up in the East Bay, in one-time bakeries, warehouses, and other converted structures.

Most visitors come to this densely populous district in search of a particular winery. None come for bucolic charm.

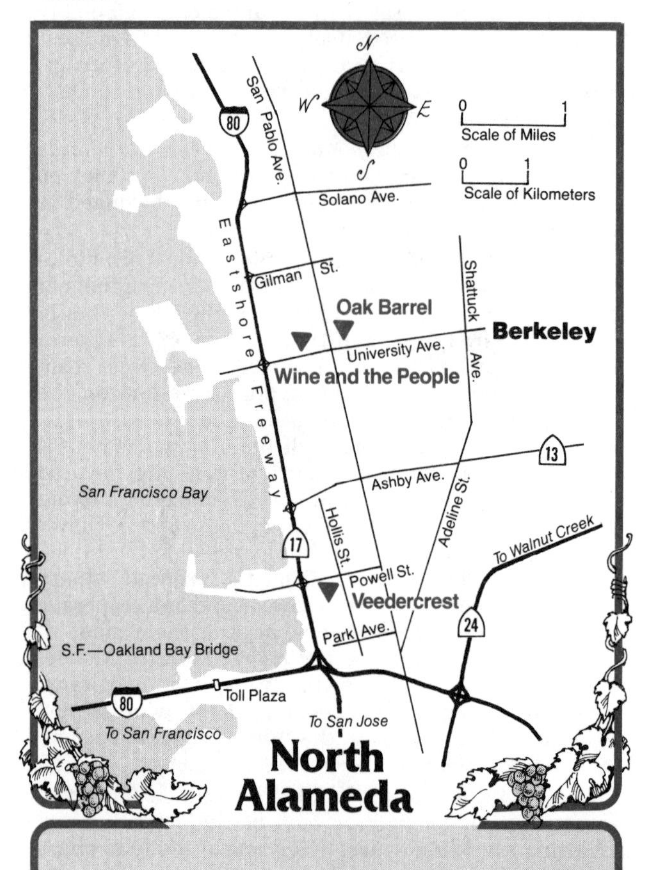

Oak Barrel. University Ave. 1 block E of San Pablo Ave. (1201 University Ave., Berkeley, CA 94702) Tel (415) 849-0400. M-Sa 10-6:30. Ta.

Veedercrest Vineyards. From I-80, Powell St. exit, E 3 blocks to SW corner of Powell St. and Doyle St. intersection (5749 Doyle St., Emeryville, CA 94608) Tel (415) 652-3103. GT by appt/Ta M-F 4-6.

Wine and the People. University Ave. 1 block W of San Pablo Ave. (907 University Ave., Berkeley, CA 94702) Tel (415) 549-1268. M-Sa 10-6, Su 11-5. Ta.

Key: GT (guided tour); IT (informal tour); Ta (tasting).

The Wineries

Like many another downtown business group, the East Bay wineries can be difficult to notice at first glance. The added fact that several are too small to court any visitors except customers buying wine means that the district is of real interest mainly to serious bibbers.

Oak Barrel is the older of two enterprises on University Avenue in Berkeley that are both wineries and suppliers to home winemakers.

There is no tour of a working winery here, but visitors can buy everything they need to start one of their own, along with wine by the barrel or bottle to tide them over while they get started. Proprietor John Bank has a tasting room that more or less doubles as a clubhouse for some of the area's home winemakers.

Veedercrest Vineyards is set somewhat apart from its neighbors in the East Bay flatlands by the fact that it is also a Napa Valley winery.

Although Veedercrest is housed in a severely modern concrete building in Emeryville, a majority of its grapes come from a sizable vineyard the company owns in the Mayacamas Mountains. The winery also buys grapes from selected small vineyards in Napa and Sonoma counties.

The winery is unmistakable with its stainless steel fermentors surrounding a building that falls somewhere between Art Deco and Moderne. Tours of the building with its below-ground cellar full of oak barrels are by appointment only, but tasting is available two blocks away in a red brick building used to store bottled wines. The roster of possibilities includes Chardonnay, Gewürztraminer, Cabernet Sauvignon, and, a rare bird, Malbec.

Wine and the People is the newer of the two companies on Berkeley's University Avenue that function both as wineries and suppliers to home winemakers.

At this one, the range of supplies stretches to include not only all of the equipment, but—in season—grapes from a wide range of California districts.

As for available wine, proprietor Peter Brehm makes small lots of Zinfandel, Cabernet Sauvignon, and other varietals—most of them from the grapes of the same vineyards that send fresh fruit to the firm for sale to home winemakers, so tastings here are doubly informative to all who contemplate making their own.

More wineries. North Alameda has three wineries with very limited visitor facilities: Fretter Wine Cellars, Montclair Winery, and Rosenblum Cellars. Fretter has the record for the smallest lot of wine offered for sale—a single case of Pinot Noir—but none of the three is large. Montclair accepts visitors only by invitation; the other two have annual open houses at which they sell much of their production.

Yet another small winery was in transition at deadline time for this book. Channing Rudd Cellars still was in Berkeley, but proprietor Channing Rudd had planted vineyards in Lake County, and anticipated construction of a cellar there in time for the 1982 harvest.

Other Than Wineries

Set in the midst of the populous East Bay, these cellars are handy to every sort of diversion from the Oakland Raiders to an afternoon at the movies, a tour of the Oakland Museum, or picnics in any of dozens of parks. The *Sunset Travel Guide to Northern California* provides detailed looks at the possibilities.

Berkeley Marina, at the foot of University Avenue, provides the handiest picnic sites. Sprawling Tilden Park has the most diverse range of possibilities.

Plotting a Route

State Highway 17—the Nimitz freeway—connects with Interstate Highway 80—the Eastshore freeway—at Emeryville. All three of the North Alameda wineries are less than a mile from the freeways. For those who would test the possibilities of public transportation, Alameda-Contra Costa Transit coaches serve the whole district. For information, telephone (415) 653-3535.

Contra Costa County

Contra Costa County contains two producing wineries in spring, 1982, which doubles the former number. The surroundings of these cellars are less urbanized than their counterparts in bayside Alameda, but hardly countrified. (See area map on next page.)

J.W. Morris Wineries have amassed a considerable history in a short while.

The firm was founded in 1975 as J.W. Morris Port Works in Emeryville. It rapidly outgrew the name when it turned to making table wines, hence its present, plural designation. By 1981 it had outgrown its original home in a handsome old brick building in Emeryville. When no suitable replacement site could be found in bayside Alameda County, the owners moved east to their current site.

One sturdy masonry building among several in an industrial park now houses ports and table wines alike. The building proper approaches its capacity for French and American oak barrels and stacked cases of wine. The stainless steel fermentors sit out back, with an appealing view of the Sacramento River.

Visitors likely will be shown around by J.W. himself, or by winemaker Jim Olsen, for this is a family concern.

The roster of wines includes Chardonnay, Pinot Noir, a pair of generics, and vintage Ports.

Conrad Viano Winery, on one edge of Martinez, has much of the air of a country winery. The family home has a rear corner of the basement set aside for tasting and retail sales. Three other smallish buildings of painted concrete block are behind that and slightly downhill. They are the winery and storage buildings.

Beyond, on the upslope, several acres of vineyard look back at the clustered structures (and several neighboring residences).

There is not enough gear on hand to call for a guided tour. A few minutes' poking about will reveal the crusher and press at the back of the hindmost building and an array of small redwood upright tanks inside it. Otherwise the scene is mostly farm tools and stored cases.

The tasting room takes longer. The Vianos have under their well-designed label Barbera, Burgundy, Cabernet Sauvignon, Gamay, Zinfandel (which they prize), Zinfandel Rosé, Chablis, Grey Riesling, and among appetizer and dessert types, Muscatel, Port, and Sherry.

The family bought the vineyard in 1920, founded the winery in 1946, and had to build a bigger cellar in 1967 and an addition in 1971. The third generation of Vianos is at work today.

There is a picnic lawn under a small grove of almonds next to the winery for those who would tarry over a bird and a bottle.

Solano County

No self-respecting geographer would identify Solano County as part of the East Bay. However, Solano County faces Contra Costa County across the Sacramento River, the two neatly connected by a bridge at Martinez and a second upstream at Antioch. Between them, the two counties have enough wineries to make an enjoyable day of touring in search of either costly varietals or bargain jug wines.

The Wineries

A short roster of wineries stretches out from Benicia on the west to Fairfield on the east, and manages to provide some genuine variety for visitors along the way.

Cadenasso Winery is a traditional stop for winebibbers who travel regularly between the San Francisco Bay area and the Sacramento Valley. The ivy-darkened concrete block walls of the main building are visible to motorists on I-80 just as they approach the Fairfield—Rio Vista—State Highway 12 exit ramp on the west side of Fairfield. Inside, an eclectic collection of oak ovals and small redwood uprights marches in four close ranks from one end to the other.

The tasting room, in the cellar beneath owner Frank Cadenasso's home, has as its entry an arched concrete tunnel. Downstairs the walls are mostly painted a vivid pink to match the company stationery.

Cadenasso began in 1906 when father Giovanni Cadenasso planted vines north of Cordelia. It continued when he moved to Fairfield to plant vines across the street from the present winery. That vineyard became county hospital grounds after the senior Cadenasso sold the land and dismantled the winery as a sensible response to Prohibition. The present site dates from 1926 (the main building came later, in 1942).

Cadenasso wines, served for tasting with great pride but no pretense, include Chenin Blanc, Grey Riesling, Chablis, and Sauterne among whites; Burgundy, Ca-

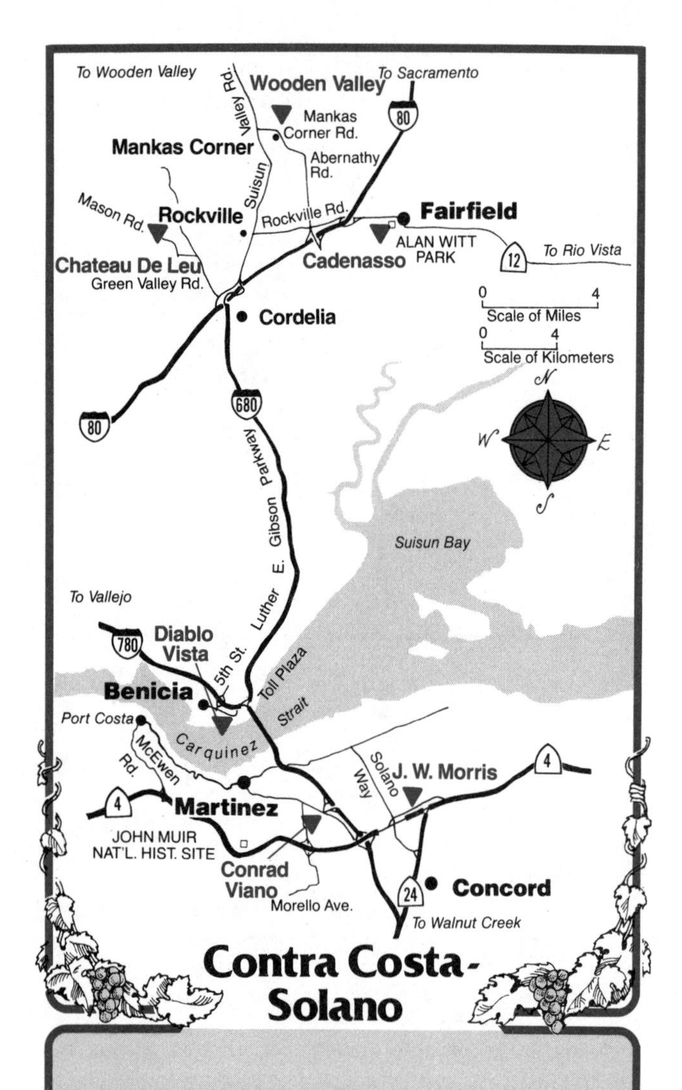

Cadenasso Winery. From I-80, Fairfield-Rio Vista/State 12 exit, S .25 mi. (P.O. Box 22, Fairfield, CA 94534) Tel (707) 425-5845. Daily 8-6. GT by appt./Ta.

Chateau De Leu. From I-80, Suisun Valley/Green Valley Rd. exit, NW on Green Valley Rd. 2 mi. to W. Mason Rd., then NW to winery at end of road (1635 W. Mason Rd., Suisun, CA 94585) Tel (707) 864-1517. GT by appt./Ta daily 11-4:30.

Diablo Vista Winery. From I-780, 5th St. exit at Benicia, S on 5th to H St., then E 3 blocks. (Bus. off.: 1610 Ridgewood Rd., Alamo, CA 94507) Tel (415) 837-1801. GT/Ta by appt.

J.W. Morris Wineries. From State 4, Solano exit, under freeway to Arnold Industrial Pkwy., E 2 mi. on Arnold to Pike Ln., N in industrial park to winery (4060 Pike Ln., Concord, CA 94520) Tel (415) 680-1122. M-F 9-5. GT/Ta by appt.

Conrad Viano Winery. From State 21, W 1 mi. on State 4, N 1 mi. on Morello Ave. (150 Morello Ave., Martinez, CA 94553) Tel (415) 228-6465. Picnic. Daily 9-12, 1-5. IT/Ta.

Wooden Valley Winery. From I-80, Green Valley/Suisun Valley exit, NW 4.5 mi. on Suisun Valley Rd. (4756 Suisun Valley Rd., Suisun, CA 94585) Tel (707) 864-0730. Tu-Su 9-5. Ta.

Key: GT (guided tour); IT (informal tour); Ta (tasting).

bernet Sauvignon, Grignolino, Pinot Noir, and Zinfandel among reds. The Zinfandel and all of the generics can be had in jugs as well as bottles, and a considerable part of each day's sale goes out the door in the generous container.

Ordinarily there are no tours. A look through the winery requires an appointment, very nearly the only formality Cadenasso allows, let alone asks. The staff is too small, though, to lay down its work without planning ahead for visitors.

Chateau De Leu nestles into an archetypal landscape in California's Coast Ranges. The building looks out across 80 acres of vines, and up to grassy hills forming the west side of Green Valley. Inside, the winery is every bit as classically Californian: stainless steel fermentors, tidy rows of French oak barrels, and a handsome tasting room finished in redwood. All of this makes the building all the more agreeable a surprise, for it is modeled on a half-timbered Alsatian country house.

In another tradition far more Californian than Alsatian, the owning Ben Volkhardt family crushed its first vintage in a half-built winery in 1981, then finished the building and the debut wines together during 1982.

All of the wines are made from the proprietor's own vines. The roster includes French Colombard, Sauvignon Blanc, Gamay, and Petite Sirah among other varietal types.

Diablo Vista Winery houses itself in, of all places, a one-time cafeteria in an old manufacturing plant in Benicia.

The proprietors say their location is ideal. First, it is handy to their homes and their source vineyards. Second, the cellar is substantially below grade, and thus easy to keep cool.

The property of the Leon Borowski and Kermit Blodgett families, Diablo Vista limits its production to Cabernet Sauvignon and Zinfandel. Appointment-only tasting tours take in every step of small-lot red winemaking from crusher-stemmer to bottling.

Wooden Valley Winery has an appealing informality about it. There is no tour. The tasting and sales room is one of four frame buildings grouped around a sizable courtyard, but is unmistakable. On weekends, especially, the court is full of parked automobiles and the tasting room full of local patrons exchanging empty jugs for full ones.

Proprietors Mario Lanza (no relation to the singer) and Richard Lanza offer several generic table wines in bottles and jugs, and a broad spectrum of varietal wines in bottles only. A complete list of appetizer and dessert wines also can be sampled.

Other Than Wineries

Solano County offers no great abundance of picnic parks or other recreational diversions close to its wineries.

One exception, directly next to the Cadenasso Winery on West Texas Street, is Alan Witt Park, a spacious collection of playgrounds and picnic lawns.

The tasting game

The names of wines do little to explain how they will taste. Colombard and Pinot Blanc do not sound much alike. Pinot Blanc and Pinot Noir sound more alike. But when you get down to cases, the wines of the first pair taste more like each other than the wines of the latter pair.

Most wineries run tasting rooms to help overcome the semantics of the business. The hosts will help organize a sequence of wines so each sample will show off to its best advantage. (Dry whites are served first, followed by rosés, reds, sweet wines, appetizers, then desserts. Sparkling wines come last.)

Newcomers usually find it useful to explore at least one candidate from each of the five classes (see the chart on page 97). Experienced tasters sometimes organize a day in the wine country just to taste one class or even one variety.

All "tasting" amounts to is making a considered judgment about whether or not a wine pleases the drinker. This is a purely personal exercise, but is most rewarding if it includes some basic tests by which professionals make their decisions.

Sight. The appearance of a wine reveals something of its character. The liquid should be clear to brilliantly clear. Young table wines should not have brownish tints (whites range from pale gold to straw yellow, reds from crimson to ruby or slightly purplish, rosés from pink orange to pink). Most dessert wines will have a brownish tint and some may even be deep amber, depending on type.

Smell. Young table wines should have a fresh, fruity quality of aroma. The many types add a wide range of subtle variations. The fruitiness may be overlaid with bouquet. (Aroma is the smell of grapes, bouquet the smell of fermentation and aging.) But one seldom encounters bouquet when drinking new wines at the winery. Appetizer and dessert wines have little aroma but substantial bouquet.

Taste. In fact, taste is simply sweet, sour, bitter, and salty. Most "taste" is an extension of smell. Some qualities can be perceived only after the wine is on the taster's palate: acidity (liveliness versus flatness), astringency (young red wines will have a tannic puckeriness in most types except mellow ones), and weight or body (light versus rich).

One further note. "Dry" describes the absence of sugar, nothing else. Dry wines are sometimes thought to be sour because acidity and tannin are more evident.

Back on the Contra Costa side of the river, the tiny, waterside town of Port Costa offers another kind of diversion altogether.

Port Costa was once a teeming Sacramento River port, but bridges and other aspects of progress caused it to become technologically unemployed during the 1930s. Beginning in the 1960s it revived itself as an antique collection of shops and restaurants, and it has played host to crowds of visitors ever since.

The village is just off State Highway 4, a few minutes downstream from Martinez.

Plotting a Route

Interstate highways 80 and 680 form a T that gets to the heart of the region from any direction.

I-680 has some agreeable moments as it slips along the flat from Cordelia down to the Sacramento River at Suisun, where the U.S. Navy's mothball fleet provides a wistful vista. But the freeways are mainly the means to get from Point A to Point B in a hurry.

The joys of driving in this part of the world belong with Suisun Valley Road, Wooden Valley Road, State Highway 121 from Cordelia to Lake Berryessa (and on across into the Napa Valley if time does not weigh heavily), and whatever connecting roads seem promising on the spot.

The Suisun and Wooden valleys, both small, look fine in all seasons. They even smell good early in March when their abundant orchards bloom a fragrant cloud of white and pink above carpets of indelibly yellow mustard and beneath canopies of blue sky.

The hills west, in this season, are bright green with new grass and dull green with old oaks.

These are old roads, narrow and curving. Summer drivers bustle along in hopes of finding some cooler place; but in late winter or early spring when the weather is balmy, some of them tend to grow forgetful of their goals. On such days the wheels of progress grind as slowly as those of justice, but the views are exceedingly fine.

The Mother Lode & Lodi

Two adjoining districts are worlds apart

For years, when a wine industry official said "Lodi," the word encompassed most of the northern San Joaquin County, Sacramento and its surroundings, and several bits and pieces of the Mother Lode.

Now Lodi pretty much means Lodi. Vineyards and wineries in the Mother Lode country have established an identity of their own under the general district name of Sierra Foothills. A whole new district is emerging in the Sacramento Delta west of Lodi, and the Sacramento Valley is becoming a separate area.

The old shorthand was forgivable. From the end of Prohibition until the early 1970s, the dozen or so wineries right around Lodi outnumbered all the others two to one. Several of them individually made more wine each year than did all those in the fringe areas combined. Lodi still dominates in total gallons, and still has the biggest wineries, but the Mother Lode now has more than twice as many cellars to visit.

The Mother Lode

The Mother Lode is that California region where local grapegrowers are most likely to say of themselves, "We don't have to be crazy, but it helps."

Theirs is an altogether different weather from that of the San Joaquin Valley floor below. Spring frosts are but one major aspect of a climate that makes grapes a dubious crop for investment. Indeed, one scientist at the University of California at Davis says that a Sierra Nevada foothill winegrower will harvest, over the long haul, approximately 25 percent of what he might expect in easier climes.

People learned this soon after 1849, when local winemaking sprang up to help satisfy the thirsts of Gold Rush miners. The rigorous climate has been a damper on would-be vineyardists since; acreage in the Mother Lode never has been large.

Still, despite the chancy economics, Zinfandel from this region has enjoyed fame in every era of California winemaking. Vines never have disappeared from the region altogether, and now they are perhaps at the zenith. Not only are vineyard acreages and the roster of regional wineries at their peaks, but cellars in many other counties are making Amador Zinfandels in competition with stay-at-home bottlings.

Even if wines from this region were less well received by connoisseurs, the Mother Lode would be worth a vinous visit. Its hills compose and recompose themselves into beautiful scenes. The whole region is full of appealing memorabilia from 1849, and full of people who keep some of that gaudy spirit. Not least, an easy friendliness pervades the small, mostly family-owned wineries.

The El Dorado district runs from Placerville south to the Amador County line, where the Shenandoah Valley vineyard district begins. Combining the two into a single tour is not only easy, but sensible. The wineries in Calaveras and Tuolumne counties are some distance away from their peers. (See map on page 133.)

El Dorado Wineries

Most of El Dorado County's wineries are small, family-owned cellars in wooded hill country near U. S. Highway 50 at Placerville, or on local roads south of U.S. 50 and east of State Highway 49.

Boeger Winery is, like a great many other California wineries, both old and new. Here, however, the contrast is easier to see than almost anywhere else.

The current winery went up in 1973, a tidy concrete block structure with stainless steel fermentors, a Willmes press and other processing gear out back, and racks of oak barrels and puncheons within.

A few yards downstream, along a creek that bisects the property, is an old stone building that orginally was the Fossati-Lombardo winery in the 1870s, but now houses the tasting room. The upper floor held a hand-cranked crusher that now sits in the tasting room. Two chutes above the tasting bar used to drop newly crushed fruit into open fermentors.

In good weather, visitors can picnic just above the creek in a spot between the two buildings, and consider how winemaking has changed.

The list of Boeger varietal wines includes Chardonnay, Chenin Blanc, Johannisberg Riesling, and Sauvignon Blanc in whites. Cabernet Sauvignon and Zinfandel are the reds. The generics are called Hangtown Gold and Hangtown Red after Placerville's original name. The wines come from four patches of grapes, one in the pocket valley that holds the winery, the other three nearby.

Incidentally, owners Greg and Susan Boeger also grow pears and apples on the home ranch.

FBF Winery shares a slope below Fairplay Road with a nursery called Famine's End. Founded in 1980, the winery presently occupies two buildings several hundred yards apart. The crushing and fermenting go on in a no-frills barn behind the main nursery building. Wines age in American oak in a block building burrowed into a sharp slope, some of which is planted to vines, some given over to nursery stock, some still wooded. Mainstays in the roster—labeled Fitzpatrick—are Chardonnay, Sauvignon Blanc, Cabernet Sauvignon, and Zinfandel. A partnership of winemaker Bill Bertram, vineyard manager Brian Fitzpatrick, and brother Michael Fitzpatrick, owns a cellar designed to grow to several times its current small size.

Granite Springs Winery nestles into an idyllic fold in gentle hills east of Somerset. Owners Les and Lynne Russell did their own construction work on a sturdy, barnlike winery building cut into a rocky slope overlooking vineyards and two ponds. An overhanging roof shelters crusher and press. Inside, stainless steel fermentors line one wall of a single, large room. Upright oak tanks and oak barrels take much of the remaining space. A cable spool is the tasting table.

The Russells first crushed here in 1981 after making wine elsewhere in 1980. Their first releases in 1982 were white Zinfandel and Chenin Blanc. Reds to be released later include Cabernet Sauvignon and Zinfandel.

Madroña Vineyards is, by a narrow margin, largest of the El Dorado wineries. As is the local habit, owners Richard and Leslie Bush did much of the construction work on a gracefully proportioned wood-sided winery cut into a long slope and shaded by a small grove of conifers. In the California tradition, construction ran right through the first crush, 1980.

A tasting room finished in natural wood overlooks both vineyards and the well-equipped main cellar from a sort of mezzanine. This allows the proprietor to conduct thorough tours without taking a step, though closer looks at stainless steel and oak cooperage are possible, too. The Madroña label covers several estate-grown varietals including Chardonnay, Cabernet Sauvignon, and Zinfandel.

Sierra Vista Winery is beyond the end of conventional roads, on one of several forest tracks. Visitors head in the right direction with help from wooden signs tacked to tree trunks wherever the track forks.

In spite of this, the winery is not remote from civilization, nor is it primitive. The rough-hewn roads are due to the fact that a high ridge is now being developed into an extension of Pleasant Valley. The winery is not primitive because its owner is a scientist.

Proprietors John and Barbara MacCready ferment their wines in one-time dairy tanks of stainless steel directly in front of a trim, 20 by 30-foot, wood-sided cellar, and age them inside the building, the whites mainly in other stainless steel tanks, the reds in American or French oak barrels. Sierra Vista is aptly named. The MacCreadys can see the Crystal Range whenever they look up from winery work.

The long-range plan is to make Sauvignon Blanc, estate Cabernet Sauvignon, and Zinfandel—the latter in conventional and late harvest styles—as the major wines on the list. Other varietals will make at least occasional appearances.

Founded in 1977 at its present tiny size, Sierra Vista is planning to increase its capacity in several phases.

More wineries. Eldorado Vineyards had a brief life in the middle 1970s, then closed. The original owner and a new partner reopened Eldorado in 1981 with a small crush, and planned to reopen for sales during 1982. The winery is located a few yards off U.S. 50 at Camino. A winery in the planning stage in 1982 was Stoney Creek, to be located on a vineyard on Fairplay Road east of Somerset.

Amador Wineries

The oldest, steadiest, and now largest of the Mother Lode wine districts is known as Shenandoah Valley. A broad, shallow dip in rolling hills east of Plymouth, it has most of Amador County's vineyard acreage, and 10 of its 15 wineries. The others are scattered, but within easy reach of this focal point.

Amador City Winery, founded in 1966, is a tasting room and small cellar housed in a building alongside State 49 in the village of Amador City. To taste here is to tour. The list of wines is basically generic.

Amador Foothill Winery is part of the new wave of Sierra foothill wineries by age and design. Husband-wife owners Ben Zeitman and Joan Sieber built their winery in time for the harvest of 1980 and designed it to be the world's most energy-efficient metal building. Zeitman, ex-NASA, made the plans with a little help from old colleagues with impeccable credentials in the subject.

Gleaming white, the passive solar structure stair-steps down a steep north slope otherwise covered in vines. Crusher, basket presses, and an off-season picnic/tasting table occupy a concrete pad at one end of the upper level. Great views are all around. Stainless steel fermentors for whites and redwood ones for reds are just inside well-insulated walls. The cooler lower level has oak uprights, barrels, and bottled wines alongside a huge bin of rocks cooled by night air. Warm daytime air establishes a convection flow as it exits through a long vent at the peak of a soaring roof.

Wines produced in this scientifically precise environment include Chenin Blanc, a white Zinfandel, and Zinfandel, the latter from nearby vineyards including one believed to date to the 1860s.

Argonaut Winery is near the village of Ione, a shade down the Sierra Nevada slopes from most of the other Mother Lode cellars.

Perhaps the smallest of the regional lot, it belongs to several partners who otherwise work in the aerospace industry. One of the partners lives at the winery site, but weekends are the only time visitors are allowed to have a look at the small cellar and its collection of oak casks. An appointment is required.

In accordance with local tradition, the list of wines is led by Zinfandel.

Baldinelli-Shenandoah Valley Vineyards makes its wines alongside and in a spruce, prefabricated metal building perched atop a knoll looking down onto Shenandoah Road.

This is an instructive example of a modern small winery. The press is an up-to-the-minute model of the horizontal basket type. The row of stainless steel fermentors alongside the cellar building has some exposed tanks, and some covered with insulating foam. Inside, the cooperage is a mixture of French and American oak barrels.

Proprietor Ed Baldinelli's first crush was 1979. The roster of wines, all from his adjoining vineyard, includes Zinfandel in every shade from white to red, and Cabernet Sauvignon.

BeauVal Wines focuses on Zinfandel in the best local tradition, but pursues the grape in all its roles, as a source of white, rosé, and red wine. Of exactly the scale to tempt home winemakers to make the next leap, this impeccable small winery has its crusher and fermentor on a patio behind the home of partners Bob and Nan Francis, while its aging cellar of American oak barrels occupies what would be the basement. The Francises will explain how large a leap is involved as well as talking about wine in general.

BeauVal made its first wines, all Zinfandels, in 1979. The owners plan to add Sauvignon Blanc and Barbera as their small vineyard matures.

D'Agostini Winery is the genuinely durable cellar in this lofty region. The first vines on the site east of Plymouth belonged to a Swiss named Adam Uhlinger, who planted them in 1856. For a good many years Uhlinger made wine under his own label. The present owners, the D'Agostini family, bought the vines and the winery in 1911, and have been on the property ever since.

Uhlinger built for the long haul. He laid stone walls and strung heavy beams. The D'Agostinis have kept his handiwork intact, though the winery has prospered substantially and required a series of additions. They also have kept several of the oak casks that were coopered on the site by a neighbor of Uhlinger.

The buildings, old and new, are set at the foot of a gentle, vine-clad slope. Beyond the 125 acres of vineyard are hills wooded more thickly than is common in California wine districts.

Tours start with the fermentors and end with the tasting room. Burgundy and Zinfandel head the list of table wines.

Greenstone Winery calls its location, well downslope from Amador's other cellars, the gateway to the Mother Lode.

The building makes a dramatic gate. Set amid vines and well back from State Highway 88, it has the sort of high, steep-pitched roof and tall gables that bring to mind prosperous farmhouses in Brittany. Greenstone will earn its name when a plywood skin tacked on just in time for the debut harvest of 1981 is covered with a distinctly green local stone. The rock is to be quarried from a site next to winery-owned vines across the highway.

Owned by two couples who like company, the winery is designed to welcome visitors to the point of having an entry road and parking area sized for recreational vehicles. An oak-shaded picnic area flanks the winery next to an area on which the owners plan to build a tasting room during 1982.

As a winery, Greenstone still is growing into its generous building. A small crusher and basket press occupy a roofed-over deck at one end. Inside is plenty of room to add to a row of four stainless steel fermentors and two short stacks of American oak barrels. Partner Stan Van Spanje is the winemaker. Karen Van Spanje and Jane and Durward Fowler also work in the vineyard and cellar.

Wines from the first crush are white Zinfandel and Zinfandel. Chenin Blanc and French Colombard were to join the roster in 1982.

Karly Winery occupies a small, well-made building next to the residence of winemaker-partner Lawrence

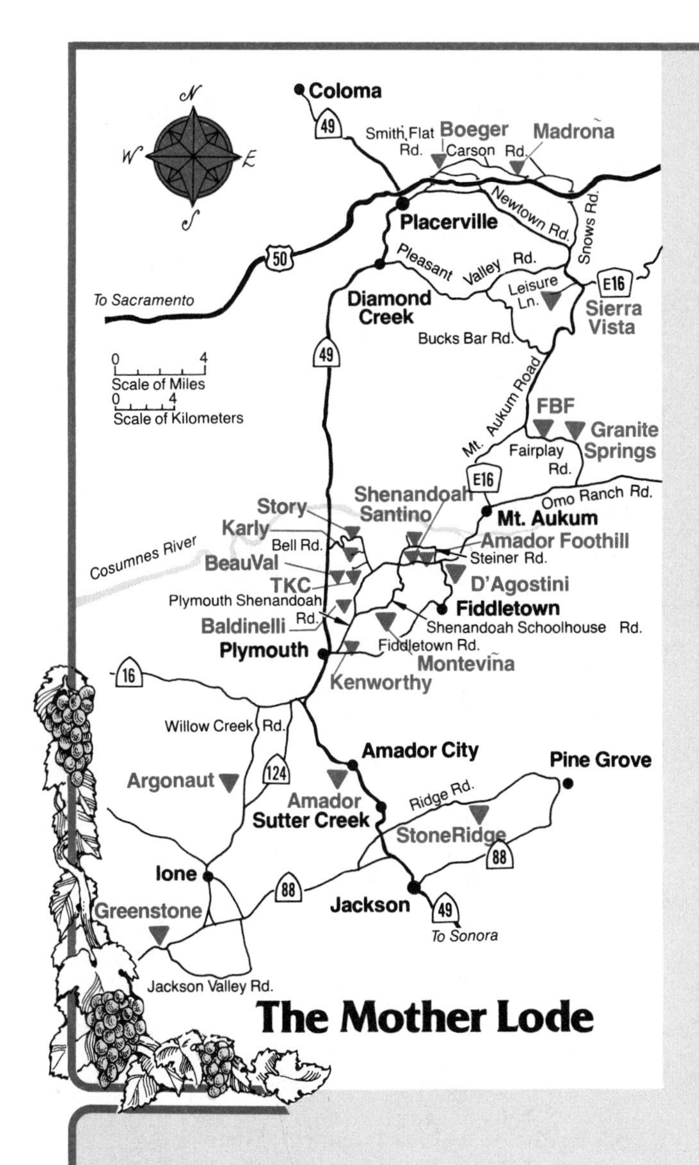

El Dorado County

Boeger Winery. From U.S. 50, Schnell School Rd. exit, N .25 mi. to Carson Rd., E .3 mi. to winery (1709 Carson Rd., Placerville, CA 95667) Tel (916) 622-8094. W-Su 10-5. Ta.

FBF Winery. From E-16/Mt. Aukum Rd., E .3 mi. on Fairplay Rd. (Fairplay Rd., Somerset, CA 95684) Tel (916) 626-1988. Picnic. W-Su by appt.

Granite Springs Winery. From E-16/Mt. Aukum Rd., E 2 mi. on Fairplay Rd. to private lane (6060 Granite Springs Rd., Star Rt., Somerset, CA 95684) Tel (916) 245-6395. Sa-Sun 11-5 or by appt. GT/Ta.

Madroña Vineyards. From U.S. 50, 5-Mile Rd. exit, N .2 mi. on 5-Mile Rd., E 2 mi. on Gatlin to private lane (P.O. Box 454, Camino, CA 95709) Tel (916) 644-5948 or 644-1154. Sa 10-5, Su 1-5 or by appt. IT/Ta.

Sierra Vista Winery. From E-16/Mt. Aukum Rd. at Pleasant Valley, W on Leisure Ln. to winery drive at end of road (4560 Cabernet Wy., Placerville, CA 95667) Tel (916) 622-7221. Sa-Su 12-5 or by appt. IT/Ta.

Amador County

Amador City Winery. On State 49 in Amador City (P.O. Box 65, Amador City, CA 95601) Tel (209) 267-5320. T-Su 10-6. Ta.

Amador Foothill Winery. From Plymouth, NE 6 mi. on E-16/ Shenandoah Rd. to Steiner Rd., then N 1.1 mi. on Steiner (Rt. 2, Box 22C, Plymouth, CA 95669) Tel (209) 245-6307. Sa-Su 10-5 (best to call ahead) or by appt. GT/Ta.

Argonaut Winery. From Ione, NE 5 mi. on Willow Creek Rd. (13675 Mt. Echo Dr., Ione, CA 95640) Tel (209) 274-4106 or 274-2882. Sa-Su by appt. only.

Baldinelli-Shenandoah Valley Vineyards. From Plymouth, NE 5.4 mi. on E-16/Shenandoah Rd. (Rt. 2, Box 7A, Plymouth, CA 95669) Tel (209) 245-3398. Sa-Su by appt.

BeauVal Wines. From Plymouth, NE 5.6 mi. to Bell Rd., N .1 mi. on Bell to Valley Dr., W .2 mi. to 10671 (Rt. 2, Box 8D, Plymouth, CA 95669) Tel (209) 245-3281. By appt. only.

D'Agostini Winery. From Plymouth, NE 8 mi. on E-16/ Shenandoah Rd. (Rt. 2, Box 19, Plymouth, CA 95669) Tel (209) 245-6612. Daily 9-5. GT/Ta.

Greenstone Winery. On State 88 3 mi. W of intersection with State 124 (P.O. Box 1164, Ione, CA 95640) Tel (209) 274-2238 or 274-4182. Picnic. Summers, Tu-Su 10-4; rest of year Sa-Su 10-4. IT/Ta.

Karly Winery. From Plymouth, NE 5.6 mi. to Bell Rd., N .25 mi. to winery drive (P.O. Box 721, Plymouth, CA 95669) Tel (209) 245-3922 or 245-3601. By appt. only.

Kenworthy Vineyards. From Plymouth, NE 1.7 mi. on E-16/ Shenandoah Rd. (Rt. 2, Box 2, Plymouth, CA 95669) Tel (209) 245-3198. Su 1-5 or by appt.

Monteviña. From Plymouth, NE 2 mi. on E-16/Shenandoah Rd. to Shenandoah Schoolhouse Rd., then E 1 mi. (Rt. 2, Box 30A, Plymouth, CA 95669) Tel (209) 245-3412. Picnic. Sales M-F 11-4; GT/Ta Sa-Su 11-4.

Santino Winery. From Plymouth, NE 6 mi. to Steiner Rd., N 1 mi. on Steiner to winery (Rt 2, Box 21, Plymouth, CA 95669) Tel (209) 245-3555. Picnic. Sa-Su 10-5 or by appt. GT/Ta.

Shenandoah Vineyards. From Plymouth, NE 6 mi. to Steiner Rd., N 1 mi. on Steiner to winery drive (Rt. 2, Box 23, Plymouth, CA 95669) Tel (209) 245-3698. Sa-Su 12-5 or by appt. IT/Ta.

StoneRidge Winery. From State 49 S of Sutter Creek, 2.25 mi. E on Ridge Rd. (Rt 1, Box 36B, Ridge Rd., Sutter Creek, CA 95685) Tel (209) 223-1761. Picnic. Sa 1-5, most Su (April-Aug.) 1-4. IT/Ta.

Story Vineyard. From Plymouth, NE 5.5 mi. on E-16/Shenandoah Rd. to Bell Rd., N 1.5 mi. on Bell to winery (Bus. off.: c/o Ann Story, 2336 Glen Ellen Circle, Sacramento, CA 95822) Tel (209) 245-6208. By appt. only.

TKC Vineyards. From Plymouth, NE 5.6 mi. to Bell Rd., N .1 mi. on Bell to Valley Dr. and winery entrance (Mailing address: 1307 Essex Cir., Ridgecrest, CA 93555) Tel (714) 446-3166. By appt. only.

Outside Map Area

Chispa Cellars. (425 Main St., Murphys, CA 95247) By appt. only.

Stevenot Winery. From Murphys, N 2.5 mi. on Sheep Ranch Rd. to winery drive (P.O. Box 548, Murphys, CA 95247) Tel (209) 728-3436. Picnic. Daily 10-4. GT/Ta.

Yankee Hill Winery. From Columbia State Historic Park, E 1 mi. on Yankee Hill Rd. (P.O. Box 163, Columbia, CA 95310) Tel (209) 532-3015. Picnic. W-Su 10-5. IT/Ta.

Key: GT (guided tour); IT (informal tour); Ta (tasting).

(Buck) Cobb. Exactly which building comes into view depends on the speed of the trip. The original board-and-batten barn of 1980 is scheduled to give way during 1982 to a larger, more substantial metal building.

Either way, the property is a pleasure to see. The buildings are well back from Bell Road amid the young vineyard, and next to a small lake. Grassy, oak-dotted hills frame the picture.

Karly's short list of wines comes partly from local grapes and partly from imports from Santa Barbara County. The locals are Sauvignon Blanc and Zinfandel; Chardonnay is the import. Cobb, a one-time United States Air Force fighter pilot, ferments his red wine in stainless steel and ages it in French and American oak, and ferments his whites in French oak puncheons.

Kenworthy Vineyards is a modern, well-built structure nested inside the faithfully preserved, irreplaceable old white barn pictured on the label.

The cellar, thus disguised, belongs to long-time home winemakers John and Patricia Kenworthy, whose first commercial vintage here was 1980. The roster is Chardonnay, Cabernet Sauvignon, and Zinfandel, some from their own young grapes, most from other growers in the Sierra foothills.

While an affable clutter of old farm implements and odds and bits of equipment surrounds the building, the interior is neat as a pin. A small fermenting room with stainless steel tanks is in an attached shed at the rear. Inside the main building is an aging cellar full of American oak barrels. The setting is a quiet delight of gently rolling vines, oak-dotted meadows, and a natural pond.

Monteviña retains its long-held title of largest winery in Amador County, and by a wide margin is the most widely distributed label among the current roster. This does not mean it is large by state-wide standards, however. Indeed, it would rank among the medium-to-small wineries in Napa or Sonoma County.

W.H. Fields and partner-winemaker Cary Gott founded Monteviña in 1973. In 1981, having outgrown the original prefabricated steel building, the owners added a handsome second building with arched windows and other Spanish touches. The original cellar still has the modern crushers, presses, and stainless steel fermentors, and still has European oak barrels stacked more than head-high in close rows. The second building, to the rear of the original, has more space for barrel aging, a bottling line, and the offices. Having grown to this size, Monteviña in 1982 established the first program of formal tours and tastings in the region. A handsome tasting room is inside the new barrel aging cellar. A canopied picnic patio is directly outside. As part of its visitor program, the winery also offers older vintages for sale.

Monteviña is an estate winery by the classical definition. All its wines come from 160 acres of vines owned by its proprietors, including one 80-year-old block. The emphasis is on Zinfandel in a variety of styles ranging from a light-hearted one made by carbonic maceration to a heavyweight meant for long aging. (To explain carbonic maceration in detail is beyond the scope of this book, but essentially it means fermenting whole grapes in clusters rather than crushed grapes separated from their stems. The idea is to achieve red wines ready for instant drinking.) Also in the roster of varietal wines are Sauvignon Blanc, a white Cabernet, Barbera, and Cabernet Sauvignon. A Port-type joined the roster in 1978.

Santino Winery is the only one in the Mother Lode built in a Spanish California style. Adobe blocks and red tile roof make it stand out in a part of the state not trod by Franciscan missionaries, whose architectural legacy is common in the coastal districts.

Architecture aside, this winery is instructive for having modern equipment in compact space, allowing visitors to grasp readily the sequence of winemaking steps. A short, fairly straight line runs from outdoor crusher, press, and stainless steel fermentors, through an aging cellar full of French oak, to the bottling line. A sparely furnished but friendly seeming tasting room is at the opposite end of the winery from the crushing and fermenting area. Just outside the tasting room, two picnic tables for visitors are in the shade of an overhanging roof.

The Santino label covers Sauvignon Blanc, Cabernet Sauvignon, and white and red Zinfandels in several styles.

Shenandoah Vineyards occupies a lofty knoll overlooking the Shenandoah Valley. The property of Leon and Shirley Sobon since 1977, the ranch belonged for many years to a prominent local family named Steiner, which directly explains the outward appearance of the place. "Stein" in German means "stone," and Mr. Steiner took his name very seriously indeed. All of the house walls and one wall of what now is the winery are of rock carted up from the nearby Cosumnes River and mortared in place by the former owners. The stonework has enough landmark status locally that old-timers come now and again to see that the new proprietors have not damaged the Steiner legacy.

The Sobons have not, though they more than tripled the size of the winery building in 1978 by adding two concrete block levels behind and below the stone and wood original, and enlarged it again in 1981. The additions are on the reverse slope of the knoll, invisible from Steiner Road.

The expanded winery is tidy and well equipped. At the upper level, crushers, basket presses, redwood red wine fermentors, and a wizard Italian juice separator (for making white wines out of black grapes) stand under a shed roof, while two rooms inside are full of barrels for fermenting and aging Chenin Blanc, white Zinfandel, and a white Mission del Sol. A small tasting room is here as well. The lower levels house several oak tanks and about a hundred American and French oak barrels for aging Cabernet Sauvignon and Zinfandel.

StoneRidge Winery is a thinking man's small cellar, designed into its site—or sites—to ease the burdens of moving both grapes and wine.

The crushing, fermenting, and pressing go on in a small shed at the high side of a hilly property. There, grapes feed into a crusher set on a platform that pivots to fill any of three open-topped redwood fermentors. On a lower level is a stainless steel tank used for the first racking. It ties into an underground line that allows new wine to flow by gravity to an aging cellar beneath the residence of proprietors Gary and Loretta Porteous.

The aging cellar has a romantic antique touch, or, rather, several of them. The Porteouses salvaged several ancient oak casks and puncheons from a one-time miners' boarding house which had made wine for its clientele in the gaudy days of the Gold Rush. These are the majority of the oak cooperage, though they are supplemented by newer French and American barrels.

Production focuses on Zinfandel from an old vineyard nearby and Ruby Cabernet from the home property.

The winery is small enough that the tasting room consists of a barrel set on end in the aging cellar. It is also small enough that an appointment usually is required to visit it. The Porteouses have no plan for their winery to grow much in the next few years.

Story Vineyard concentrates on Zinfandel, in the best tradition of this region, but also makes a white wine from mission grapes as a limited-production specialty.

This is an instructive small winery. Founded by the late Eugene Story and continued by his family, the yellow brick building on Bell Road is flanked by a 50-year-old vineyard. Between the first row of vines and the main door, crusher and press occupy a concrete pad. Inside, a row of temperature-controlled, stainless steel fermentors runs along one wall while racks of American oak barrels take up most of the rest of the space. A small bottling line is at the rear. Thus, the cellars allow the process of winemaking to be seen from beginning to end without moving a step, though for clear looks at some of the details it is advisable to stroll a few feet.

Story founded the business in 1973 as Cosumnes River Vineyard, and built the cellar in the following year. He changed the name to Story in 1979 after finding that almost nobody but locals could pronounce Cosumnes.

TKC Vineyards is a looming presence from either Bell or Shenandoah Road in spite of its being buried almost to its roof in a small knoll. A pair of substantial doors flanked by retaining walls makes an impressive, highly visible facade. In time, the winery will be capped by the residence of proprietors Harold and Monica Nuffer, but, for now, they commute from China Lake.

TKC made its first Zinfandel in 1981. The owners plan to continue as specialists in that variety. The name, incidentally, comes from the initials of three Nuffer children.

Calaveras-Tuolumne Wineries

Two readily visitable small wineries are close to the Calaveras-Tuolumne county line, one near Murphys in Calaveras County, the other on the Tuolumne side near Columbia.

Stevenot Winery may have as romantic a site as a winery can have in California. The road to it runs up to a ridge above Murphy's main street, passes Mercer Caverns, then plunges down a tree-clad slope to the bottom of a deep gorge. There owner Barden Stevenot's vineyards begin right next to the road. His cellar is hidden away behind them, beneath a looming outcrop of rock.

Except for being housed in a notably picturesque hay barn, the winery proper is a typically well-equipped, modern California cellar. Visitors are encouraged to have leisurely looks at the working gear, which includes horizontal basket press, stainless steel fermentors, and French oak barrels.

The tasting room is across a small clearing on the lower level of a wood-frame, unpainted house that ought to be in movies, preferably ones about The Last Frontier. In it visitors may sample Chenin Blanc, Cardonnay, Cabernet Sauvignon, and Zinfandel among other varietals, mostly from local grapes.

Yankee Hill Winery, a mile east of Columbia State Historic Park, is the property of the Ron Erickson family. It originally was Columbia Cellars, built by another owner in 1972.

The Ericksons offer vintage-dated Zinfandel, Grenache, and several generic table and sparkling wines under the original Columbia label. They also offer picnicking under an arbor alongside a small wood-sided building that serves both as tasting room and cellar.

More wineries. Several other wineries are in the planning stage. One more Calaveras County winery, Chispa Cellars in Murphys, exists and has been producing tiny lots of wine since 1977 at the upper end of the main street in Murphys.

Other Than Wineries

The Mother Lode, like several other California wine districts, gains considerable appeal from having a romantic nineteenth century history. Unlike the others, the early appeal was only slightly vinous. The real story in these parts was gold.

Though large-scale mining is in the distant past, the countryside still shows a good many signs of the time: headframes of old mines, washes from sluicing opera-

tions, and, not least, towns with some uncommon architecture dating back to an era of easy spending.

The landmarks are too many, in too many different places, to be covered here. An engaging guide is the *Sunset* book, *Gold Rush Country.*

Plotting a Route

One U.S. highway and a plethora of state highways ascend from the San Joaquin Valley floor to intersect with State Highway 49, the Mother Lode's north-south artery. The fastest way up is U.S. Highway 50 from Sacramento to the intersection with State 49 at Placerville.

Of the slower state routes, State Highway 88 from Lodi to Jackson is ranked by more than a few connoisseurs at the head of the list for scenic beauty. Almost as attractive is State Highway 16 from Sacramento to Plymouth. The latter road has the further advantage of arriving in the heart of the most vinous part of the Mother Lode.

Within the region, winery visitors can make a tidy and efficient loop by using U.S. 50, State 49, and Amador County Road E16 (which becomes Pleasant Valley Road in El Dorado County). Nearly all of the wineries in Amador and El Dorado counties are on these routes, or very close to them. The Calaveras and Tuolumne wineries are near State 49 some miles south of the loop.

Lodi, town & country

Lodi is a genuine Central Valley agricultural center. Most of its 35,000 people live in tidily kept, tree-shaded residential districts around the main shopping area. Vineyards and other farmlands come right up to the edge of town.

Local farmland is, by force of geography, compact. Lodi nestles within the angles formed by the meeting of the Sacramento and San Joaquin rivers. To the east, the Sierra Nevada foothills form the third leg of a triangular boundary. Though other crops grow here, grapes predominate. The town long has been a table grape center, a brandy capital, and a natural source of sherry types. In more recent times, new grape varieties produced by the University of California at Davis have helped refocus local production toward table wines.

The Wineries

For one reason or another, Lodi has been—and still is—a traditional home for wineries owned by cooperatives of grape growers. Two of its visitable cellars are co-ops. Probably because so many of its growers have a piece of the co-op action, Lodi has lacked for small, family-owned cellars in recent years. But that appears to be changing. Three of its visitable cellars are indeed family-owned, and small.

Barengo Vineyards, known a bit less formally by local visitors as just Barengo's, looms up alongside Acampo Road in an expansive and rather graceful brick building which dates back to 1868.

It became the Barengo winery in 1944 when Dino Barengo bought it to establish his own business. The property now belongs to Verdugo Vineyards, Inc., after two brief interim ownerships during which the winery was modernized and its capacity more than doubled from Barengo's day. The new owners are continuing both trends and sprucing up the grounds as well.

After years of being a tantalizing presence beyond the tasting room window, the winery is open to tour. The crushers and fermenting tanks sit in open air behind the old still house. Inside the brick-walled, wood-beamed main cellar, visitors can look through the long series of cellars, some filled with stainless steel storage tanks, others with an agreeable mixture of redwood and oak cooperage ranging in size from 50,000-gallon tanks down to 50-gallon barrels.

One of the winery's long-time specialties is Ruby Cabernet, which founder Barengo helped pioneer as a varietal wine beginning in 1949. (It is a UC-bred offspring of Cabernet Sauvignon and Carignane.) Other specialties include a flavored after-dinner drink called Cremocha, and Dudenhofer, a woodruff-flavored white patterned after German May wines, but distinct from them. The list—all of it open for tasting—continues through a broad range of varietal and generic table wines and dessert wines under the Barengo and Lost Hills labels.

The name Barengo also is associated closely with wine vinegar made in the traditional Orleans method, which is slow aging in barrels. That process takes place in a sizable cellar separate from the winery. The tasting room staff will explain vinegar as well as wine.

Across from the tasting room door, under a row of trees, several picnic tables are available on a first-come, first-served basis.

The firm has several tasting rooms around the state. It will forward a list on request.

Borra's Cellar is one of two recently established small family wineries in Lodi. It may be the only one in California with an aging cellar that can be entered through a good, old-fashioned storm cellar door, the kind that angles up against a wall to cover the stairs beneath.

An appointment is required to get through that door to see neatly stacked rows of American oak barrels, or to have a look at the tasting room and bottling line in the upper story of what used to be a family residence but now is a winery from top to bottom. Proprietors Stephen and Beverly Borra can be talked into strolling out beyond an equipment shed to show the crusher, press, and fermentors. The latter include both open-topped redwood and stainless steel tanks. The family vineyard stretches away beyond them. The Borra's Cellar label is used mostly for Barbera and Carignane from those vines.

Coloma Cellars operates from an adobe-faced building on the State Highway 99 frontage road just north of Lodi.

Visitors to the small aging cellar find a variety of table, dessert, and specialty wines available for tasting.

There are no tours of the cellar or the adjacent building where grape concentrate is produced for home winemakers. The company has several tasting rooms elsewhere in the state, and will provide a list.

The label, incidentally, originated in the Gold Rush town of Coloma.

East-Side Winery, known by its labels as Royal Host or Conti Royale, has its tasting room inside a retired 50,000-gallon redwood wine tank.

The vessel, tailored to its new purpose with a man-sized door and interior varnishing, still gives a clear impression of how it feels to be inside a wine tank. It gives the optical illusion of being bigger inside than outside.

The main winery buildings stretch southward from the roadside tasting room. As is often the case with cellars built in the 1930s, the architecture does not conform to romantic notions of a winery. Still, at East-Side, the scenic deficiencies are only external. The interiors are full of handsome cooperage, all of it in admirably clean and orderly surroundings.

East-Side, as much as any winery in the district, reflects increasing local interest in making table wine. Members of the grower cooperative that owns it have responded strongly to new grape varieties developed at U.C. Davis. The Royal Host and Conti Royale labels appear on varietal bottlings of Emerald Riesling, Ruby Cabernet, and the rarer Gold. (Gold, a muscat-derived grape, was originally intended to be eaten fresh, but it would not ship successfully. The wine resulting from it falls within the general classification of light, sweet Muscat.)

East-Side demonstrates equally well the lingering and probably unquenchable Lodi enthusiasm for making Sherry. In one building on the comprehensive tour is a large and informally organized Sherry solera.

After the tour, which is long, and the tasting, which can encompass a substantial list, visitors can retire to picnic tables just outside the tasting tank. On the lawn, tables are shaded by a mixture of tall trees. Family groups need give no advance notice, but larger groups are required to reserve in advance. The grounds will accommodate no more than 100.

Guild Wineries & Distilleries, largest producer of wine among California's cooperatives and one of the state's farthest-flung associations of vineyardists, has its ancestral home and much of its presence in or near Lodi.

For visitors, the action is all at Central Cellars just off Victor Road (State Highway 12) on the east side of town.

A modern, spacious, and cool tasting room is in front of the main aging cellar. Some of Guild's visitors limit their explorations to this oasis, especially when the summer sun heats Lodi into the 100°F/38°C range, or when winter rain pelts the countryside. However, the hosts willingly conduct tours in the worst of weather as well as the best.

Visible in the big cellars during the tours are concrete storage tanks of great capacity and steel tanks of still greater volume, a complete Charmat Champagne cellar, a huge bottling room that clanks and rattles at

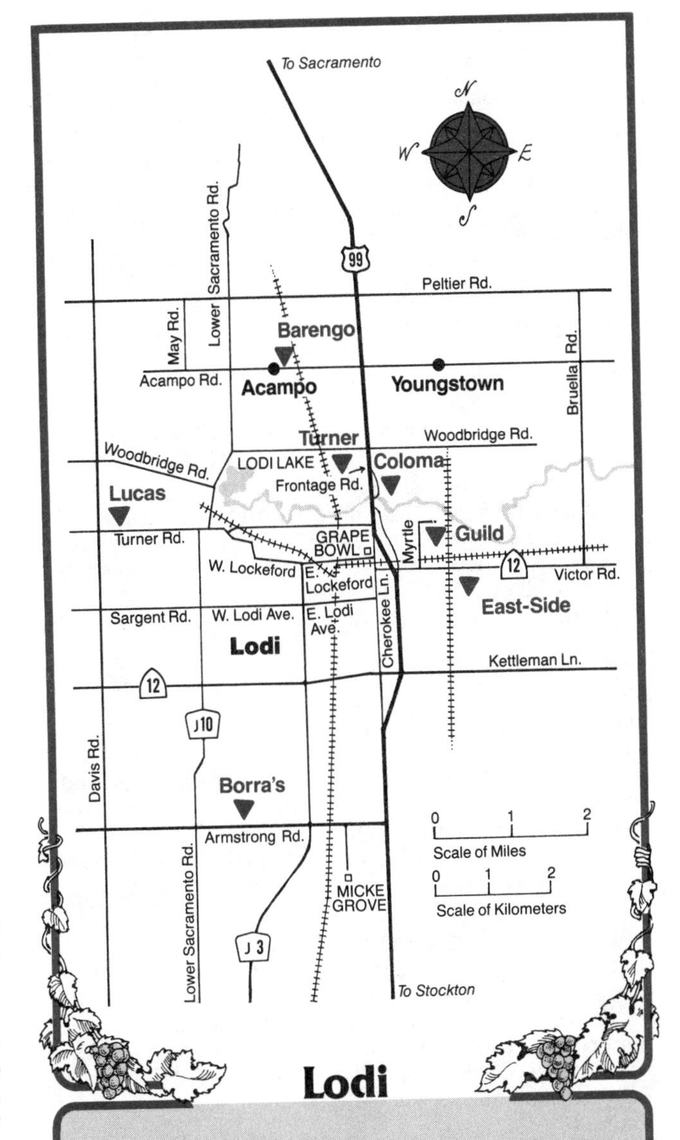

Barengo Vineyards. From State 99, Acampo exit, W 1 mi. on Acampo Rd. (3125 E. Orange St., Acampo, CA 95220) Tel (209) 369-2746. Picnic. Daily 9-6. GT/Ta.

Borra's Cellar. From State 99, Armstrong Rd. exit, W 2 mi. on Armstrong Rd. (1301 E. Armstrong Rd., Lodi, CA 95240) Tel (209) 368-5082. Appt. only.

Coloma Cellars. On State 99 east side frontage road N of State 12 (P.O. Box 478, Lodi, CA 95240) Tel (209) 368-7822. Daily 9-6. Ta.

East-Side Winery (Royal Host). From State 99, E on State 12-East 1 mi. (6100 E. State 12, Lodi, CA 95240) Tel (209) 369-4768. Picnic. Daily 9-5. GT/Ta.

Guild Wineries & Distilleries. From State 99, E on State 12-East .5 mi. to Myrtle Ave., N .5 mi. to winery. (One Winemasters' Way, Lodi, CA 95240) Tel (209) 368-5151. Daily 10-5. GT/Ta.

The Lucas Winery. From State 99, Turner Rd. exit, W 3.5 mi. to N. Davis Rd., N .1 mi. to winery (18196 N. Davis Rd., Lodi, CA 95420) Tel (209) 368-2006. Picnic. Nov-Dec daily noon to sunset, by appt. remainder of year.

Turner Winery. From State 99, Woodbridge exit, W .5 mi. on E. Woodbridge Rd. (3750 E. Woodbridge Rd., Woodbridge, CA 95258) Tel (209) 368-5338. Daily 10-5. GT by appt./Ta.

Key: GT (guided tour); IT (informal tour); Ta (tasting).

a furious enough pace to satisfy *The Sorcerer's Apprentice,* and, not least, the cased goods warehouse. There is an immense amount of wine at Guild, and the people there have worked out ingenious arrangements for dealing with it. For example, a sunken lane goes straight through the middle of the warehouse. It is just wide enough to accommodate flatbed truck and trailer rigs and just deep enough for forklifts to drive right on and off the flatbeds to load them.

No grapes are crushed at these premises. That goes on at other Guild locations in Lodi, Fresno, and Bakersfield. However, the firm maintains a display vineyard adjacent to the Winemaster's House. In this vineyard the proprietors have planted three or four of each of the wine grape varieties recommended for California. Nowhere else can visitors see with so few steps how varied is the vine.

Back in the tasting room, Guild offers a full line of table, appetizer, dessert, and sparkling wines. Most are under the affiliated Cresta Blanca (see Mendocino chapter) and Cribari (see Fresno section of San Joaquin chapter) labels. Guild also makes a good deal of brandy and, uniquely, a grape vodka called Silverado.

The Lucas Winery is Lodi's smallest cellar.

David Lucas makes wine mostly for local customers, having started in 1978. Much of it he sells each autumn to a mailing list. What is left sells at the cellar door, first-come, first-served, between Thanksgiving and Christmas. Home winemakers are welcome in harvest time, when David and Tamara Lucas sell grapes from their 30-acre vineyard of old zinfandel vines. Visitors with appointments are welcome all year around.

The crusher and press are housed in an old-fashioned redwood barn during the off-season and are pulled out in the open air during harvest. Stainless steel fermentors occupy a roofed area behind the barn. Two small, tidily kept frame buildings between the barn and the proprietor's residence hold a tasting room and several small racks of barrels full of aging Zinfandel, some white, some light, some full-bodied, and some late harvest.

Turner Winery is a curious outgrowth of changing tides in California wine. For years an anonymous bulk plant, it was bought in 1979 by a family of vineyardists from Lake County who wanted an immediately efficient home for their sizable acreage of grapes.

In the absence of any old cellars close to home, they went afield to Lodi. The winery they bought had been built in 1935 on the site of a still older winery, then modernized at several junctures before its sale to the current owners. The Turners offer tours of their big, plain-faced winery only by appointment and only to groups, but their Lake County wines are available for sampling by all comers in a pleasantly decorated tasting room. The list includes Chardonnay, Chenin Blanc, Sauvignon Blanc, Cabernet Sauvignon, Petite Sirah, and Zinfandel.

More wineries. In the course of poking around Lodi, one is bound to encounter other wineries. Most are marked by the tall towers that house their column stills. (Lodi is a center for beverage brandy as well as for the production of dessert wines.)

One of the most architecturally striking wineries in the district is on Woodbridge Road at Bruella. Once the Cherokee Co-op, later Montcalm, still later Filice, it now belongs to Robert Mondavi. Two or three other Lodi wineries are purely in the bulk trade and not open to visit. These include Woodbridge Vineyard Association and Community Winery (United Vintners) in the northwest quarter of town, and Liberty Winery in the northeast quarter.

Other Than Wineries

The year-round attractions of the wineries are supplemented by an annual festival with an uncommonly long name—the Lodi Grape Festival and National Wine Show. It takes place all over town on a weekend in mid-September, usually the one following Labor Day.

Most of the festivities are in the Grape Bowl, a fairground near State 99 northeast of Lodi. Wineries mount exhibits, and the local wine growers' association sponsors daily wine tasting in the midst of general farm displays and the most widely advertised feature of the festival, the grape mosaics.

The mosaics are what their name suggests—pictures or designs wrought by placing grapes one at a time on wire mesh. Panel sizes range up to 5 by 10 feet. Club women spend hours plucking thousands of grapes and poking them into words and pictures that follow a preannounced theme. (A typical motif is "early California.") Grapes come in a wider range of colors than many people would suspect. The mosaics are as much a lesson in grape physiology as they are folk art.

Elsewhere on the grounds concessionaires operate the usual quick-food stands and carnival rides.

The main event is an hours-long parade with bands, floats, and drill teams. It assembles on the west side of town, winds through the business district, and finishes up 2 or 3 miles later under the summer sun at the Grape Bowl.

Several wineries hold open house during the festival just as they do all year. But they augment their staffs to run comprehensive tours for festival crowds that have numbered 50,000 to 60,000 in recent years.

Lodi has two recreational parks. Lake Lodi Park, on Turner Road a mile west of State 99, rings the municipal lake, a diverted part of the Mokelumne River. Trees shade the shore and picnic tables. The park has rental boats and swimming beaches.

Micke Grove, south of town in a large stand of valley oaks, has a small zoo, gardens, and fine picnic sites. It is west of State 99 on Armstrong Road.

For a listing of restaurants and accommodations in the area, write to Lodi District Chamber of Commerce, P.O. Box 386, Lodi, CA 95240.

Plotting a Route

The town of Lodi straddles State Highway 99, the quick route from almost any of the other Central Valley towns north or south.

For visitors coming from the San Francisco Bay region, the freeway route is Interstate Highway 580

Sherry: variations on the theme

As a word, "Sherry" is not a great deal more precise than, say, "nuts." Both cover a vast ground (and they go well together).

The most noticeable difference from one Sherry to the next is in degree of sweetness. Some relatively dry ones are intended as appetizer drinks. Others, very sweet, come under the dessert category. In California the appetizer Sherries for the most part are labeled "dry" or "cocktail." The dessert types mostly go forth as "Cream Sherry."

Sherry begins being Sherry when the winemaker adds a bit of brandy to a newly fermented dry white wine. The purpose is to stabilize the wine so it will not turn to vinegar when it is exposed to oxidation, the next step.

After this initial step, California winemakers produce their various Sherries in several ways, adding still more distinctions of flavor than sweetness.

Many "bake" it, though the word suggests more heat than they in fact apply. The usual limits are 120° to 140°F/49° to 60°C for 45 to 120 days. Air space is left in the barrel or tank. Heat and air together produce the darkened color and characteristic flavor. Sweeter Sherries are made by blending in a certain amount of Angelica or a similar wine after the base Sherry has been baked. The wine may or may not be aged further after baking.

A variant method is the long aging of partly filled barrels without the unusual warmth. In this instance, oxygen and wood together form the flavor.

A radically different method involves cultivating a specific yeast as a film floating atop aging Sherry in a partially filled barrel or tank. The yeast, "flor," produces a distinctive flavor of its own. The yeast, oxidation, and the wood of the barrels all come together to form the characteristic flavors of this type of Sherry. In the case of flor Sherries, the initial addition of brandy is very slight and is augmented at the end of the aging period.

In California several wineries use a variant method developed at the University of California. It is called "submerged yeast culture," an unromantic but accurate designation. Instead of a film of yeast being allowed to form and then work very slowly, a yeast is introduced into the wine and episodically agitated so it is present throughout the wine. The method, faster than film flor, produces a characteristic yeast flavor but without the wood flavor associated with film flors.

Whichever of these methods it uses, a winery may establish a "solera." Solera indicates only that a barrel is never emptied of all its wine. Rather, a certain fraction is removed for bottling, then a newer wine is added to the remaining part.

through Livermore to Tracy, then north along the connector Interstate Highway 205 to Interstate Highway 5. To change from I-5 to State 99, you can continue on State Highway 120 to Manteca, or make a brief descent onto one local road. Lathrop does the job as well as any, connecting with I-5 about 4 miles north of its junction with I-205.

Another speedy but fairly scenic route between the San Francisco Bay area and Lodi combines Interstate Highway 80 as far east as Fairfield, then the two-lane State Highway 12 from Fairfield to Lodi. At one point the road offers an overview of the aircraft based at Travis Air Force Base. It also offers endless opportunities to study small boats while they pass under the river bridge at Rio Vista.

A slower, still more scenic variation of the I-80/State 12 route between the Bay region and Lodi stays closer to the Sacramento River delta for a longer time. This route requires getting to the Contra Costa County town of Martinez by whatever means, then working east to Antioch on State Highway 4, and from there to Rio Vista along the levee road, State Highway 160. At the Rio Vista Bridge, change to State 12 for the final leg into Lodi.

Within the neighborhood of Lodi, getting around requires little effort. West of State 99, Turner, Woodbridge, and Acampo roads serve well for east-west travel. The main north-south roads other than the freeway are De Vries and Lower Sacramento.

East of the freeway, things spread out a bit more, but the same east-west roads continue, with the important addition of Victor Road. The north-south roads are Kennefick and Bruella.

Within these grids the terrain is flat, given over mainly to vineyards, but with occasional surprises such as a line of olive or palm trees, or an old dry river course with its bottom full of vineyards and an occasional home garden.

Sacramento and West

For years Sacramento had the odd winery or two hidden away in back corners, but was mainly notable for being the state capital. The city proper still has its same handful of wineries, but its suburbs have sprouted almost twice as many.

Much of the interest is some miles to the southwest, near the Sacramento River delta town of Clarksburg, where a fairly large winery has some substantial vineyard acreage to go with it. Nearby Davis, home of the University of California's Department of Viticulture and Enology, has a visitable cellar. So do the towns of Winters and Woodland.

For all the growth, wine touring in and near Sacramento remains a matter of visiting a cellar at a time rather than trying to cover the whole route because the wineries are scattered across so large a landscape.

The Wineries

The range in size and character among Sacramento area wineries is as great as in far more crowded districts.

Brookside Winery's Sacramento facility was founded as Mills Winery in 1910, had its second set of owners in 1946, then became a part of the Cucamonga-based Brookside Vineyard Company in 1968 (see page 154).

The cellars are open daily for self-guided tours and tasting. A limited number of wines, mostly dessert types, still are available for purchase by the barrel, an original distinction of Mills. All Brookside wines are available for tasting and sale.

Caché Cellars belongs to a growing tradition in California, that of the winery housed in a former dairy.

In this case the architecture, to borrow a line from Duke Ellington, "ain't much to look at, ain't nothin' to see." But the winery within transcends both the building's exterior and the plain fields around it in the flats west of Davis.

Owner-winemaker Charles Lowe chose the inexpensive building and site so there would be more money left to fill it with stainless steel fermentors and a varied collection of American and French oak barrels, and to fill them with wines from grapes purchased across much of the state. The roster, to give some idea, includes Chardonnay from Monterey, Sauvignon Blanc from San Luis Obispo, Pinot Noir from Sonoma, Zinfandel from Amador, and Carnelian from not far away. The Carnelian, incidentally, is made with the technique called carbonic maceration (see page 134). The first crush was in 1979.

R & J Cook Winery is the great pioneer in a surprising new wine district around Clarksburg, in the Sacramento River delta country.

The winery is typical of modern small cellars in California: a big horizontal basket press, stainless steel fermenting and storage tanks inside and out, and French and American oak barrels for final aging. Neither is the part concrete block, part wood frame lean-to cellar building any sort of surprise. A ranch house with Tudor touches is somewhat unusual, but the real surprise is vines growing right to the dry edge of delta levees. The view from a tree-shaded, levee-top picnic area—across water but down to vines—is not easy to find anywhere else in the world. Owners Roger and Joanne Cook are pleased to explain why the deep, sandy soil here is an ideal environment for wine grapes.

The roster of wines from their vines includes Cabernet Sauvignon, Merlot, and Petite Sirah among reds. Among the whites are three Chenin Blancs, made semi-dry, dry, and barrel-fermented dry. Together they make a most instructive tasting in how winemaking affects varietal flavors.

Frasinetti and Sons dates back to 1897, a long career by local standards. Founder James Frasinetti died in 1965 at the age of 91. His sons and grandsons continue the family tradition.

After the original building burned to the ground in 1924, it was replaced by a utilitarian collection of corrugated iron structures. During the early 1970s, the family added warm-hued stucco faces to the main cellar and bottling building, made a handsome tasting room, and otherwise turned the property into a peaceable, even serene, island at the end of a busy industrial street running alongside a railroad track.

There is no tour, only tasting of a longish list of table and dessert wines.

Gibson Wine Company is best known as a pioneer in the making and marketing of fruit and berry wines, including one from kiwi, but the firm also makes a range of table, dessert, and sparkling wines.

There is no tour of the substantial winery, started in 1943 by Robert Gibson and continued since 1960 by a grower cooperative, but the wines may be sampled at the Gibson tasting room a mile south of the winery, next to State 99 at Grant Line Road.

Orleans Hill Vinicultural Association, temporarily housed in a rented part of the old Woodland Olive Products processing plant, is one of those tiny wineries that tempt home winemakers to make the jump, in this case for a particularly good reason.

Owners James and Carol Lapsley are the staff, having graduated to the bonded ranks in 1980 after a decade as home winemakers. (Prudently, they keep other jobs. James organizes wine courses at U.C. Davis extension.) A small crusher and an ingenious, home-built hydraulic press are the main pieces of processing gear. American oak barrels serve both as fermentors and aging vessels for Lodi and Amador Zinfandel made in a range of styles from white to red.

The name comes from a long-ago vineyard of Arpad Haraszthy (see the Buena Vista entry, page 35) near the village of Esparto. The vineyard's name came, in turn, from a grape variety called Orleans, which allegedly has some flavor kinships with white riesling, and which the Lapsleys hope to see replanted for their use.

Winters Wine Company occupies a fine brick building which did time in the Gaslight Era as the dining room of the Winters Opera House.

Owner John Storm has installed within its walls a typical small, modern winery in which he makes a broad range of wines from a remarkably local assemblage of vineyards. Included in the roster are a Petite Sirah from century-old vines at Orleans Hill (see Orleans Hill Vinicultural Association, above), a Johannisberg Riesling from Suisun Valley, and a Chenin Blanc from Winters. There are also varietals from Napa and Amador counties. There is, alas, no Port under the jug label, Storm Cellars.

More wineries. Two small wineries in the Sacramento district round out the roster. Harbor Winery is the property of a college teacher of literature named Charles Myers, who makes small lots of varietal table wines from Napa and Amador grapes, and a rare dessert wine from mission grapes grown in Amador. The cellar in a riverfront building at the edge of the city has been active since 1972 but is not open to tour.

Bogle Vineyards is a much smaller neighbor of R & J Cook near Clarksburg in the emerging Delta district. A producer of Chenin Blanc, Petite Sirah, and a proprietary rosé called Merritt Island Rosé after the vineyard location, the family-owned winery is open only by appointment.

Other Than Wineries

Though the Department of Viticulture and Enology at U.C. Davis is not open to the public, it deserves a bow from any appreciator of California wine who whistles past on I-80 or cruises by on State Highway 128 on the opposite side of the campus. The campus, 14 miles west of the state capital, is a pretty place to while away an hour or two in the midst of a great many trees and even more bicycles.

It would stretch matters to say that all of California's technical progress in winemaking owes itself to the academicians at Davis, but the school had a lot to do with creating the spirit of enlightened inquiry that marks professional vintaging in the state.

Some of the most visible results of the work at Davis are noted here and there throughout this book. But some of the most important results of the school's research are not covered because they have to do with such esoteric (but vital) matters as the roles of tannins in red wines, or the tensile strengths of main stems in grape clusters.

Plotting a Route

At the hub of Interstate Highway 5, Interstate Highway 80, U.S. Highway 50, and State Highway 99, Sacramento is not hard to find.

Most of the district's wineries are fairly close to one or another of these freeways. The exceptions, at Clarksburg, also are in the only part of the district that could be called scenic. State Highway 160 cuts west from I-5 at Sacramento and passes through Clarksburg on its way to a junction with State Highway 12 at Rio Vista.

Brookside Winery. From U.S. 50, Bradshaw exit, N .25 mi. to winery (9910 Folsom Blvd., Sacramento, CA 95827) Tel (916) 366-9959. Daily 10-6. IT/Ta.

Caché Cellars. From I-80 W of Davis, Pedrick Rd. exit, N 2.3 mi. on Pedrick Rd. to winery drive (Route 1, Box 2780, Davis, CA 95616) Tel (916) 756-6068. By appt. only.

R & J Cook Winery. From Clarksburg, SE 2.8 miles on Netherlands Rd. to winery drive (P.O. Box 227, Clarksburg, CA 95612) Tel (916) 775-1234. Picnic. M-F 9-4 or by appt. GT/Ta.

Frasinetti and Sons. On Frasinetti Rd., .5 mi. S of Florin Rd. and W of SP RR tracks (P.O. Box 28213, Sacramento, CA 95828) Tel (916) 383-2444. M-Sa 8:30-7. Ta.

Gibson Wine Company. Tasting room at junction of State 99 and Grant Line Rd. (Elk Grove, CA 95624) Tel (916) 685-9211. Daily 10-7. Ta.

Orleans Hill Vinicultural Association. From I-5, Pendegast/State 113 exit, N two blocks (1111 Pendegast St., Woodland, CA 95695) Tel (916) 662-1928. Sa 9-5 or by appt. GT/Ta.

Winters Wine Company. From I-505, State 128 exit, W .3 mi. to Main St., S .7 mi. to winery (15 Main St., Winters, CA 95694) Tel (916) 758-2150. Daily 10-6. GT by appt./Ta. (Outside map area.)

Not on Map—Restricted Visitor Facilities

Bogle Vineyards. (Route 1, Box 276, Clarksburg, CA 95612) Tel (916) 744-1139. By appt. only.

Harbor Winery. (7576 Pocket Rd., Sacramento, CA 95831) By written appt. only.

Key: GT (guided tour); IT (informal tour); Ta (tasting).

San Joaquin Valley

California's biggest vineyard of them all

California barn

The San Joaquin Valley is not wine country in the compact sense of the north coast counties, where wineries may be as thick as six per square mile. But this huge and implausibly diverse agricultural empire is wine country on a scale the coastal regions cannot match. Its 35 wineries produce something like 70 percent of the state's annual volume of wine. Fresno County alone sends 700,000 tons of grapes to wineries in a good year, compared to 320,000 for all 14 coast counties combined.

Not unexpectedly, this vineyard of the giants requires its visitors to wear seven-league boots. Some 200 miles of State Highway 99 separate Modesto on the north from Bakersfield on the south. In all that space, only 15 cellars had visitor facilities in the spring of 1982. What is more, the area's distance from other major population centers matters to all but valley residents. Modesto is 95 miles southeast of San Francisco; Bakersfield 111 miles north of Los Angeles. For these reasons most winery visits come as diversions, either during travels between coast and mountains, or on north-south vacation trips.

The handful of survivors from the family farm era of winemaking lend spice to visits, but in the main the tourable wineries fit the size of this great valley.

In business terms, the San Joaquin is one huge district because the large wineries draw grapes from the length and breadth of the valley. For visitors, though, the region divides into at least three parts. The focal points are Modesto, Fresno, and Bakersfield.

Modesto & surroundings

Modesto and the wine business did not get together until the 1930s, but the two have prospered mutually since. The city's population doubled between 1950 and 1960, and has doubled again. The total now surpasses 105,000. The production of wine has grown faster than that.

Modesto is well equipped to handle visitors in numbers. A gateway to Yosemite National Park, it has substantial numbers of motels and restaurants, most of them ranged along McHenry Boulevard and Yosemite Avenue.

The Wineries

No great distance separates Lodi from Modesto, but in those few miles the pattern of winery ownership changes markedly. Lodi is a capital of grower cooperatives. Modesto does not have a single one.

E & J Gallo is far and away the dominant winery among the eight that ring Modesto. Some that seem small next to Gallo have impressive size when measured against the average cellar of other districts. A pair of genuinely small premises still give the region a diverse character.

Four wineries welcome visitors in one way or another. Bella Napoli and Delicato Vineyards are on or near the freeway, State 99. Cadlolo and Franzia are east of the freeway on State Highway 120.

Bella Napoli evokes an era that seems to be passing in the San Joaquin Valley. The winery, a separate structure at the rear of the family home, is in every respect a small, old-fashioned country enterprise.

Because of this, proprietor Lucas Hat cannot encourage a tourist trade in the usual sense. There are no tours or tastings, only the agreeably uncomplicated opportunity to stand in the courtyard amid whitewashed farm buildings and buy a supply of country red or white in bottle or jug.

Lucas is the second generation of Hats—the family name is Neapolitan—to make Vine Flow table wines for sale to a mainly local trade.

The wines come from a sizable vineyard surrounding the house and winery. Hat takes only a small part of his crop for his own use. The rest he sells to a larger winery.

Cadlolo Winery, in the town of Escalon, presents a fresh face to the world. The main building of concrete and red brick looks almost new beneath its coat of pale cream paint. Almost the only signs of age are an old-style evaporative cooler on the roof, and a mature tree shading the front wall. But the building dates from 1913 when L. Sciaroni launched a winery on the site. Charles Cadlolo held the reins from 1937 until 1955. His sons, Raymond and Theodore, maintained the business until 1980. The new owner of these still-small cellars is Dorothy Walton.

The owners' pride in the premises is evident in more than the freshly painted appearance of the main building. The crusher alongside one wall has a well-scrubbed air. The interior of the winery is just as tidy.

Not-quite-formal tours (sometimes interrupted for a bit of work on the part of the guide) start at the crusher and go all the way through to the bottling department. Tasting is in a casual room just to one side of the main cellar, within sniffing range of its aromatic redwood tanks full of wine. On hand for sampling are several generic table wines, and an equal number of appetizer and dessert wines.

Delicato Vineyards occupies a very considerable plot of ground just alongside the southbound lanes of State 99, on a frontage road near Manteca.

Signs give ample warning before the freeway exit leads onto what is very nearly a private lane. The winery has on each flank a residence of one or another branch of the owning family, the Indelicatos. (Given the family name, the proprietors must have taken great delight in naming the place. He who doubts the authenticity of the reverse twist has only to read the names on the mailboxes on either side of the winery.)

Delicato has grown greatly over the past 15 years. At one time an informal tour could cover all the ground within a small, iron-sheathed winery building in a very few minutes. Now guided tours, launched from a modern textured-block tasting room, take in impressive arrays of outdoor stainless steel fermentors and storage tanks—almost 22 million gallons worth—and such esoteric contrivances as rotary vacuum filters. The immaculately clean original cellar, full of redwood tanks, is on the route as is a much enlarged bottling line. This tour is the most complete and informative of any offered by a sizable producing winery in the district. The wide range of Delicato wines includes varietal and generic table wines; appetizer, dessert, and sparkling wines.

Franzia Winery is on State 120 east of Ripon. An attractively designed and furnished tasting room sits in the midst of a decorative block of vines next to the highway. The several large buildings of the winery proper stand farther back, amid larger blocks of vines.

Giuseppe Franzia, having emigrated from Genoa, started his family in the California wine business in 1906. After the untimely intervention of Prohibition necessitated a second start in 1933, Giuseppe and five sons built the enterprise up to an annual production of 15 million gallons by the time the family sold to a corporate owner in 1971. The new proprietors have kept things growing.

The company offers tours of its vast, mechanically efficient plant only by appointment. Appointments are generally limited to groups.

The tasting room, meanwhile, is open to all. Franzia wines include a broad spectrum of generic and varietal table wines, several sparkling wines, and vermouth.

A tree-shaded picnic ground on lawns adjacent to the tasting room is open to casual drop-in visitors when it has not been reserved for groups. It's a good place to enjoy a deli lunch with your wine choice.

More wineries. Visitors to Modesto are likely to notice other wineries on the landscape.

By far the largest winery in Modesto (and one of the largest in the world) is E & J Gallo. At the present it is not open to visitors. Alas for that, because the Gallos have come from small and perfectly ordinary beginnings to a dazzlingly complex center for making wine under the most rational of conditions with the most efficient of equipment. Nothing is left to wayward chance. The Gallos even have their own bottle manufactory on the premises, yielding glass made to their own patented formula.

Gallo's made-on-the-spot bottles receive a complete range of varietal and generic table wines, sparkling wines, and appetizer, dessert and flavored types made from grapes grown the length and breadth of the state.

(Continued on next page)

. . . Continued from page 143)

The firm owns huge vineyard acreages in Modesto, Livingston, and the Sierra foothills, buys still more grapes on contract, and also buys the entire wine production of grower cooperatives in the Central Valley, Sonoma, and Napa.

Even though there is no admittance, serious students of California wine owe themselves a drive past the headquarters and winery on Fairbanks Avenue in the southeast quarter of Modesto. There is no crushing at this facility: that goes on at other Gallo wineries west of Livingston and in Fresno.

Another sizable winery in the district which bottles wine but does not have visitor facilities is JFJ Bronco. At its Ceres location, the winery makes a wide range of varietal and generic table wines.

A. & L. Pirrone Vineyards operates a substantial, durable bulk winery alongside State 99 at the town of Salida. It has been a family cellar since 1936; the vineyards date from 1923.

United Vintners has an old, little-used winery on State Highway 120, about equidistant between Franzia to the west and the town of Escalon to the east. This, the original Petri winery, is never open to visitors. Instead, UV welcomes visitors at Asti in Sonoma County (see page 43) and at Inglenook in the Napa Valley (see page 77).

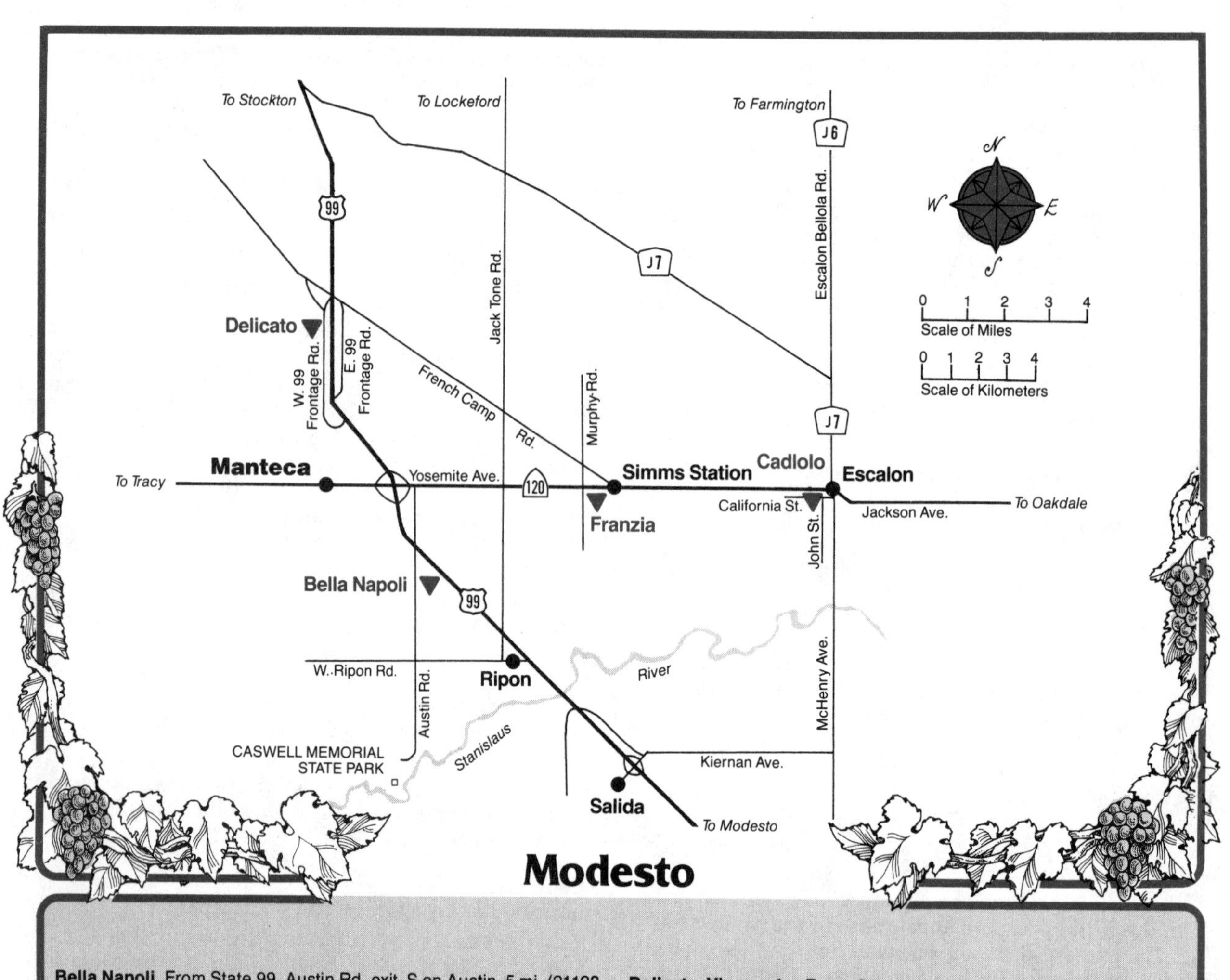

Bella Napoli. From State 99, Austin Rd. exit, S on Austin .5 mi. (21128 S. Austin Rd., Manteca, CA 95336) Tel (209) 599-3885. Daily 9-5.

Cadlolo Winery. From State 120 at W side of Escalon, S on McHenry Ave. across RR tracks, W on California Ave. 100 yards to winery (1124 California St., Escalon, CA 95320) Tel (209) 838-2457. M-Sa 8-5. IT/Ta.

Delicato Vineyards. From State 99, French Camp Rd. exit, S on westside frontage rd. .5 mi. (12001 S. Hwy. 99, Manteca, CA 95336) Tel (209) 982-0679. GT F 2 and 4 or by appt./TA daily 9-5.

Franzia Winery. From State 99, E 4.5 mi. on State 120 (P.O. Box 697, Ripon, CA 95366) Tel (209) 599-4111. Picnic. GT by appt/TA daily 10-5.

Key: GT (guided tour); IT (informal tour); Ta (tasting).

Other Than Wineries

Unlikely as it may seem, Modesto is in the midst of a great deal of water. The Tuolumne and Stanislaus Rivers join the San Joaquin just west of town. Just to the east, folds in the hills harbor three major reservoirs with recreational developments.

These reservoirs, along with Yosemite National Park, draw a great many vacationers through the Modesto district. But for casual visitors, they are too far away to combine with winery visits.

Caswell State Park solves that problem. It extends along 4 miles of the Stanislaus River west of Salida. The river, shallow here, has a number of swimming holes. Picnic sites under spreading oaks are 10 to 15 degrees cooler than nearby farm fields. To get to the park, exit west from State 99 on Austin Road 2 miles south of Manteca. The park is about 5 miles west of the freeway.

Each of the major towns in the district has a tree-shaded municipal park for quick picnics or a lazy afternoon nap.

For a list of overnight accommodations, write to the Modesto Chamber of Commerce, P.O. Box 844, Modesto, CA 95353.

Plotting a Route

All of the wineries open to visit in the Modesto area are either on the freeway, State 99, or the two-lane road, State 120. These two roads form an awkward, toppling T. State Highway 108, another two-laner, runs from State 120 at Escalon into Modesto, the third leg of a triangle that can turn a tour of all five wineries in the region into a tidy loop for anyone starting and finishing in Modesto.

On the San Joaquin Valley floor, these and all other roads are flat, with few or no curves.

The visual interests are subtleties on a vast canvas. A shift from row crop to orchard is gross change, especially when February and March light the orchards with blossom. Random occurrences of single oaks or small clusters in the fields produce eerie perspectives on a misty day. There is a prodigious number of unpainted, decaying small barns to consider in this era of large-scale agriculture. Residential architecture ranges from a rare brick colonial to a profusion of board-and-batten cottages.

To get into the region from the San Francisco Bay area, use Interstate Highway 580 to Tracy, Interstate Highway 5 to its junction with State 120, then the state route to get to or across State 99.

From Los Angeles, I-5 intersects both State Highway 132 into Modesto, and State 120.

Fresno

The highest point in Fresno is the 20th floor of a downtown hotel. Look out from that floor on a typical heat-hazy day in summer, and no hill of stature will appear in view. Fresno is flat.

The city has grown big enough to have traffic jams and other nonagricultural qualities. (In the last census, its 215,400 population was enough to rank it ninth largest among California cities, 73rd largest in the nation.)

Yet it manages to have charms. The main street of Fresno's original business district, fading a few years ago, has been turned into a spacious shopping mall with fountains, many trees (and shaded sitting places), and 20 specially commissioned sculptures. Nearby, a big convention center of unusual architecture is the stage for attractions both home-grown and imported.

To the north of the original city center, West Shaw Avenue has become a long, often architecturally distinctive, sequence of shopping centers and office buildings.

The central city may have begun to acquire a certain urbanity in this era of large-scale and mechanized farming (everybody in the Central Valley calls it "agribusiness" these days), but Fresno is, nonetheless, a farm center. The talk in the coffee shops has to do with one crop or another.

Among those crops, grapes figure most prominently. Fresno and neighboring counties north and south produce enough raisins for the Western hemisphere and enough table grapes for much of the United States. In recent years the district's share of wine production has slipped below its old level of 50 percent of all California wine, but only because other districts have added vineyards more rapidly than has Fresno.

Traditionally the production has leaned toward Sherries, Ports, Muscats, and other sweet dessert wines. The long, sunny summers favor sugar-laden grapes with their ancestral roots in Portuguese or Spanish soils. Here, as in Lodi and Modesto, specially developed warm-climate grapes for table wines are replacing other varieties or supplementing them.

Reading the founding dates of wineries, an innocent might assume that winemaking did not get going in Fresno until 1936 or so, as in the case of Modesto. Blame Prohibition for creating yet another false impression. A man named Lee Eisen planted the first vineyard in the district in 1873. (Three rail-sitters of the day volunteered to eat the entire crop, which they might have done the first year but never thereafter.) Grapes have flourished in Fresno from Eisen's time on, and a good many have gone into wine since 1876.

The Wineries

The Fresno district covers an awesome number of square miles from Madera on the northwest to Cutler on the southeast. Within that vast expanse, fewer than a dozen wineries welcome visitors. But sparse as the numbers might be, the wineries are of such diverse character as to make a complete sampler of everything from giant to miniature, from generalist to specialist, from ultramodern to entirely traditional.

Cribari Winery is located in the colorful complex of brick buildings built as the Roma Winery.

(Continued on next page)

. . . Continued from page 145

When a man named John Cella was developing Roma in the post-Prohibition era, he meant to have a giant of a winery. The fact that the property is laid out on a grid of streets attests to his ambition. The winery is not the giant it once was because standards have changed, but it is big, covering more ground than many newer places. It is also a good deal more colorful than many contemporary wineries.

Cribari is now owned by Guild Wineries & Distilleries (see the Lodi section, page 137).

The proprietors took a huge, brick-walled aging cellar, removed the tanks from it, and turned it into a reception and tasting hall for visitors. Fanciful flags and pennants hang from the lofty ceiling and on some of the tall walls. Hourly tours leave from this reception hall.

The route is along B Street to 4th, across to C, then back. Along the way it passes Cribari's huge crushers, dejuicers, and temperature-controlled, stainless steel fermenting tanks. Finally, in the brandy distillery, the tour provides the only close-up look at column stills to be had in all California.

Available in the tasting room is the full line of Cribari table, sparkling, and dessert wines.

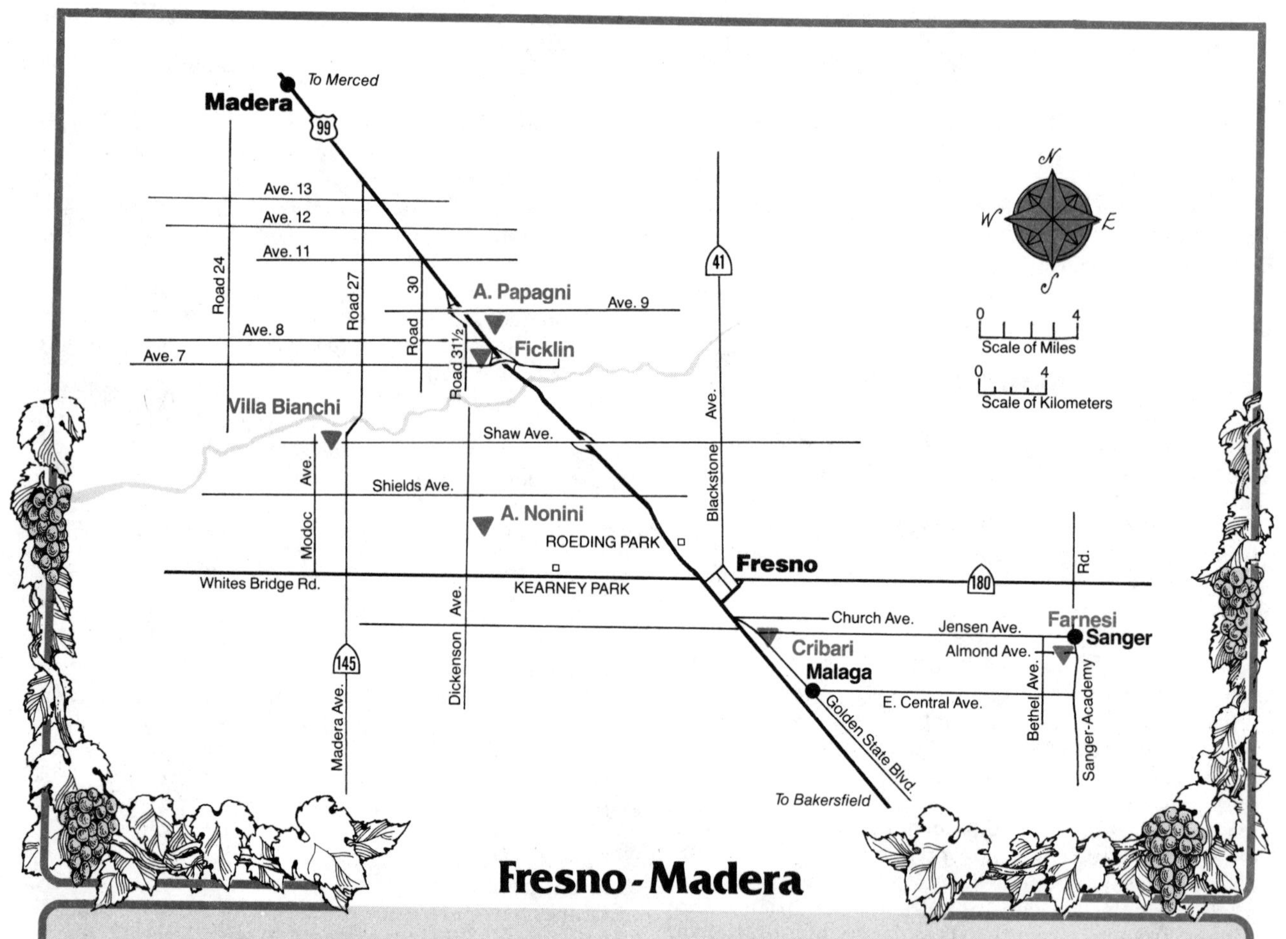

Fresno - Madera

Cribari Winery. From State 99, Jensen Ave. exit northbound or Ventura Ave. exit southbound, change for Golden State Blvd. to Church Ave., then E .25 mi. to winery (3223 E. Church Ave., Fresno, CA 93714) Tel (209) 485-3080. Daily 10-5. GT/Ta.

Farnesi Winery. From Jensen Ave. in Sanger, S on Bethel Ave. .5 mi. to Almond Ave., E on Almond to winery (2426 Almond Ave., Sanger, CA 93657) Tel (209) 875-3004. M-F 8-5, Sa 8-12. Ta.

Ficklin Vineyards. From State 99, Ave. 9 exit, E on Ave. 9 to Rd. 30, S on Rd. 30 to Ave. 7 1/2, E to winery (30246 Ave. 7 1/2, Madera, CA 93637) Tel (209) 674-4598. GT by appt.

A. Nonini Winery. From State 99, McKinley Ave. exit, W 7.5 mi. to Dickenson Ave., then N .5 mi. to winery (2450 N. Dickenson Ave., Fresno, CA 93705) Tel (209) 264-7857. M-Sa 9-6. GT/Ta.

Angelo Papagni Winery. In SE quarter of Ave. 9 exit from State 99 (31574 Ave. 9, Madera, CA 93637) Tel (209) 674-5652. GT by appt.

Quady Winery. Road directions given with appt. (Bus. off.: 321 W. Yosemite Ave., Madera, CA 93637) Tel (209) 673-8068. GT/Ta by appt. (Not on map)

Villa Bianchi Winery. From State 99, W on Shaw Ave. to Modoc Ave., N on Modoc to winery (5806 Modoc Ave., Kerman, CA 93630) Tel (209) 846-7356. M-F 8-4. IT (except during crush)/Ta.

Outside Map Area

California Growers. From Cutler, S to intersection of Rd. 128 and Ave. 384 (P.O. Box 21, Yettem, CA 93670) Tel (209) 528-3033. M-F 8-5.

Key: GT (guided tour); IT (informal tour); Ta (tasting).

Farnesi Winery in Sanger is a small family enterprise founded in 1935 by a transplanted Tuscan named Corado Farnesi, and carried on since 1951 by his nephew, Danny Farnesi. The younger Farnesi, having had the benefits of practical instruction from the founder and academic work at Fresno State University, runs the winery alone in all seasons except harvest-time. Then the whole family joins in making two red table wines to satisfy a local clientele.

The winery, in an adobe building across the street from a row of tidy residences, requires no tour. The proprietor will talk shop over a cordial glass.

Ficklin Vineyards, out of Madera, is one of the smallest wineries in the Central Valley, and certainly the most single-minded.

The specialty is a Tinta Port made entirely from four selected Portuguese grape varieties. Not only is it the specialty: it is nearly the sum of winery production. (The owners started making Emerald Riesling and Ruby Cabernet in the 1960s mainly for their own table, but this remains a very casual part of the enterprise.)

The Ficklin family ranch dates back to 1911, when Walter Ficklin, Sr. arrived in the Fresno area and immediately launched into grapes and other fruit growing. Wine entered the picture in the early 1940s when Ficklin responded to a request by scientists at the University of California at Davis to plant trial blocks of several Portuguese grape varieties that had shown promise in university tests.

David Ficklin, after studying at Davis, began as the winemaker and winery manager. He continues in those roles, assisted now by his son Peter, also a Davis graduate. The vineyardist is Steven Ficklin, son of the now-retired Walter Ficklin, Jr.

The winery was founded in 1946, and in 1948 the first wine was made from tinta cao, tinta madeira, alvarelhao, and touriga grapes. The alvarelhao grapes since have been abandoned in favor of souzao.

The main cellar, small and low in a flat sea of vineyards west of State 99, is of adobe block fashioned on the site by the family. It is a substantial tribute to the traditional bent of the Ficklins. So is a handsome cellar full of fat oak barrels and puncheons. However, the family is only bent toward tradition, not bound by it. For example, they have done away with their original concrete fermentors in favor of more practical stainless steel tanks. And they have abandoned binning their bottled wines in favor of storing them in their case boxes to minimize handling.

The Ficklins sell their Tinta Port (along with small lots of Emerald Riesling and Ruby Cabernet) in a retail room next door to the cellar. Because the winery and ranch are owned and worked by the family, the Ficklins can offer tours by appointment only, when their days are not too full of jobs that need doing immediately.

A. Nonini Winery, on the west edge of Fresno, was founded in 1936 by A. (equally appropriate for Antonio and wife Angiolina) Nonini, and since has passed to the hands of three sons, Geno, Gildo, and Reno. The third generation now is entering the family winemaking arena.

Since the Noninis own all their own grapes, they lay claim to having the only estate-bottled wines in Fresno County. Production is limited to table wines, including Barbera and Zinfandel as well as generics.

A tour of a tidy wood-frame cellar takes in every step from crushing to bottling, ending up in a fittingly informal tasting room housed in a cottage just in front of the cellar's front wall.

Along with Bella Napoli, Cadlolo, and Farnesi, this is one of the last four survivors of a once-abundant roster of family wineries catering to a local trade. This one has not lost a bit of flavor from the days when Basque shepherds would fill botas, or buy barrels on the way from winter to summer pastures, and back. It is still possible to buy Nonini wine in small barrels, or to have your own filled.

Angelo Papagni Winery tucks into one quarter of a freeway cloverleaf just south of Madera.

The buildings went up in 1973–1975. Though the exterior walls are unornamented workaday warehouse metal, this is an impressive place. The Papagni crushing facility rivals the nearby freeway cloverleaf for size. Inside, stainless steel fermentors and aging tanks share space with an imposing collection of oak barrels.

The property was designed to make vintage-dated varietal table wines, including the rarely produced Alicante Bouschet and Charbono among reds, Chardonnay and Chenin Blanc among whites, and Moscato d'Angelo as a signature among the sparkling wines.

Full-fledged tour and tasting facilities lie in the future. Meanwhile, the proprietors will give tours by appointment. Anybody lucky enough to wander through when the winemaking staff is tasting in the lab may be invited to share a glass.

Quady Winery has recently joined Ficklin in Madera as a specialist in making Port, but the tack is somewhat different.

Where the older winery makes what might be called wood Ports, Quady produces vintage Ports. The differences between the two depend most on aging and blending. Wood Ports are blended from different vintages which have spent greater and lesser amounts of time aging in barrel. True vintage Ports come all from a single vintage, and are bottled after approximately two years in barrel.

Proprietor Andrew Quady offers looks at Port from the perspective of the vintage style in the small, wood-frame winery building behind the family residence. The only other Quady wine is a dessert type called Essencia, made from Orange Muscat grapes.

Villa Bianchi Winery is one of the newer labels in the Fresno district, launched in 1974 in a 1930s winery refitted to the state of the art for the purpose.

Just for the romance, owner Joseph Bianchi saved an old still tower fitted out to please the taste of a Henry the Eighth. Otherwise the property has been made into a modern San Joaquin-style cellar, but not quite a typical one: Villa Bianchi operates with a patented process for both red and white wines that keeps grapeskins and seeds out of contact with the juice as it ferments. Tour guides explain the details as part of a complete exploration of the premises.

The tasting room lets visitors judge the results for themselves. The roster includes French Colombard, a white wine from Grenache, and Zinfandel, as well as generics.

More wineries. The California Growers winery, launched in 1936 as a cooperative and owned since 1973 by the Setrakian family, offers neither tours nor tasting in its large winery near Cutler, but does sell wine at retail weekdays. The Growers and Setrakian labels cover varietal and generic table wines and brandy.

A good many more large wineries operate within this sprawling district. Included in the roster are these: California Products, E & J Gallo, Guild, Sierra, Vie-Del, and Viking in Fresno; Almaden in Kingsburg; Bisceglia (Canandaigua), Paul Masson, and Mission Bell (United Vintners) in Madera; Cella (United Vintners) and Mt. Tivy (The Christian Brothers) in Reedley; and Selma in Rio Vista. These wineries have no visitor accommodations of any sort. They do not even sell wines at retail.

Other Than Wineries

Fresno has two excellent parks and a mysterious underground grotto as alternate diversions to winery tours.

Roeding Park, 157 acres tucked between the freeway, State 99, and State 99-Business and between Olive and Belmont Avenues, is a tree-shaded, quiet respite from the valley sun. There are several areas for children, including a storyland, a zoo, an amusement arcade, a sizable pond with rental boats, and spacious picnic areas beneath tall rows of eucalyptus.

Kearney Park is 7 miles west of Fresno on Kearney Boulevard. It is a huge, county-operated picnic park on the grounds of the old M. Theo Kearney estate. Several large areas are set aside for group reservations. Interspersed between these are a great many small areas for first-come, first-served family use.

The mysterious underground grotto of Baldasare Forestiere is north of Fresno, two blocks west of State 99 on Shaw Avenue. Forestiere was a Sicilian possessing Herculean powers with a pick and shovel. After digging for 38 years, he ended up with a maze of tunnels that runs beneath 7 acres of surface ground. The deepest rooms are 25 feet below ground and 20 degrees cooler than summery afternoons up top.

For information on accommodations and restaurants in the area, write to the Fresno Chamber of Commerce, 2331 Fresno Street, Fresno, CA 93721.

Plotting a Route

For people in the San Joaquin Valley, State Highway 99 is the obvious means of approaching Fresno-area wineries from either north or south. Anyone starting from the San Francisco Bay area can get across the coast ranges most efficiently on Interstate Highway 580, though State Highway 152, the Pacheco Pass Highway, is more scenic and only slightly slower.

In addition to being the basic approach route, State 99 is also a useful thread in getting from one winery to another since it makes a long, diagonal slice through the region that somewhat parallels the sequence of cellars.

Generally speaking, none of the roads leading to the wineries provides stunning scenery. The possible exceptions would be those roads in the Reedley-Sanger district that get close to the course of the Kings River. These lead past changing terrain and brightened colors.

Bakersfield

Bakersfield is the urban anchor for the southern end of the San Joaquin Valley. Unlike Fresno and other valley cities, Bakersfield is as involved in drilling for oil as it is in growing crops. In fact, it is not at all uncommon to see the bobbing heads of pumps at wells between vine rows. The other instantly noticeable fact of local life is a general passion for country and western music.

Grapes have been a part of Kern County agriculture for a good many years, but most of them went for table use or raisins until late in the 1960s. Then, new grape varieties and new grapegrowing techniques began to open new avenues in this hottest of California wine regions, and wine became a prime interest rather than an afterthought.

The Wineries

It is easy for visitors to get a taste of wines in this region. Three of its six wineries maintain tasting rooms. Seeing how the work gets done is harder, since only two offer tours, and then only by appointment.

Giumarra Vineyards first opened to visitors in 1974, at the same time the family-owned winery released its first vintage-dated varietal wines from local vineyards.

The winery occupies the western end of a long line of buildings near Edison. The other structures house other aspects of a diverse farming business, and there are enough of them that it takes a couple of minutes to drive from the property entrance to the sculpted concrete building that houses the bottling lines and tasting room.

On the second floor, the tasting room allows visitors to watch work on the bottling line while they sample from a list that includes Chenin Blanc, Riesling, French Colombard, Cabernet Sauvignon, and Pinot Noir.

Groups can arrange for walking tours of the crushing area and aging cellars.

LaMont Winery has been a pioneer in Kern County winemaking in several ways. It started as a family-owned bulk winery in 1945, then was bought by a grower cooperative in 1966. During years as a cooperative, the winery was named Bear Mountain after a conical peak that looms up just behind a rambling array of cellar buildings and open-air steel fermenting and storage tanks. Also during that time, the winery began producing varietal table wines under the LaMont label, the latter name borrowed from a nearby town. These wines marked the first concentrated effort to produce and sell table wines from the Bakersfield district. LaMont became the name of the property in 1978 when it was bought from the grower cooperative by John Labatt, Ltd., a Canadian firm which owns a major brewery and three wineries in its home country.

Under the new owners, LaMont continues to produce varietal table wines, including Chenin Blanc, French Colombard, Gewürztraminer, a Rosé of Barbera, and Ruby Cabernet.

Visitors can arrange to tour the winery. The tasting room is open to all comers, even people who arrive by airplane, for this is the only tasting room in the state with an adjacent airstrip. Because the strip is private, fly-in visitors must write ahead to the winery for a "hold harmless" agreement.

Sierra Wine Corporation made its first face-to-face approach to the public early in 1982 when it bought the former A. Perelli-Minetti & Sons winery at Delano, but the company has been a major factor in the bulk wine trade for many years with wineries elsewhere in the San Joaquin Valley.

The recently acquired winery buildings do not lend themselves to touring because they cover so much ground and also lack pathways safely out of way of the work. However, there is tasting.

A visitor center in front of the sprawling winery complex was built by the former owners as an architectural tribute to a wine tank and a general tribute to the idea of recycling. A round, redwood building, it uses staves from a one-time wine tank as an exterior wall, interwoven grapestakes as a ceiling, and other winery equipment for various details in the construction. The only material not salvaged from winery or vineyard is redwood for the interior walls.

Sierra's flagship wine is called Philip Posson Sherry after the veteran Sierra winemaker who produces it. Other Sierra-produced table and dessert wines also are available under a range of labels.

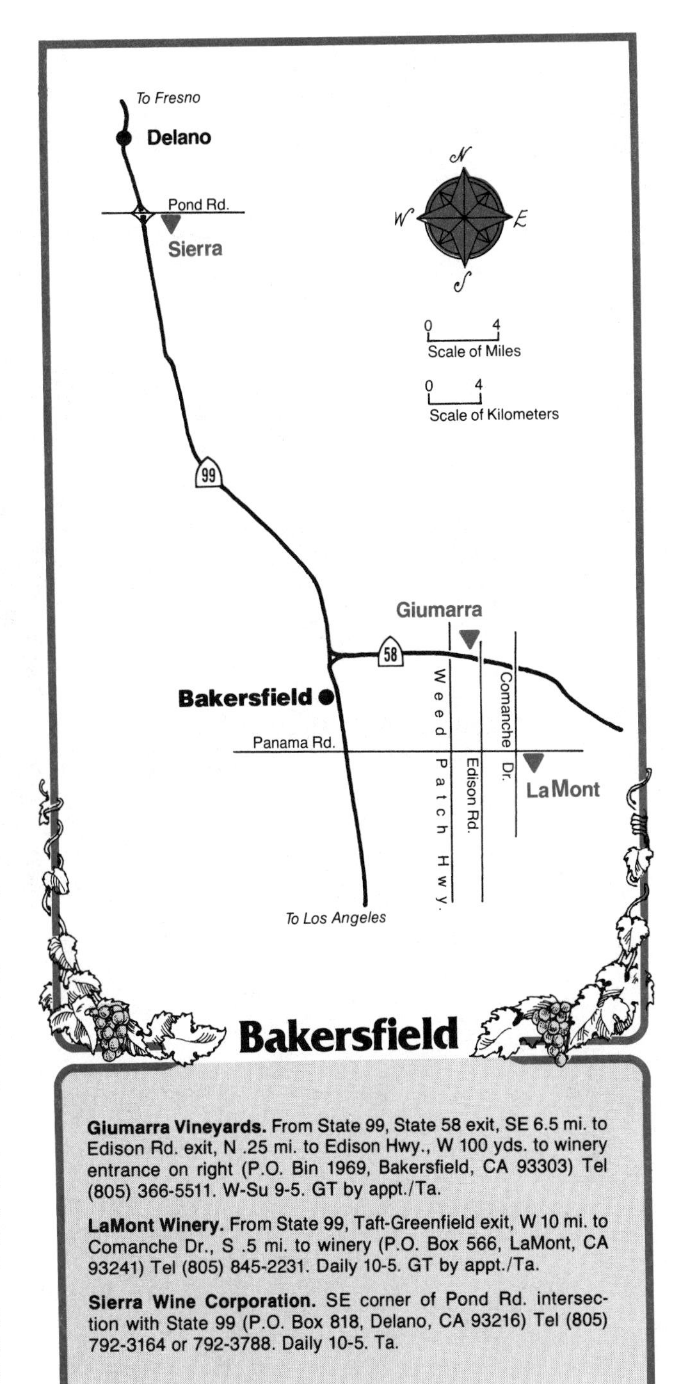

Giumarra Vineyards. From State 99, State 58 exit, SE 6.5 mi. to Edison Rd. exit, N .25 mi. to Edison Hwy., W 100 yds. to winery entrance on right (P.O. Bin 1969, Bakersfield, CA 93303) Tel (805) 366-5511. W-Su 9-5. GT by appt./Ta.

LaMont Winery. From State 99, Taft-Greenfield exit, W 10 mi. to Comanche Dr., S .5 mi. to winery (P.O. Box 566, LaMont, CA 93241) Tel (805) 845-2231. Daily 10-5. GT by appt./Ta.

Sierra Wine Corporation. SE corner of Pond Rd. intersection with State 99 (P.O. Box 818, Delano, CA 93216) Tel (805) 792-3164 or 792-3788. Daily 10-5. Ta.

Key: GT (guided tour); IT (informal tour); Ta (tasting).

More wineries. Three wineries in the region make and move wine only in bulk. The most visible of them is an Almaden winery alongside the freeway, State 99, at MacFarland. The others are Delano Cooperative and a dessert wine cellar belonging to Guild Wineries and Distilleries (see page 137).

Southern California

New frontiers back where it all began

Time and the restless tide of population in Southern California have caused a whole series of shifts in vineyards of this oldest of California's wine growing regions.

Father Junipero Serra planted the first vines at the mission in San Diego circa 1769. As early as 1831 Jean Louis Vignes planted the first commercial vineyard in what is now downtown Los Angeles. All traces of these and some other early districts are long gone. The one reminder of early times is a small room at Mission San Gabriel, kept more or less the way it was when the Franciscans were making wine in it.

At present the greatest concentration of vineyards is in the Cucamonga district east of Los Angeles, between the San Bernardino County towns of Ontario and Fontana. However, as population pressures grow more severe with each passing year, this region too suffers a steadily tightening squeeze.

In searching for new land to plant, several vineyardists have turned south to Temecula in Riverside County; others have looked still farther south, to Escondido, only a few miles from the old mission in San Diego.

Running ahead of this shift in vineyard sites is a shift in winery location. Temecula now has more wineries to tour than does Cucamonga.

Temecula

The Temecula district started all in a rush as a winegrowing area when a real estate development operation turned much of the southwest corner of Riverside County into Rancho California and simultaneously encouraged buyers to plant grapes on their parcels.

The first small plantings in 1968 quickly expanded to 2,000 acres. By 1981 the total approached 3,000 acres. The first winery, built in 1974, now has six neighbors, with more in the planning stages.

This is relentlessly hilly country. The section where the vines grow is a sort of catch basin for what little runoff water there is from a sparse annual rainfall. It also draws cool, moist sea breezes through a gap in the hills to the west. The combination makes the local climate as pleasant for people as it is for vines. The climate notwithstanding, Temecula has tended to business, rather than developing into a vacation retreat.

The Wineries

The short roster of young wineries offers remarkable diversity of size and architectural style.

Callaway Vineyard & Winery started the new trend in winemaking south of the Tehachapi Mountains. It pioneered the shift toward small, estatelike wineries producing varietal table wines.

Occupying a series of rolling knolls east of Temecula, the winery and vineyards were founded by retired business executive Ely Callaway, who planted his first vines in 1969, built the first cellars in 1974, and sold his much-enlarged properties to Hiram Walker Resources, Ltd., the Canadian distillers, in 1981.

The present winery looms up from the top of a sharp rise above Rancho California Road. Its tall, white walls are unbroken by windows except on the west face, where the visitors' hall is a light and airy room. Around back, a short length of metal wall and another of concrete block reveal the original size of the building.

From custom-made crusher to continuous dejuicer and press, stainless steel fermentors, and centrifuge, this is a first-rate example of a modern California winery. It differs from most of its peers in aging its white wines only in German oak, although it has American, French, and Slavonian cooperage for its reds and some experimental wines. The tour staff gladly explains the hows and whys of this wood-aging program.

Each hourly tour finishes with a sit-down tasting of selected wines. The winery particularly encourages group visits, and will arrange special tastings and tours, given enough advance notice.

Wines include White Riesling (regular and late harvest), Sauvignon and Fumé Blanc, Chenin Blanc (regular and late harvest), Cabernet Sauvignon, Petite Sirah, and Zinfandel.

Picnickers may make use of a well-designed area behind the winery on a first-come, first-served basis, except when it has been reserved for a group.

Cilurzo Vineyard & Winery was launched only in 1978, but the Cilurzo vineyard goes back to 1967. Its oldest block has the first commercial vines planted in Temecula.

The two-story cellar building is cut into one of the infinity of sandy hillocks that make up this part of Rancho California, its plywood hide painted almost the same hue. In the time-honored way of hillside wineries, grapes arrive at the uphill side for crushing, and new juice flows to fermentors below. A tidy cellar full of oak barrels nestles in an angle formed by two perpendicular rows of stainless steel fermentors. Amid stored cases of wine and bottling gear on the upper story is an affable, informal tasting room.

Hollywood lighting director Vincenzo Cilurzo and his wife Audrey started growing grapes almost on a whim, fell into home winemaking, and ended up taking winemaking courses at the University of California at Davis. (The depth of their involvement can be measured not only in the winery, but in the name of their daughter, Chenin.) The winery came as the inevitable final step. One of the Cilurzos will lead the tour after which visitors can go uphill from the cellars to a tree-shaded picnic area next to a small pond.

The roster of Cilurzo wines includes Chenin Blanc, Cabernet Sauvignon, Petite Sirah, and a proprietary blend of Chenin Blanc and Petite Sirah called Chenete.

Incidentally, the label briefly was Cilurzo & Piconi, but the Piconis now have their own winery a short distance away. (See page 152.)

Filsinger Vineyards and Winery is not only family owned, but family built. Whenever they could spare time from demanding regular jobs, Bill and Kathy Filsinger planted vineyards, built cellars, and made wine.

Moved by stories of earlier generations of family winemaking in Germany, they began with vines in 1974, first made wine in 1980, and opened for sales and visitors in 1981.

The white stucco, Spanish colonial-style building housing their tasting room and bottled wines has tile floors, a handsomely carved bar, Casablanca fans, and other refined details that make it one of the most pleasant places to visit in the district. The winery proper hides a hundred or so yards away behind a small knoll. A prefabricated metal building with a wood frame extension, it is not the architectural equal of its companion structure, but remains an instructive example of what a small, modern winery should be. The proprietors do not press visitors to look through it, but they and their winemaker are glad to show it off to those who ask.

The wines are Emerald Riesling, Chardonnay, Fumé Blanc, Gamay Beaujolais, and Petite Sirah.

Hart Vineyards is a small winery by the modest standards of a district full of small wineries, and almost a one-man cellar. The boxy, brown, plywood-covered cellar perches on a shelf cut into a typical Temecula sandy knoll directly next to the one Callaway Vineyard & Winery is on. In contrast to the neighbor, to step through the front door here is to see all there is of equipment.

Owner-winemaker Joe Hart welcomes visitors when he has wine to sell. When he has none, he posts a "sold out" notice on his roadside sign, and, like as not, spends the day elsewhere at more fruitful tasks.

The list from the first vintage, 1980, included Chardonnay, Sauvignon Blanc, Cabernet Sauvignon, and Zinfandel.

Mesa Verde Vineyards, for the moment, is the most easterly of the wineries along Rancho California Road. Like several of its neighbors, it is the property of a young couple. Keith and Lynne Karrup own their own vineyards and winery, and manage vineyards for local independent growers.

The cream-colored stucco winery building sits square atop a little knoll a short distance away from a Spanish-style building that houses the tasting room and a small wine shop and delicatessen. The Karrups do not insist on cellar tours, which would, in any case, be brief. To the left of the main door are the stainless steel fermentors, to the right oak barrels, and to the rear the crusher, press, and other working gear.

The small, attractively furnished tasting room looks onto a patio through windowed doors. Visitors are free to wander in and out, tasting at their own pace from a list that included Johannisberg Riesling and Gamay Beaujolais as the first releases, and will have Cabernet Sauvignon and Zinfandel beginning early in 1984.

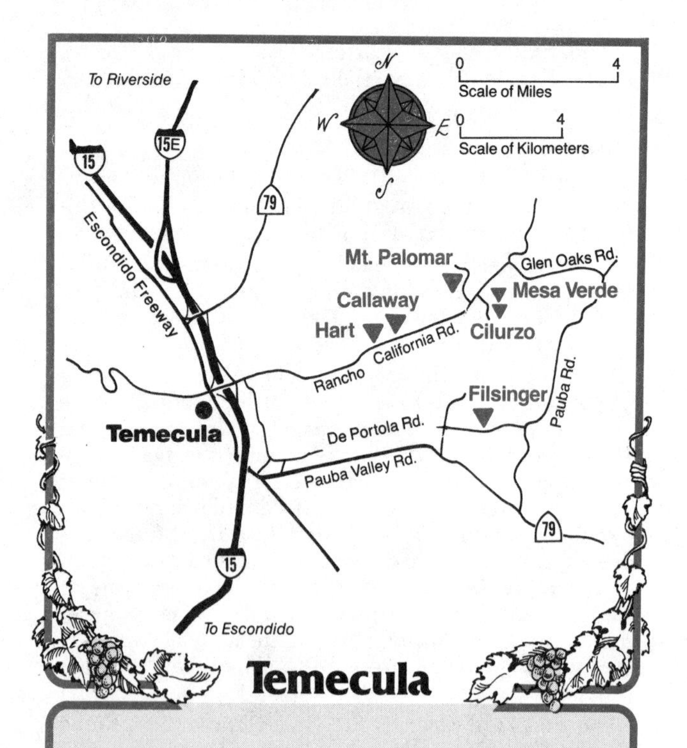

Temecula

Callaway Vineyard & Winery. From I-15, Rancho California Rd. exit, E 4 mi. (32720 Rancho California Rd., Temecula, CA 92390) Tel (714) 676-4001. Picnic. M-Su 10-5. GT/Ta.

Cilurzo Vineyard & Winery. From I-15, Rancho California Rd. exit, E 5.5 mi. to Calle Contento, S .25 mi. (41220 Calle Contento, Temecula, CA 92390) Tel (714) 676-5250. Sa-Su 9-5, weekdays by appt. GT/Ta.

Filsinger Vineyards and Winery. From I-15, SR-79 exit, E 4.8 mi. to Anza Rd., N .5 mi. to De Portola Rd., then E 2.8 mi. (39050 De Portola Rd., Temecula, CA 92390) Tel (714) 676-4594. Sa-Su 9-5, weekdays by appt. GT/Ta.

Hart Vineyards. From I-15, Rancho California Rd. exit, E 3.8 mi. (41300 Avenida Biona, Temecula, CA 92390) Tel (714) 676-6300. Daily by appt.

Mesa Verde Vineyards. From I-15, Rancho California Rd. exit, E 5.8 mi. (34565 Rancho California Rd., Temecula, CA 92390) Tel (714) 676-2370. Daily 9-5. IT/Ta.

Mt. Palomar Winery. From I-15, Rancho California Rd. exit, E 5.3 mi. (33820 Rancho California Rd., Temecula, CA 92390) Tel (714) 676-5047. Picnic. Daily 9-5. GT/Ta.

Not on Map—Restricted Visitor Facilities

GlenOaks Cellars. (40607 Los Ranchos Circle, Temecula, CA 92390) Tel (714) 676-5831.

Key: GT (guided tour); IT (informal tour); Ta (tasting).

Mt. Palomar Winery announces itself by means of a loudly painted, upright redwood wine tank perched on a grassy slope above Rancho California Road. The winery proper hides on the reverse slope.

The property of John Poole, Mt. Palomar is set efficiently into a side slope, much as old cellars were in turn-of-the-century Napa or Sonoma. The crusher-stemmer feeds grapes down into a gallery containing stainless steel fermentors and an automatic Vaslin press. This is where the new ends: the fermentors feed new wine into a cave full of venerable oak oval casks and barrels. (Outdoors is a sun-baked solera for sherry types.)

Tours cover all of these points, as well as a small bottling line, ending up in the tasting and sales room. The owner has thoughtfully added a small deli to the tasting room in compensation for the remoteness of his site. Picnic tables outside the cellar door are available to first-comers.

The Mt. Palomar wines available for tasting include Chenin Blanc, Sauvignon Blanc, Cabernet Sauvignon, Petite Sirah, and—rare bird—a dessert Cabernet Sauvignon made after the fashion of Ruby Port.

More wineries. GlenOaks Cellars is a tiny winery owned by scientist Hugo Woerdemann. Housed in an expanded garage next to his home, it is visitable only by appointment. However, selected wines, bottled under the Hugo's label, are available for tasting at Mesa Verde.

Under construction during 1982 is the Piconi Winery. After making wines elsewhere, proprietor Dr. John Piconi anticipates a first crush at his own cellar in 1982, with the earlier wines due on the market immediately. The winery is to be open for visitors as soon as wines are available.

Plotting a Route

Nothing could be simpler than organizing a day of winery touring in Temecula. Rancho California Road exits east from Interstate Highway 15 at the town of Temecula about midway between Riverside and San Diego. All of the region's visitable wineries but one lie along that road within six miles of the freeway. The lone exception is found on a parallel road three miles to the south.

Escondido

Escondido is the agricultural heart of San Diego County. A dramatically hilly countryside between sea on one side and desert on the other, it gets enough water to grow avocados, citrus, and some grapes.

Once highly respected for its wines, the district dwindled almost to extinction as a vineyard after Prohibition, but is now making a modest comeback.

Not quite large enough to call for a pilgrimage, it is close enough to San Diego to make a pleasant day trip. It also can be visited in combination with Temecula, some 27 miles to the north via Interstate Highway 15.

The Wineries

Escondido has two persistent old-time cellars plus a single newcomer.

Bernardo Winery is one of the old-timers, and a surprising place in almost every respect. Tucked into a narrow draw behind a classy country club development, the property looks a bit like a main street movie set from an old western. More than merely looking the part, the place is actually a village of shops, of which the winery is one.

Visitors can buy indoor plants, worked silver, antique mirrors, and heaven knows what all else in addition to wine.

Winery and tasting room sit on the uphill side of the main street, at its intersection with a side road. Both are wooden buildings, welcoming and more than faintly time-worn. Tours of the cellars are informal, offering an instructive look at a working example of a basket press, and other equipment not often in use these days.

Some long-aged dessert wines lead the tasting room lists.

Ferrara Winery dates from the same era as Bernardo and has a similar cellar full of old upright redwood tanks and some kindred wines. It also has the warm, familial air that makes visitors feel notably welcome.

It differs in singleness of purpose. No galaxy of shops surrounds the winery, which hides away at the end of a quiet residential street not far from the downtown.

Ferrara also differs from Bernardo in having a few surprisingly contemporary touches, not the least of which is an elegant stainless steel crusher-stemmer.

A small patch of vines marks the property. The winery is tucked in behind the family home and can be seen only from two doorways—one leading to the fermentors, the other to the aging cellar. Tasting goes on in a comfortable building between house and cellar.

San Pasqual Vineyards is the new boy in town, different from its old neighbors in every way.

On the road leading to the San Diego Zoo's Wild Animal Park, the winery is a plain, fabricated steel building set atop a knoll at one corner of its vineyards. The property of a local partnership, it dates from 1976.

The vines, within an agricultural preserve, are the source of San Diego County's only estate-bottled, vintage-dated, varietal table wines. At informal weekend open houses, the winery staff explains the modern, well-equipped cellars and offers tasting from a roster that includes Chenin Blanc (dry and off-dry), Fumé Blanc, Semillon, Muscat Canelli, and Gamay. The proprietors also have an arbor-shaded picnic area for visitors to use.

Plotting a Route

Local vinous geography is almost as simple as at Temecula. The three wineries are accessible via three consecutive exits from Interstate Highway 15. None is more than a mile off the freeway.

For information on accommodations write to the Escondido Visitors & Information Bureau, 720 North Broadway, Escondido, CA 92025. The San Diego Convention and Visitors Bureau, 1200 Third Avenue, San Diego, CA 92101, offers county information.

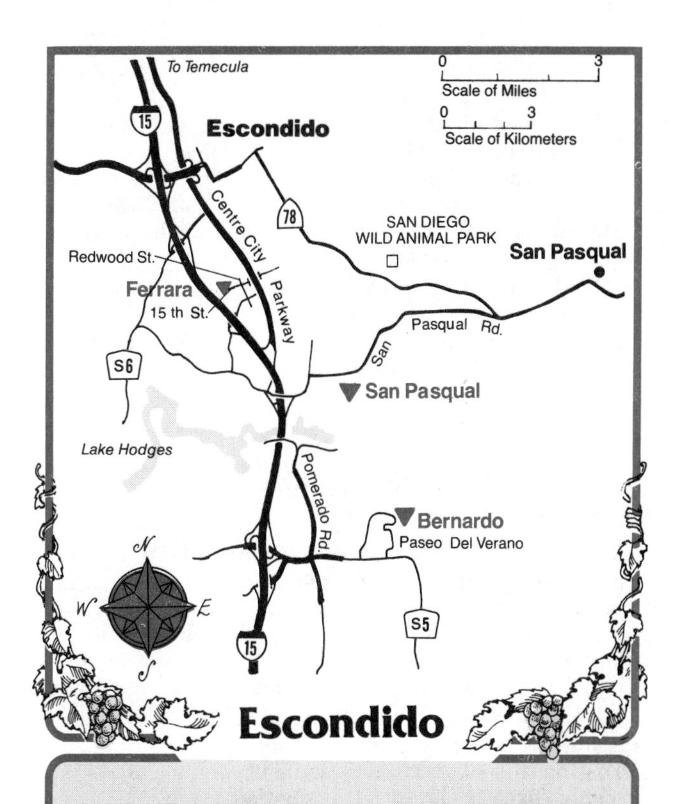

Bernardo Winery. From I-15, 7 mi. S of Escondido, Pomerado Rd. exit, E to Paseo Del Verano (make U-turn after overshooting; no direct left), then N 1 mi. to winery (13330 Paseo Del Verano Norte, San Diego, CA 92128) Tel (714) 487-1866. Picnic. Daily 7-6. IT/Ta.

Ferrara Winery. W on Felicita from Centre City Pkwy., rt. on Redwood to 15th St. (1120 W. 15th St., Escondido, CA 92025) Tel (714) 745-7632. Daily 9-6:30. IT/Ta.

San Pasqual Vineyards. From I-15, 3 mi. S of Escondido, Via Rancho Pkwy. exit, NE 1 mi. to San Pasqual Rd., then E (13455 San Pasqual Rd., Escondido, CA 92025) Tel (714) 741-0855. Picnic. Sa-Su 11-5, weekdays by appt. GT/Ta.

Key: GT (guided tour); IT (informal tour); Ta (tasting).

Cucamonga

A wide, relatively unpopulated strip separates Ontario from Fontana. Within it lies nearly all of the present-day Cucamonga wine district.

Cucamonga hardly exists as a specific place; it is an intersection of Archibald Avenue and Foothill Boulevard, or a post office. The more general description of the area these days would be Pomona Valley. But wine goes back to the 1830s in Cucamonga, and that will be the name of the wine district for as long as its vines endure.

Whatever its name, this is a curious countryside. The San Gabriel Mountains rise sharply on the north, effectively forming a wall on that side of the valley. At the foot of these mountains, a gently sloping and remarkably even alluvial fan runs more than a mile before it flattens out and becomes true valley floor. To the south, a less imposing range of hills called the Jurupas marks the limit for grapevines.

Industry and population press in from both east and west. In the late 1960s, San Bernardino County had 23,000 acres in bearing vines. By 1980 the figure had dwindled to 7,300, the owners of many of these acres allowing vines to die by inches while they await a day of higher land prices.

Still, 7,300 is a considerable acreage, and the history of the vine in this district is long and strong. Furthermore, just because vines are in trouble does not mean wineries are. In these times of fast, efficient transport, grapes are being brought from elsewhere to keep wineries active hereabouts.

The Wineries

It has been a habit among Cucamonga proprietors to play the part of the traditional country winery, selling much—sometimes all—of their production at the cellar door. The custom continues, even though some of the larger cellars have had to build extra doors in favorable locations to make supply and demand come out right.

Get down to business, and there are three full-fledged producing wineries to visit in the Cucamonga district. Tasting rooms, with and without aging cellars attached, expand the roster by another three.

Pierre Biane Winery, also known as Cucamonga Vineyard Company, is a remarkable restoration, and therefore a remarkable winery to visit.

Built before the turn of the century by a pair of brothers named Vai, the winery carries California Bond No. 1. Until its current owner, Pierre Biane, acquired it in 1977, it *looked* like the first winery ever bonded in the state. But since Biane's arrival, he has built spanking new cellars in, on, and around the old-timer. As a result, they give a look at the most modern of equipment side-by-side with some genuine museum pieces.

Brand new refrigerated stainless steel fermentors stand in tidy rows alongside ancient open sumps with old brine pipes, once used as chillers, running through them. Just across a walkway, a handful of open-topped redwood fermentors stand empty and disused, more mute testimony to how things used to be done here. It is a longer walk from the old crushers to the new ones with their companion dejuicers and continuous presses, but the contrast is not lessened by the stroll.

Tasting goes on in an old aging cellar, emptied out and spruced up for the purpose. (No wines remain from the old days for contrast with the new production. A man can't hang on to everything.)

Cucamonga Vineyard Company plans to focus on table wines (both varietal and generic) and sparkling wine. There will be some specialty sherry types.

Brookside Vineyard Company says it is in Guasti. In fact, it nearly is Guasti.

The winery buildings are numerous and spread out over an uncommonly large plot of ground. Interstate Highway 10 sets limits on the north. Ontario International's main runway borders Brookside on the south. Turner Road on the east and Archibald Avenue on the west are the other limits to the main property. And there is more of Brookside than bewilders the eye at headquarters: two fermenting wineries and an aging cellar are elsewhere in the district.

The proprietors have made things easy for visitors. Only two of the home winery buildings are open. One is the stone-walled tasting room and retail shop. The other is the handsome main aging and bottling cellar.

Tours of the aging cellar depart from the tasting room. On weekdays, signs do the guiding; on weekends, a host or hostess leads the way.

The cellar is a startling structure. Looping curves atop the end walls suggest Roman inspiration. Built of dark gray river rock that must once have been abundant here, it measures 100 by 600 feet, suggesting Herculean ideas more than mere mortal ones. Inside those 3-foot-thick walls the two major points of interest are a huge underground cellar full of barrels—in their turn full of sweet wines—and a museum of the winery's long, complex history.

The winery that is now called Brookside was built as the Italian Vineyard Company by Secundo Guasti in the 1880s. As IVC, it was the biggest winery in the world just before Prohibition, with 5,000 acres of vines all in a block.

Meantime, Brookside had its origins in the same decade, but was built in Redlands by Emile Vache. Another Frenchman, Marius Biane, married the boss's daughter, then inherited the business. Biane's sons took the Brookside name with them when they revived the then-defunct Guasti property in the 1950s.

Bianes owned Brookside until 1972, when it was bought by Beatrice Foods, Inc. In 1981, Beatrice sold the winery to Chesapeake Industries, a manufacturer of doors based in Orange County. Under both corporate ownerships a third-generation Biane, Rene, has run the winery.

Wines on hand in the tasting room are labeled Assumption Abbey (produced under an agreement with the Benedictine order), Brookside, and Vache. Under one or more of these labels the company offers a wide range of table, appetizer, dessert, and sparkling wines.

In addition to providing tastes indoors, the winery will sell bottles for picnics at tables on a tree-shaded lawn facing the tasting room.

For those who cannot get this close, Brookside has another 30 tasting rooms, most of them in California, some outside the state. The company will forward a list upon request.

J. Filippi Vintage Company, on the edge of Fontana and at the end of a row of industrial concerns, encourages visitors to limit their inspection of the premises to the tasting room, which is comfortably airy.

The working winery has grown right through the walls of its original building in a series of additions, with the result that there is no easy path to follow through it. The earliest walls date from 1934. The most recent additions—a row of foam-insulated stainless steel storage and fermenting tanks—stand outside of all the walls. Persistent visitors may have a look inside, where the working equipment is mostly modern.

(Continued on page 156)

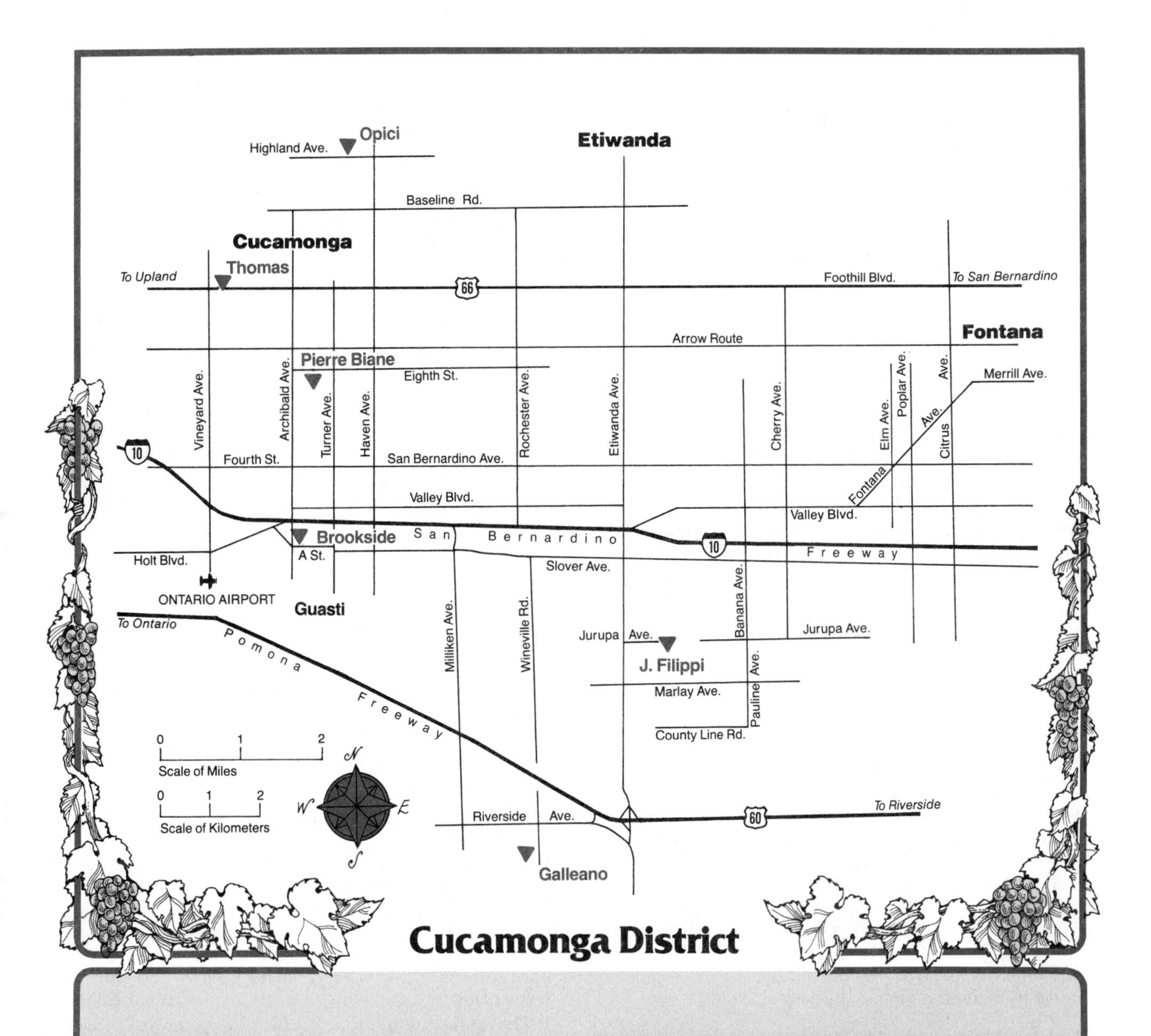

Cucamonga District

Pierre Biane Winery. From San Bernardino Fwy. (I-10), Archibald Ave. exit, N to Eighth St., E to winery (10013 E. Eighth St., Cucamonga, CA 91730) Tel (714) 987-1716. Ta.

Brookside Vineyard Company. From San Bernardino Fwy. (I-10), Archibald Ave. exit, S 2 blks to A St. (9900 A St., Guasti, CA 91743) Tel (714) 983-2787. Picnic. Daily 8-6. IT weekdays, GT weekends/Ta.

J. Filippi Vintage Company. From San Bernardino Fwy. (I-10), Etiwanda Ave. exit, S 1 mi. to Jurupa Ave., the winery drive (P.O. Box 2, Mira Loma, CA 91752) Tel (714) 984-4514. Picnic. Daily 9-6. Ta.

Galleano Winery. From U.S. 60, Etiwanda Ave. exit, S to Riverside Ave., W to Wineville Rd., S to winery (4231 Wineville Rd., Mira Loma, CA 91752) Tel (714) 685-5376. M-Sa 9-5. GT/Ta.

Opici Winery. From San Bernardino Fwy. (I-10), Haven Ave. exit, N 4 mi. to Highland Ave., then W .5 mi. (10150 Highland Ave., Alta Loma, CA 91701) Tel (714) 987-2710. Th-M 10-6. Ta.

Thomas Vineyards. From San Bernardino Fwy. (I-10), Vineyard Ave. exit, N 2 mi. to Foothill Blvd. (8916 Foothill Blvd., Cucamonga, CA 91730) Tel (714) 987-1612. Picnic. Daily 8-6. IT/Ta.

Outside Map Area

San Antonio Winery (Los Angeles). From City Hall in downtown L.A., NE 1.5 mi. on N. Main St. to Lamar St., E to winery (737 Lamar St., Los Angeles, CA 90031) Tel (213) 223-1401. Picnic. M-Sa 8-7, Su 10-6. IT/Ta.

Key: GT (guided tour); IT (informal tour); Ta (tasting).

. . . Continued from page 154

On hand for tasting are a number of table, sparkling, and dessert wines. The varietal table wines are produced elsewhere. The generic types are made here, as are several dessert wines, including a specialty called Marsovo (Marsala with a trace of egg in it). The labels are Joseph Filippi and Chateau Filippi.

The winery and adjacent family homes are surrounded by an expansive vineyard, all well trained, much of it planted since the mid-1960s. It makes a startling contrast to the dead and abandoned vines across Etiwanda Avenue and elsewhere in the immediate neighborhood.

The Filippi family maintains six tasting rooms elsewhere in Southern California. They will send a list of addresses on request.

Galleano Winery, after years of shy withdrawal from public attention, opened a tasting room in the early 1970s and now offers tours as well.

Founded by Domenic Galleano in 1933, the property is a perfect evocation of the sort of small, family enterprise that once dotted this whole countryside. The main cellar has tidy rows of ancient redwood tanks, plus some oak. Crusher and presses also go back to an earlier day.

The tasting room is housed in a modest frame building at the rear of a courtyard formed by the main cellar on one side and the family residence on the other. Within, visitors may taste the pride of the house, a local Zinfandel, usually with one of the owning Galleanos as host. The roster of wines includes other varietals, generics, and some dessert wines. Galleano wines are sold nowhere else.

Opici Winery has a tasting room open to the public. Tucked away at the end of a street next to a platoon of Alta Loma tract homes, the square, flat-roofed, cream-colored building offers a surprising range of wines made in facilities located elsewhere in the district and state.

This is headquarters for the company, which sells most of its wine along the Atlantic seaboard, limiting the home audience to this one outlet. The lone opportunity to taste and buy at the source is congenial.

Thomas Vineyards, in Cucamonga, is housed in the oldest winery building still standing and in use in California. At least part of the adobe structure dates to 1839, when Governor Juan Batista Alvarado of Mexico deeded the property to a winegrower named Tiburcio Tapia. (The east end of the building dates only to 1969, but is a faithful restoration of the original, which washed away in a flood.)

The wines, labeled Thomas Vineyard and Old Rancho, are available for tasting and sale only on the premises. Visitors are free to wander through an aging cellar full of fine old oak ovals, and out back, where there is a modest collection of old winemaking equipment.

Other Than Wineries

The most notable tourist attraction other than wineries in this region is the annual Los Angeles County Fair. It runs the last two weeks of September, the right time for a companion look at the new vintage in progress. The grounds are located north of Interstate Highway 10 in Pomona.

A number of motels and restaurants can be found in the area. For specific information write to the Greater Los Angeles Visitors and Convention Bureau, 505 S. Flower Street, Los Angeles, CA 90071.

Plotting a Route

The towns of Ontario and Upland run into one another so smoothly that the change is imperceptible to all but devoted readers of roadside signs. Together, the communities straddle every major east-west road between Los Angeles and the state line. For visitors to wineries, the most useful of these are Interstate Highway 10 (the San Bernardino Freeway) and Foothill Boulevard, a moderately fast four-lane commercial road that once was part of the much-sung-about Route 66.

The whole district is divided into a tidy gridwork by local roads. The most useful of the north-south arteries are Vineyard, Archibald, and Etiwanda avenues.

Los Angeles

Early in the history of wine in California, a sizable vineyard grew where Union Station now stands. Times have moved so far that even the railroad station is now on its way to being a part of the local past.

Los Angeles hardly can be called "wine country" in any general sense. But hardy San Antonio Winery can and does advertise itself in most years as the only producing winery within the city limits of Los Angeles.

San Antonio Winery, with increasing ease, perseveres as a producing winery in spite of its downtown Los Angeles location. The development of field crushing means that the owning Riboli family can bring unfermented grape juice via road tanker from Santa Barbara, Monterey, or other Central Coast vineyards for fermenting in the industrial surrounds of Lamar Street.

The walk-through tour of the winery shows the new developments alongside bits and pieces of equipment from the old days, when they brought whole grapes in trucks from Cucamonga. The clearest evocation of the old era is a big crusher-stemmer, still anchored to its original spot in a room that has been transformed into an Italian restaurant. The clearest evocation of the new era is at the rear of the main cellar: a fermenting room full of stainless steel tanks. Between the two rooms—physically and in time—are the wood aging cellars, filled mostly with redwood tanks, but also including a growing collection of oak barrels.

One of the redwood cellars has an agreeably eclectic collection of old winery tools.

In the tasting room, visitors can assess an extensive line of wines of all types, from varietal table wines to flavored dessert specialties. A picnic ground with space for 100 adjoins the main cellar.

San Antonio maintains tasting rooms elsewhere in Southern California. The proprietors will provide a list on request.

It all begins with vines in the sun

A grape starts out in spring all acid and no sugar. As it ripens its acid level declines and its sugar level rises.

The winemaker's task is to harvest the grapes when the ratio of sugar to acid is right. The desired ratio differs from one class of wine to another. Port and other dessert types come from grapes with higher sugar and lower acid then grapes used for red table wines. Champagne, on the other hand, calls for unusually low sugar and very high acid.

In the end it comes down to the interactions of climate and grape variety. There is a "right" climate for each variety—or, more precisely, a right range of climate. California has richly diverse and complicated climate patterns. Furthermore, vineyardists in the state grow 130 varieties of *Vitis vinifera* in one amount and another.

After a long study, researchers at the University of California at Davis defined five climate zones based on heat summation. (Heat summation is the total number of degree-days above 50°F between (and including) April 1 and October 31. The measuring stick for degree-day calculations is mean temperature. For example, if the mean temperature was 70°F for 5 consecutive days, the summation would be: $70 - 50 = 20 \times 5 = 100$ degree-days.)

The five climate zones:

Region I (2,500 degree-days or fewer). Occurs in Anderson Valley, Carneros, Felton, and Gonzales, as examples. The university recommends table wine grapes as best suited to the region, especially such varieties as chardonnay, pinot noir, and white riesling.

Region II (2,501-3,000 degree-days). Occurs in Glen Ellen, Hollister, Oakville, and Greenfield, as examples. The university recommends table wine grapes for this region also, especially cabernet and sauvignon blanc. In both this region and Region I, in fact, it recommends nearly all of the grapes used in familiar varietal table wines.

Region III (3,001-3,500 degree-days). Occurs in Cloverdale, Livermore, Calistoga, Paso Robles, and Ukiah, as examples. This begins to be the margin between purely table wine country and dessert wine country. The recommended table wine varieties include barbera, ruby cabernet, sauvignon blanc, and semillon. The university gives qualified recommendations for many others, depending on specific local conditions. It also recommends a good many of the familiar muscats and some sherry and port grapes, again depending on precisely measured local climate factors.

Region IV (3,501-4,000 degree-days). Occurs in Guasti, Livingston, Lodi, and Modesto, as examples. The balance goes over to dessert wine grapes. Nearly every muscat, sherry, and port grape earns a univerity recommendation in this region. Among table wine grapes, emerald riesling, French colombard, barbera, and ruby cabernet get clear recommendations. As the presence of emerald riesling and ruby cabernet indicates, this is a region for which many of the UC hybrid varieties are bred. As the national demand for table wine rises and the university program progresses, this region is turning more and more toward making table wine.

Region V (4,001 degree-days or more). Occurs in most of the southern San Joaquin Valley, from Madera to Bakersfield, and much of the Cucamonga district. All of the sherry and port grape varieties carry university recommendations in this region. It will probably always produce a great part of California's dessert wines, but the hybrids and a few other varieties, coupled with advances in vine-training techniques, make table wines a possibility in the warmest of these vineyards.

Index

Photographers

David Bartruff: 25 top. **Morton Beebe:** 2. **Ron Botier:** 10 top, 16 top, 23. **Gene Dekovic:** 17 top. **Lee Foster:** 30 bottom right. **Peter Fronk:** 28 top, 30 bottom left. **Hal Lauritzen:** 18, 20 top, 31 bottom. **Luther Linkhart:** 11 top. **Fred Lyon:** 1, 31 top. **Jack McDowell:** 6 bottom, 17 bottom, 19 top right, 21 top, 26, 27 bottom, 30 top. **Ted Streshinsky:** 4, 5, 6 top, 7, 8, 9, 10 bottom, 11 bottom, 13, 14, 15, 16 bottom, 19 top left & bottom, 20 bottom, 21 bottom, 22, 24 top, 25 bottom, 27 top, 28 bottom. **Bob Thompson:** 3, 12. **Dick Warton:** 24 bottom. **Darrow M. Watt:** 29, back cover.